MAY 1 1 2015

P9-CKU-602

NAPA COUNTY LIBRARY
580 COOMBS STREET
NAPA, CA 94559

NICHOLSON

ALSO BY MARC ELIOT

Michael Douglas: A Biography

Steve McQueen: A Biography

Paul Simon: A Life

American Rebel: The Life of Clint Eastwood

Song of Brooklyn: An Oral History of America's Favorite Borough

Reagan: The Hollywood Years

Jimmy Stewart: A Biography

Cary Grant: A Biography

Down 42nd Street: Sex, Money, Culture, and Politics at the Crossroads of the World

Take It from Me: Life's a Struggle, but You Can Win
(with Erin Brockovich)

To the Limit: The Untold Story of the Eagles

Death of a Rebel: A Biography of Phil Ochs

Kato Kaelin: The Whole Truth
(The Real Story of O.J., Nicole, and Kato from the Actual Tapes)

Walt Disney: Hollywood's Dark Prince

Rockonomics: The Money Behind the Music

Down Thunder Road: The Making of Bruce Springsteen

NICHOLSON
A BIOGRAPHY

MARC ELIOT

CROWN
ARCHETYPE
NEW YORK

Copyright © 2013 by Rebel Road, Inc.

All rights reserved.
Published in the United States by Crown Archetype, an imprint of the
Crown Publishing Group, a division of Random House LLC, a Penguin
Random House Company, New York.
www.crownpublishing.com

Crown Archetype with colophon is a trademark of Random House LLC.

Library of Congress Cataloging-in-Publication Data
Eliot, Marc.
  Nicholson : a biography / Marc Eliot. — First edition.
    pages cm
  1. Nicholson, Jack. 2. Motion picture actors and actresses—United States—
    Biography. I. Title.
  PN2287.N5E45 2013
  791.43028'092—dc23
  [B]   2013018044

ISBN 978-0-307-88837-2
eISBN 978-0-307-88839-6

Printed in the United States of America

Title page photo courtesy of mptvimages.com

Book design by Lauren Dong
Jacket design by Nupoor Gordon
Jacket photography: Archive Photos/Getty Images

10 9 8 7 6 5 4 3 2

First Edition

*In Memory of Andrew Sarris,
we miss the passing of our great teacher, friend, critic,
and historian, and for the late Karen Black,
whose input was enormous and whose cooperation was
unending. And always for baby cocoa bear.*

Contents

Introduction 1

Part One
Hard Ride to Easy Rider
7

Part Two
Flying over Chinatown Straight On to the Cuckoo's Nest
107

Part Three
The Good Life
165

Part Four
Return of the Joker
199

Part Five
A Few Good Roles
235

Part Six
Sunset on the Boulevard
263

x CONTENTS

FILMOGRAPHY   295

AWARDS   303

NOTES AND SOURCES   313

ACKNOWLEDGMENTS   331

INDEX   335

"There is James Cagney, Spencer Tracy, Humphrey Bogart and Henry Fonda. After that, who is there but Jack Nicholson?"

—MIKE NICHOLS

◆ ◆ ◆

"Marlon Brando influenced me strongly. Today it's hard for people who weren't there to realize the impact that Brando had on an audience. . . . He's always been the patron saint of actors."

—JACK NICHOLSON

◆ ◆ ◆

"He's our Bogart. He represents this whole period of history in a way Bogart represented the '40s and '50s on film."

—HENRY JAGLOM

◆ ◆ ◆

"When I started off, there were 25 people walking around L.A. in red jackets who looked exactly like James Dean, because he was very extreme and quite easy to imitate—which missed the point entirely."

—JACK NICHOLSON

◆ ◆ ◆

"He has a great deal of respect for women, and I would think was one of the pro–women's lib type people."

—BRUCE DERN

◆ ◆ ◆

"What would it be like to fuck Britney Spears? I can answer that question: Monumental. Life altering!"

— JACK NICHOLSON

NICHOLSON

INTRODUCTION

"One never really recovers from his own birth."

—JACK NICHOLSON

JOHN JOSEPH "JACK" NICHOLSON JR. WAS BORN APRIL 22, 1937, AT home in New Jersey, according to his official record of birth, which lists his parents as John and Ethel May Nicholson. Growing up, Jack called Ethel May "Mud," short for "Mudder," Jackspeak for "Mother."[1]

Ethel May was the stalwart family breadwinner. For many years she worked as a hairdresser out of a second-floor room of the small family house in Neptune City, until eventually she made enough money to expand her business, move the brood to a better neighborhood, and open a string of modestly profitable beauty parlors.

John J. Nicholson was nothing like Ethel May; he had no money and little ambition. He found jobs intermittently doing handiwork. While Jack was still a baby, John's drinking became too difficult for Ethel May to put up with and she kicked him out of the house. After that, he lived hand to mouth, often sleeping on park benches and occasionally under the boardwalk. He showed up at Ethel May's mostly on holidays, when she let him in to have dinner with the family. Although Jack rarely saw him, this was the man he believed was his real father.

Various other men drifted in and out of the family house during

---

[1] Early on, Jack liked to make up his own language by shortening words to make them sound funny and keep, or sometimes heighten, their meaning. Later, when he moved to L.A. and hung out with the postbeat/Kerouac crowd, he began to incorporate more "beat speak" into his already colorful "Jackspeak." "Beat speak" is essentially musical in origin, coming out of the sound of jazz and early a cappella rock and roll.

this time, including Don Furcillo-Rose, a dark-haired, dapper, sharp-dressed fellow with a great smile. He had been Jack's older sister June's boyfriend just before her abrupt departure from the family home to fulfill her dream of being in show business. The charming and good-looking Furcillo-Rose, ten years June's senior, was a sometime musician who played with various pickup bands along the Jersey Shore, where they likely first met.[2]

Apparently, Ethel May did not like Furcillo-Rose sniffing around June, and whenever she caught them together she warned him to stay away from her underage daughter or she would have him thrown in jail. After June left home, Furcillo-Rose still occasionally came around, but he was never warmly welcomed by Ethel May, or Lorraine and Shorty, her other daughter and her husband, but Mud knew Furcillo-Rose and June had grown very close, so she occasionally let him sleep over in June's empty room. He was, in his way, after all, part of the family.

Little Jack also never liked Furcillo-Rose, the way he reeked of whiskey and cigarettes, the way he was always whispering to Ethel May so no one else could hear him. Furcillo-Rose never said much to him. Jack did adore Lorraine and George W. "Shorty" Smith. "I had Shorty, as good a father [type] as anybody's ever going to get or need."

Lorraine was the opposite of June in every way. She was not outgoing and not a dreamer; she preferred being a stay-at-home wife. She had married Shorty as soon as it was legal for her to do so. They had gone together since she was seven and he was eleven. In his spare time, which was plentiful, since regular work was hard for him to find, he taught Jack everything a real father would normally teach a boy: how to lift the toilet seat when he peed, how to catch a grounder on the nearby sandlots. *Keep your knees closed when the ball is hit. Let it come to you and wrap it in your glove with your other hand.* In his earlier days Shorty had taken dancing lessons with June, at her insistence, so she could have a partner who wouldn't be groping her all the time, and it

---

[2] Don Furcillo's stage name was Don Rose. He is often referred to in books and articles as Don Furcillo-Rose.

had left him unusually limber. In high school he played a little foot-ball, although he was too small to make first string. He earned his pay as a brakeman for Conrail, but was laid off too many times to be able to call it a career. At the height of World War II he decided to join the merchant marines for the three squares, a place to sleep, and a regular paycheck that he always sent back to Lorraine.

Jack had no memory of June, but he always remembered all the stories told about her around the dinner table at the family house. "My sister June was another story," he told *Rolling Stone*. "She left home at sixteen," the same year Jack was born. "She was a show dancer for Earl Carroll and knew Lucky Luciano. She married one of the test pilots on the American team that broke the sound barrier. . . . Then June went to California, got some interesting jobs, met some interesting people. And died. Very young. Cancer."

Jack told this to the magazine as if it were an outline for a screen-play, a fantasy with a storyline that ended in tragedy, June the beauti-ful but doomed princess. Jack was also still a teenager when he, too, decided to leave home and head west, in search of his own dreams of show business glory. He said he wanted to be an actor. Like June, he had a fanciful imagination hinged to a lack of real opportunity.

When he first arrived in L.A. he briefly stayed with her, until he got a regular job and moved out. After taking some acting classes, he found some work in independent films. His early "rebel" roles led him to big-ger parts with better scripts, and although it took many hard years to happen, he eventually became a star. He was lauded by fans and critics alike for his attractive onscreen persona and how he always seemed to be playing himself, no matter what the role. People went to his movies to see him as much as to see the film. Audiences loved Jack—or the movie persona they believed was Jack.

Acting came naturally to him and with good reason. His Americana childhood was a diorama of deception. Nothing in the Neptune City house was exactly the way as it had seemed. Everyone in his childhood had played a role, and they did it well. Jack didn't learn how to act from Marlon Brando or even Stanislavsky. He learned from June, Lorraine, John, Shorty, Don, and most of all, Ethel May.

♦ ♦ ♦

ALL THE GREAT movie stars, and Jack is unquestionably one of the greatest, are really two people: the private person offscreen and the famous actor on it who plays the characters that audiences love him for. This duality makes it difficult for audiences, and sometimes film critics and historians, to differentiate between the characters actors play and the character of the actor who plays him. The trick for screen actors is to convince us they are who they aren't and they aren't who they are; the contradiction for those performers looking to reveal the "truth" to their audiences is by playing people they are not. Acting is the art of the artificial.

The continuum of Jack's character, smiling, cool, hip, intense, and articulate, showed up in virtually every one of his movies, until one day in 1974 he learned his family's terrible secret, the reality behind all that "acting," something so deep, so dark, and so deceptive, it changed everything about his life, and therefore everything about his acting. The final film he made before he found out this secret was *The Last Detail*, in which the character he plays, Billy "Bad Ass" Buddusky, believes he is invulnerable. He is tough, funny, cocky, and inherently instinctive. He is innocent when the film begins and he remains so, even as he comes to recognize the contradiction of his responsibilities. In the first film he made after that, *Chinatown*, the character he plays, J. J. Gittes, is a detective, a symbol of authority. Gittes, too, is tough, funny, cocky but vulnerable and inherently cerebral. To audiences, this was the better, meaning more ingratiating, performance. Audiences adore attractive vulnerability in their heroes.

But to Jack, the differences were more than surface sensitivities. His acting style hadn't grown; Jack the personality had changed because Jack the man had changed.

In between, he made *The Passenger* for Antonio Antonioni, before *Chinatown* but released after. It is a film whose main character has no clear identity and spends the entire film in search of himself. This journey serves as the transition between the characters "Bad Ass" Buddusky and J. J. Gittes. The liberation of the aptly named David Locke is the link between the two. Set in the background of the Chad civil war, a perfect metaphorical backdrop for this film, Locke comes across a dead body at his hotel and assumes the person's identity, literally and figuratively becoming him. In *Chinatown*, Gittes starts off as an innocent, but when the film ends he is, in Blakean terms, experienced. In real life, Jack had taken a bite of the forbidden fruit when he learned the family secret and paid the price.[3] For the rest of his life, no character he ever played would again be so easy, simple, or innocent. This is what people really mean when they talk about the difference between Jack's early performances in his "personal" films and his later ones in more commercial, mainstream movies.

After 1974, with one or two exceptions, he never again played a purely romantic lead. And in real life, while women continued to be a source of both pleasure and pain for him, true love was something he could never fully accept, believe, or trust from them. His seventeen-year relationship with Anjelica Huston, the woman able to get closest to him, was a series of hellos and good-byes, angers, frustrations, and, on both their parts, infidelities strewn throughout their time together. It is significant that in the end they both wound up alone.

What follows, then, is the story of Jack Nicholson the movie star and Jack Nicholson the man. Jack the personality made sixty-two films, during which Jack the man kept playing the one role he had tried to reconcile with and perfect his whole life. Who he really was.

Himself.

---

[3] The remarkable similarities between what Jack discovered in real life and the plot of *Chinatown*, written by his friend at the time Robert Towne, was something Jack called a coincidence, as the film was written before he found out. However, a close check of the chronology of events shows that Jack did know it before *Chinatown* was written and very likely helped Towne shape his screenplay into something more autobiographical (for Jack) than originally intended.

Part I

Hard
Ride
to
Easy
Rider

PREVIOUS PAGE: Dennis Hopper, Peter Fonda, and Jack Nicholson in Hopper's 1969 *Easy Rider. Courtesy of Getty Images*

"I have the blood of kings in my veins . . ."

—JACK NICHOLSON

JACK NICHOLSON GREW UP IN NEPTUNE CITY, A SMALL BOROUGH in Monmouth County, New Jersey; it is situated approximately fifty miles south of Manhattan near the Jersey Shore and Asbury Park, the colorful mecca of carnival dreams and penny arcades that so captured the imagination of the local children of South Jersey's working class. Asbury Park needs no further mythic atmospherics than have already been provided by its fertile crop of countless local dreamers-made-good, most notable among them—besides Jack—Bruce Springsteen, Danny DeVito, and, a step or two back in time, the most commercially successful film comedy duo of its day, the burlesque-trained team of classic skinny straight man and lovable tubby *stupido*, Bud Abbott and Lou Costello.[1]

Because Ethel May's house was constantly filled with women coming and going to have their hair done, and the children they brought along to save babysitting money, amid all the hustle and bustle and female gossip, young Jack had trouble finding his own little corner in this noisy, chemical-smelling house. As Jack later said, being surrounded by all that estrogen, "It's a miracle I didn't turn out to be a fag." Sometimes if he could, he would sneak off and lose himself in the sands of the shore, walking aimlessly through its many cheap and tawdry sideshows.

Two other things he could do by himself were read comic books and

---

[1] Lou Costello was born farther north, in Paterson, New Jersey.

collect baseball cards. Jack was a boy who lived inside his superhero dreams. Escapism helped alleviate the loneliness borne of being surrounded by so many people at the house and yet being alone so much of the time. As a result, he had frequent temper tantrums that were partly a cry for some attention of his own. According to his sister Lorraine, when Jack couldn't get his way about something, his tantrums "rocked the house like an earthquake." One Christmas, he took a crosscut saw and sliced off a leg of the kitchen table. In return, Ethel May gave him a lump of coal for his present. Jack screamed and hollered until she gave him his real present, and then he calmed down. Another time, when she was on the phone, he lay down on the floor and began kicking and screaming until she hung up. "Later on," Jack recalled, "I became conscious of very early emotions about not being wanted—feeling that I was a problem to my family as an infant. You see, my mother and father separated just prior to my birth . . . it must have been very hard on my mother . . ." It would take decades for Jack to understand why he had those feelings.

Like most boys his age, Jack idolized Joe DiMaggio and had all his cards. One time Jack was sent to the grocery store for bread and milk and instead spent the money on the newest issues of *Sub-Mariner, Human Torch, Captain Marvel,* and *Batman* comics. He loved Batman the most because of his extended human skills rather than superhuman skills or supernatural powers. And the character of the Joker. When he came home, Ethel May spanked him and took all the comic books away.

And the seeds of sex were clearly planted in Jack from a very early age. "I was very driven. I remember being at least mentally sexually excited about things from childhood, even sooner than eight, in the bathtub. I mean, I had a large appetite."

AND THERE WAS also the movies. Young Jack spent nearly every Saturday afternoon at the local movie house, the Palace, devouring the cartoons and the episodic serials with endings that seemed impossible for the hero to survive—cliff-hangers constructed to guarantee the return of every kid in the audience the following Saturday for another marathon of celluloid, soda, popcorn, and miracles.

Even though there were some hard financial times, "I never felt poor," Jack recalled. "In Neptune there was a slightly rougher, lower-middle-class region and a more upper-middle-class one. Ethel May Nicholson was smart enough to move [us] to the better area . . ." With her business thriving, in 1950, when Jack was thirteen, she moved the entire brood a crucial two miles south to Spring Lake, a better neighborhood on the other side of the tracks, sometimes called the Irish Riviera of the Jersey Shore. She set up home and shop at 505 Mercer Avenue just in time for Jack to enter Manasquan High School, one of the stronger academic public schools in southern New Jersey.

It was a big deal to everyone except Jack when Ethel May bought one of the first TVs on the block, a black-and-white box with legs. Jack preferred the Saturday morning big-screen movies over the blurry, talky content of the small flickering screen. He wasn't impressed with the likes of *The Adventures of Superman* or *The Lone Ranger.* To him, they were better in comic books, or in his animated imagination, than on TV. Even when some of the other kids from the neighborhood crowded in to watch the new picture-and-sound marvel in the living room, Jack could not have cared less.

He hadn't yet had his adolescent spurt (such as it would be); he was still shorter than most of the other boys and carried a thick layer of baby belly fat. He would eventually lose most of it but would never grow as muscular as he wanted to be, or tall enough to play basketball, his favorite sport. With the extra pounds and the diminutive height he earned the taunting nickname "Chubs" from the other students. And he suffered from an unusually extreme case of acne. His skin was covered with blemishes that would permanently scar and pit his face, shoulders, chest, and back, causing him throughout most of his film career to never allow himself to be filmed without wearing a shirt unless the lighting was favorable and his body and face makeup was expertly applied.

At Manasquan he proved a good student—smart, cerebral, and analytical—but what meant most to him was what he lacked: the size and physical strength to play ball. He also tried out for football but proved too small and too soft for that game as well and had to settle instead for the job of the baseball team's equipment manager, reduced to carrying bats, balls, and gloves for the team's players. "He wanted to be an athlete, and was probably frustrated about not having been a little bigger, a little taller, maybe even a little older at the time. He was always the youngest in the group. . . ," recalled one classmate. Instead, he wrote about the teams' games. What did come easily to him, he discovered, was writing. He liked descriptive prose, capturing the action as if he were playing right alongside the team. Writing a great sentence was almost as good as making a slam-dunk. Almost.

By 1953, his junior year, sixteen-year-old Jack, with his dark Irish good looks—despite his acne—his new, leaner, and more muscular body, and his sharp, witty tongue, went from being the runt to one of the most popular boys in his class. For the first time the girls at school began noticing him—"Chubs" became "Nick" (short for Nicholson)— and his broad smile, which seemed always now to be plastered across his face as if cut open by a can opener. And while his teachers were always suspicious of what they perceived as some mischievous prank behind it, along with his general air of newfound arrogance, the worst thing they could find to accuse him of was smoking. He had developed a two-pack-a-day habit he would never be able to break. They warned him that smoking would stunt his growth. He laughed but would never grow taller than 5'9½"—smaller than Steve McQueen, smaller than Paul Newman, smaller than Robert Redford, the same size as Robert De Niro, taller than Al Pacino and Bob Dylan.

After failing to make any of the teams, he eventually turned to acting in school plays, something that didn't require the size and strength of athletics. He tried out for one in the spring of his junior year and discovered he not only liked performing but was pretty good at it. His first show, *Out of the Frying Pan* by Francis Swann, was a broad comedy about young kids trying to make it as actors on Broadway. It had had a successful Great White Way run in 1941, after which Swann's youthful characters became a staple of high school productions for much of the

1940s and 1950s, before giving way to more contemporary fare. Jack had a small role in *Frying Pan*, but it was satisfying enough to persuade him to sign up in his senior year as a regular for the school's drama club.

After hours, between rehearsal schedules, to earn cigarette money Jack worked as an usher at a local movie theater, the Rivoli in Belmar. There the brightness of the day and the attention he got in school by acting turned into the darkness of the movie theater, where he was able to pay attention to real actors over and over again, studying their every move, trying to figure out how they did what they did, and how he could do it too. He also worked as a part-time lifeguard in the warmer weather, at nearby Bradley Beach (always wearing a swim shirt to keep his acne-filled chest skin covered), a job that gave him the pleasurable task of watching pretty young girls sunbathe in bathing suits.

In his senior-year production, Jack landed the role of one of the crazies in John Patrick's *The Curious Savage*, originally written as a screenplay for the silent screen legend Lillian Gish about an old woman committed to an insane asylum where she is surrounded by lunatics, one of whom, Hannibal, was played by Jack. He was so good in it that at graduation he was voted "Best Actor" by his classmates.

Despite his increased, thespian-generated popularity with girls and his lifeguard gig, he still couldn't actually get one to go with him. Always quick with a joke or a smirky comment, he became something of the class clown throughout high school, and his quick wit eased a lot of his frustration. If he couldn't attract girls with his physical prowess, he could get them at least to come closer by making them laugh, and as a result he was surrounded his senior year by what were for him all the prettiest look-but-don't-touch cuties. Sandra Hawes, the senior class's "Best Actress," the princess to Jack's prince, remembers, "He would hang around with the most popular girls in high school . . . because he was fun to be with . . . even though he never really had any love life . . . he was probably the only one who didn't have to have a girlfriend . . . he was a kidder, a joker, always cutting up." His verbal athletics earned him the new nickname "The Weaver" for his ability to move in and out of stories and always manage to find a way to tie them all together at the end. Even then he had the habit of licking his lips between groups of words.

His good-guy popularity also got him elected vice president of the senior graduating class, despite the fact that by now his everyday costume of choice was more fit for a budding rebel—a pair of dirty jeans and a motorcycle jacket became his uniform after he saw László Benedek's *The Wild One* when it opened in December 1953, starring Marlon Brando as a motorcycle-riding bad boy who possesses a killer smile he fully flashes only once, at the so-called happy ending of the film. The school's authorities frowned on Jack's outfit, but they chose to look the other way. He was about to finish school that June; it made no sense stirring any pots at the last minute.

HE GRADUATED FROM Manasquan in June 1954. By then he had saved enough money from working at the movie theater and as a lifeguard to buy himself a used 1947 Studebaker (Jack liked to brag that he was such a good handicapper that his regular visits to the Monmouth racetrack all through high school had won him the money to buy it). It was only when he applied for his driver's license that he discovered for the first time there was no record anywhere of his birth, which he had always assumed had happened at home, like his sisters. As far as the state was concerned, Jack Nicholson did not exist. To solve the problem, Ethel May filed a Delayed Report of Birth with the New Jersey State Health Department. In it she listed Jack's birth date as April 22, 1937, at 1410 Sixth Avenue in Neptune City, New Jersey. According to it, Jack was indeed born at home. She listed herself, Ethel Rhoads, as the mother and John Joseph Nicholson as her husband and Jack's father.

It gave Jack the official documentation he needed to get his license, but, as he was later to discover, like so much of the rest of the family's history he believed and believed in, none of it was true.

"I got into acting by being a fan . . ."

—Jack Nicholson

[WHEN I WAS OLD ENOUGH] I HEADED WEST TO SEE SOME MOVIE stars and got work around the studios . . . when I say 'fan' I don't mean I was an autograph hound or anything like that . . . Everybody in my age bracket [were] Marlon Brando fans."

Jack's decision to spend some time in Los Angeles came because of an invitation from the unlikeliest of sources, his sister June. She was living now in Inglewood, a low-rent section of L.A. County on the outskirts of Hollywood. Her journey west had not been a smooth one. Over Furcillo-Rose's objections, two months after Jack was born, she determined to leave New Jersey to pursue a career of her own in show business. She joined one of the remaining vaudeville circuits that traveled from Philadelphia, down to Miami and back north and west to Chicago. In 1944, at the age of twenty-five she gave up on making it as a dancer and wound up working in a defense plant in Ohio. There she met and married Murray "Bob" Hawley, a divorced test pilot (who may or may not have broken the sound barrier) but who definitely came from money. Over the next few years they had two children, a son and a daughter, and relocated to Southampton, New York, the playland of the Northeast rich. All was well until one day, without warning, Hawley left June and the children and took up with another woman. Dejected, June returned briefly to New Jersey before setting out to Los Angeles with her two children in tow, hoping to start another new life.

When Jack graduated from high school in the spring of 1954, as a present June sent him an invitation to spend the summer with her in

Hollywood and a plane ticket to get there. Jack jumped at the chance not only to be with his sister but to walk the same streets and breathe the same air as his screen idol Marlon Brando.

Curiously, and despite his popularity, he told none of his neighborhood friends from school about his journey west. It was as if, after all, they meant nothing to him, that they had made his life more difficult than it had to be, especially the girls. He was still a virgin when he left for California. Jack promised Ethel May he would return in two months and enroll at the University of Delaware, where his high grade-point average had earned him an offer of an engineering scholarship.

IT DIDN'T TAKE long for June to regret having invited Jack, and for him to regret accepting. Her apartment was already small with her and the two children, and smaller with Jack in it, especially since he hung around all day, sullen, slouchy, sleeping late, and eating whatever was in the small refrigerator. The only time she had a break from him was when he walked over to the nearby Hollywood Park to indulge in his favorite pastime, playing the ponies. On days he didn't have enough money for the track, he ventured out by bus to Hollywood to explore its fabled streets. He couldn't get over all the little aqua-and-green houses.

The dream-factory town was built by the first-generation movie moguls who took over the orange groves that covered acres of cheap land and turned them into studios and built these little houses for the employees, from the makeup staff to the actors and actresses. Small businesses sprang up to service the two necessities of most studio actors and technicians—coffeehouses where they could smoke and drink cupfuls of hot, steaming caffeine on their way to work, and bars where they could retreat in the evenings and juice it up until closing time. At eleven every night the town shut tight. Filmmaking began at dawn.

By 1935 the party had moved west to a strip of undistracted, unregulated land between Hollywood and Beverly Hills on Sunset Boulevard known as the Sunset Strip. It had no police department and no local government, and sex and alcohol were plentiful. Many of the cafés and clubs on the Strip were owned by the actors themselves, and for those who couldn't couple up for free, there were brothels all over the place, their main attraction the unusually beautiful girls who worked there, many of them bit players at the studios during the day, "starlets," as they preferred to be called, waiting for their big break and in the meantime needing a way to pay their bills.

The major Hollywood studios had a decades-long lock on what could be made and what could be seen; they produced the films, distributed them, and owned the theaters that showed them. That iron grip began to loosen in 1948, when the Supreme Court declared Hollywood an oligopoly, and because of it the look of films soon began to change. The arrival of independent films signaled the beginning of the end of the censorial Production Code, and Hollywood, but not necessarily the majors, began to make more interesting movies, exploring subjects beyond the boy-meets-girl fare that had dominated the studios' Golden Age. At the center of these new films were new stars, and no one was more explosive than Marlon Brando.

In July 1954, shortly after Jack arrived in Hollywood, Elia Kazan's *On the Waterfront*, starring Brando, opened in theaters and replaced Johnny Strabler with Terry Malloy as the newest rebel of American movies, a virile but vulnerable tough guy in search of his own tortured soul.

Brando changed forever the image of what an American male movie star was, by lowering the age and raising the temperature of the definition of onscreen masculinity. As Terry Malloy in *Waterfront*, Brando's performance turned on Jack and a whole generation of young starstruck boys just like him who wanted to be the next Marlon Brando.

DESPITE THE FACT that he felt crowded in June's tiny apartment and didn't especially like her constant fixing of his hair, and asking him if he'd had enough to eat even when he emptied the fridge, and if he had changed his underwear, more like a mother than a sister, he didn't mind it all that much. "There were certain things about my relation-ship with her," Jack recalled years later. "Body English. And I remember thinking, when my sister doted on me, what was she worried about?"

Despite Mud's insistence that fall that he return east to start college, Jack knew there was no turning back. When the summer ended he de-cided to trade in his chance to get a higher education in favor of learn-ing a few life lessons. He found himself a small inexpensive apartment in Culver City, a few miles south of Hollywood, where he would sleep until late afternoon if he felt like it, without June's constant nagging, then get up and go to the part-time job he'd found to pay for it, restock-ing inventory in a toy store on Hollywood Boulevard.

After work he might grab a bite at Romero's Coffee Shop on Wilshire, a hangout for a lot of the new self-styled rebel wannabe actors. Jack's outgoing personality allowed him to easily ingratiate himself into their circle, where he loved to sit around and talk with them about movies in his flat monotone New Jersey voice. They all enjoyed hearing him ana-lyze that scene in *Waterfront* where Brando as Terry picks up the glove that Eva Marie Saint as Edie accidentally drops while they're walking and talking. Terry picks it up and tries to put it on his own hand, in ef-fect to get under her skin. What made the scene even more special for Jack was that it was improvised. Saint really had accidentally dropped the glove during filming and Brando just went with it. Method-acting, of which this was a perfect example of "being in the moment," was nirvana to him and the rest of these caffeine critics.

And if Jack got lucky, he might even try to pick up one of the little beauties in tight sweaters and black jeans sitting at a nearby table, their chins in their palms, listening to his every word in rapt attention. He may have thought about it, but he never had the courage to try.

Or he might head over to one of the other Googie-style coffee-houses and bars where other nests of wannabes frequented, or the Unicorn, the Renaissance, Chez Paulette's, Barney's Beanery, the Rain Check—a good place to play a game of unhurried darts—Mac's, Luans. He loved hanging with the "puries," as he called them in Jackspeak, the L.A. young actors whose own hip culture was emerging around them. "I was part of a generation that was raised on cool jazz and Jack

Kerouac, and we walked around in corduroys and turtlenecks talking about Camus and Sartre and existentialism . . . we stayed up all night and slept till three in the afternoon . . . We were among the few people around seeing European pictures . . . L.A. 'puries' were people very expressive of the L.A. culture—the overstuffed hamburger, the 18,000 ice-cream flavors, the Hollywood electric whiz-bang kids . . ."

Or, if he was really broke, he might walk east on Sunset, past La Brea, to one of the many storefront pool halls tucked between the tattoo parlor and the whorehouses, and hustle up enough money to make that month's rent.

But by 1955, after Jack had spent a year scrounging and being alone among the coffeehouse cliques, L.A. was beginning to lose some of its allure. Hanging out with the boys was fun, but it wasn't enough for him. He had not been able to get close to anyone, boy or girl. He didn't want to spend the next twenty years drinking coffee, smoking cigarettes, and getting off on the sound of his own voice. He wanted to be where the real action was, to somehow break into the business, no matter how menial a position he might be able to get. Anything had to be better than sleeping all day and bullshitting all night. He would rather return east and go to college, like Ethel May was still pushing him to do. "I had no [real or meaningful] friends. I was living on my own . . . I had this job I kind of liked as a messenger. I was living in this apartment in Culver City. I'd already seen the two movies in town and I had no car . . . I felt as grim as Vincent van Gogh . . ."

Everything changed one day when a tip from a fellow he'd met at one of the pool halls he frequented led him to MGM's mandatory Labor Relations Deck in Culver City, where, his friend told him, he could apply for a job, and probably get it if he didn't care what it was. He didn't, as long as he could smell the same air the studio's movie stars did. As he later recalled, "I had [already] bought a [plane] ticket on my birthday to go back . . . I thought, 'Well, nothing's happening much [in L.A.]. I better go back [east] and get serious. And while I was down buying the ticket I got the job at MGM." At the last minute, as he was already packing, he got a call that he was hired full-time as an office worker for MGM's animation department.

He started May 5, 1955; his salary was thirty dollars a week, his job to do things like sorting the fan mail for Tom and Jerry, MGM's cartoon cat-and-mouse answer to Disney's Mickey Mouse and Donald Duck. He soon realized that the work (and the money) wasn't much different than at the toy store. There he worked with stuffed animals, here animated ones, but at least now he could legitimately say he was in show business. He quickly got used to seeing all the real-life MGM stars roaming about the storied Culver City studios, where there were, supposedly, more than in heaven.

"I saw everybody. I was on those sound stages a lot . . . Monroe, Bogie, Hepburn, Brando, Spencer Tracy, everybody worked there in the time I was there. It was hog heaven for me. I laid out on the lawn one day to try and get a look at Lana Turner's underpants . . ." Jack made it a point to address everyone by his or her first name, from the lowliest sweepers (even lower than him) to the top executives, his words always accompanied by a smile.

He was now able to afford a better place to live, a small above-a-garage apartment in Culver City he shared with another wannabe actor by the name of Roger "Storeroom" Anderson, who also worked at MGM, as a gofer. Like Jack, Anderson was yet another wannabe Brando from back east who after finishing high school decided to move to L.A. to strike it rich in Hollywood. The place was awful; the sound of the garage doors opening and closing at all hours nearly drove the two of them crazy, and the smell of gasoline seeping up through the floor made them sick to their stomachs, forcing them to keep the windows open during the often chilly L.A. nights.

Because he was earning a regular salary, Jack felt comfortable enough to ask Mud for a loan, which he promised he would pay back, so he could buy a car. Public transportation in Southern California then (as now) was woeful, and when Mud realized he wasn't coming home, she sent him $400. As soon as he got the money he went out and bought a used Studebaker.

Jack loved his car and drove it everywhere, even to the track, where, one day, after playing his hunches, he came back to the parking lot to find that it was gone. It was a bitter reminder that Hollywood wasn't only the land of dreams; it also had its fair share of reality.

AT MGM, JACK fit in easily with the other workers, but he wanted to get himself out of the cartoon division as soon as possible and into the acting one.

One of the more apocryphal-sounding stories Jack himself promulgated for years was how he got his first break. He claimed he was riding in an elevator at MGM and the veteran producer Joe Pasternak (*Destry Rides Again, Summer Stock, The Great Caruso,* and others) happened to be on it, began staring at Jack's pleasant face, asked him point-blank if he wanted to be an actor, and Jack said no.[1] Later on he would explain that he had been so flustered that he meant to say yes, but before he could correct himself Pasternak got off the elevator. Later on, Bill Hanna, one of the important animators in the cartoon department, who had taken a liking to Jack, listened to his relating of the incident and laughed when Jack said he'd said no. Hanna then told him about the one essential fact of Hollywood life: that you never say no to anyone, no matter what the proposition. Fortunately, Pasternak had ignored his response (or hadn't heard it) and in May 1956 he arranged for Jack to take a screen test at MGM.

Which he failed miserably.

The report that came back on him was strong; it acknowledged his good looks, the terrific smile, his slight, athletic build, and his beautiful, magnetic hazel eyes. But the negatives were stronger: a notable lack of experience—MGM did not consider high school plays legitimate credentials, unless they were talking about a beautiful young blonde who wanted to be an actress—and a flat-toned voice driven by a pronounced

---

[1] Stories like this abound in Hollywood. The most famous is that Lana Turner was sitting at the soda counter of the legendary Schwab's drugstore and was discovered by the publisher of the *Hollywood Reporter,* impressed by her "abilities," meaning the tight sweater she was wearing at the time. Jack has always insisted his elevator story actually happened.

New Jersey accent. He was instructed to take speech and acting lessons and told they would reconsider him in six months.

It was a setback, and Jack was depressed about it. Hanna felt sorry for him and hooked Jack up with a friend, Joe Flynn, another then-struggling character actor who had opened up a little acting school to support himself and that competed with the dozens of other workshop storefronts on Hollywood Boulevard. During this time Hollywood had almost as many acting schools as coffee shops. Most were attended by actors on the G.I. Bill, which paid for the classes. Flynn, whose portly physique and sharp tongue would eventually land him jobs as a regular and familiar face-without-a-name in dozens of TV sitcoms until he hit it big with 1962's TV goofball sitcom *McHale's Navy*, had developed a strong student following. Hanna arranged an audition for Jack.

The first thing Flynn told him was not to do anything about his accent, that it was what made him stand out from all the other per-fect-diction hopefuls. Each sentence Jack spoke faded at the end, as if his vocal engine had run out of gas, but that was okay. And there was something else Flynn noticed about Jack. His eyes seemed to match his words. As he spoke, his eyebrows arched up and down. Flynn did not often see a face as uniquely expressive as Jack's. It had a charismatic attraction, something that can't be taught in acting classes. "I think I knew the power of my smile by the time I was five or six," Jack remembered. "Once I started looking at myself, though, I thought, 'I've got to keep my lips closed. Otherwise I look like an inebriated chipmunk.'"

Flynn suggested that Jack skip the lessons and instead find a place he could do some real acting and get some solid experience under his belt. At the time MGM underwrote a place called the Players' Ring, a small, 150-seat repertory company on Santa Monica Boulevard, as a way to discover and develop new talent. With a good word put in from Flynn, Jack was hired for their production of *Tea and Sympathy*, a play that had had a successful run on Broadway in 1953 and would be made into a movie in 1956. To get the two-line part they wanted him for, Jack had to agree to also sweep the floors of the tiny stage every night after the show and perform other menial tasks, all for the royal sum of fourteen dollars a week.

The rest of the cast was made up of young, good-looking hopefuls, all unknowns on the brink: Michael Landon, who would go on to play Little Joe in the long-running *Bonanza* and two other long-running series for NBC; Robert Vaughn, who would go on to be TV's *The Man from U.N.C.L.E.*; Robert Fuller, who would land several series roles playing cowboys (*Laramie*, *Wagon Train*); and Edd Byrnes, Edd "Kookie" Byrnes when he landed a regular role on *77 Sunset Strip* and became a fifteen-minute teen sensation because of the way he was always combing his hair on the show.

A fifth player, a real actor, dropped out early in the production. He had already appeared in George Stevens's *Giant*, co-starring the very hot and very dead James Dean, Jack's newest favorite actor after seeing him in Nicholas Ray's *Rebel without a Cause*. The fifth player had also appeared in *Rebel*, landing the part on Dean's recommendation. His name was Dennis Hopper.

EVEN JACK, BY far the least experienced of all the company's players, managed to get work off his brief appearance in *Tea and Sympathy*. He was called in again by MGM's casting department; after seeing him in it, they gave him a small part in *Matinee Theatre*, an afternoon live sixty-minute drama the studio produced out of L.A. It wasn't that Jack had been so great in *Tea and Sympathy*. TV ate actors, and every young out-of-work wannabe in Hollywood sooner or later landed on *Matinee Theatre*. Jack's episode was broadcast September 3, 1956. He was ecstatic.

Two weeks later Jack was fired by MGM, along with everyone else on his floor, when the studio decided to shut down its animation division.

Once again Jack was on his own, broke and alone, just another out-of-work Hollywood actor scrounging for parts. His appearance on *Matinee Theatre* earned him membership in AFTRA (the American Federation of Television and Radio Artists) and because of it his name was listed in the Academy Players Directory, a kind of Sears catalog of actors and actresses. Out of that he scored a few more live local TV spots and shows like *Divorce Court*, sometimes playing the defendant, sometimes the claimant. It didn't really matter; everyone on these shows was utterly faceless, forgotten the minute their "case" was resolved.

Barely scratching out a living, Jack continued to hang at all the regular actor haunts. He had breakfast every morning sharing a booth at Schwab's Pharmacy, the legendary drugstore/soda fountain, with whatever actor or musician happened to be there. He spent afternoons at Romero's, and most evenings hustling pool. One day he happened to run into fellow MGM-exer Luanda Andrews and another friend, Jud Taylor, and they told him a spot was opening up in Jeff Corey's acting class. Corey had been a fairly successful New York method-trained Shakespearean stage actor in the 1930s, came to L.A. and had a solid film career until 1951, when he was brought up before the House Un-American Activities Committee, after which he found himself on the dreaded blacklist and did not appear in another movie for twelve years. To support himself during that time he taught acting out of his garage. His list of students included Robert Blake; Carole Eastman, a young, good-looking woman interested in learning about acting to better write for the screen; Robert Towne, who had ambitions to both write and direct; Sally Kellerman; James Dean (whose mere attendance before his untimely death instantly elevated Corey's reputation to near-mythic proportion after it); and a host of other actors and writers who would go on to successful careers. Many of them later attributed their success to having studied with Corey.

Jack wanted in, but soon enough was hearing the same old thing from Corey that he had everywhere else, except from Flynn—about his funny voice and accent. Corey insisted he had to get rid of it, that it made him sound callow. He practiced day and night until Corey was satisfied enough to admit him to the one available seat left in the current enrollment.

Jack always considered Corey one of the best teachers he'd ever had, acting or otherwise. He remembered Corey saying, "When an actor takes on a part, he or she should feel free to assume they have 85% in common with them . . . if you can't drop the character within 10 minutes after the performance, then you're in trouble, you've invested psychically in it in a way that's not good for you as a person." Jack could dig it. This was acting talk he understood. Especially the 85 percent. Only what do you use, he wondered; how do you measure that?

What became immediately apparent to Jack was how the other actors seemed to all want to emulate James Dean, who himself had seemed, before his death, to be emulating the Great God Brando. They all dressed in jeans, T-shirts, sneakers, and zippered or leather jackets, and spoke with their heads down while their eyes stared straight ahead. During breaks or after classes, having coffee somewhere, the boys in the class chatted about their other cultural touchstones, the 1950s beat writers and poets: Kerouac, Kesey, Ginsberg. Jack immediately made it his business to read their work, to find out what it was that these boys liked so much about them.

The girls in Corey's class were another story: soft and creamy and career-minded, hoping to break into the movies. And they were not the least bit interested in getting laid, at least not by any of these horny wannabes.

Except for one, Georgianna Carter, a blond southern girl with a great smile. The first time Jack laid eyes on her, he decided she was for him, and he pursued her like crazy. She knew it and didn't mind at all. "I liked him a lot," she later remembered, "and pretty soon I couldn't do without him. He was a year younger than I. He was very boyish and had a very soft look about him." Georgianna happily took Jack's virginity.

They quickly became a couple, always arriving at and leaving Corey's class holding hands, and when Corey moved his classroom to a storefront in Hollywood at Western and Fernwood, Jack and Georgianna and some of the others volunteered to help move furniture, paint walls, do whatever was necessary to help, having fun doing it.

Then one day a new member joined the class. His presence would prove auspicious; it would change both his and Jack's lives forever, in ways neither one could ever have foreseen.

"Early on, I would say that Brando was a big hero of mine. Castro was a hero. I like Galbraith. Dylan. Joe DiMaggio was one when I was a kid."

—JACK NICHOLSON

B Y THE MIDFIFTIES, THE STUDIO SYSTEM WAS SLOWLY DYING BUT not yet dead. As original-looking, different-feeling, and popular as the new postwar films were, they still conformed to traditional studio standards to maintain their box office appeal to mainstream audiences. Fred Zinnemann's 1952 *High Noon* resolves all its complex and psychological issues by that most fundamental of old-school methods, the classic cowboy movie shoot-out. *On the Waterfront,* too, is, above and beyond all its other socially relevant issues, a conventionally redemptive love story.

In the 1950s, coinciding with Jack's arrival in Hollywood, a handful of film producers were looking to break studio precedent. With the help of a Supreme Court–ordered weakening of the lock the studios had on production, distribution, and exhibition and an influx of young people willing to work for little money and take the big risks the majors wouldn't, or couldn't, this new generation of filmmakers became the pioneers of the burgeoning independent movement in film. They were the real rebels of Hollywood.

One of these was a young, good-looking fellow by the name of Roger Corman. Like so many of his generation, he was film-literate, having grown up on the movies before the onset of television, and a total cinematic nonconformist. His importance to the independent film movement in the 1950s cannot be overemphasized. "Corman was one of those guys in the early years of the New Hollywood who grew up loving the John Fords, the Howard Hawkses, the Alfred Hitchcocks, and, later, the French New Wave, the Swedes, all the film avant-garde who had something new to say and a different way of saying it," recalled Michael Medavoy, a major Hollywood player who has worked within the studio and also as an independent.

According to film critic and historian David Thomson, "One of the things that had been happening in the fifties was that Roger Corman had been doing a lot of exploitation films, biker films, drug films, and he had a coterie around him. Those films were extraordinarily cheap because Corman was cheap, but they made a lot of money. Say what you want, Corman proved one thing, that there was a teenage audience out there and they were ready to deal with films that had sex, rock and roll and drugs, that were becoming increasingly common in ordinary American experience."

And from film historian and biographer Peter Biskind: "Corman provided everyone of that generation their first opportunities to write, act, and direct. Roger Corman was the closest thing to an institution. There were no film schools in those days. He just threw you into the deepest end of the pool. He pushed you out there and you had to perform."

One thing everyone agrees on, no matter what they may think of his films, is that Corman was a young visionary in an industry run by old and ossifying functionaries. Here is Roger Corman in his own words: "It was difficult being an independent producer/director during my early days, which were at the height of the studio system's last years of dominating American film. It was very difficult at first for me to get financing and second to get any sort of decent distribution, but I managed."

Roger Corman was born in Detroit, Michigan, in 1926, and by his account was interested in movies as far back as he could remember. His parents moved to L.A., and he and his younger brother attended Beverly Hills High School. Roger then went on to Stanford, intending to major in industrial engineering, with time out for a stint in the Navy. After the war, he completed his degree and landed a job at U.S. Electrical Motors in Los Angeles, but lasted there only four days, realizing this was not the direction in which he wanted his life to go. "I began work on Monday and quit on Thursday, telling my boss 'I've made a terrible mistake.'"

Corman had studied engineering to learn about the mechanics of filmmaking, not engines. After quitting his job, he tried to break into producing, but the opportunities were few and far between. "The only job I could get after that in films was at Twentieth Century-Fox as a messenger. I worked my way up to story analyst. I read scripts and commented on them . . . as the youngest reader I was given the most hopeless scripts to cover."

A frustrated Corman quit Fox; scraped together enough money from friends, family, and anywhere else he could; and in May 1954 produced his first solo independent film, *Monster from the Ocean Floor*, for a pittance, directed by an unknown, Wyatt Ordung.[1]

Roger listed himself as the producer, but in fact he was much more than that; he was the hands-on one-man crew, arriving before every day's shoot to help set up, staying behind after to help break down. He was willing to get on his knees and scrub the floor, if that was what it took to get his film made. Medavoy recalls, "The idea was to save money, and Roger figured the more he did himself, the less he would have to pay someone else."

Monster didn't break any box office records, but made enough money to allow Roger to produce another film. He then tried the sports car racing genre with 1955's *The Fast and the Furious* co-directed with Eduard Sampson and starring John Ireland, a fairly well-known journeyman actor.

Roger was now beginning to understand how Hollywood really worked. He realized his biggest hurdle was the lag time between putting up the money to make a film and having to wait for it to open to

---

[1] Five months prior to Monster from the Ocean Floor's release, Corman co-produced Nathan Juran's Highway Dragnet with Herb Meadow and Jerome Odlum for Allied International Pictures, an outgrowth of the '40s Monogram Pictures.

(hopefully) recoup the investment. "I could see the problem . . . you raised the money, you made the picture, then you had to wait for the picture to earn its money back before you could make another picture." Just as it appeared his producing career was about to come to a fast and furious end, two other independent producers, Sam Arkoff and Jim Nicholson, at the time starting a new independent film company together, American International Pictures, originally called American-Releasing Corporation, offered to lease the completed negative for *The Fast and the Furious* and use it for their startup production. To make the deal, Corman asked for·and got guaranteed up-front production money for his next three pictures that AIP could distribute. That solved both AIP's and Corman's problems: AIP now had a guaranteed flow of product, and Corman had a way to fund his films.

Roger still felt there was one element to the filmmaking process he didn't know enough about. "I had learned the use of the camera and other useful technical qualifications of directing a movie but did not know enough about acting. So I enrolled in Jeff Corey's acting class. Not to become an actor, but to learn about acting . . ." Corey admitted him as a professional observer. Corman's focus soon fell on one actor.

Jack remembers, "[Corman] came into the class, serious as a heart attack . . . He was a one-man band." As is often the case, the special students take the most abuse from their teachers. With Jack and Corey, it was no different. When Corey admonished Jack one time to "show me some poetry" with his acting, Jack snapped back, "Maybe, Jeff, you just don't see the poetry I'm showing you."

It was that confrontation that first brought Jack to Corman's attention. He loved his attitude. Being an antiauthoritarian himself, he applauded this actor's willingness and ability to stand up to Corey. Not long after, Corman offered Jack the starring role in his next scheduled film, *The Cry Baby Killer*. He gave the part to him on his twentieth birthday. Corman had no doubt that he had chosen the right actor. As Corman put it, "I was absolutely certain Jack was going to be a star." Besides Jack's demonstrated intensity, Corman also liked his offbeat good looks, different from the homogenized studio-manufactured male heartthrobs of the day, the Robert Wagners and the Rock Hudsons. He knew before a foot of film had been shot that he had found someone special.

The Cry Baby Killer was a misunderstood-youth story that runs at top speed, *Rebel without a Cause* on amphetamines. "Times were changing," Corman said. "The major studios really didn't understand. The audience was looking for a different type of film. One that spoke their language. If we were going to make pictures about young people, we needed a young person to star—and Jack Nicholson was the one." The Jersey jerk in Jack's voice sounded genuine to Corman—a youthful toughness cut with a thin slice of panic. *The Cry Baby Killer,* Corman's twenty-fifty film, was shot in ten days, on a total budget of $7,000, out of which Jack was paid $1,400, more money than he had ever made from acting in his life.

Despite the fact that AIP couldn't find an exhibitor for the film for the next eighteen months, Jack was ecstatic about being in a real Hollywood movie playing a James Dean–like character. "I hadn't really worked before, I figured this is it!" But despite the film's eye-grabbing tag—"YESTERDAY A TEEN-AGE REBEL TODAY A MAD-DOG KILLER!"—when it finally was released it wound up on the bottom half of double bills, made no money, and quickly faded away.[2]

Jack didn't make another movie for nearly two years. With nothing else on his plate, he joined the Air National Guard, knowing that in peacetime there was little likelihood of his ever being called up for combat duty. While he was doing his basic training in Texas, he received mail almost every day from Georgianna, saying how she missed him and couldn't wait for him to come back to L.A., but he was far more interested in the letters that Mud sent: clips from the local *Asbury Park Press.* It was the only real coverage *The Cry Baby Killer* got: "Small-town boy makes good"–type stories all about him.

◆ ◆ ◆

[2] *The Cry Baby Killer,* made in 1956, was released in August 1958. After its brief theatrical run, it was sold to television, where it eventually made back its investment.

JACK SPENT EIGHT weeks in basic that felt to him like eight years, and he couldn't wait to get back to California. This taste of military discipline was enough to last him for a lifetime. When he was released, he still had six years of Air Guard duty waiting for him, and air training a couple of days a month. Because it was in L.A., his unit had its fair share of entertainers. He got close to Bruce Ballard, the lead singer of the Four Preps, who, like Jack, was always up for a good time, and they managed to find ways to entertain themselves during the hours they belonged to the Air Force. They drank, smoked a little pot, and, even though Jack was going with Georgianna, chased after the waitresses who worked in the coffee shops near the Reserves base. They quickly gained a reputation among the others as champion skirt-chasers. Jack and Bruce always wore their uniforms when they went out, believing they were pussy magnets.

MUD, MEANWHILE, decided that if Jack really wasn't going to come back to New Jersey, she would move to Los Angeles, to be near him and June. She left her businesses to Lorraine and Shorty to look after, hoping they could keep them going. Not long after she arrived in L.A., she moved with June into a small but comfortable duplex on Whitsett Avenue in North Hollywood, in the San Fernando Valley, and June went to work at a local J. C. Penney.

Jack, meanwhile, was sharing a new apartment with a couple of friends; otherwise Mud could have stayed with him. While in Texas he had given up his half of the place above the garage to save on rent. When he was invited by two of his coffeehouse pals—Bronx-born Don Devlin, whose father was an actor and producer Jack hoped to follow into the business, and Harry Gittes, who wanted to break into the producing end of movies—to move in with them in a big apartment they had taken at Fountain and Gardner in West Hollywood, Jack immediately went for it. He could have moved in with Georgianna, who more than once suggested it, but the thought of being in another cramped apartment with a woman was not something that struck him as a good idea. He liked Georgianna well enough, but he didn't want to be with her all the time. That was something people called marriage, and he wasn't ready for anything like that.

If he was hoping for a little peace and quiet, he didn't get it in what was later described as "the wildest house in Hollywood." There was round-the-clock partying, drinks, drugs, sex, lots of tea (of the smoking kind), and beautiful, hot, willing girls who loved to get just as high as the boys and have a good time. The refrigerator never had any food in it, just milk (for Jack's sometimes sensitive stomach), beer, and pot in the freezer to keep it fresh.

Sally Kellerman, another Corey alum and an as-yet-unknown actress, was one of the girls who liked to hang at the house, and whose big break wouldn't come until 1970 when she played "Hot Lips" Houlihan in Robert Altman's film *M*A*S*H*. She was always showing up at all hours to cry on Jack's shoulder about some love-gone-wrong. Jack, with his heavy-lidded eyes, happily provided his shoulder for her. According to Harry Dean Stanton, a good-looking then-out-of-work actor and folk-singer and one of the house regulars, Jack was always tipsy and ready to offer any comfort he could to whatever woman needed it: "Whenever I think of Jack from that period, I always see him with a cheap red wine on his lips."

Another out-of-work hangout friend Jack regularly ran into on the coffeehouse and bar circuit was a rail-thin, wild-haired wannabe director by the name of Monte Hellman, who had now somehow managed to raise $25,000 for a half-written script and wanted Jack to help him finish it. He agreed, and the two worked intensely on it for weeks, with Hellman paying Jack for his time. Corman read the screenplay and liked it but thought it would be too expensive to make, and instead offered Hellman a chance to direct *Beast from Haunted Cave*, an independent, low-budget, twelve-day shoot for Corman's new ancillary company, Filmgroup, to be produced by Roger's brother, Gene Corman. Corman created it because he wanted to loosen the ironclad grip of AIP. *Beast from Haunted Cave* was made in 1958, but without AIP Corman couldn't get distribution for a year.

Hellman had wanted to use Jack in *Beast*, but Corman had other ideas. He used Michael Forest in the lead. Two years after *The Cry*

Baby Killer, Corman finally had another role he thought was better than *Beast* for Jack. *The Wild Ride* (aka *Velocity*) was a California-based drama directed and line-produced by Harvey Berman, based on the same West Coast drag-racing craze that had been the tragic center-piece of *Rebel without a Cause*. It was another Corman neo-teen delinquent film, and the second time he used Jack as his imitation Dean.

Corman: "I had met this other acting teacher who had an acting school in Northern California, and who had been working with his students to make a short film. He approached me about being involved, assuring me it would cost very little because he could supply the crew from his students and most of the cast. I developed the script myself [with Ann Porter, Marion Rothman, and Burt Topper]. I also chose the director of photography [Taylor Sloan] and the leading actors. Even though I hadn't used him after *The Cry Baby Killer* I knew Jack could act, and this was the first script that came along since I thought he was right for the lead. Jack had a lot of intensity and I always thought he would make a great youthful psychotic."

Corman also cast Georgianna in the film, hoping some of her and Jack's real-life chemistry would transfer to the screen. He paid them each two hundred dollars a week, from a total budget of $12,000, and shot the whole thing on a vacant racetrack in the Sonoma Valley.

The film centers on a psychotic biker gang leader, Johnny Varron, played by Jack, who causes the death of several police officers when he sadistically forces them off the road. At the same time, Varron warns one of his gang members, Dave (Robert Bean) to give up his girlfriend, Nancy (Georgianna), and spend more time with the gang because he is starting to be seen as a chicken. Things quickly resolve in this fifty-nine-minute flick, as Johnny falls for and is eventually redeemed by Nancy. According to Jack, he looked for whatever good qualities he could find in this woeful script to humanize his performance. "I think in all my movies all the characters have something to say, and that's how you give a larger picture. I believe in the positive philosophy of all my characters . . ."

When the film was finished, Georgianna said she wanted to meet Jack's family. He dutifully introduced her to Mud, who, like Georgianna, took the visit to mean they were headed toward marriage and made a real effort to embrace her. Jack also introduced her to June, who took an instant liking to her. They began calling each other every day, chatting, June always asking how Jack was doing.

Sure enough, soon after meeting Mud and June, Georgianna started talking to Jack about maybe making plans for the two of them to tie the knot. That was it for him. He had no time for or interest in domesticity. He considered himself an artist, the romantic loner. His thing was making movies, not babies. He told her so, and Georgianna quietly disappeared from his life.

THE WILD RIDE managed to get booked mostly on the bottom side of drive-in double or triple bills up and down the California coast.[3] Hellman agreed to work on *The Wild Ride* as Corman's editor and unofficial and uncredited co-producer. It was while on location during production that Hellman and Jack got to know each other better. Their personalities were very different, but they shared a love of independent film, Brando, Dean, and the Beats. Hellman was the quiet one, observant, always looking as if he were lost in thought a million miles away. Jack, on the other hand, was one of the most outgoing actors on set. He was something of a backslapper and loved a good time. Hellman believed Jack was talented, smart, and "very wry and funny but very cynical." Just as in high school, on set Jack liked to make jokes that made everyone laugh out loud.

As they grew closer, Hellman realized how smart and how frustrated Jack really was. "Jack already had a reputation among his other friends as being the crowd 'intellectual.' He was big on quoting from *The Myth of Sisyphus*, Camus's ode to absurdity. He carried a copy of it in his back pocket, and told me working in these films was like trying to push a boulder up the side of a mountain, believing if he kept pushing he would find stardom at the top. Like Camus, he told me, he had come to discover the joy of pushing as its own reward and that was

---

[3] The film is now in the public domain.

the real reason he appeared in these cornball quickies. I also think he really needed the money."

Jack's attraction to Camus was more than Sisyphean. The author was French/Algerian and was profoundly affected by the War for Independence that broke out in Algeria against the French. Camus's first novel, *The Stranger*, published in 1942 when he was only twenty-nine years old, made him world famous. He was an intellectual, a modern Absurdist writer whose work anticipated everything from Joseph Heller to Bob Dylan to the Beatles. He was a rock star of a writer, young, good-looking, angry, and brilliant. Jack could relate to all of that. In 1957, Camus won the Nobel Prize in Literature, that world's equivalent of an Academy Award. But what really cemented it for Jack was the beautiful Camus's shocking death early in 1960, just prior to production on *The Wild Ride*. Camus was killed in a car crash, a scenario that placed him in the same eternal and eternally romantic pantheon of Jack's other early-death hero, James Dean.

Not long after *The Wild Ride* wrapped, Jack was cast in his third film, his first away from Corman, Richard Rush's *Too Soon to Love*. Rush had heard about Jack from American International Pictures and offered him a part in the film, based on a first-time script by László Gorog, Rush, and a then-unknown Francis Ford Coppola, and AIP wanted Jack to star. The role of the villain in this cheapie was meant to be *Romeo and Juliet* meets *Rebel without a Cause*. To Jack, Corman was John Ford compared to Richard Rush.

He then happily accepted Corman's next assignment, a small part in something called *The Little Shop of Horrors*, a monster movie about a man-eating plant, produced and directed by Corman for his Film-group. Corman did *Shop* as an experiment, to see if he could shoot a feature in less time than a half-hour TV show, which normally (then) took three days. To save money, Corman had his cast and crew all climb over the fences at the old Charlie Chaplin Studios on La Brea and used the facilities without permission.[4]

---

[4] The studio complex was later turned into the A&M recording studios, and still later bought by Jim Henson Productions.

Corman: "It was actually shot in two days and a night and all the actors, including Jack, only had one day's rehearsal. It came about because at one of my other film screenings, there was a moment of horror that made the audience gasp. I thought, that's perfect. And then a funny thing happened. Some of them laughed. I thought, what have I done wrong? Then I realized I hadn't done anything wrong. I had gotten the scream I wanted, and then the audience released the remaining tension by laughing. That's when I first saw the connection between horror and comedy. I then made a picture called A *Bucket of Blood* as a comedy and it was a huge success."

Even though Jack was cast in the film, he had no idea what it was about or even what part he had until he showed up for the first day of rehearsals. Corman wanted him for Wilbur Force, a nerd who goes to the dentist and winds up wrestling with him and his equipment (borrowed by Corman from his own dentist). Much of the scene was improvised, and it was head and shoulders (and teeth) above the rest of the film, and today it is the only scene most people remember. It eventually inspired a hit musical film and Broadway show. [5]

Jack's bit in *Shop* was so good it helped get him his first part in a studio film: Irving Lerner's screen adaptation of one of the books in the trilogy of James T. Farrell's Depression-era opus, *Studs Lonigan*. Farrell was a writer Jack liked, and this was a film he really wanted to do. Unfortunately for him, the title role he thought he was being offered went to Christopher Knight, yet another James Dean look-alike. Jack got one of the lesser roles, Weary Reilly. An unknown actor who had a flair for impersonation, Frank Gorshin, played Kenny Killarney. This is Jack's version of how he was cast as Weary: "The reason I got it, I think, is that readings consisted of improvising situations from the book, and I was the only actor in Hollywood with the stamina and energy to [have actually] read the 700-page trilogy . . . and I was pretty strong in improvisation, because I'd studied with Jeff Corey."

Unfortunately, the film failed to capture the novel's sweep, power,

---

[5] Although they were based on the original film, Corman had nothing directly to do with the later musical film and Broadway versions.

or intensity and struggled to find an audience. Although it was not a success, and James T. Farrell would fade from the requisite reading lists of college English curricula, it was the first time Jack was mentioned in reviews from mainstream critics. At twenty-three years old, he also marked a private milestone, the first year he logged thirty days as a paid actor. He knew this because he marked every day he worked in a little two-inch black address book he kept in his back pocket.

EVEN WHEN HE wasn't working, which was most of the time, he had plenty going on. He had hooked up with Sandra Knight, a twenty-year-old blond California native he had first noticed when she was a messenger at MGM, and then again in Martin Landau's acting class he had lately been taking, while she was still going with young actor Robert Blake, which was why Jack hadn't moved on her then. He didn't want to tangle with the vicious-looking Blake.

Knight, too, was now occasionally working behind the scenes for Roger, and they ran into each other on one of Corman's sets. They started chatting, and when Jack heard she and Blake had split up, he immediately asked her on a date. She accepted, he took her out, and they wound up spending the night together. The speed and the intensity of it (and the freedom Knight had with her own body, and his) made him feel certain that he had found the love of his life.

The beautiful, earthy, and sensual Knight was born in Pennsylvania and grew up in Venice, California, one of L.A.'s beach areas known for its bohemian lifestyle. Knight bore such a strong physical resemblance to Georgianna that, until they were actually introduced, many of Jack's friends thought at first she *was* Georgianna.

Blake, meanwhile, found out Knight was with Jack and let it be known that he intended to kick his ass for "stealing" his girl. Jack's friends repeatedly warned him to steer clear of Blake, which he did.

Jack wanted to break down any remaining emotional or physical barriers between him and Sandra. She had taken a new drug called lysergic acid diethylamide, or LSD, that unleashed one's inhibitions and Jack wanted to try it. With Sandra's enthusiastic support, he went to see psychiatrists "Oz" Janiger, Mortimer Hartman, and Arthur Chandler, all of whom had begun using LSD in their practices.

Jack's experiences with the drug were life-changing. He believed after taking it the first time that he had seen the face of God. He also had castration fantasies, homoerotic fear fantasies, and revelations about not being wanted as an infant. "All of your conceptual reality gets jerked away and there are things in your mind that have in no way been suggested to you," Jack said later on. He also had vivid insights about his childhood, with visions of not being wanted by his mother. And while tripping, he could confront the persistent problem of premature ejaculation that had plagued him ever since he had begun sleeping with Georgianna (and would never fully overcome). All of these visions and revelations were connected, like the wire that links individual posts to a fence. Jack would continue to take LSD for years.

Three weeks after Jack's first acid trip, Sandra proposed to him and he accepted. They tied the knot on June 17, 1962. Jack asked Harry Dean Stanton to be his best man. Sandra's maid of honor was Millie Perkins, a slim, dark-haired beauty whose breakthrough came in 1959 when she was cast in the lead role in George Stevens's *The Diary of Anne Frank*.

As Jack later remembered, "While the ceremony was going on, that part of me that, at night, half believes in God, was looking upward and saying, 'Now, remember, I'm very young, and this doesn't mean I'm not ever going to touch another woman.' It's a humiliating thing and a horrible thing, allegedly, to admit to, but I remember this very clearly."

They had no honeymoon. Instead, both went immediately back to work: she in a small role in Roger Corman's lowbrow take on Shakespeare's *Richard III* called *Tower of London*, he working on but not acting in Corman's 1963 adaptation of Edgar Allan Poe's poem *The Raven*, often incorrectly remembered as Jack's debut in films.

As it happened, Corman had built expensive Gothic-style sets and had the studio space rented through the following Monday but temporarily ran out of money the Friday before and had to halt filming. Jack remembers, "I said, look, Roger, these [elaborate] sets are going to be up over the weekend, so can I use the same sets for free [to direct a few pages of script]? He went and got [Leo Gordon and Jack Hill] to write something." Corman said yes.

Something, but no one was quite sure what. Unlike Richard Matheson's comparatively well-written script for *The Raven*, the screenplay for what Jack named *The Terror* was an out-and-out disaster. It is the film that Jack always names without hesitation as the worst of his career. Boris Karloff, who was in *The Raven* and agreed to give Jack two days for his film, remembered that by late Sunday night, "As [the magnificent sets from *The Raven* were being pulled down around [us] Jack was [still] dashing around with a camera two steps ahead of the wreckers." He was filming some additions to his script he had written himself at the last minute, a few pages of plot, in the hopes he could pull the film together. He couldn't.

After that, everyone connected with *The Raven* had to cool their heels while Corman worked on the finances. It took him another nine months to come up with sufficient funds to complete the final outdoor scenes, on location up at Big Sur.

At least some of the first part of the film was directed by Francis Ford Coppola, until he left for another job that paid more money. Monte Hellman also directed some scenes (a great deal of it, he claims) until he, too, left for a better-paying job. Corman directed the rest of the film himself. He brought the principals back for eleven days to complete the film. Jack and Sandra arrived together, but they had little to do except enjoy the scenery and observe the methodical madness of moviemaking, Corman-style, and each other.

Sometime during those eleven days, Sandra told Jack she was pregnant.

CHAPTER  4

"I never dug [being in Corman's films]. I'm not a nostalgic person. They were just bad. The people who never saw my [early] movies are better off in life than I am, but like all other actors, I needed the work . . . they were the only jobs I could get. Nobody else wanted me."
—JACK NICHOLSON

B Y THE EARLY SIXTIES, THE MAJORS WERE BEGINNING TO CATCH on to and up with Corman. They were attracted to his ratio of low budgets to high profits. Twentieth Century-Fox created a small subdivision called Associated Producers to crank out movies that mostly fell between A-features, the studio's standard fare, and B-movies like the ones Corman was making.

Jack, meanwhile, asked the debacle of *The Terror* Corman how he could get himself a real screenwriting job. Corman's advice was simple: write something easy to film, with no fancy sets or special effects, and make it a thriller. Shortly thereafter, Robert Lippert asked Corman if he knew a good screenwriter and he suggested Jack, who in turn brought Don Devlin in with him as a partner. Devlin had actually written and sold a screenplay he also acted in, *Anatomy of a Psycho*, a cheapie independent released in 1961, directed by Boris Petroff. Jack felt more secure working with an experienced co-writer. It helped him to have another voice there to develop ideas and throw dialogue back and forth to test it out loud.

Lippert hired them for $1,250—for both—and turned them loose to write an easily shootable script. Jack came up with a plot and some dialogue for what became *Thunder Island*, while Devlin did most of the actual scripting. The film, about a political assassination plot set in the Caribbean, starred the voluptuous Fay Spain, and Gene Nelson in the part Jack had originally written for himself. The reason he didn't get it, Lippert said, was that he liked Jack better as a writer than as an actor, and besides, he wasn't a big enough name, which was why Nelson, who was a star at the time, got the part.

Shortly after completing *Thunder Island,* Jack received a call from Mud with the news that June had taken ill. He dropped everything and went to visit her at Cedars of Lebanon Hospital. The doctors told him June was dying of cervical cancer and an especially aggressive breast cancer and warned him not to be shocked when he saw her. He was. She weighed eighty pounds and was skeletal. He couldn't bear it. The last time he'd seen her, when he'd introduced Georgianna to her, June had looked terrific. They talked for a few minutes, and then he kissed her on the forehead and left. He never went back to the hospital and never saw June alive again. The day-to-day job of seeing her through to her death fell to Mud. As she lay nearly unconscious, June suddenly asked to see, of all people, Georgianna. She was the only girl Jack had ever introduced her to, and they had become close, with June perhaps still believing this was the woman Jack was going to marry. Mud told Jack, and he said he would call Georgianna and ask her to visit his sister in the hospital.

When Georgianna answered the phone, Jack quickly explained that this wasn't a romantic call, that he was married now and about to become a father, that the reason for it was that June was dying and had asked to see her. Georgianna immediately went to the hospital, and, like Mud, visited June every day until she died on July 31, 1963, at age forty-four.

Thunder Island was released in October 1963, a little more than two months after June's passing and a month before the killing of John F. Kennedy. After Dallas, no one wanted to see a film about an assassination, and it quickly disappeared from theaters. Jack and Devlin had proved a good creative match, but when the film failed to find an audience, it put an end to their writing partnership.

That August, Jack flew to Acapulco, Mexico, to start work in Josh Logan's *Ensign Pulver*. He had managed to land a small role in the Warner Bros. production, and although the part was tiny, it was by far his biggest mainstream production so far. *Ensign Pulver* was based on the character played by Jack Lemmon in the 1955 screen version of *Mister Roberts*, directed by John Ford and Mervyn Leroy (and an uncredited Logan), originally produced on Broadway by Logan, from Thomas Heggen's best-selling semiautobiographical 1946 novel.

The film was shot off the waters of Acapulco, in Puerto Marques, aboard a retired naval cargo ship. The crew was played by up-and-coming studio contract players. Jack was the least well known and his role in the film was the smallest, while its star, Robert Walker Jr., struggled in the lead. Jack remembered Walker from the old coffeehouse cliques. His father was a famous movie star who committed suicide in the early 1950s. Walker had waited a long time for his big break, and when it finally arrived, it became clear from the start that Logan had picked the wrong actor for the lead. Although he looked remarkably like his father, the difference between the two was that Junior had no talent.

Shooting progressed at a snail's pace. With little to do, Jack passed the time getting stoned. Pot was easily available in Mexico, and soon all the ensemble players were smoking every day, part of the reason they come off a little goofy-looking in the film.

The film's female lead still wasn't cast. With Sandra pregnant, Jack suggested to Logan he consider her best friend, Millie Perkins. Logan tested her and gave her the part as the gorgeous young nurse who drives Pulver gaga.

Not surprisingly, without Fonda, Cagney, and Lemmon reprising their roles, and with the film resting solely on the shoulders of Walker, Jack, most of whose scenes didn't make the final cut, didn't have to wait for the film's release to know that he had just finished participating in what the cast had called the Manhattan Project: the making of an atomic bomb.

◆ ◆ ◆

THE SAME DAY Jack returned to Los Angeles Sandra gave birth to a daughter they named Jennifer. He immediately gave her a nickname, Ona, presumably after Ona Blake, daughter of Urizen in William Blake's mythology. Ona was the only name Jack would ever call her as a child.

During the filming of *Pulver*, Jack had become friendly with one of the cast, Larry Hagman, and now Jack and Sandra began socializing with Hagman and his wife. The Nicholsons lived in a modest bungalow near Plummer Park on the outskirts of Hollywood, where they had moved to make room for baby Jennifer. Hagman's situation was a little different. He came from acting royalty—his mother was the famed Broadway and movie star Mary Martin. He kept a beach house in the Malibu colony, where the Nicholsons loved visiting them on weekends, when it was always party time, the best champagne flowing plentifully. Sandra quickly found her own version of paradise in the Hagmans' out-of-a-magazine kitchen. She enjoyed standing barefoot in it and concocting various exotic dishes, more often than not laced with a little pot.

But it was Jack to whom everyone gravitated. His charismatic presence was the best thing in these weekend get-togethers. Word quickly spread about the soirées, and soon everybody who was anybody in the business wanted an invitation. When the Hagmans moved, Jane Fonda and her then-lover, film director Roger Vadim, who had recently relocated to the beach, happily took over the hosting chores, throwing regular beach bashes for some of Hollywood's biggest names. And when Fonda and Vadim had had enough, they passed the baton to John and Michelle Phillips of the Mamas and the Papas, who lived in Bel-Air, and threw even more extravagant parties than the Hagmans or the Vadims. Regardless of who was hosting, the Nicholsons were there every weekend.

Jack loved to party with Hollywood's crème de la crème, but work was still the most important thing. In 1964 he co-wrote another screenplay, this time with Monte Hellman, called *Epitaph* (aka *To Hold the Mirror*), about a couple of unemployed actors, one of whom is searching desperately for someone willing to perform an illegal abortion. They took it to Robert Lippert at API. While Lippert hemmed and hawed (and eventually passed), Fred Roos, a former agent and now an up-and-coming independent producer associated with Medallion Pictures, yet another of the new independents, had commissioned a screenplay of his own, *Back Door to Hell*, and wanted Jack to star in it.

Set during World War II, by Richard A. Guttman and John Hackett, *Back Door to Hell* focuses on three young soldiers scouting an island held by the Japanese before the main Allied forces will attempt to take it. Jack's American character can, inexplicably, speak fluent Japanese. Jack read it and agreed to do it, but only if the film could be directed by Monte Hellman. Jack, always loyal, didn't want to leave Hellman with nothing to show for all the work they had put into *Epitaph*, and he knew that Hellman still wanted to direct. Roos agreed and hired Hellman.

Back Door to Hell was shot on location in the Philippines, which, according to Hellman, "in those days was like the Wild West. You'd go into a gas station and the attendant would have a forty-five automatic in his belt. It was rough and tough and exciting. A terrific experience." Roos wanted them to make two movies while they were there, one for theaters and one for TV, and was looking for a second script. Hellman said he had one all ready to go and Roos gave it the green light—the long-dormant *Flight to Fury*. With Jack's help, they revised it to make it work in the Philippines. In it, Jack played another psychopath. In the end, after ample carnage, his character kills himself.

The pace was nonstop. "Three weeks for one, a short break, and three weeks for the other," Hellman remembered. But despite some interesting touches of directorial stylistics on Hellman's part and Jack's intense performance, when they were released, both films faded quickly. *Back Door to Hell* played briefly on the bottom half of Robert Aldrich's eerie 1964 *Hush . . . Hush, Sweet Charlotte*, which was itself a dressed-up B-movie. *Flight* played only a few times on TV before disappearing. *Flight to Fury* is notable as Jack's favorite of the twelve pictures he made from 1958 through 1964, all the way back to *The Cry Baby Killer*. He loved playing psychopaths, and he thought this was his best one yet.

Despite the failure of these two films, work kept coming Jack's way.

His next film, *The Shooting* (not to be confused with Don Siegel's 1976 John Wayne vehicle, *The Shootist*), was a western Jack described as a "McLuhan mystery," the first of two cowboy films Jack and Hellman would produce for Corman under his new Proteus Film banner. Jack would produce and act in them, Hellman would direct, and they would each write the screenplay for one.

They brought Corman the idea at a meeting at the old hat-shaped Brown Derby on Vine Street, just south of Hollywood Boulevard. Corman was eager to get them back into the fold and offered them the same two-picture deal that Roos had given them, more than Corman usually paid. At the meeting, he asked only one question: What were the plots of the films? The first was *The Shooting*. The second Jack remembered was "the one I wrote. We called it *Ride in the Whirlwind*. We kind of sold it as an *Attack of Apache Junction*, or something, with a lot of stagecoaches and Indians. And *The Shooting*, we sold as *African Queen* in the desert." Before dinner was over Corman had given them the green light, as long as there were "lots of tomahawks and ketchup," which Jack assured them there would be.

Corman: "I agreed to let them make these two low-budget westerns with Monte directing and Jack co-writing them and also starring. It was a big assignment, and later on we all agreed to hire Carole Eastman, our classmate from Jeff Corey's acting classes, to help write the script for one of the films." It was a good thing. Hellman didn't want to write any of *The Shooting*, so he could concentrate on directing it. Jack and Eastman ("Speed" in Jackspeak, for the slow pace of her writing) began working on it in a tiny office on the second floor of the Writers' Building, in Beverly Hills, Eastman under the name Adrien Joyce, after her literary hero, James Joyce. She wanted to reserve her real name for films she wrote by herself. *The Shooting*, to her way of thinking, was not a true Carole Eastman film.

She was an exceptionally good-looking woman, a former ballet dancer and fashion model with long, thick blond hair; she was preternaturally thin and most resembled a swan. She definitely had the face to become an actress but decided early on she really wanted to be a screenwriter. She had dozens of phobias, which may have limited her career opportunities. She wouldn't fly in planes, she wouldn't ride in cars unless she drove, she didn't like her picture being taken, she chain-smoked, and, as Peter Biskind pointed out, despite being hit on by men and women constantly, no one ever knew her to have a lover of either sex. In a time when paisley headscarves, short skirts, high boots, and free love were overrunning Hollywood, she refrained from all that; she dismissed current fashion as culture communism. She always dressed down in jeans, shirts, and sneakers.

Jack gave her the concept for *The Shooting*, while he worked with Hellman on the plot points of *Ride in the Whirlwind*. The budget for the films was $75,000 each. Corman put the money up himself, and because of it, he warned Jack and Hellman that if they ran even one dollar over budget, they would have to make it up out of their own salaries.

The Shooting, filmed in Utah, looks like the first western film where nearly everybody involved in it, except Corman and one or two other of the straight, nondrug contingency, was taking psychedelics during the entire shoot. It is an incomprehensible fury of a film, with an indecipherable plot. There were lots cowboys on horses, lots of guns fired, and lots of people (maybe) dying. It is a fascinating attempt at bending a genre (and a couple of minds). Hellman cut out as much of Eastman's dialogue as he could, including the entire first ten pages of her script, feeling that her plot interfered with the "pure" visual impact of his film.

They tried the same thing without Eastman in *Ride in the Whirlwind*. They shot it in Utah, and Jack later described it as a very classy, Ingmar Bergman–styled "existential western." Monte Hellman was more specific. He called the film "a horror picture in the form of a western, something like Henry King's *The Gunfighter* reconceived as a horror film . . . We shot them literally as one movie. Carole was writing one while Jack and I were writing the other, we went off and found the location that served both pictures, and we shot them back to back."

Mythic, no backstories, the two films are decidedly experimental, with nary an Indian or ketchup bottle in sight. Jack and Hellman had managed to produce two color westerns for the agreed-upon $75,000 apiece, and when they went a little over budget, Corman, true to his word, took it out of their pay, so that Jack and Hellman (not Eastman, who was on salary) wound up making a total of $5,000 apiece. Corman liked what he saw onscreen and believed that as a team Jack and Monte and Carole were on to something, even if he, or they, weren't exactly sure what.

Jack and Monte thought they knew. Their films were about rebellion, cut with acid, and the soul of Kerouac riding shotgun on their shoulders. Jack later said, "As a young Turk, resenting that I had to be nice for the audience . . . I considered it artistic pandering . . . when [Monte and I] made [*Ride in the Whirlwind*], we said, 'Well at least we aren't having the guy read the Bible around the campfire.' That's because for guys who grew up in the '50s, that sort of scene would have been considered kissing the public's ass."

Corman managed to sell the two films together as a package to the Walter Reade Organization for TV distribution in the United States and sent Jack to the 1966 Cannes Film Festival to exhibit them out of competition, hoping to find a foreign theatrical distributor for them. Jack recalled, "That was the first time I went there. They didn't know me, but [Jean-Luc] Godard befriended me the first night—he came to the first screening and after that I was a 'member of the delegation' of *Cahiers du Cinema* . . ." That delegation included François Truffaut, Eric Rohmer, and Claude Chabrol. Godard had told Jack how much he liked *The Shooting,* and suddenly this struggling actor found himself rubbing shoulders with members of the panthcon of the French New Wave.

Jack also discovered for the first time how much the French revered Roger Corman's films, in a way Americans didn't, and eagerly anticipated the reception of the pair of westerns that he had brought with him. To satisfy the crowds that wanted to see *The Shooting,* the better-received of the two, Corman four-walled (rented) a theater in Paris around the corner from the Arc de Triomphe, where *The Shooting* played to packed houses for a year.[1]

---

[1] Some foreign distributors expressed interest in acquiring the film, but a legal dispute Corman had with his backers over the foreign rights prevented it from happening for several years. Playing only in Paris, the film became something of an underground sensation.

Jack liked Cannes so much that he decided to stay until his expense money ran out and he had to leave behind the high of the croissant for the reality of Hollywood Boulevard, where he had nothing much else going for him. Both *The Shooting* and *Ride in the Whirlwind* had bombed badly in the States, despite Cannes, thus ending another creative partnership for Jack, this time with Eastman and Monte Hellman.

Hellman saw the experience differently: "That year was the most productive of my life," while Jack saw it as a failure. The difference in their perspectives was, essentially, a difference of personalities. Jack had come to think of success as a function of box office, Hellman as an aesthetic evaluation. At this time, Jack had had enough of rebellion and wanted to permanently join the mainstream, while Hellman shunned it, and would for the rest of his career.

Mike Medavoy recalled, "Monte was a real talent, but he was also a cipher. No one could ever figure him out. He could have been a great studio director, but he wanted to go his own way. Only nobody, maybe even him, could figure out what that way was. Jack, on the other hand, was being pulled into bigger movies, where I think he belonged. He was a big personality that was ready for the stardom he so desperately wanted. He had the indefinable something that we call talent. Everybody wants it, a lot of people think they have it, very few actually do. Jack had it."

BEFORE HE'D LEFT for Cannes, Jack and Sandra had been fighting a lot about money or more precisely their lack of it. Upon his return, with empty pockets and spent dreams, their battles grew more intense. At Sandra's insistence, they went to see a therapist together. They each took acid before the first session, which probably didn't help.

One day while they weren't talking to each other, Jack decided to fix the brakes on the car himself; to save thirty-five dollars, he bought new drums and tools and did the job on the front lawn. While he was struggling with the brakes, the phone rang. He went inside, wiping his hands on a rag before he picked up the receiver. It was Corman. He wanted Jack for a gangster picture called *The St. Valentine's Day Mas-*

sacre. Nothing new there. What was new was that it was going to be for a major studio. Twentieth Century-Fox had signed Corman to a contract, and that meant more money for everybody, and use of all their props, costumes, and stagehands. Most important, the studio promised to leave everyone alone, insisting they were buying Roger Corman because they wanted a Roger Corman–style movie. And, he told Jack, he wanted him to play one of the killers in the infamous holiday garage executions. Jack thanked him profusely. He really needed the money, he said, and to get out of the house for a while, because he and Sandra were driving each other crazy.

He had only one line in the picture, but he made it a good one. When another gangster notices one of the killers (Jack) greasing his bullets with garlic, he asks why. Jack says, "The bullets don't kill ya. Ya die of blood poisoning."

He had made it up on the spot, and Corman loved it. So did audiences. This otherwise scripted gangster film brought Jack more attention than all his other roles combined. It also earned him more money than ever before, courtesy of Corman. He was aware of Jack's deepening financial troubles that were threatening to bring down his marriage. He hadn't really needed him in the movie, but Corman figured hiring him was better than giving him a handout.

AFTER MASSACRE, CORMAN returned to independent filmmaking, still smarting over the studio's broken promise that he could make the film his way. What angered him the most was that when he had tried to cast Orson Welles as Al Capone, the studio had said no. (Jason Robards Jr. got the part.) He finished the film, exercised his out clause, and left Fox.

Corman now wanted to create a new series of independent films about motorcycle gangs that took their cue from 1953's *The Wild One.* It was a genre that had been around for more than a decade but had faded, despite Brando's iconic performance, because the film hadn't done all that well at the box office. Forever searching the headlines for subjects for films, Corman began to read about a new phenomenon, the most celebrated and baddest of all motorcycle gangs, Hells Angels, led by the charismatic Ralph Hubert "Sonny" Barger Jr.

Corman: "The Hells Angels were very much in the news. I got in touch with Sonny Barger and told him I wanted to do a film called *All the Fallen Angels*. Barger gave the OK, and Jim Nicholson and Sam Arkoff at AIP approved the idea immediately." Corman used many Hells Angels from the Venice branch to flesh out the backgrounds on their bikes, because they had the best choppers and it was cheaper to pay them "extra" money than to rent real Harleys.

Corman originally wanted George Chakiris to star in the film. Chakiris had won a Best Supporting Actor Oscar in 1961 for his performance in the ersatz street musical *West Side Story* (it played better on the stage), after which Chakiris's career cooled off and Corman figured he could get him on the cheap, until he discovered that Chakiris couldn't ride a motorcycle. Corman then called Peter Fonda, who he knew could ride, and offered him the lead instead, a character called Heavenly Blues. Peter, the son of screen legend Henry Fonda, drifting along the edges of mainstream Hollywood filmmaking for years, eagerly accepted the offer.

To play the part of Joe "Loser" Kearns, Corman chose one of Jack's friends, Bruce Dern—"Derns" or "Dernsie" in Jackspeak—and he also cast Nancy Sinatra, turning the film into something of a clarion call to the next generation, to the kids who'd never heard of Henry Fonda and wouldn't be caught dead listening to Frank Sinatra.

To help with the making of the film, Corman hired the then-unknown Peter Bogdanovich to be his assistant director and uncredited co-writer and Monte Hellman, whose career had stalled, to edit. The director Richard Rush's had fallen even further. Corman put him in charge of props.

And Jack was offered nothing—no acting, no writing (Charles B. Griffith wrote the screenplay), no assisting. Corman had originally asked Jack to write the film but wouldn't pay him what he wanted. His only contribution to the film was a better title. He thought *All the Fallen Angels* required too many marbles in the mouth, and suggested to Corman the simpler and better *The Wild Angels*. The title combined Brando's *The Wild One* with the motorcycle gang's name, Hells Angels.

Corman loved it, as Jack knew he would. But he was still angry and disappointed at otherwise being shut out of the film.

When production finished, Corman sensed he might have something special on his hands. He exhibited the film in competition at the Venice Film Festival, where it failed to please the *cineaste* crowd. Undeterred, he brought it back to the States, where it quickly found an audience among the young.

The Wild Angels, Corman's sixty-first film, was among his biggest hits. Made for $360,000, it took in $15.5 million worldwide, and was the seventeenth-highest-grossing American film of 1966. It also single-handedly redefined "youth" films, taking them off the clean white beaches and putting them on the gritty blacktop roads.

After the success of *The Wild Angels*, everybody wanted to make a copycat biker movie. *The Rebel Rousers*, produced and directed by Martin B. Cohen, starred Bruce Dern, whose biggest film to date had been *The Wild Angels*. Even Jack also took a role in *The Rebel Rousers*. It was so bad it didn't get released for three years.

When Fonda passed on the 1967 follow-up to *The Wild Angels*, *Hells Angels on Wheels*, Corman cast Jack as a new character, Poet, a disillusioned and disaffected gas-station worker who searches for the meaning of life from the seat of a Harley-Davidson. Fonda had turned Corman down because he'd wanted more money than Corman was willing to pay. But that was only part of the reason. Fonda really wanted to produce his own biker film.

With Jack in the lead, *Hells Angels on Wheels* proved infinitely better than *The Wild Angels*. Fonda looked good as a biker but was a bit dull as an actor, and Dern was at best a journeyman, with a horsey face and a funny way of using his hands, as if he were twisting dials every time he spoke a line of dialogue. But although the film was twice as good, because of the crowded market and diminishing returns, it grossed only half as much as the original.

NOT LONG AFTER the completion of *Hells Angels*, Jack's already shaky marriage to Sandra collapsed. There had never been enough money, they lived in relative squalor, in Sandra's opinion, unfit for raising a child, and his career was still going nowhere. But what finished it for Sandra was Jack's inability to keep it in his pants. She heard about another affair he was having and decided she wasn't going to live like this while he was out partying it up. For his part, he just couldn't put up with the pressure of matrimonial monogamy. His constant affairs were fuel for his tender ego and release for his ongoing feelings of entrapment. During the filming of *Hells Angels on Wheels*, Jack had started an intense affair with a young beauty, Mireille "Mimi" Machu (real name I. J. Jefferson), a flower-power-child-meets-go-go-dancer type who had a small part in the film. She was a younger, sweeter, and hotter version of Sandra.

In June 1967, Jack and Sandra formally separated. Alone, she got deeper into mysticism and the work of Jiddu Krishnamurti. Jack's friend Harry Dean Stanton, also into Krishnamurti, urged Jack to read him, saying that it might be the path to save his marriage. He tried it and also delved into some of the various fads and movements that Sandra swore by, one of which was Reichian therapy, the only therapy (besides a few visits to the marriage counselor with Sandra) Jack was ever willing to try. It actually did draw him deeper into himself but no closer to Sandra. One of Jack's female friends, Helena Kallianiotes, whom he knew from the coffeehouse days and who occasionally worked as a dancer while skimming along the edges of the independent film movement, but with whom he never slept, put it best describing why Jack's and Sandra's marriage fell apart: "She fell in love with God and Jack couldn't compete."

Sandra eventually relocated to Haight-Ashbury, San Francisco's hippie/mystic mecca, and took baby Jennifer with her. With his wife and child gone, Jack moved in with Harry Dean Stanton, who now had a small rental in Laurel Canyon, just north of Hollywood.

If Jack was distressed by the loss of Sandra and Jennifer he didn't show it, at least not directly. And he denied that Machu had anything to do with it. He told *Playboy*, "My marriage broke up during the period when I was acting in a film during the day and writing a film at night. I simply didn't have time to ask for peace and quiet or to say [when we fought], 'Well, now, wait a second, maybe you're being unreasonable.' . . . It ended before I was ready to be out of it. She felt that I wasn't worth her time. She'd had it. It was very sudden, very abrupt. I was unprepared. I couldn't cope with all the emotion that was released as the result of being cashiered . . . our marriage was lived out rather than failed."

JACK WORKED FOR Corman again in 1967 on another motorcycle movie, *The Trip*, but this one was different because Jack wrote the entire script himself. Corman produced and directed *The Trip* in three weeks. Corman gave one of the lead roles to Dern, a move that made Jack bristle. He complained to Corman that he had written the role of John (his real first name) based largely on himself, and that he, Corman, had given it to Dern only because he was his favorite actor.

"Bruce was *one* of my favorite actors," Corman said. "I wanted every actor in *The Trip* to have a certain look, and to be able to ride a motorcycle really well. There are too many action pictures made where the hero can't jump on a horse and you have to make that cut so the stuntman can ride away. I wanted my actors to be able to do their own riding. Bruce and Peter Fonda were both expert cyclists and Jack wasn't. Despite what anyone may think, that was the only reason, simple and clear, that he was not in the film."

Jack quickly cooled off and regained some perspective. "By now, Roger and I were back in synch," he said. "Hey, the man's supporting my whole life, how could I not be in synch with him? He had asked me to write *Hells Angels on Wheels*. I said, Roger, you know we're pals and this and that, can't you pay me a little more than scale? Scale plus five dollars and I would have relaxed. No. And I didn't write it. To write *The Trip*, though, he said all right and gave me a little more and I did it."

Also in the film was Dennis Hopper. "I had known Jack and Peter prior to [*The Trip*]," Hopper recalled, "when we were all doing motorcycle pictures at AIP [and in acting classes] . . . I made a thing called *The Glory Stompers* and Peter had made *Wild Angels*. I knew Jack as an actor, but I also knew him as an excellent screenwriter." Dennis, who played Max, everyone's favorite dealer, had been recommended for the part by Fonda, who agreed to be in *The Trip* because he needed bridge money while he continued to look for funding for his own biker film.

To better acquaint himself with the subject matter, Corman agreed to take an acid trip. Jack wrote the highly personal and character-rich screenplay on acid as well, completing it shortly after Sandra left. The film had a touch of the European exotica about it that he had taken from his *Cahiers* experience at Cannes. Later on, when Bosley Crowther reviewed the film for the *New York Times*, he picked up on its art-house look as much as its drive-in attraction. "If *The Trip* is a fair indication of what one sees when high on psychedelic drugs, take it from me the experience is not very different from looking at some of the phantasmagoric effects in movies like [Federico Fellini's] *Juliet of the Spirits . . .*"

The film also referenced Ingmar Bergman and Jean Cocteau, and there was even a tongue-in-cheek homage to the earlier Corman horror flicks during one of Fonda's hallucinations. (Corman had the sets warehoused and wanted to use them in the film because they were free, and he had Jack find a way to write them into the screenplay. They became part of one of Fonda's trips.)

When Corman expressed little enthusiasm for filming the second-unit scenes in the desert, Hopper and Fonda volunteered and Corman gave them his blessing. Hopper took the director's chair and Fonda played producer, and they shot a number of scenes, few of which were actually in Jack's original script. It was the first time they had worked together creatively as a team.

It wouldn't be their last.

THE TRIP WAS ultimately perceived by most critics as too pro-drugs at a time when it was a growing problem among the country's young. The film's criical failure was a big disappointment to Jack, who had so emotionally invested himself in his screenplay. He was certain, now, after fifteen pictures in nine years, that he was not, after all, going to be the next Marlon Brando or James Dean or Robert Riskin to Corman's Frank Capra. His feelings of failure were reinforced when he had recently been up for Roman Polanski's *Rosemary's Baby*. Casting went down to the wire before director Roman Polanski chose John Cassavetes over Jack to play the part of the devil/husband. When he found out, Jack got stoned with Harry Dean Stanton to the point of immobility.

ON WEEKENDS, HARRY Dean liked to throw sex parties that started on Friday night and ended sometime Monday morning that gathered the hottest starlets and all the available young men, some single and some not, who wanted to get whacked out and share beds filled with these naked, luscious, beautiful women. Lately, though, Harry Dean had had to literally pull Jack out of his room to join in. Most of the time, while the action was hot and heavy in the other rooms, Jack would prefer to stay by himself, in his bedroom, furiously pounding out his next screenplay.

Jack had also agreed to help out with the script of another psychedelic movie for AIP, *Psych-Out*, directed by Richard Rush and filmed by László Kovács, the same team that had directed and filmed *Hells Angels on Wheels*. The film was officially written by E. Hunter Willett and Betty Ulius, adapted from an original story, and, despite Jack's input, they won the valuable WGA (Writers Guild of America) credit. It burned Jack that even though he had put up a fight to get his name included in the writing credits, he couldn't get enough support from Rush and Kovács, and his name was left off.[2] The cast included AIP and Corman regulars Susan Strasberg, Bruce Dern, Adam Roarke, Jack, and Henry Jaglom, a transplanted East Coast newcomer to Hollywood's independent film scene, a wannabe writer-director learning the business via the Corman/AIP route.

Jack was immediately drawn to Jaglom; he was smart, articulate, and obviously a mover. He liked Jaglom's knowledge of film and his ability to slice through Hollywood's invisible wall between the outsiders

[2] Screen credit is important in Hollywood for negotiating future fees.

and the insiders as easily as a knife through warm butter. And Henry liked everything about Jack that everybody else liked: his charm, his smile, his intellectual strength, his acting intensity, and his love of a good time.

One evening after work, Jaglom ran into Jack, who was hanging out stoned and alone at the Old World ice cream parlor on Sunset Boulevard. Jaglom was with Karen Black, an actress he'd met in New York and brought out to L.A. to find her movie parts. He introduced her to Jack. According to Black, "Our eyes met, something happened, and he wound up walking me back to my little apartment in Hollywood that I had recently moved into. I was really poor. There were a lot of kids in the complex my house was in so I put a little teeter-totter in my living room. It only got about a foot off the floor. No sooner did we get to my place than Jack went straight for the teeter-totter. He got on one side and I got on the other. I remember we stared into each other's eyes, and he said, 'Blackie'—he always called me 'Blackie'—I might be interested in you.' That was fine, except that I was interested at the time in [actor] Peter Kastner and told Jack so. Besides, I think I was too fat for Jack. He really liked those skinny blond twenty-year-old model-type actresses, like Mimi Machu, whom I thought he was going out with at the time anyway."

One day not long after, Jack took an incoming call from Mimi, long distance. She was phoning from Florida and her message was short and sweet. They were finished. Jack heard the click in his ear as the phone went dead. Overcome with emotion, he hung up the phone as he fought back the tears. "I was with her for . . . in love, and when she dumped on me, I couldn't even hear her name mentioned without breaking into a cold sweat." He didn't know what happened, but he was sure it had something to do with another man. Or woman. It was okay for him to proposition Karen Black, but the thought of Mimi with someone else ripped him apart.

He was inconsolable. To try to get his mind off Mimi, he spent several nights sitting alone in various screening rooms, watching advance prints of other studios' films, or at Doug Weston's nightclub the

Troubadour, on Santa Monica and Doheny, just east of Beverly Hills and adjacent to the super-hip Dan Tana's restaurant. The Troubadour's front bar was the center of the L.A. social scene and the heart of the so-called California soft rock sound. It was filled at all hours with musicians: the Everly Brothers, Linda Ronstadt, Don Henley and Glenn Frey before they were Eagles, and a lot of young actors and actresses and their agents. This was a new scene for Jack, and he loved it. He easily fell in with the musicians, and they helped alleviate the pain of Mimi's kiss-off.

PSYCH-OUT'S PLOT HAD something to do with a deaf flower child (Strasberg) looking for her lost hippie brother (Dern), who is accompanied by Jack. Music from the likes of Strawberry Alarm Clock and The Storybook dotted the soundtrack. The film was produced by a young up-and-comer, Dick Clark, a TV rock-and-roll hot-shot looking to expand into movies. Coincidentally, he was the one at the WGA hearing whose testimony, that Jack's material was too far-out and Willett's and Ulius's wasn't, had lost Jack his valuable screen credit.

The film did not do well, and Clark, who would go on to be an extremely powerful producer on television with an uncanny ability to sense what would appeal to across-the-board audiences and what wouldn't, claimed the reason was that the hippie pot-smoking generation had already morphed into the rougher heroin-and-coke scene, that the utopia of early innocent hippiedom had collided with the real world of Vietnam, heroin, cocaine, and Hells Angels. He was right. By the time *Psych-Out* was released, box-office flower power was a thing of the past.

It was another bitter failure for Jack. He began seriously thinking about giving up acting altogether and concentrating solely on writing. Or maybe give up the whole business and look for a real job that paid a decent salary.

Fred Roos, meanwhile, had moved on to television and landed a position as a network sitcom-casting director. To help Jack out, he put him in a few shows, work that he abhorred but needed for rent money. Roos got him two episodes of *The Andy Griffith Show*. "I always sort of stunk on television," Jack later recalled.

But even as he was kicking shit in Mayberry, a hurricane of creative change was about to rip through Hollywood. Peter Fonda had since partnered with Dennis Hopper on Fonda's as yet unproduced biker film that, after a couple of false starts, when they finally got it made, would go on to become a cultural phenomenon that changed the way Hollywood looked at independent films and the people who made them.

Out of it would emerge a character actor in a relatively small part who wasn't even supposed to be in the movie at all, to become Hollywood's newest overnight star sensation.

His name was Jack Nicholson.

"Being stoned takes a lot of your energy away, and that's difficult. The only thing I can really say being stoned has helped me with creatively is writing . . . it's easier to entertain yourself mentally. It produces a lot of shit, too."

—JACK NICHOLSON

THE PROJECT THAT EVENTUALLY BECAME 1969'S *EASY RIDER* BEGAN years earlier with two separate sets of friends who didn't know each other but had one thing in common; they all wanted to make movies. Thirty-five-year-old Berton "Bert" Schneider and Bob Rafelson ("Curly Bob" or "Curly" in Jackspeak) were the suits, well-off film industry businessmen who longed to make art; thirty-one-year-old Dennis Hopper and twenty-eight-year-old Peter Fonda were the rebels who disliked mainstream Hollywood but longed to make mainstream money.

Bert Schneider, basketball-tall, Malibu blond, steel-blue-eyed, and movie-star good-looking, had a golden Hollywood connection. He was the son of Abraham Schneider, who, in 1958, following the death of the legendary iron-fisted Harry "King" Cohn, took over as president of Columbia Pictures. A year later the senior Schneider also assumed the presidency of Screen Gems, Columbia's TV division, and brought in his son, Bert, to run it and serve as its treasurer. But Bert was not satisfied. He dreamed of producing movies like the Europeans did, personal films filled with power and emotion.

His good friend Bob Rafelson, the son of a successful milliner, had bouncer-broad shoulders, sinister dark hair, and unconventional good looks. He had longed to be a legitimate member of the beat generation, but family pressure mandated that he go to college and get a good-paying job, if not making hats, then doing something productive. Rafelson dutifully attended Dartmouth, majoring in philosophy. After graduation he was drafted and stationed in Japan, where in his down time he worked part-time as a disk jockey, translating Japanese films, and was an advisor to the Shochiku Film Company. In 1959, upon completion of active duty, he returned to the States, married his high school sweetheart, and found a job writing for New York's pre-PBS Channel 13, including *Play of the Week*, produced by David Susskind. In 1962 he moved with his wife, Toby, to Los Angeles, where he eventually landed a job at Revue Productions, the TV branch of MCA, and worked under the personal supervision of studio head Lew Wasserman. When he had a falling-out with Wasserman, Rafelson moved to Screen Gems, where he met and befriended Bert Schneider.

One time, during a mutual whining session over their creative frustrations with the corporate film business, Schneider suggested they start their own independent company. They quit their Screen Gems jobs and formed Raybert, a production house with a catchy name, no projects, and a single employee, Steve Blauner, Schneider's best friend from childhood, a full-on bald-headed hippie with a long straggly beard and beads around his neck. He had been Bobby Darin's road manager before joining Raybert.

One day in 1965 Rafelson had a brainstorm. A big Beatles fan, he stood up from his desk, walked into Blauner's office, and grandly announced, "I want to make *A Hard Day's Night* as a TV show!"

Television, he knew from his brief time working at Screen Gems, was sorely in need of fresh programming that spoke to a younger audience. In the sixties, years before the 1981 arrival of MTV, except for shows like Ed Sullivan's Sunday night ritual hour of reflective pop culture, rock and roll hardly existed on the small tube. Rafelson regularly attended film screenings, and often ran into Jack Nicholson at them. Jack was on all the lists and tried to see as many films as he could. According to Rafelson, "When I liked a picture, I'd stand in the dark and applaud and whistle like mad [and] I noticed that another person was doing the same thing." That was Jack. One time the two looked at each other, laughed, and decided to go for coffee and talk about the film they had just seen. "I'm a New Wave baby," Jack said later on. "So I got very stimulated by foreign film. All the great moviemakers, Truffaut, Godard, Resnais, Bresson, Vigo . . . These filmmakers woke my generation up to the broadness of the medium . . ." Rafelson asked Jack what he did for a living, and Jack said he was a screenwriter who did a lot of scripts for Roger Corman, and occasionally some acting too.

Each was impressed by the other's knowledge of film, and they soon discovered they were fellow travelers. When they finished their impromptu meeting, they exchanged numbers and agreed to stay in touch.

SCHNEIDER KNEW exactly where to get the $225,000 they needed to make the pilot for the TV show. He went directly to his father and easily persuaded him to have Screen Gems give him a development deal for something he called *The Monkees*. Rafelson, meanwhile, was a big fan of the Lovin' Spoonful and had originally wanted them to star in the show as themselves, but the band, which had a string of successful singles, wanted too much money and all the royalties from any original music they contributed to the show, and refused to grant permission to use any of their hits as part of the series. He then decided it would be easier and cheaper to create a new group and simply lease pop tunes from the writing stable at the Brill Building, the famous Manhattan songwriting mecca. To handle the acquisition of songs, Raybert entered into a deal with Don Kirshner, the head of the music division of Screen Gems. Kirshner then used some of the best songwriters in the business to write tunes for the group, including Carole King and Gerry Goffin ("Pleasant Valley Sunday"), Neil Diamond ("I'm a Believer"), and Tommy Boyce and Bobby Hart ("Last Train to Clarksville").

The next step was to find four boys to play the members of the band. On September 8, 1965, Bert placed the first of three days of ads in *Daily Variety* and the *Hollywood Reporter*:

Madness!! Auditions.
Folk & Roll Musicians—Singers for acting roles in new
TV Series. Running Parts for 4 insane boys, age 17–21.
Must come down for interview.

Out of the 437 hopefuls who showed up at Raybert's offices to audition, Bert, Rafelson, and Blauner settled on an obscure folksinger
named Peter Tork, starving guitarist Michael Nesmith, and British
stage performer Davy Jones, who had played the Artful Dodger in the
West End production of *Oliver!* and also had a career as a jockey. Micky
Dolenz, the fourth member of the ersatz band and a professional actor,
managed to skip the cattle call in favor of a private audition with
Schneider and Rafelson and was quickly added to the group.

The Monkees debuted on NBC September 12, 1966, and ran for two
seasons (fifty-eight episodes), until March 25, 1968. By then, the band
had become a pop phenomenon, having sold 23 million albums during
the show's run, and made Schneider, Rafelson, Don Kirshner, and all
the hired songwriters into millionaires several times over.[1] All except
for the Monkees themselves, who were salaried actors, didn't write their
own music, and were barred from the studio when their vocals were
mixed in with the music tracks. Predictably, the boys felt both exploited
and trapped.

By the start of the show's second season, the four actors who played
the Monkees weren't the only ones disenchanted with the show.
Schneider and Rafelson were as well. They saw it slowly taken over by
Kirshner, who to their minds had destroyed their hip, satirical concept
and turned it into one of the most predictable and boring TV sitcoms
of all time, sticky and blown out of proportion with what came to be
known as "bubble-gum music."

Rafelson had one last desperate trick up his sleeve. He decided to
make a feature film starring these same Monkees, in the style he had
originally intended the show to be rather than the lame imitation it

---

[1] In 1967 the Monkees reportedly outsold the Beatles' and the Rolling Stones'
albums combined.

became. Micky Dolenz: "We all agreed we didn't want to do a ninety-minute version of the Monkees TV show. We wanted to do something we couldn't do on television, to get out there a little bit."

TV had given Raybert money and position in Hollywood; now Schneider and Rafelson wanted to validate it by making a movie. To do so, Schneider knew he would need the coolest, hippest writer around. After going through lists of names and unable to find anyone who satisfied the both of them, Rafelson then remembered the fellow he had met at the foreign film screenings who said he was a screenwriter for Roger Corman. Bob got in touch with Jack, and after a brief meeting at Raybert's offices, Schneider asked him if he was sure he could write this kind of material. Jack said, confidently and with a bit of an edge, "I can write any movie about anything." Schneider and Rafelson had especially loved his script for *The Trip* and told Jack they were looking for that same psychedelic trippiness for their deconstruction of *The Monkees*. After they all agreed on a title—the smirky sex/drug double entendre *Head*, Jack was officially hired.

There was something else besides a love for foreign filmes that Jack and Bob had in common. They both lusted after young women. Rafelson was a notorious ladies' man, despite the fact that he was, on the surface at least, still happily married to Toby. He preferred young, willing, and beautiful blondes, of which there was no shortage in Hollywood. Jack was less selective as long as they were young and hot. They began foraging into the seamy side of the Hollywood night hunting for women.

During the writing of the script, Jack, Bob, and Bert regularly got stoned and dropped acid together. From the beginning, the screenplay was a drugged-up mess, much of it cobbled together during a weekend visit to a resort in Ojai, California, where the Monkees, Rafelson, and Nicholson brainstormed into a tape recorder while stoned on marijuana. Jack then took the tapes to his room and used them as the basis for his screenplay. He wrote the first draft under the influence of LSD. Between sessions, the team took long walks to discuss the script, and, to further bond (as if any more were needed), they attended several Lakers home games together at the Fabulous Forum in Inglewood. Raybert had six season courtside seats.

As Rafelson later recalled, during the writing of the script, "Jack used to act out all the parts. He'd hold me captive with his performance of whatever the scene was. And I kept staring at him and then said, 'You know what? The next movie I do I'm going to do with you as the star.'"

Not just Rafelson but everyone involved with the project was drawn to Jack, for his talent, his likability, his energy, and his creativity. Micky Dolenz remembers that during production, "He just started hanging out all the time, on the set and at my house all the time, getting to know my family. Obviously, he was doing his homework, getting to know the boys and what the whole Monkees thing had been about. I thought Jack did a wonderful job scripting the movie. And, despite what people think from the look of it, the whole thing was scripted. Also, by that time, the band was grumbling about not being treated as a real band—which it wasn't—and some of that dissatisfaction made it into the movie."

In the finished film, Dennis Hopper is wandering around in the background in one or two scenes. Helena Kallianiotes, Jack's friend, performs a belly dance. Frank Zappa appears with a cow. Victor Mature shows up as the Jolly Green Giant. Even Annette Funicello makes it into a couple of scenes. In his script Jack also made fun of the Beatles' guru phase (which may also have been a jab at Sandra's spiritual conversion).

Hundreds of extras were brought in for a big birthday scene. To do the choreography, Rafelson hired Toni Basil. "Bob knew me socially, from my work as a choreographer and also as a filmmaker. He was great to work with because he was so collaborative. I was mostly involved with the songs and the dancing. I choreographed two numbers, including Davy Jones's 'Daddy's Song.'"

According to Micky Dolenz: "They were looking to deconstruct not just the Monkees, but all of Hollywood, using the Monkees as a metaphor. They wanted to shake things up, to start an independent film movement, and *Head* was intended as their big step. Victor Mature represented the fake, old Hollywood, and the Monkees were supposed to represent the new. As the film came together, we all got glimmers of the Jack Nicholson personality audiences would soon come to know.

"I remember we were in the Bahamas for a few days, and Jack was doing the second-unit directing, a lot of underwater stuff. One night we got dressed up in very hip, sixties-style Nehru jackets, to go gambling at a big, formal casino. We were stopped at the door by a big, tough bouncer, who told us we couldn't get in without a shirt and tie. Jack didn't get excited, he didn't go off on him or anything. Instead, he stood there and debated with the guy, explaining in a very intellectual way that three quarters of the rest of the world considered these clothes fashionable, so why couldn't this casino? I think our long hair, we were all wearing our hair very long, had something to do with it too.

"Despite his patience and reasoning, we never got in, but I remember thinking to myself that this was a side of Jack I hadn't seen before, that nobody had seen before. We knew him as a bit of a wild guy, who loved to have fun and had no respect for bullies or any kind of hollow authority figures. Reasonable Jack, that was a new one on me."

Head premiered in New York on November 6, 1968, and nationwide November 20. Rafelson and Schneider came up with a campaign to promote the film built around a poster of a head with the word *head* on it. They plastered them on every lamppost in Manhattan up until an hour before the film's premiere, when the two were arrested for damaging public property. To their dismay, the film did poorly and quickly disappeared from theaters. It took years to make back its $750,000 cost and could not be described as anything other than a disaster for Raybert's initial foray into feature filmmaking. Even Jack didn't like the final result and summed up his feelings after the opening this way: "I hope nobody ever likes it. I'm going to remake it with the Beatles . . ."

IN JANUARY 1968, Hopper and Fonda joined forces and chose a new screenwriter for Fonda's biker movie they were now calling *The Loners.* Terry Southern was a successful satirist as both a novelist and a screenwriter; his previous screen work included Stanley Kubrick's *Dr. Strangelove, or How I Learned to Stop Worrying and Love the Bomb* (1964) and (with Ring Lardner Jr.) Norman Jewison's star vehicle for

Steve McQueen, *The Cincinnati Kid* (1965). His 1958 satirical novel, *Candy* (written with Mason Hoffenberg), was a huge success in print and later, in 1968, onscreen.

Fonda then approached Roger Corman and asked him to be the film's executive producer. Corman loved it—*The Wild Angels* meets *The Trip*—and told Fonda and Hopper he thought they were sitting on a gold mine. While *Head* was still filming, as soon as Southern had a finished script, Corman took it to AIP for funding. According to Corman, "I was sure I could get all the funding we'd need from AIP. We all attended a meeting, and sure enough AIP loved the idea but wanted a rewrite from Southern with less emphasis on drugs. And one more thing, one of the executives warned us, in front of Hopper, whose reputation in the industry was not good, if the film fell even one day behind schedule because of him, the funding would be immediately canceled. I saw the looks on Dennis and Peter's faces and knew that the executive had made a major mistake. After the meeting, the two made their displeasure quite clear to me." Corman soothed their anger and assured them he could fix everything.

Corman had left the meeting confident he would get a green light upon the presentation of an acceptable budget and shooting schedule and a commitment to come in at or under that budget. A day later, Corman called AIP to reassure them that Hopper would not be a problem. AIP said that was fine and then asked to see the revised first draft before making their final commitment.

WHEN HOPPER BEGAN complaining about the stalling and the runaround he believed *The Loners* was getting from AIP, Jack suggested they come see him at Raybert and maybe Schneider, Rafelson, and Blauner might be interested in their project.

A meeting was set up, but not for *The Loners*. Fonda didn't want to jeopardize the pending deal at AIP and convinced Hopper they should pitch Raybert a different movie. Hopper suggested a film version of Michael McClure's political satire, *The Queen*. When they showed up for the meeting, Jack invited them to come into his office to smoke a joint while they waited for Schneider, who had not yet arrived. He had recently injured himself in a skiing accident and was walking on crutches, which slowed his getting around. When he did get there, Jack, Schneider, Rafelson, Blauner, and Jaglom all went into Schneider's office to listen to what Hopper and Fonda had to say. After making their pitch, Hopper asked for $60,000 in development money for *The Queen*.

After a heavy pause, Schneider asked what else they had, which meant he was passing on that one. Jack then told them about *The Loners*, which he thought was the reason for the meeting. Schneider already knew about the deal at AIP from the trades and also that Hopper wasn't happy there. "How's your bike movie coming?" he asked. When Hopper angrily declared they were being dicked around by AIP, Schneider, Rafelson, and Blauner all looked up. After a few seconds of silence, Bert asked Hopper to tell them about it.

Five minutes later Fonda and Hopper had a deal with Raybert.

Schneider agreed to give them the $360,000 seed money they wanted to make *The Loners*: eleven profit points each for Hopper and Schneider (Southern was not in attendance and his points were not set), and $40,000 immediately for Hopper and Fonda to make a test reel. Depending upon how that reel came out, Schneider would give them the remaining $320,000.

Schneider knew he was taking a big chance—Hopper had the worst reputation in Hollywood, and Fonda was untested as a producer—but Bert was willing to put his money where his mouth was. Raybert was in and Corman and AIP were out. Jack felt bad for Corman, but he understood better than anyone how the movie business operated. It could be cutthroat when it came to stealing projects and luring talent. Besides, this wasn't his deal; he had only brought the project to AIP, which had not put up any front money, and money was what made a deal real.

Schneider popped open a bottle of expensive champagne to celebrate.

Hopper and Fonda left the next day for New Orleans, with Toni Basil (Mary) and Karen Black (Karen) and to fill out the female parts of the test reel. Hopper would be Billy (Billy the Kid), and Fonda would be Wyatt (Wyatt Earp, aka Captain America). The plan was to film an extended acid trip during Mardi Gras for as long and as far as the $40,000 would take them. Jack would go along as the watchful eyes of Raybert.

Trouble began the first day in New Orleans. Everyone was up at six A.M. to try to blend in with the Mardi Gras festivities and shoot some wild footage, and then film a scene at the cemetery, but no sooner did everyone assemble when Hopper, already flying without a plane, declared himself to the crew as the greatest director who ever lived, and worse, said that they were nothing more than flunkies on his film. Several crew members quit the project right then and there. When shooting finally resumed at a local cemetery, so did the chaos. "We were all in our Winnebago," recalls Karen Black, "and we were all looking for where all the people were marching down the streets for Mardi Gras and we could never find it. If you look at the film now you'll see that Toni, Dennis, and I are never actually in the parade. I'm in there once.

"It was a confused mess. Toni and I are sitting in the Winnebago while everyone else was doing, I think it was coke at this point. And there was a lot of wine. And they were blasting rock-and-roll music constantly. It was crazy. Dennis kept on looking out the window making funny remarks to passersby. That's when I began to think this film was going nowhere."

According to Basil, "In the first scene in the cemetery I was on the ground and I saw Karen Black and Dennis coming toward me and I said, 'Oh shit!' I was ready for anything. But as the scene came together, it occurred to me that there was something very familiar about it. And then I realized that Dennis, who was heavily into experimental filmmaker Bruce Conner, was modeling the scene after a similar, experimental one that Conner had done. The cemetery scene wasn't as haphazard, or spontaneous, or out of control as everyone always thinks."

The next day in New Orleans, a stoned-out Hopper tried to get Fonda to be further in touch with the essence of his character by reliving his mother's suicide on camera. He thought it would provide great footage for the test reel. Fonda didn't want to do it, thinking Hopper was going way too far. The two had a blistering fight, until Fonda gave in, climbed up on a statue of the Madonna, and mumbled a line or two to his "mother," asking her why she'd done it. Hopper screamed. He loved it. From then on Fonda no longer was talking to Hopper.

By the time they all returned to L.A., Fonda wanted to quit the project, but Rafelson persuaded him to stay with it by telling him that in their absence, Schneider had persuaded Columbia to distribute *The Loners*, in return for which they would advance the entire $360,000 budget. There was no way out now, Rafelson told Fonda; he couldn't pull out without creating major legal problems for everyone and hurt some of his friends, since Raybert had already deposited Columbia's check in the bank and paid itself back the $40,000 it had given to Hopper to finance the test reel.

A reluctant Fonda flew to New York City, where he kept a town house on the East Side, to do some work on the script with Terry Southern. When a paranoid Hopper heard about it he angrily flew to New York as well, not wanting to be left out of anything that had to do with "his" film.

He arrived at Fonda's place, where he was told by the housekeeper that Peter, Terry, and actor Elmore Rual "Rip" Torn Jr. had all gone to Serendipity 3, a nearby restaurant on East 60th Street that was a favorite among the New York hip/cool crowd. Torn was a young, good-looking Broadway actor who had signed on to play George Hanson, the football-helmeted, alcoholic ACLU lawyer that Billy and Wyatt meet on the road. He had come along to help out with his scenes.

Hopper burst through Serendipity's front door like it was a saloon and went directly to the table where Fonda, Southern, and Torn were eating and drinking. At the top of his lungs and oblivious to the rest of the patrons, he demanded to know why he hadn't been invited to the meeting and, for that matter, why they weren't all back at the house writing instead of goofing off, eating ice cream sundaes, and wasting production money. Hopper then made a derogatory comment aimed directly at Torn about Texans, knowing that Torn was from Temple, Texas. He said he couldn't even take a stopover in Dallas because they cut long hair off hippies with a razor down there. Torn smiled and tried to cool Hopper out, saying all Texans weren't assholes, and stuck his hand out to shake. Hopper then called him a motherfucker, grabbed a steak knife off the table, made a half lunge for Torn, and missed. Torn then told Hopper: "I'll wait for you in the street. Bring your guns. Bring your knives. Bring your pals, and we'll find out in about three seconds who the punk is."

Hopper never came out. The next day Torn quit the picture.[2]

Hopper next tried to get rid of Southern, saying the new script wasn't as good as it should have been. When Hopper called Schneider in L.A. to get Southern fired, he refused, claiming Southern was the biggest name attached to the project. Hopper's attempt proved unnecessary. After giving Fonda a new and better title for the picture, *Easy Rider*, Southern, too, had had enough and quit.[3]

Fonda and Hopper had yet another falling-out about how to divide the newly available profit points that Southern's departure had created. Unable to reach an agreement, each later claimed the other had threatened his life.

Back in Los Angeles, when Schneider heard that Torn had quit, without consulting Fonda, Hopper, or Bob, he approached Jack about taking over the role of Hanson. He offered him $392 a week ($508 less than Torn was getting). It was a small role but a gem, and Jack grabbed at it. He later claimed that despite the film's thus-far chaotic production, he was eager to be in *Easy Rider* for two reasons. The first was: "Almost everyone wanted me out of acting. Not because they thought I wasn't good. To do the kind of acting I was doing was a waste of energy.

---

[2] Hopper appeared on *The Tonight Show* in 1994 claiming Torn hadn't quit but was fired because Torn had pulled a knife on him. Torn sued Hopper for defamation and won a $475,000 judgment against Hopper. It is unclear if he ever actually collected the money.

[3] An easy rider is a man who lives off a hooker's earnings. He isn't a pimp, but a boyfriend or a husband whose partner's earnings make his life an easy ride. Southern maintained throughout that despite quitting, he had written the entire script. The screenwriter credit on the film went to Southern, Fonda, and Hopper, but the only money Southern ever saw from *Easy Rider* was his initial $3,500 payment. When he quit, he surrendered his agreed-upon percentage of the film's future profits.

People thought I could be putting that energy into directing, writing, and producing . . ." This was his chance to prove them wrong. The second was: "There hasn't been a motorcycle picture yet that hasn't made [a lot of] money. It had [what was left of] Terry Southern's writing, it had motorcycles, the open road, Dennis Hopper and Peter Fonda as a pair of drifters. What more could you ask?"

The character of Hanson was Southern's creation. From the beginning he had felt there needed to be a third, sympathetic character in the film, one that balanced out the other two, who would be able to articulate a lot of what Wyatt and Billy felt but weren't capable of putting into words. Southern later claimed he had based Hanson on a small-town lawyer who was a recurring character in several of Faulkner's novels.

Schneider had another reason for wanting Jack to be in the film. He knew that although Fonda and Hopper were at each other's throats, they both liked Jack a lot, and Schneider was counting on Jack to make sure one didn't kill the other before the picture was done.

Not everyone was as certain as Jack was that he could pull it off. Hopper had strong reservations, believing Jack was too East Coast to be able to play a Texan, and in a paranoid rant, accused Schneider of purposely sabotaging his movie. Despite Hopper's objections, Jack's training and experience gave him both the discipline and the desire to play Hanson. He was stoned during the entire key "campfire" scene (*Playboy* reported that he smoked 155 joints during the time it took to film it) and for most of the making of the picture. To capture the Texas speech pattern, he listened over and over again to a recording of Lyndon Johnson. Jack: "That long scene by the campfire, about the UFOs and so on, I did with a script. It's hidden under that coat you see there. It looks improvised but most of it was written in advance . . ." The famous Three Stooges, flapping-his-arms-like-a-chicken-and-going-"nik-nik-nik" bit, which Jack did whenever Hanson drank, he picked up from one of the crew, who occasionally did it during breaks. It is one of the more memorable moments of the beautifully acted monologue.

◆ ◆ ◆

JUST AS PRODUCTION was wrapping, late in 1968, Jack learned that his divorce from Sandra had at long last become final. The lawyers divided up everything as equally as they could. Sandra took her Mercedes that she had bought before they were married; Jack kept the yellow Volkswagen he had bought for himself after the Studebaker was stolen. They had a total of $8,000 in savings, which was split in half. Jack agreed to pay whatever alimony and child support he could, and Sandra agreed to weekly visitations in the settlement. But as soon as the divorce was finalized she moved to Hawaii, making it all but impossible for Jack to see his daughter. Because of the alimony and child support, Jack could no longer afford his share of the rent on the apartment he was sharing with Harry Dean and had to move out. He slept mostly on friends' sofas, when he couldn't find a girl to keep him warm in her bed.

And Mud now wanted to buy a trailer. She asked Jack for the money and even though he didn't have two nickels to rub together, he promised her he'd get it for her.

IT TOOK SEVEN weeks to shoot *Easy Rider* and seven months to edit all the footage into something resembling a final cut. With *Easy Rider* nowhere near being released, and desperately needing money, Jack took a job acting in a studio film he was previously offered that he had absolutely no interest in.

Vincente Minnelli was directing a movie version of a 1965 Broadway musical dud called *On a Clear Day You Can See Forever*, loosely based on a 1956 best-seller sensation called *The Search for Bridey Murphy* by amateur hypnotist Morey Bernstein, about a patient he claimed he was able to put under and send back to an earlier incarnation of herself. Because they couldn't get the rights to *Bridey Murphy*, Alan J. Lerner and Frederick Loewe, the team that had adapted Shaw's *Pygmalion* into *My Fair Lady*, based their musical instead on an obscure 1929 play by John L. Balderston called *Berkeley Square*.

On a Clear Day You Can See Forever opened on Broadway in June and stayed on the boards for eight months. Even before it opened, Paramount paid Lerner $750,000 for the film rights, and the fast-rising producer Bob Evans signed red-hot Barbra Streisand to play the role of Daisy Gamble, the girl who "goes under."

Evans had decided the show needed to be updated, made more contemporary, with some mention of student protests that were happening all over the country at the time, to try to bring in a younger audience. He came up with a new character for the film: Tad Pringle, Daisy's stepbrother, an articulate, cynical hippie—or what passed for one in Hollywood. Evans knew he had found his Tad when he saw Jack in a screening of *Psych-Out*, the last film he appeared in before Hanson in *Easy Rider*.

Jack reluctantly took the part, but not before some hard negotiating with Evans. "I set up a meeting with the [then unknown] Jack Nicholson . . . He starts talking to me, and I don't understand a word he's talking about. But every time he smiles, I can't take my eyes off his smile. So I say, 'Listen, kid, how would you like to play opposite Barbra Streisand in *On a Clear Day You Can See Forever*? I'll pay you $10,000 for four weeks' work.' He had never earned more than $600 [*sic*] on a picture his whole life. He looks at me and says, 'I just got a divorce, and I've got to pay alimony. I have a kid. I have to pay child support. Can you make it $15,000?' So I say, 'How about $12,500?' He throws his arms around me and says, 'I love you.'" Jack was so grateful he kissed Bob Evans on the lips. (The film's male lead, Italian-born French star Yves Montand, who could barely speak English, was paid $400,000.)

Even though the film was something of a financial godsend for Jack, he hated everything about it—the script, the square (to him) score, and most of all his manufactured "hip and cool" character, who even sings a song with a sitar. Because he wasn't a trained singer and couldn't play the instrument, Jack talked the song through and faked playing the sitar, an instrument popularized in the West by Ravi Shankar and the Beatles. "I don't know a movie that needs to cost $12 million," Jack said before *Clear Day* opened. "I've only done that one big-budget 'A' film because I was desperate for money, and I wouldn't be in the movies if that's what making movies is like. I've got twelve years' experience in all phases of filmmaking. I did please Vincente Minnelli because in my own theory of acting, I must please the director, and I think Minnelli is good, but each night [of shooting] I was unhappy." It was an experience Jack wanted to forget, and he wished it would just go away. He used his salary to send money to Sandra and Jennifer and to buy Mud a pink-and-white trailer, even though he still didn't have a place of his own.

By EARLY WINTER 1969, after endless battling between Hopper and Fonda over every detail, including the film's sudden, shocking ending—Hopper had wanted them instead to ride off into the sunset, an argument Fonda won—*Easy Rider* was finally ready for release. Raybert held a first screening at Columbia and of the few executives who bothered to attend, almost all left by the end of the first half hour, not willing to sit through any more of a movie that clearly had no beginning and no middle, and felt as if it would never end.

Raybert reluctantly took the film back and asked Hopper to recut it. He did, again and again. He was obsessed with editing a film he couldn't finish. He took whole scenes out, put them back in, rearranged them, added outtakes. When Fonda saw Hopper's new version, he angrily complained to Schneider that all of his scenes had been cut out by Hopper, and all of Hopper's were left in.

Karen Black defended Hopper's version of the film. "I feel Dennis was enormously inspired. He had incredible intention, like a machine. He was going to get his vision of life on film, no matter what. That's why the film is great. I kind of loved Dennis."

She was in the minority.

An INCREASINGLY EXASPERATED Schneider then sent Hopper and Fonda to neutral corners and hired Henry Jaglom to take over the editing of the film. According to Jaglom, "[Schneider] told me, 'We're having a little problem here with *Easy Rider,* it's four hours long and Dennis loves it the way it is. Would you take a look at it? I can't release a four-hour film.' . . . I went to a screening and for reasons I still don't understand, I was the only one who wasn't stoned. Everybody else [was and] loved it. Each scene went on for twenty minutes, and the riding shots dragged on for three or four [soundtrack] songs. [When I began to cut the film] Jack [who was a pretty good editor, and whom Schneider allowed to edit his own scenes] was in the next room with his editor, and we were working from front to back and back to front." [4]

Hopper's version differs from Jaglom's: "I edited it for a year, and then Bert Schneider said he didn't like it the way it was at that time. He came in himself and did some things on it. Henry Jaglom did some things on it. Bob Rafelson did some things on it. There were quite a few different people who worked on it . . . the scenes that are in it are the same as when I had it in my film."

The group managed to get the film down to ninety-five minutes. This version completely freaked out Hopper, who screamed to Schneider, in front of Fonda, that his cinematic work of genius was ruined, that his movie looked now like a made-for-TV film. "*His* movie," Fonda muttered after Hopper's outburst. "I thought it was *our* movie."

COLUMBIA'S EXECUTIVES reluctantly returned for another screening and this time approved the new, much shorter edit, although they remained mystified as to what the film was about and expressed their concern that it wouldn't find an audience. In the weeks that followed, as they struggled to figure out how to position the picture for release, a buzz spread through Hollywood about a new biker film coming out with Bob Dylan's songs (sung by others) on the soundtrack and a performance by Jack Nicholson that was so great it was going to bury

[4] Schneider offered Jaglom either a small salary or nothing up front and a percentage of the film. Jaglom took the salary, a decision that would eventually cost him millions.

everything else that year. Not long after, Abe Schneider remarked to his son that he didn't know what the film was about but he was sure it was going to be a hit.

According to Peter Biskind, when Bruce Dern was making Sydney Pollack's 1969 *They Shoot Horses, Don't They?* with Jane Fonda, they were talking during a break about what new films were coming out and she said, "Wait'll you see Peter's movie, you're gonna freak out, 'cause there's a guy in that movie who is so fantastic! Somebody has finally made a good biker movie."

Bruce jerked his head back. "Whaddya mean a biker movie? We made all the biker movies. I did eleven of them. It's over for biker movies."

"This one is different."

"Who's in it?"

"Dennis, and this guy Jack Nicholson."

"*Jack Nicholson?* I gotta pay attention to *Jack fuckin' Nicholson?*"

IN THE SPRING of 1969, Bert Schneider brought *Easy Rider* to Cannes, where Jack, Peter, and Dennis were treated like rock stars. It was there that Jack first met Peter Guber, who would play a significant role in Jack's future: "I had just become chairman of Columbia Pictures that year, which was why I went to Cannes. That's where I first met Jack Nicholson, because *Easy Rider* was being distributed by us." They were up against Costa-Gavras's uber-political *Z*, which would go on to win the Jury Prize over *Easy Rider*. Lindsay Anderson's *If* won the highest prize, the Palme d'Or. Nonetheless, it was *Easy Rider* that caused a near riot among audiences. Dennis Hopper easily won Best First Work (*Prix de la première oeuvre*) by a new director, and the French film festival's recognition of his performance instantly converted Peter Fonda from a journeyman B-movie actor into the "John Wayne of biker films." (For however briefly it lasted, Fonda was a legitimate Hollywood sensation.)

But it was Jack, at that first screening, who felt the excitement from the audience from the first time he came onscreen. He heard the room laugh out loud at his goofily charming monologue by the campfire and then gasp in horror at his unexpected and brutal murder. As the lights came up and he stood to take a bow, the crowd was screaming and cheering. He grinned and thought to himself, *I'm a movie star!*

"Since my overnight stardom, if you can call it that, I can't go around picking up stray pussy anymore."

—JACK NICHOLSON

A S HE KNEW IT WOULD AFTER THE REACTION AT CANNES, *EASY Rider* made Jack Nicholson Hollywood's newest golden boy. Now every studio and producer wanted him. One thing Jack was sure of, he would never again embarrass himself playing a doofus in the service of a Barbra Streisand in a dopey film like *Clear Day*. Those days were over.

Jack then received a call from his sister Lorraine. Less than a year after he had bought her the trailer, Mud was back in New Jersey, in a hospital in Allenwood. She was dying, Lorraine told him, and he needed to come back immediately. Jack was surprised; not only did he not know she was sick, but with all that was going on he wasn't even aware she had left L.A. Nor did he have any idea what happened to the trailer. Jack was not the kind of son to call his mother every day or go over for dinner on Sunday.

He went to Rafelson, who arranged a mini-publicity tour for Jack in Manhattan, and as soon as he arrived in New York, after checking into his hotel, he hired a car to take him to the New Jersey nursing home three miles from the house where he had grown up. He got there just in time to watch her die. Mud passed away on January 6, 1970. When Jack returned to Los Angeles he talked to no one about it.

Early that same year, the Academy announced its nominations for the past year's best movies and performances. Jack was thrilled to learn he was nominated for an Oscar for Best Actor in a Supporting Role.

The first thing he did was call Mimi Michu, who was still in Florida. Now that he was successful, he felt ready to ask her to come back to L.A. and be with him. For her part, with nothing else going on, whatever it was that had caused her to dump Jack was no longer an issue, so she decided a free trip to L.A. might not be so bad. She hung up the phone, packed her bags, and started making arrangements to fly to L.A. on Jack's nickel of course

Bert, for one, was not surprised. He knew she still rang Jack's bells the way few other women could. As she once described their sexual proclivities, "We were two maniacs." Jack concurred: "I'm interested in sex. I'm preoccupied with sex. I love it."

He welcomed her back to Los Angeles with outstretched arms, and once again they became inseparable.

PRIOR TO THE night of the 1970 Oscars, Rex Reed wrote a profile of Jack for the *New York Times* and gave him a light corrective knuckle-rapping, while expressing more than a little disdain for the independent movies that had made him: ". . . Nobody ever noticed him until *Easy Rider*. The movies he's been in have all been low-budget go-out-and-grab-a-movie B flicks. Motorcycle flicks. Beach blanket bikini flicks. Horror flicks. The kind of trash only a mother or a *Cahier* critic could sit through and love. Yet, out of the anti-establishment *Easy Rider* he became a hero for two cults. The anti-establishment B-flick under-ground digs him because he's the proof that something good can come out of all that American-International garbage. And the over-30 crowd digs him too . . . There was something so touching about his alcoholic Southern aristocrat searching for a philosophical grass-roots identity with the new hip and the new cool in his faded fifties Ole Miss football jersey, that made them want to revel in their own squareness . . ."

Mimi accompanied Jack to the Old Gray Lady, in New York's mid-town, where Reed conducted the interview. She sat behind Jack and to the right, directly in Reed's line of sight. She flirted outrageously with him, something that Jack quickly became aware of that made him furious. The angrier he got, the funnier Mimi thought it was, both the flirting and the anger. None of it had any effect on Reed, other than to confirm to him that Jack must have been desperate for attention when he met this one.

THE ACADEMY AWARD ceremonies were held on April 7, 1970, at the Dorothy Chandler Pavilion, part of the Los Angeles Music Center. For the second consecutive year the Academy departed from tradition and instead of having one host to lead the audience through the numerous awards and ludicrous dance numbers designed more for the TV audience ratings than anything to do with the movies, they used what they described as "Seventeen friends of Oscar." Unfortunately, Jack couldn't be there because he was on location with a new film, *Drive, He Said,* that he was directing but not appearing in. He took Mimi with him on location, to ease the pain of missing the big night.

Peter Fonda did show and so did Dennis Hopper, with Michelle Phillips on his arm. Hopper wore a velvet double-breasted tux and white ten-gallon cowboy hat and looked completely out of place at the ceremony. Hopper couldn't resist poking his finger in the eye of the Hollywood mainstream. Henry Fonda, one of the giants of that mainstream, there to support his son, was outraged when Hopper put his hat on at one of the postceremony dinner parties and kept it on the entire meal. "Any man who insists on wearing his cowboy hat to the Academy Award ceremonies and keeps it on at the dinner table afterward ought to be spanked."

Easy Rider was nominated for two awards—Jack's performance and Best Original Screenplay (Dennis Hopper, Peter Fonda, Terry Southern). The latter went to William Goldman for *Butch Cassidy and the Sundance Kid*—the consensus being that Goldman won because *Easy Rider* sounded too improvised to have been a real screenplay.

Jack lost Best Supporting Actor to Gig Young for his portrayal of a sleazy contest runner in *They Shoot Horses, Don't They?*, a period piece about Depression-era marathon dancing contests. The crowd roared when Young's name was announced, demonstrating how the old-school voting members of the Academy felt about the new independent film movement and especially the game-changing *Easy Rider*. But it really didn't matter. Everyone knew what film and which actor was that year's real winner. Among the Best Supporting Actor nominees—Anthony Quayle, Elliott Gould, Rupert Crosse, and Young, Jack was the only one whose star was on the rise.[1]

Shortly before the night of the awards, Jack shared his feelings about them with one reporter. Speaking of his own experience: "I've always wanted to be a movie actor and the only kind to be is a big one." Meaning he would like to win. After he lost, he told another, "I liked the part [in *Easy Rider*] but I didn't know it would change my life . . . There was no demand for what I did, I always had to fight for what I got. [Before I did it] there was no demand for young unknown actors anywhere. In fact, you're suspect. People think you're avoiding going to work. In Los Angeles you say you are an actor and they think you're a gigolo of some kind, it's a way of impressing girls." No matter how self-righteous the rest of it sounded, the impressing-girls part was right on the money.

Not long after the Awards, Schneider changed the name of their company from Raybert to BBS (Bert, Bob, and Steve Blauner, who was made a one-third partner. Bert considered Steve a valuable asset and didn't want to lose him to another company). They moved into plush new digs on La Brea, not far from Charlie Chaplin's original studios, complete with a fifty-seat private screening room.

Soon enough the halls were filled with producers, writers, editors, and directors walking determinedly in and out of offices and hallways, calling one another "babe" and "doll." Secretaries yelled out loud about long-distance calls to their bosses. Gorgeous actresses nervously sat in a reception room that was decorated by Schneider with French posters from the student riots of 1968, framed splendidly in chrome, and a large black-and-white Peter Max mural.

Jack, although he was not an official member of the new company, shared free office space with filmmaker Henry Jaglom. Schneider and

---

[1] Anthony Quayle for Charles Jarrott's *Anne of the Thousand Days*, Elliott Gould for Paul Mazursky's *Bob and Carol and Ted and Alice*, Rupert Crosse for Mark Rydell's *The Reivers*, and Young. *Easy Rider* won nothing.

Rafelson loved having the creative energy of Jack's newfound success in the house.

Jack, meanwhile, after the Awards, had found a real house for himself that he liked, but because he was still broke—his earnings from *Easy Rider*, especially the piece of the back end given to him by a grateful Schneider after Jack was nominated, still hadn't started coming his way—Schneider gave him a $20,000 advance to buy the $80,000 two-story, eight-room A-frame atop Mulholland Drive, with sliding glass doors and a swimming pool that offered a spectacular view of both the Hollywood side and the San Fernando Valley that at night turned Jack's backdrop into a gorgeous blinking light show.

And it had something else. On a slightly elevated plot of land, next door and half a level up, on the other side of where the road forked, lived Marlon Brando. That sealed the deal for Jack.[2]

This generous like-a-brother aspect of Schneider's relationship with Jack offered an insight into both their personalities and backgrounds. Bert was from a privileged background; his father helped grease a lot of skids for his son to become a success in the movies. Jack was born into near poverty and had no father to speak of. As was true of many young men of the wealthy, Schneider liked to give his friends extravagant gifts. That was the bright side of it.

The darker side was the need to purchase friendship and, in Jack's case, loyalty. Schneider's new star had had a hand in every previous BBS production—he had helped write *Head*, he played a crucial role in *Easy Rider*, had directed *Drive, He Said*, and he was about to star in *Five Easy Pieces*. Bert knew everyone in Hollywood was going to come after Jack, and he wanted to exploit their emotional tie to ensure their business one.

After closing, Jack promptly furnished his new digs with used props, a gigantic bar, an original Marilyn Monroe nude calendar that hung in

---

[2] Another of Jack's nearby neighbors was Charlton Heston. This strip of Mulholland would become known in Hollywood as "Bad Boy Alley" because of Nicholson, Brando, Rafelson, and Warren Beatty, who also lived on Mulholland. Charlton Heston was not considered one of the bad boys. Almost immediately, Brando threw up a chain-link fence between his property and Jack's.

the living room, and a large jar filled with shredded dollar bills, his favorite conversation piece. Not long after, studio executive Peter Guber came to pay him a visit at his new home and got lost on Mulholland Drive trying to find the fork in the road that led to it. "I had the address," Guber recalled. "It wasn't very far from my house. I drove down his road but couldn't find the number. Then I saw a big, fat guy planting roses on the side of this road. I called out, 'Mister, mister.' He didn't turn around, but asked me what I wanted. 'Where's Jack Nicholson's house?' At that point he stood up, and I saw who it was. 'Oh fuck,' I said to myself. 'It's you! Marlon Brando!' 'Who did you expect?' he asked. I said, 'Jack Nicholson,' and he said, 'Well, I ain't Jack Nicholson. He lives down there.' He pointed down the road, then turned his back and went back to his roses.

"I eventually found the house, and Jack invited me in. I was there to talk about some project, I don't recall which, it was early on, and as we talked I couldn't help notice all these [Fernand] Légèrs leaning against the walls, on the walls, like a bunch of old newspapers. 'You're into art,' I said to him. He smiled and said, 'You might say that.'"

Jack's first big checks had just started to arrive and he had gone on an art-spending spree; the paintings were the only things he owned that he really cared about. The rest of the house looked like it was furnished from a thrift shop. Mimi helped him pick out the junk, not the art.

As money continued to roll in, Jack added a balcony off the second-floor bedroom at the far end, above the pool. He liked to wake up, open the new doors, and dive into the deep end. He also added a black open-air Jacuzzi, which took three years to finish because of the difficulty of getting it to pass code in earthquake-prone L.A. Eventually they had to cut its base directly into the house's bedrock foundation. When it was finally completed, Jack liked to take a swim, relax in the Jacuzzi, and dry himself in the warm late-afternoon breezes. Life was good.

It got better when Schneider gave Jack two impossible-to-get court-side season tickets to the Lakers, right next to the two that belonged to Dunhill Records owner Lou Adler.[3] Adler was, like Jack, a basket-

---

[3] The tickets are still in effect today.

ball freak, and they immediately bonded, meeting each night before a game to grab a bite, or have a drink, before heading to Inglewood to enjoy the game. They also loved young and beautiful women almost as much as they loved Laker showtime. The Los Angeles Lakers, formerly the Minnesota Lakers (hence the team's name), joined the NBL (National Basketball League) in 1947 and soon had their first superstar, the future legend George Mikan. In 1949 the NBL merged the BAA with the NBA. The Lakers moved to L.A. in 1960.

Jack was mesmerized, along with the rest of the country, by the memorable 1969–1970 finals that pitted Wilt Chamberlain and Jerry West, the stars of the Lakers, against the Knicks' indomitable Willis Reed. For Jack there was an extra kick; it was like watching his old hometown (on the East Coast) against his new adopted one, Los Angeles. The Knicks won in dramatic fashion in seven games, a series no one, especially Jack, would ever forget, and it cemented his love of the game.

And the season tickets, more even than the loan for the house, assured his loyalty to Schneider.

FIVE EASY PIECES was co-written (with Carol Eastman as Adrien Joyce based on an original story by Eastman and Bob Rafelson) and directed by Rafelson with a budget at just under $900,000. It is a film about the struggle of its protagonist, Bobby Dupea, who is part working class and part upper class, at home in both places but unable to relate to either. Dupea's struggle to find his place and his identity, thanks to the script, Rafelson's direction, and Jack's performance, is at once powerful, provocative, emotional, dramatic, and very entertaining. Drawing a direct line between himself and Bobby Dupea, Jack told *Newsweek*, "I've taken all the drugs, balled everybody, gone everywhere . . . the search for me and for the character is compulsive . . . There's never been a time in my life when that wasn't going on. I suppose that's partly the coincidence of when I was born and where, plus whatever fantasies I have as a person. So naturally, I feel the search is a way in itself. Looking for validity is not a big detective story but a continuing thing . . ."

Among the film's many memorable scenes, the most unforgettable

was the one in the diner. It became a signature Jack Nicholson moment, the perfect bridge between actor and character connected by
Jack's needs and his innate rage. Bobby and his girlfriend, Rayette
(Karen Black), pick up two lesbian hitchhikers, played by Helena Kallianiotes and Toni Basil—both now regulars in the BBS family of recurring players. A little farther on, they stop at a roadside diner to get a bite
to eat. All four look at menus. Bobby knows what he wants: "An omelet,
no potatoes, tomatoes instead, and wheat toast instead of rolls. Some
toast." The waitress stubbornly refuses to fill his order because it's not
on the menu. Bobby then orders a chicken salad sandwich and tells the
waitress to hold all the extra ingredients, so he can get what he originally wanted. When she asks him where he wants her to hold it, he says
between her legs. Furiously, she asks him if he sees the right-to-refuse-
service sign. In response, an equally furious Bobby asks her if she sees
this sign, and with his two hands he sweeps the table clean, sending
everything flying. During a script meeting where Jack and Carole were
trying to find a scene to express Bobby's rage, Jack reminded her about
something similar that had happened to him and Rafelson a couple
of years earlier at Pupi's, a coffee shop on the Sunset Strip, when Jack
exploded at a waitress. Out of that came the diner scene.

Although it has an improvisational feel to it, according to Kallianiotes, Rafelson wanted the scene played exactly as he had blocked
it out, but Jack told her to use her acting instincts. "Jack started the
scene. Defending him to the waitress, I rose and delivered the line to
the waitress, 'Hey Mac.' The director, Bob Rafelson, told me to say the
line seated. Then I heard Jack's voice call out, 'That's her instinct . . .
Curly, *maan*, adjust your camera.'"

When Jack was later asked by Gene Siskel of the *Chicago Tribune*
about *Five Easy Pieces*, he said, "My character was written by a woman
who knows me very well. I related the character to that time in my life,
which Carole [Eastman] knew about, well before *Easy Rider* when I
was doing a lot of second-rate TV and movies . . . So in playing the
character, I drew on all the impulses and thoughts I had during those
years when I was having no real acceptance."

Five Easy Pieces is more of an extended character study than a film with a detailed plot. It concerns a period of self-contemplation, difficult to capture on film, that leads to major change in the life of Bobby Dupea, a self-exiled classical piano player from a well-to-do talented musical family, whose self-esteem has fallen so low he works on oil rigs and has a gum-chewing, country-tune-humming bimbo of a girlfriend, Rayette, played superbly by Karen Black (Jack had insisted that Black play Rayette). Shortly after Bobby's rigging pal Elton (Billy "Green" Bush) is arrested, Bobby learns from his sister that his father has suffered a stroke, and he decides to try one more time to reconnect to his family.

The title of the film is something of a double entendre, referring at once to the Chopin piece that Bobby plays superbly, if too easily, on the piano, his musical talent diminished in his own mind by the very ease at which it comes to him, and the five women he is involved with in one way or another during the course of the film.[4] If *Easy Rider* is about the politics of the counterculture, *Five Easy Pieces* examines the politics of the crassly cultured. Bobby has always rejected his family's hollow elitism, but the low-level desperation of Rayette's clinging fills him with self-loathing.

When he tells Rayette he is going home and that she can't go with him, she tells him she is pregnant. Bobby gets into his car and throws what will become an increasingly familiar sight in Jack's movies, a cyclonic fit. Then, spent and defeated, and weak, he reluctantly goes back and gets Rayette out of bed and, against his better judgment, takes her with him. It is clear she loves him unconditionally, at whatever level she is capable of loving. Whether he can return any of that love, or whether he can love at all, is one of the essential questions of the film.

Five Easy Pieces, shot almost entirely in sequence, is, as historian Douglas Brinkley points out, "*On the Road* gone wrong." It's Kerouac's wanderlust intermingled with a Bergmanesque rondo of adult sexual relationships topped with a dose of Chaplinesque expressionism—early on, when Bobby is stuck in traffic, he climbs on the back of a pickup truck and starts playing an upright piano like a happy madman.

---

[4] In the film, Bobby plays two Chopin pieces, one Mozart, and one Bach.

Karen Black remembers working on the film as an experiment in "ecstasy," especially in her scenes with Jack. "I was so happy making that movie. Of course, I fell in love with Jack again, but neither of us was available—he had a girlfriend, or he was married, I don't remember, and I was still with Peter Kastner . . . all the way up the West Coast, while moving from one location to the other, we'd stop in hotels, and at night we'd dance. Jack was a great dancer—he'd stick his butt out and bend his legs and really get into it . . . nothing ever happened between Jack and me, because, as I say, we were both taken.

"Another time I remember, I had a line as Rayette in the car about how she would take better care of Bobby than anyone else, and feeling that she would never say that, that she would never make a comparison like that. Bob stopped the shoot and we discussed this one sentence for easily more than an hour. That was his and the BBS way."

The most difficult scene for Jack to shoot was when Bobby finally meets with his father and tries to talk to him, even though the father cannot speak because of his stroke. Rafelson wanted Jack to cry. Jack refused, and it nearly turned into a brawl. Jack insisted that crying in the scene was phony acting-school stuff. Rafelson countered by insisting it would be Jack's Oscar moment. Jack finally and reluctantly did it—his way. After many takes, pulling deeper into himself each time, he was able to arrive at a place where he could cover his face and appear to sob. Ultimately, whether he really did cry is less important than the fact that he could convincingly *act* as if he did.[5]

Although he was still going with Mimi, during production Jack became secretly and heavily involved with Susan Anspach, who plays a young and beautiful pianist engaged to Bobby's brother and has a brief but heated onscreen flirtation with Bobby. Two and a half weeks after the film premiered on September 11, 1970, Susan gave birth to a baby boy. Although she denied it for years, everyone in Hollywood seemed somehow to know that Jack was the father. He claimed not to be sure

[5] Or not. Susan Anspach later told a reporter that during the shoot Jack was heavily into cocaine, and that he used it to do the scene. He did thirty-nine takes to get it right. "Jack took one toot every six takes. He frequently left the set to snort."—Robert Sellers, *Hollywood Hellraisers*, p. 122.

himself, even after Anspach told him herself at a party not long after the night of the 1971 Oscars. She named the baby Caleb, after James Dean's character in *East of Eden.* In 1974, Anspach married another actor, who adopted the boy and gave him his last name, but Jack secretly continued to send child support payments to Anspach.[6]

THE OPENING OF Jack's two films bracketed the summer. *On a Clear Day* opened on June 17, 1970, and grossed only $14 million, with all the available heat going to Streisand. Jack's one song was mercifully cut from the film's soundtrack, much to his relief and delight, and although the reviews were dismal, he was completely ignored by the critics and the film did nothing to damage the late-in-coming but post–*Easy Rider* lightning momentum of his career.

MADE ON A budget of $1.6 million, almost twice what the tax shelter had mandated, the balance made up by the principal of BBS, *Five Easy Pieces* opened on September 11, 1970, to mixed-to-good reviews and grossed $18 million in its initial domestic release, making it the second straight box office hit for Jack and BBS. In December, *Newsweek* did a promotional cover story on Jack, a milestone first for him. In the interview, he credited Eastman for the high quality of the screenplay, alluding only indirectly to Rafelson's earlier, unthought-through version: "The original script, as written by Bob Rafelson, had Bobby and Rayette going off a cliff in their car, with only Rayette surviving . . . we didn't continue with that ending because we weren't happy killing people off. I don't like killing off people in movies . . . in every movie I made [before *Five Easy Pieces*], practically everyone was killed off, but we didn't want to rely on that . . ."

After *Easy Rider,* and before *Five Easy Pieces*, Jack had told Schneider that he wanted to try directing again, and he quickly found a property for him. It was called *Drive, He Said,* a 1964 novel about college

---

[6] Caleb was born September 30, 1970. James Dean died on that day in 1955.

basketball and campus protest politics by Jeremy Larner. Jack read it and liked it, and Schneider obligingly secured the film rights for him. Schneider was aware of a commitment Jack had already made to Mike Nichols ("Big Nick," in Jackspeak) to be in his upcoming *Carnal Knowledge*. After Jack's performance in *Easy Rider*, Nichols had publicly declared him "the most important actor since Brando" and wanted him for *Carnal Knowledge* badly enough that he agreed to wait until Jack was available.

For *Drive, He Said*, Bert moved Steve Blauner into the co-producer slot. Peter Guber, now vice president of Columbia, the film's distributor, while not directly involved with the production, considered himself "a cheerleader and a supporter of Jack and the film." Bert then handed the entire project over to his brother, Harold, to work with Blauner and executive-produce (he is uncredited in the film).

Rafelson was less willing than Schneider to give Jack everything he wanted. He was wary of those he considered Jack's hangers-on, like Fred Roos, whom Jack had worked with during the Corman years, and who had since become a casting director, and his good friend Harry Gittes. Bob had no use for Roos or Gittes; the latter served as Jack's unofficial agent, meaning Bob had to deal directly with him about the business of the film. This last development was too much for Rafelson, who went straight to Jack and Bert and gave them an ultimatum: either Jack must stop using Gittes as his agent or BBS would not continue with *Drive, He Said*. Jack pulled Gittes off the financial watch. To make it up to him, he found Gittes a small part in the movie.

Jack then insisted on rewriting Larner's script himself. Rafelson agreed it wasn't very good (he had already rewritten it once with the help of Robert Towne and Terrence Malick, both uncredited). Larner was furious, but contractually there was nothing he could do. (However, even with all the work that was done on it, the script still didn't work.)

Schneider, as a further gesture of goodwill, then hired a bunch of Jack's friends besides Gittes to fill out the cast, all of whom accepted scale just to be in a Nicholson project. Bob Towne, the writer, played the cuckolded husband married to Olive (Karen Black), and the part of Coach Bullion, at Jack's insistence, went to Bruce Dern, for whom Jack arranged separately to receive a thousand dollars a week for the part. He wanted to do something to help kick-start Dernsie's financial situation caused by his stalled career. Henry Jaglom played Conrad, one of the hard-ass professors, and newcomer William Tepper, a recent UCLA film school grad who had played a little high school basketball, was cast as Hector, the film's star athlete.

Set at the height of the Vietnam War, the film centers on two friends and fellow students, the apolitical, good-looking Hector and his not-so-good-looking pal Gabriel (Michael Margotta), who is extremely political and being hotly pursued by his local draft board (and offscreen by Mimi, who carried on hot and heavy with him behind Jack's back for almost the entire production).

Between shooting baskets, Hector has an affair with Olive, a gorgeous professor's wife, and (not at the same time) watches his naked girlfriend roam around his dorm. Meanwhile, Gabriel, freaking out over his imminent induction into the military, tries to convince everyone he is a first-class moron, setting reptiles free from the school lab. When that doesn't work, he takes it to another, dangerous, and quite moronic level as he tries to rape Olive. The end of the film sees him being taken away in cuffs. Prison, not Vietnam, is his fate, and the film's timely message suggests that there is no real difference for America's youth of the day between the two.

It quickly became apparent while filming that nothing was right about the script, and more rewrites were needed. This delayed the shoot for more than a month. Labor problems also plagued the production.

During the downtime, Jack returned to Hollywood. While the rest of the production remained on location at the University of Oregon, where the film was being shot, Jack decided to operate his own personal casting couch to find the perfect girl for the brief nonsexual nudity that takes place in the film. High on dope, grinning from ear to ear, Jack had the most beautiful starlets in Hollywood come to his office at BBS as he sat between his poster of Bob Dylan on one side of his sofa and a large photo of a nude woman on the other and made each disrobe for him. Some were more eager than others, but all disrobed and endured Jack's near-medical examination. He saw more than a hundred girls before he chose June Fairchild, an actress who had been in *Head*, likely someone he had in mind for the part all along.

Back in production, Jack shot the sex scene in a car, where one of the participants has a vocal orgasm; another scene showed male frontal genitalia that violated a "no nudity" clause he had agreed to in return for the right to shoot directly on the university's campus. That produced a brouhaha that threatened to again shut down the film.[7] Jack later explained, somewhat ambiguously and not altogether accurately, what had happened this way: "I want to make only X-rated films . . . [seriously,] I knew we weren't supposed to do it, but one very early Sunday morning I went out with the cameraman, a friend, the actor, did the bit and then split. Someone ratted, but we had already gotten the film out of the state across the border . . ." To *Playboy*, he later said this about nudity in American films: "If you suck a tit, you're an X, but if you cut it off with a sword, you're a PG . . . I don't think there's anything dirty about sex . . . I didn't want to do a 'Romper Room' movie . . . we got in trouble because you weren't supposed to hear the sound of an orgasm. In England they wanted me to cut one line from the movie: 'I'm comin'.' I refused and the movie was never shown there. No one cared that a character in the picture was nude all the time. . . . [She was] nude for no purpose. I was sick of convention. I just put a nude woman in for no reason. For that movie I also wanted to do a symphony of dicks . . . I thought it might have been a good title sequence but the cameramen wouldn't shoot it."

There may have been another reason Jack wanted the film to hover

---

[7] It initially received an X rating by the MPAA. Columbia had never previously released an X-rated film and challenged the MPAA's decision. Ramsey Clark was a member of the law firm that handled Columbia's successful appeal. Nothing was changed, nothing was taken out, and the film's rating was changed to R. Jack called it a victory for anticensorship. He also refused to cut the nudity or the orgasm scene for Canada or England, and as a result the film was not released in theaters in either country.

near the notorious X. He never wanted a movie of his to be shown on television, a medium he hated. In the days before cable, videocassettes, DVD, and streaming, movies that came to broadcast TV too soon were considered box office failures (most of them were). He wanted to make movies that could be shown only in the theaters. Peter Guber took a supportive stand, backing Jack's sexual ideas, but with one eye on protecting the studio: "We were enthusiastic about the film and stood totally behind it, with a safety wall. I was not really creatively involved with any elements of the production at all."

To Jack, *Drive, He Said* had all the same rebellious elements of his best Corman films, but when it opened, after *Five Easy Pieces*, audiences didn't buy it. Instead of antisocial or politically radical, it came off as dated, hollow, pretentious, and ineffective. As a (re)writer, Jack failed to provide his story with sufficient dramatic buildup or any kind of logical progression of the plot. As a director, he failed at illuminating the story's subtext, and his frame lacked cinematic tension. Because of it, all the characters came off two-dimensional and vapid, and Gabriel's final rape freak-out lacked any sense of moral outrage or ironic desperation, little more than a pornographic adolescent wet dream.

With all the delays, and the death of Ethel May, the production, originally scheduled for thirty days, stretched past two months. During the time Jack was away from the set, he kept hearing rumors that Mimi, whom he had given a small role, was having an affair with Margotta. When Jack got back, he tried to get her to stop; she ignored him, until one day she showed up on set with a black eye. The next day she left, telling Jack they were through, and once again he went crazy over losing her, performing his own tragic opera for anyone who could bear to listen to it again. Harry Dean remembers how Jack was "almost incoherent. I've never seen such despair."

They were back together a week later.

It was obvious almost from the start that Jack was in trouble as a director. Normally the coolest cat on the set, he was in over his head. As Karen Black recalls: "The production was disorganized and because of budget problems they couldn't give Jack enough people to do all the other work. There were not enough hats to let Jack concentrate only on directing. This had to be done, that had to be done, and Jack wound up doing most of it and he just couldn't handle it all by himself. It's the plague of independent filming, and also part of what makes independent filmmaking so exciting, like that old Chinese saying, 'The worst part of you is also the best part of you.'"

Despite the production's cost escalations, Schneider, who was in charge of the budget for this film, said nothing and kept paying the bills. In the spring of 1971, he finally showed a rough cut of *Drive, He Said* at Cannes, where it was hooted at by angry audiences. When Jack was brought out as the director after the screening, he was booed off the stage. It didn't help that any moral antiwar conviction the hero might have had was lost by his attempted rape of an innocent woman, a metaphor of America's involvement in Vietnam that didn't work at all. *Drive, He Said*'s moral imperative about the war came out exactly the opposite of what Jack had wanted it to be.

Besides its weak script, the film lacked two essentials needed to become a hit. One was Jack's onscreen presence. He might have been able to pull off one of the two leads and generate sufficient box office to have the film at least break even. Both Tepper and Margotta had zero presence. The other was timing. What had seemed relevant and dramatically justifiable in the sixties simply didn't resonate the same way in the seventies. The American public had grown weary of Vietnam, and the reaction at Cannes was a harbinger of things to come. *Drive, He Said* never gained traction at the box office, and it was finally released June 13, 1971, on the bottom half of a double bill with Columbia's rerelease of Paul Mazursky's 1969 hugely popular ode to free love, *Bob and Carol and Ted and Alice*.

Jack had arrived at Cannes with a big smile plastered on his face and the gorgeous Michelle Phillips, late of the Mamas and the Papas. Michelle had since married and divorced Dennis Hopper not long after she had shown up at the Oscars with him for *Easy Rider*. A few days later after the wedding they'd had a fight that ended with Hopper punching Phillips, and she ended their eight-day marriage. Phillips dropped her line back in the water. The two were first introduced by Lou Adler, who had originally signed the Mamas and the Papas to his Dunhill Records and made them stars. He did it in the hopes that Michelle might be able to turn off Jack's Mimi-driven obsession. He was right. Jack was dazzled by Michelle's hippie/glam look, dropped Mimi for good, and started going with Phillips.

Jack took Michelle to Cannes with him. As soon as John Phillips, Michelle's ex, heard about it and that Mimi was available, he tracked Mimi down and began sleeping with her. And everyone from Malibu to Melrose knew it. Including Jack, which was exactly what John Phillips wanted.

IMMEDIATELY FOLLOWING *Drive, He Said*, Henry Jaglom asked Jack to play a small part in his first directorial effort, *A Safe Place*, and with nothing else on his plate he said yes.

Jaglom had played a small role in *Drive, He Said*, and now, as payback, Jack took the role of Mitch in Jaglom's *A Safe Place*. Jaglom couldn't pay anything. Jack didn't mind. Jaglom had taken SAG minimum for *Drive, He Said*. Jaglom gave Jack a color TV for his services. He could use it to watch Lakers games, the only thing on television he watched.

Jack improvised all of his scenes in one day. There was no written script for his character, so he worked off descriptions fed to him by Jaglom. The good part was that he was going to co-star opposite the luscious Tuesday Weld and the great Orson Welles. Welles had long been a pariah at the studios and was perennially in need of funds to produce his own movies. Jaglom gave him a chance to flex for the screen, something he all too rarely got the opportunity to do.

A Safe Place is simply beyond comprehension. There is so much "filmmaking" going on in it that the whole movie gets buried behind zoom shots, single-take shots, tracking shots, shots of reflections through water, high-angle shots, low-angle shots, everything but shots that offer a narrative continuity to tell the film's plot. *A Safe Place* made

Drive, He Said look like *Gone with the Wind* (and *Drive, He Said* made *Easy Rider* look like *The Birth of a Nation*).

There are pot scenes, seminude orgy scenes, hippie clothing, and lots of candles, all of which displaces the film back to the sixties, in a script loaded with words, words, words, camera angles, camera angles, camera angles that mean nothing, nothing, nothing.

It is also notable as the first film in which Jack's hair loss is visible, as well as a slight but hard-to-miss weight gain that he would now battle throughout the rest of his career. In *A Safe Place* he is shot in basically two modes; moving across a rooftop in medium close-up as the camera pans left to right, keeping him in frame, and in a two-shot in bed with Weld (rumors ran rampant on the set that they were having sex with each other throughout filming). Jaglom uses a soundtrack peppered with Édith Piaf and Charles Trenet, suggesting some kind of connection to the n*ouvelle vague*, but the only time the film has any vibrancy, Welles's presence notwithstanding, is when Jack appears onscreen. His magnetism is undeniable, even in a pretentious mishmash like this.

Here, in his own words, is how Jaglom conceived *A Safe Place*: "I personally had two very different influences—improvisational theater, which I started out in, and European films, including Fellini, Godard, Bergman, a new kind of cinema . . . I first did it as a play at the Actors Studio in New York in 1964, with Karen Black playing the Tuesday Weld part and I played the part that Jack played. Philip Proctor did the same part on stage and screen . . . Karen Black was my girlfriend at the time. I got connected to Tuesday Weld and wrote the play about a character who is one third Tuesday, one third Karen, and one third me . . . I was interested in exploring the inner, unexpressed life of women . . . who were not represented in Hollywood films . . . After the success of *Easy Rider* I went to Bert Schneider and told him that I wanted to make a film too. He said okay and I told him it was going to be based on my play *A Safe Place* and he said 'Fine.' . . .

"Jack comes in, fucks the girl, fucks the picture, and fucks the audience, and then disappears, like the Orson Welles character, the magician . . . it's about the magic of our lives . . ."

A *Safe Place* did nothing at the box office. Jack's only official comment on his one-day shoot for *A Safe Place* was, "My stuff was great."

THAT SUMMER OF 1970, Helena Kallianiotes showed up at Jack's doorstep with an unexplained black eye. He asked no questions, but figuring Kallianiotes was the victim of some sort of physical abuse, perhaps from her broken marriage, he let her move in. "Pick yourself a bedroom," he told her. In return for running the house and handling the daily chores, he told her she could stay as long as she wanted. She was, in many ways, Jack's perfect nonwife. She wasn't the only houseguest Jack had ever had, but the most permanent. His door was always open to all his friends: Dernsie, Bob Evans, Roman Polanski. Whenever they needed a place to be discreet, Jack's was it. They also loved to come over and hang by the pool, get stoned, and trade film-business stories.

Jack especially liked Helena's social ease and popularity. She was connected to the Hollywood hip and took him along to places he hadn't been before, out of the coffeehouses and bars to more interesting places. She introduced him to Mick Jagger, Bob Dylan, Cat Stevens, and John Lennon, all regulars at places like the Chateau Marmont and the Beverly Wilshire bar Hernando's. Through her he met and had affairs with several of L.A.'s most coveted women, including folk/rock goddess Joni Mitchell.

Not at all bothered by Kallianiotes's residency in Jack's house, Michelle, never the jealous or possessive type, rented a house near Jack's for herself and her daughter, which suited him just fine.[8] He could be free and involved at the same time. Jack also called Dennis to tell him he was seeing Michelle. The last thing Jack wanted was to have Hopper hear about it from someone else (which he probably already had, since everybody in Hollywood knew everything Jack did) and come after him, or the both of them, with a gun. He was capable of it. Plus, the permanent paranoia resulting from the recent Tate/LaBianca murders, the handiwork of the infamous Charles Manson and his band of

---

[8] Some reports have Jack buying the house.

followers, had made everybody in Hollywood acquire guns, and Jack was sure Hopper knew how to use his. For a time, Jack slept with a hammer under his pillow.

Hopper only laughed when they finally spoke, telling Jack that Michelle was his headache now.

Jack had known Sharon Tate and occasionally had dinner with her and her husband, director Roman Polanski, at El Coyote, a popular Hollywood Mexican restaurant. A year after the murders, in 1970, the trial began, and Jack managed to secure passes to watch the proceedings in person. He was fascinated by Manson's persona and the crazy way he looked during the proceedings. The whole ghoulish thing was run like a public circus. It amounted to courtroom pornography, and Jack, who was there almost every day, couldn't get enough of it.

EARLY IN 1971, Jack was nominated for Best Actor for his performance as Bobby Dupea in *Five Easy Pieces* and this time he made it his business to be there. To celebrate, Jack bought a brand-new super-expensive $23,000 Mercedes-Benz 600, to park next to his 1967 yellow Volkswagen. His friend Harry Gittes noted, "You can tell Jack's mood by which car he uses. One part of him is definitely a street person [the Volkswagen], a guy who loves to go to Lakers basketball games and harass the opposition, or prowl dingy bars on Santa Monica Boulevard. The other part is the show-biz celeb [the Mercedes] . . . trying to make time with the world's most glamorous women." He also began picking up everyone's tab whenever he ate with them: breakfast, lunch, or dinner. He became addicted to expensive Cuban Montecristo cigars, which he bought by the boxload whenever he was in Europe or Canada, smuggling them home in his luggage. And Jack became more of a user of cocaine because, as he told *Playboy*, "Chicks dig it sexually."

The 43rd Annual Academy Awards were held on April 15, 1971, once again at the Dorothy Chandler Pavilion. This time thirty-two stars shared the hosting duty, in an attempt to liven up the proceedings (it didn't). Besides Jack's nominations, *Five Easy Pieces* received three other nominations: Karen Black for Best Supporting Actress, Rafelson and Joyce (Eastman) for Best Original Screenplay, and Rafelson and Richard Wechsler for Best Picture.

The overwhelming favorite that year in all the categories was Franklin J. Schaffner's *Patton*, old Hollywood's seemingly never-ending celebration of World War II. George C. Scott's performance in the title role was a testament to his ability as an actor, and everybody in the house, including Jack, stylish in a black custom-tailored suit with a black tie and black shirt, with Michelle in an eclectic yet lovely outfit by his side, knew it. Scott won but didn't show up, and he refused the Oscar when he received word it had been awarded to him. He was, reportedly, at home in New York City watching a hockey game when someone called to tell him the news.

Scott may not have cared, but Jack was disappointed. He was 0 for 2 now at the Oscars and beginning to wonder if the Academy establishment was ever going to recognize him.

BBS MANAGED TO take Bogdanovich away from Corman by offering him more money. Bogdanovich wanted to make a movie out of writer Larry McMurtry's semiautobiographical novel *The Last Picture Show*, and Bert Schneider gave him the money to do it.[9]

Schneider thought the thirty-one-year-old Bogdanovich was a legitimate talent and a great addition to BBS's expanding corral, which included Jack, Carole Eastman, Henry Jaglom, Robert Towne, and Rafelson. In a way, BBS had turned itself into a higher-class version of Corman's operations. If Corman had pioneered the independent movement in the Hollywood of the 1950s, BBS in the late 1960s and early-to-mid 1970s brought it into the mainstream.

---

[9] Bogdanovich had made *Targets* for Corman; it was the product of a contract Corman held on Boris Karloff that had a few days left on it. Bogdanovich's job was to come up with a story built around Karloff. The film was released in 1968, but Corman held it back for several months because of the assassinations of Martin Luther King Jr. and Robert Kennedy; it later became a cult film. Corman had wanted a Hitchcock-type movie, the only real directive he gave the young director. Bogdanovich also made another quickie exploitation film for Corman in 1968 called *Voyage to the Planet of Prehistoric Women*.

The Last Picture Show, a look at a dying Texas town as seen through the eyes of three young boys, was released on October 22, 1971, four months after *Drive, He Said,* and grossed more than $29 million in its initial domestic release. The following year it was nominated for eight Academy Awards, including one for Best Director (Bogdanovich), and won two, Ben Johnson for Best Supporting Actor and Cloris Leachman for Best Supporting Actress. Despite the failure of *Drive, He Said* (released after *Five Easy Pieces*), it kept BBS at the top of its game. But it wasn't destined to stay there much longer. The wheels of pop culture were turning, and BBS was about to start rolling downhill and take the first wave of independent movies with it.

DENNIS HOPPER HAD also wanted to make his own film, something called *The Last Movie.* He boldly walked into BBS's office and demanded that Schneider let him make it for him. As Hopper later explained to Peter Biskind, the film was about "a stunt man in a lousy Western. When his movie unit goes back to the States, he stays on in Peru to develop a location for other Westerns. He's Mr. Middle America. He dreams of big cars, swimming pools, gorgeous girls . . . But the Indians . . . see the lousy Western for what it really was, a tragic legend of greed and violence in which everybody died at the end. So they build a camera out of junk and reenact the movie as a religious rite. To play the victim in the ceremony, they pick the stunt man . . . [it's] a story about how America is destroying itself."

To his shock and amazement (but nobody else's), BBS turned him down. Rafelson, especially, had had his fill of Hopper and felt no need to reenter that particular filmmaking asylum. It marked the end of Hopper's association with BBS.

Still, the outsize and unexpected box office success of *Easy Rider* prompted most of the majors to start so-called youth divisions that hopefully would turn out movies like *Rider* that would appeal to younger audiences, be made for less than a million dollars, and avoid using expensive mainstream stars. Universal's new division was run by former MCA recording executive Ned Tanen and former TV executive Sidney

Sheinberg. They signed up a slew of projects, the first being Dennis Hopper's ironic (and prophetic) title *The Last Movie*, which was set to co-star Peter Fonda (as an actor only), Henry Jaglom, Michelle Phillips, and Kris Kristofferson. Tanen and Sheinberg, hoping to catch a part of the cultural tidal wave of *Easy Rider*, welcomed Hopper with open arms and pocketbook. They also signed Peter Fonda and his first post–*Easy Rider* project, *The Hired Hand*, and even a film by Jack's old friend from the Corman days, Monte Hellman, *Two-Lane Blacktop*, which substituted '55 Chevys for motorcycles and otherwise was essentially a copy of *Easy Rider*, with James Taylor and Dennis Wilson of the Beach Boys in the Peter Fonda and Dennis Hopper roles.

The first three films released under the Tanen/Sheinberg banner were Frank Perry's *Diary of a Mad Housewife* (1970), Miloš Forman's *Taking Off*, and Hellman's *Two-Lane Blacktop*. *Housewife* and *Taking Off* each did moderately well, critically and at the box office, and turned a modest profit because of their limited budgets. *Two-Lane Blacktop* did less well, grossing $800,000. Fonda's film, which he directed and starred in, managed to break the million dollar gross feeding off the success of *Easy Rider*, but left no lasting impression on audiences and was quickly forgotten. The big blow came with the failure of *The Last Movie*. Originally budgeted at $850,000, the film's cost escalated when Hopper decided to shoot most of it on location in Peru, and wound up grossing only $1 million, far below what it needed to break even. Released in 1971 to mixed-to-poor reviews, it confirmed to Universal that splitting up Fonda and Hopper was like using Stan Laurel without Oliver Hardy. *Variety* was the first to declare that the new emperors of Hollywood had no blue jeans when it declared, with undisguised glee, that the *Easy Rider* "craze" was over.

Would-be independent filmmaker George Lucas remembers that, after the failure of *The Last Movie*, "I went to every studio in town [to get funding for *American Graffiti*] and nobody wanted anything to do with it. Eventually Universal picked it up, thanks to the very last vestige of one of those studio offshoots that had sprung up in the Sixties after *Easy Rider*. Universal decided not to make any more of those kinds of films. Dennis Hopper had just made *The Last Movie* for them in the Andes [mountains of Peru] and pretty much killed off the whole thing he'd started with *Easy Rider . . .*"

JACK, MEANWHILE, was licking his wounds after the failure of *Drive, He Said* and hoping his directing fiasco didn't damage the momentum of his acting career. He had promised Nichols he would do *Carnal Knowledge,* but now Nichols was not ready. Instead, Jack seriously considered playing Napoleon in a film bio to be called *Waterloo,* directed by Stanley Kubrick. "He had a lot of revolutionary ideas about how to approach a costume picture . . . a lot of his work on *Napoleon* went into *Barry Lyndon.* He called me on the phone . . . 'I'm thinking of doing a film on *Napoleon.* And my plans involved having only English actors. But I broke my leg and while I was in bed I saw *Easy Rider.* Because of your performance I'm going to adjust the way I do the picture. Would you be interested in playing Napoleon?'" However, money problems plagued the project. Jack offered to help raise what Kubrick needed but was turned down by him. The project was fatally stalled.

Mike Nichols called to say he was now ready to begin production on *Carnal Knowledge* at Joseph E. Levine's Avco Embassy, the same company that had made Nichols's *The Graduate.* Jack said he was too.

Carnal Knowledge begins in the 1940s and spans twenty-five years in the life of two roommates at Amherst College, Jonathan (Jack) and Sandy, played by Art Garfunkel ("Art the Garf" in Jackspeak), who had temporarily broken away from Paul Simon and their megasuccessful pop duo Simon and Garfunkel to accept the role as the bombardier, Captain Nately, in Nichols's film adaptation of Joseph Heller's massively popular *Catch-22.* Nichols then wanted him back to co-star opposite Jack. Garfunkel had just the right combination of innocence and passivity, which deepened the contrast between Sandy and the conniving, perennially dissatisfied Jonathan.

The role of the sexually ambivalent Smith student Susan went to Candice Bergen. After Jane Fonda turned down the role of Bobbie it went to the fabulously sexy Ann-Margret in what was undoubtedly the best performance of her career. Stage and screen actress Rita Moreno played the dutiful embodiment of middle-aged Jonathan's fantasy fuck, a small but powerful role and performance.

The film opens with a voice-over question from Jonathan to Sandy that sets the philosophical and emotional exploration of the film: Is it better to love or to be loved? The answer, by way of Jules Feiffer's brilliantly cynical screenplay (the script was originally written for the stage, intended for Broadway, but Feiffer could not get it produced) and Nichols's single-take direction, is that it is impossible to be either. As the audience soon discovers, Jonathan is desperate to be loved, enough to put getting laid (his version of love) above loyalty, while Sandy longs to love in that way college boys dream of while they write lousy poetry in their notebooks.

Soon enough, Sandy falls for the angelic-looking but standoffish Susan, a student at Smith who, after a long and frustrating struggle with Sandy, still won't sleep with him but gives him a compromise hand job, just enough to keep him interested. That night, back in the dorm, Sandy brags to Jonathan about what Susan did to him. Nichols's next razor-sharp, perfectly timed jump cut has a drooling Jonathan on a hallway pay phone calling Susan and arranging to go out with her. They meet and begin a blazing sexual romance without Sandy knowing, until Susan, realizing Jonathan is only in it for what he can get off her, drops him and (eventually) marries Sandy. There is a whiff of Freudian homoeroticism here, the sharing of one woman by two friends being an indirect way of having sex with each other, underscored by the two boys sharing single beds in their dorm, each talking about his female conquests that turns the other one on. The first act ends with Sandy unaware that Jonathan has slept with Susan.

In the film's second act, the boys are now in early middle age. Jonathan is single, a successful money manager, while Sandy, a doctor (a specialist!), is unhappily married to Susan. Apparently, the sex has long gone out of their marriage and he is horny but trapped, by both social convention and his own inability to overstep the careful bounds that

Susan has laid out. To others, the marriage is perfect. To Sandy it is perfectly boring. Jonathan then gets involved with a red-haired bimbo with big tits (Jonathan's main requirement of his women), Bobbie (Ann-Margret), good-looking but helplessly dependent, who pushes him to "shack up," and when he reluctantly lets her move into his Upper West Side apartment, she then presses him to get married, with disastrous results. In one of their more tempestuous arguments, she complains of having nothing to do, that she wants a baby, and Jack has an explosive fit (his best onscreen one yet), climaxing with the most unforgettable line of the scene, the movie, and possibly the seventies: "I'm taken! *By me!*"

The fight is shown in a single take, the first and only one Nichols shot. Jack goes balletic as he moves about the apartment flailing, yelling, and screaming, while Bobbie sits on the bed, pilled up, boozy, watching in horror. Audiences were at once shocked and mesmerized.

Afterward, as Sandy keeps complaining to his friend about how the sex has gone out of their lives, Jonathan proposes a solution. Jonathan has a hot friend, Cindy (Cynthia O'Neal), good-looking in that Upper East Side style and looking for action. He fixes Sandy up, and soon they're mating like rabbits. This kicks off Jonathan's old competitive/jealous/greedy streak, fueled by his grass-is-greener complex, and while having Sandy and Cindy over for a double date, he takes Sandy aside and suggests they swap partners for the night. He convinces Sandy and sends him into Bobbie's room. Jonathan then makes his pass at Cindy, who turns him down, at least for now, but leaves the door and everything else open.

When Jonathan realizes he isn't going to get laid with Cindy that night, he goes back to his room, hoping it's not too late to stop Sandy, who is now on the phone, calling for an ambulance. Bobbie has OD'd and Sandy is trying to save her life. Eventually, she recovers, Jonathan marries her, and she soon leaves him and hits him up for all the alimony she can squeeze out of him.

The film moves into its third act, with the men bemoaning their fates as they walk along Park Avenue. Sandy's marriage is still there and not there, and Jonathan has given up all hope of ever becoming "*Playboy* magazine's ideal man." What fascinates him now is a beautiful ice-skater in Central Park he likes to watch from a distance; she is his ultimate ice-queen fantasy of female sexual perfection.

In the film's truly shocking climax, Jonathan visits a beautiful woman, Louise (Rita Moreno), with whom, it appears, he has at last found the perfect mate, a hooker who follows a sexual script, and who sends Jonathan into another fit when she flubs a line. They start the scene over and he lies back on her sofa, allowing her to talk him into a difficult-to-achieve erection. As Louise works on him, Jonathan's mind drifts into a fantasy about the ice-skater as the film ends.

Jack and the other cast members made a vow to stay off pot for the duration of the production, to make sure they were pinpoint sharp, to match Nichols's precise direction. Jack smoked his Montecristos instead.

CARNAL KNOWLEDGE opened on June 30, 1971. The film received mixed reviews; its overall emotional darkness and sexual cynicism didn't compute with most of the daily write-a-review critics. It wasn't a big studio production; it had relatively no action, no plot, and plenty of near-explicit sex and big-star nudity, which were still relatively new to the movie mainstream.[10]

One Hollywood producer had this to say about it: "The film was written by one Jewish guy and directed by another, and Arthur Garfunkel was the onscreen Jew. The producer, Joseph E. Levine, was also Jewish, and not especially well-liked in Hollywood. He was the Jewish

---

[10] Not that the film didn't have legal problems that may have hurt it at the box office. A theater in Albany, Georgia, showed the film on January 13, 1972, relatively late in its run, and the local police served a search warrant on the theater and seized the print. In March 1972, the theater manager was convicted of the crime of "distributing obscene material." His conviction was upheld by the Supreme Court of Georgia. On June 24, 1974, the U.S. Supreme Court found that the State of Georgia had gone too far in classifying material as obscene in view of its prior decision in *Miller v. California*, 413 U.S. 15 (1973) (the *Miller* standard), and overturned the conviction.

Roger Corman, the difference being that everyone loved Roger and his pictures, even his exploitation flicks were harmless cartoons. Both *The Graduate* and *Carnal Knowledge* dealt with topics like incest and marital infidelity that turned off a lot of people in Hollywood, and because of it—maybe it hit too close—*Carnal Knowledge* had absolutely no support at the Academy, which itself, of course, is largely Jewish and saw the film as a testament to self-hate; the ultimate Jewish guy [Garfunkel] who wants to assimilate with the ultimate *shiksa* [Candice Bergen, or "Bug" in Jackspeak]. Thank God for Jack Nicholson."

Carnal Knowledge came in at number thirty in a magazine compilation of the year's best movies; William Friedkin's policier *The French Connection* came in at number one. *Carnal Knowledge* was the sixth-highest-grossing film of the year, and took in $18 million domestically, $29 million worldwide.[11]

Jack had given his best performance yet and it helped Nichols take his place as a legitimate American auteur. Jack later admitted, revealingly, to *Playboy* that, with Nichols's encouragement, he'd allowed Jonathan to get closer to his own reality than any other character he had played to date.

And, as that producer had predicted, it was all but ignored at Oscar time. Jack did not receive a Best Actor nomination, and Nichols was passed over as Best Director. Only Ann-Margret was nominated, for Best Supporting Actress.[12] Despite the Academy's snub, *Carnal Knowledge* is the film that confirmed that thirty-four-year-old Jack Nicholson was the best American film actor of his generation.

After its release, Jack took a deep breath and, through his new agent, Sandy Bresler, turned down a number of lucrative offers, including the role of Michael Corleone in Francis Ford Coppola's 1972 *The God-*

[11] The top ten highest-grossing films of 1971 were Norman Jewison's *Fiddler on the Roof,* William Friedkin's *The French Connection,* Robert Mulligan's *Summer of '42,* Guy Hamilton's *Diamonds Are Forever,* Don Siegel's *Dirty Harry,* Mike Nichols's *Carnal Knowledge,* Stanley Kubrick's *A Clockwork Orange,* Alan J. Pakula's *Klute,* Peter Bogdanovich's *The Last Picture Show,* and Robert Stevenson's *Bedknobs and Broomsticks.*

[12] Cloris Leachman won Best Supporting Actress for *The Last Picture Show.*

father, which went instead to Al Pacino and made him a star. He also turned down *The Sting*. "The same year I turned down *Godfather* and *The Sting*," he later told Peter Bogdanovich. "A lot of that was because of what else I felt I had to be doing. I was perfect for *The Godfather*—I don't think I would have turned it down today [2006]. But at that time it was like Tony Franciosa and Ben Gazzara were the only Italians acting. I felt like, the Italian actors should have it—it was very idealistic of me." As for *The Sting*, he said, "I liked the project, I liked the period and I knew it would be commercial. But I wanted to put my energies into a movie that really needed them." Jack also turned down the younger priest in William Friedkin's *The Exorcist* and the assassin in Fred Zinnemann's *The Day of the Jackal*.

There was one role he really regretted saying no to. "I could kill myself [for turning down] *The Great Gatsby* . . . Since I was 18 years old people said I should do Gatsby." The part went instead to Robert Redford, in Jack Clayton's flat 1974 version of F. Scott Fitzgerald's novel.

But to close friends he admitted that the real reason for turning everything down was that he was exhausted. He had made twenty-six movies in thirteen years and needed a breather, to regain his strength and to see what, if anything, was still out there for him.

As it turned out, it was only the end of the beginning.

JACK NICHOLSON
ONE FLEW OVER
THE CUCKOO'S NEST

Part II

Flying
over
Chinatown
Straight
On to the
Cuckoo's
Nest

Fantasy Films presents
A MILOS FORMAN FILM · JACK NICHOLSON in "ONE FLEW
Starring LOUISE FLETCHER and WILLIAM REDFIELD · Screenplay LA
Based on the novel by KEN KESEY · Director of Photography HASKELL
Produced by SAUL ZAENTZ and MICHAEL DOUGLAS · D

R RESTRICTED   NOW AVAILABLE IN SIGNET PAPERBACK AND VIKING/COMPASS

PREVIOUS PAGE: Lobby poster for *One Flew Over the Cuckoo's Nest*. *Courtesy of Rebel Road Archives*

"I'm a fairly common man, a New Jersey personality. I don't exude aristocracy or intellectualism. But I try to give the common man some extraordinary facet."

—Jack Nicholson

Bert Schneider had separated from his wife in February 1971. Fed up with his insatiable lust and unstoppable pursuit of women, his drugging, and the increasingly shady (to her) circle of radicals and who-knows-who he surrounded himself with, she couldn't take it anymore and asked him to leave. Schneider moved into a small bachelor pad he kept for himself in Benedict Canyon. His neighbor there was the lovely Candice Bergen, also a friend of Henry Jaglom's; he was the first to bring her to one of Schneider's regular seminude Benedict Canyon back-to-bachelorhood reveries, complete with the requisite number of champagne-swigging revolutionaries, drugs of all types, and nitrous oxide, the latest craze among the celluloid/rad set.

At that same party, he reintroduced Jack to Warren Beatty. The two had first met in Canada and they immediately hit it off. After running with him for a couple of weeks, Jack soon dubbed Beatty "Master B" or "the Pro" for his ability to bed women. Beatty, meanwhile, nicknamed Jack "the Weaver" for his ability to tell a good story. With Beatty's magnetic looks and Jack's articulate charm, they made a formidable duo cutting through the starlet populace of Hollywood like two love musketeers. Who was the better swordsman? According to Bob Evans, no slouch himself in the skirt-chasing department, there was no question it was Jack. "He [was] a very big player. Not even Warren Beatty has been so successful with women." Another time Evans added, "I've been at parties where Jack's been there. Warren's been there, Clint Eastwood's been there, Bob Redford. All the girls go to Jack."

JACK WANTED TO do a project for Michelangelo Antonioni that had gotten bogged down by delays and previous commitments of the Italian director. While waiting, he spent the summer adding a $40,000 addition to his house, for Michelle and her daughter, Chynna (by John Phillips). To make room, Helena Kallianiotes was moved into a small shack on Jack's property.

UNLIKE SCHNEIDER, WHO had grown tired of making movies, Rafelson wanted to continue BBS and direct movies through its title umbrella. He had a script he liked, *The King of Marvin Gardens*, but despite his having hit it big with *Five Easy Pieces* there was no rush by any of the studios to work with him. Even his best films were not hugely successful at the box office, and he had developed a reputation as difficult to work with. Even Jack was hesitant to do another film with him, but when Rafelson asked, out of loyalty Jack said yes. Loyalty was Jack's great personal strength and professional Achilles' heel. Over the objection of Sandy Bresler, Jack accepted the deal and agreed to take SAG minimum. Bresler still insisted his client get a piece of the back end, and Rafelson agreed.

Although Jack didn't know it, he hadn't been Rafelson's first choice. Bob had wanted Al Pacino, but he kept wavering. Before Pacino could make up his mind, Jack had accepted the part of David in *The King of Marvin Gardens*.

In addition, Bruce Dern's career was still going nowhere, and, as Jack knew, the role of Jason Staebler, David's more flamboyant brother, was a potential star-maker for him. Jack wanted Rafelson to give Dern the role. Rafelson said okay if Dern promised to try to control his distracting hand gestures that showed up in every character he played. Dern packed his wife and two dogs in his car and drove cross-country to southern New Jersey for the duration of the location shoot.

The King of Marvin Gardens was made in typical BBS fashion—on the cheap, mostly on location, this time in Atlantic City, which was in post–Miss America decline and years away from its legalized-gambling resurrection. Jack was happy to be there, near enough to Neptune City for him to drop in occasionally on Lorraine and see how she and Shorty were doing. He normally tried to come home once a year, and after *Easy Rider* he could do it on someone else's nickel, to promote a movie. This was the first time, however, he brought a woman with him to New Jersey. At his invitation, Michelle came along for the duration of the shoot.

To prepare for his role, Jack packed the essentials, and a crate of his favorite albums—George Harrison's *All Things Must Pass*, Strauss waltzes recorded by Fritz Reiner and the Chicago Symphony, *Rimsky-Korsakov's Greatest Hits*, some Dylan, a couple of Cat Stevens albums, and a Lee Michaels.

Gardens, in many ways, complements *Five Easy Pieces*—except nothing in *Gardens* works cinematically, and without Eastman's touch the script cannot compete. It is a family drama and takes place in an isolated house where the family comes together to try to work out their differences.

David (Jack) is the host of a radio talk show, nerdy and toothsome (and balding), whose brother, Jason (Dern), has a get-rich scheme that will necessarily involve them with some shady characters and ultimately results in Jason's death. The film opens on a Kovács-lit close-up of Jack, who could be testifying at a trial or confessing to a priest for all anyone knows, before the camera pulls back and reveals that he is talking into a microphone. He is a small-time radio DJ.

According to Jack, this is the breakdown of his character: "The character was sort of what I call a one-roomer. He's Kafkaesque. He lives alone. He is a radio monologist. He's an intellectual and he's been institutionalized. He's involved strongly in the absurdities of life. He's not really in with society, he's like a bystander. He's very laid-back. Most of his thinking and verbosity relate to his work and not to his life. He's a watching character in life."

Much of the film was shot in an old hotel, which was cheaper than building sets, but because of it, camera movement was necessarily minimal, and it stopped whatever visual flow the film might have had.

Michelle had been a few days late in arriving, and when she found the entire cast was holed up at a nearby Howard Johnson's, she insisted she and Jack find a place of their own, somewhere on the beach. Jack didn't want to look like he was on a star trip to the rest of the cast and crew, but to keep Michelle happy he agreed. The next day he took her to a football game at Manasquan High, to show her where he grew up as a child, and afterward for a walk in the sand, but Michelle wasn't into nostalgia. Instead she kept pressing him to find them a place until he finally said he decided he didn't want to leave the hotel after all, that it would make him look like too much of an elitist. Michelle threw up her arms, exploded, called him a "stupid Irish Mick," and turned and left him standing there in the sand while she went back to the Howard Johnson's, packed her bags, hopped into a taxi, and caught the next flight from Newark Airport back to L.A.

What Jack didn't know at the time, and what may have been part of the reason her temper was so mercurial, was that her hormones were out of whack. She was pregnant with his baby. A month later she miscarried.

WITH MICHELLE GONE, even in Atlantic City, the constant flow of locals and groupies ("chippies" in Jackspeak) helped fill Jack's sexual void, and there were plenty, as he was a big star, but he was still upset about Michelle and it showed. For Jack, it was a tired replay of his female abandonment-induced pain. According to his friend Harry Gittes, "Jack always has the same dynamic with women, tremendous push-pull. He was pulling away for the first three fourths of the time. Then eventually the girlfriends pull away—who can have a relationship with an actor who goes on location with beautiful women, wanna fuck 'em, and, start chasing them. The key word is control."

To one unnamed friend, Jack summed up his loss this way: "[Michelle]'s the only one who makes my wee-wee hard."[1]

---

[1] It was a fascinating rondo. Michelle, who had been married to Hopper, then lived with Jack, next appeared on an episode of the TV game show *The Dating*

◆ ◆ ◆

AUDIENCES DIDN'T GO for *Marvin Gardens*. Despite Rafelson's unbridled enthusiasm for it, and the film's being chosen to open the 1972 New York Film Festival on the strength of Jack's name, it was eventually pulled, and bombed at the box office.[2] Critics were divided but mostly negative, unable to put their finger on what was wrong or right about the film. Andrew Sarris wrote a review in the *Village Voice* on November 9, 1972, that was more entertaining and clarifying than the film itself. It said, in part, that "the big problem with *The King of Marvin Gardens* is not that Rafelson saw too many Fellini movies, but that in casting Jack Nicholson and Bruce Dern as the two fraternal leads he provided more angst than any movie could digest. And since *The King of Marvin Gardens* oscillates hopelessly between catatonia (Nicholson) and megalomania (Dern), the audience is left stranded on a lonely sandbar of alienation. There seems to be a gap in the movie between what its makers feel and what they choose to communicate to the audience. I say seems to be because the two mystifying female onlookers (Ellen Burstyn, Julia Anne Robinson) at the spectacle of brotherly bathos seem to switch their moods as often and as capriciously as their underwear . . ."

The King of Marvin Gardens followed a distinct BBS theme that had begun with *Easy Rider*, the independent "buddy" film. The theme continued in *Five Easy Pieces*, at least for the first half hour, before Dupea's friend is arrested, setting off Bobby's decision to try to return

---

Game and won a trip to Asia with some guy she barely knew, either before or after the trip. She then dated French actor, director, and screenwriter Christian Marquand, who directed the film version of Terry Southern's novel *Candy*, which starred Marlon Brando. She next began a relationship with Lou Adler, one of Jack's best friends, who had been previously dating Britt Eckland, with whom he had a child. After leaving Adler, Michelle lived for a while with Warren Beatty.

[2] Jack fought hard to keep the film out of the early fall festival, because it meant delaying its opening for six weeks, and it would then be surrounded by other big fall commercial films, denying it the kid-glove platform-release treatment that it needed to find an audience. Eric Rohmer's *Chloe in the Afternoon* opened the festival after *Gardens* was pulled.

once again to his upscale roots. *Drive, He Said* centers on the relationship between the two male roommates, and *Marvin Gardens* is about the tenuous bond between two brothers. Even Bogdanovich's *The Last Picture Show* has two buddies at its core, who eventually do battle over the same girl. In some ways, this structure also reflected the successful, if complex relationship between Bert and Bob: Bert was always more business-oriented than Bob, Bob more the self-styled creative artist. And yet, by the time of *Marvin Gardens*, Schneider was no longer interested in Bob, at least not as a filmmaker, and no longer cared about producing films when, as he saw it, America was on the eve of destruction. The film marked the start of the final descent of BBS, which had only one more major movie left in it.

Jack was infuriated by the film's critical and commercial failure. "I usually don't think critics can hurt a movie, but that one they hurt . . ." *The King of Marvin Gardens* proved a creative and commercial failure for Jack.

IN THE SUMMER of 1972, Jack had agreed to star in a Hal Ashby remake of Tay Garnett's 1946 version of James M. Cain's classic noir novel, *The Postman Always Rings Twice*, to be called *Three-Cornered Circle*, playing the leading role of Frank Chambers, made famous by John Garfield in Garnett's version. Garfield's co-star had been the smoldering Lana Turner, unforgettable in her incandescent turban and tantalizing white shorts. She drove Garfield and every male who saw it crazy with her come-hither performance as Cora, the sexually frustrated wife of an older man who owns a dingy roadside diner.

To play Cora in his version, Jack insisted on Michelle Phillips. Knowing how sexual her ambition was, and how ambitious her sexuality was, he thought that offering her the role and working together might rekindle their romance. Ashby said yes, knowing that if he wanted Jack, he would have to take Michelle. However, Jim Aubrey, the head of MGM at the time, which was financing the film in return for distribution rights, rejected Phillips out of hand. Jack, in a fit of anger, abruptly left the project and Ashby dutifully followed him out the door. Jack then tried to move the project to Peter Guber at Columbia, who passed on *Postman* but signed Jack to agree to star in and Ashby to direct another project the studio already had, a military police drama titled *The Last Detail*, with a screenplay by Jack's good friend Robert Towne, adapted from the novel by Darryl Ponicsan. Both Jack and Ashby said yes, which put an end to *Three-Cornered Circle*.

Producer Gerald Ayres had paid Ponicsan $100,000 for the rights to his novel and hired Towne to write the screenplay. Although Columbia and Guber, then head of American production, was enthusiastic about the project from the get-go, he could only give it a yellow light, halfway between a dead-stop red and a go-ahead green, mainly because of the script's heavy use of the F-bomb, necessary, according to Towne, because the film was about a bunch of rough Navy guys and that was the way they talked. Jack refused to sign his contract until the film was an official go, although he maintained he would definitely sign on when it was.

According to Peter Guber, "I was totally involved with this film but in the first seven minutes, there were 342 'fucks.'" The original novel had used the F-bomb innumerable times, and with countless variations, giving it a military authenticity that Guber thought read better than it would play onscreen. These were the Nixon years, and everybody in Hollywood was aware of Nixon's disdain for the film industry, his "enemies lists," and his history of involvement with the blacklist, and Guber was hesitant about pushing the government too far. A film that portrayed MPs as foul-mouthed louts might not be the best way for Columbia to go. "The project broke down several times," Guber recalled. "Jack was the only one who could save it."

Guber believed a big star might make the production work, and if Jack was not going to sign on, Guber wanted Burt Reynolds, huge at the time, who could bring some authentic "good old boy" to the role of Billy "Bad Ass" Buddusky, along with Jim Brown, a former football great, as "Mule" Mulhall and David Cassidy as Larry Medows, the prisoner they have to deliver to military prison. Guber also flirted with the idea of firing Towne and bringing in a new writer who would not resist toning down the language of the script as well as simplifying the plot to make it more accessible to a broader audience not familiar with the ways of the military.

It didn't help anything that while the studio was trying to reduce the number of *fucks* in the film, hoping to put a ceiling on them at twenty, Ashby was busted in Canada trying to cross the border back into America holding a considerable amount of pot. He had traveled there to scout inexpensive locations and picked up some "supplies" along the way. According to Guber, "I had fly to Canada and get him out of the hoosegow. It was a total nightmare."

After Ashby's bust, the project was on life support, until Ayres, with the film at a very pale yellow, managed to get Jack to sign his contract, after which Columbia gave it a $2 million green light, a modest amount but enough to get the film into production while the rest of the deal, including the language issue, was resolved, and dialogue such as "I *am* the motherfucking shore patrol, motherfucker!" was reluctantly approved by the studio.

In the film, a teenage kleptomaniac sailor convicted of petty theft, Larry Meadows (Randy Quaid), is being taken from his base in Norfolk, Virginia, to the prison compound in Portsmouth, New Hampshire, by two career sailors, "lifers," shore patrolmen Billy "Bad Ass" Buddusky (Jack) and "Mule" Mulhall (Otis Young).[3] They quickly learn that the boy had the bad luck to be caught stealing from the favorite charity of the commanding officer's wife and was convicted and sentenced to eight years in the brig. On the way, Billy and Mule decide to send Meadows off with one last healthy dose of freedom during the five-day journey that included a beer blast, a brawl in Penn Station with a couple of Marines, and, when they discover that Meadows is still a virgin, getting him laid at one of the sleaziest (and therefore, to Billy, the best) brothels in Boston.

---

[3] When Jack agreed to be in *The Last Detail*, he wanted either John Denver, the singing star who had a great quality of innocence about him that Jack thought was perfect for the role of Larry Meadows, or John Travolta, another young TV actor who could also project innocence well. Neither had made a feature film at the time. In the end, Jack reluctantly agreed to Quaid, although he was concerned if Quaid had enough experience or "innocence" to pull off the role.

Then the unexpected happens. Having had a taste of real life, Meadows decides he won't be able to stand eight years of confinement, and, despite the fact that Billy and Mule have relaxed their custody of him and treated him as a friend rather than a prisoner, he decides to flee. Billy and Mule quickly recapture him, are sympathetic, and consider letting him go, but they know that if they do, they will wind up in the brig, in effect doing Meadows's time for him.

Towne's script is brilliantly realized by Ashby, whose edgy, nervous direction illustrates the tension between authority and rebelliousness, obligation to duty and love of fellow man. And as far as Guber is concerned, "Jack was a force of nature in this film."

Because of the film's salty language, and the behavior of all three sailors, the film received no cooperation from the military. Most Hollywood films about the armed forces enjoy at least some measure of cooperation, including being allowed to film on bases and using soldiers or sailors as extras, backgrounds of real equipment and ships, and military assistance to make the script more accurate. *The Last Detail* was shot in Toronto from November 1972 to March 1973, in the dead of the Canadian winter, where the weather was so cold it nearly froze everyone's coffee during breaks.

To keep warm and stay high, which he was most of the time, Jack stayed close to Ashby. The two chain-smoked joints during the entire shoot as if they were Marlboros. Perhaps because he was so stoned, Jack bragged offscreen to the few women in the film that his Navy uniform costume was custom-fit to emphasize his dick. He liked it that way, he said, it helped his character.

His co-stars Quaid and Young physically towered over Jack, which emphasized his 5'9½" height, but in every other way Jack soared above them. His charisma was the glue that held this unlikely trio together.[4] Here was Jack, charming, smirky, and at his best, showing off his singular ability to carry a nongenre film to mainstream audiences and,

---

[4] Rupert Crosse, originally cast as Mule, had something of a nervous breakdown before the film began shooting and was replaced by Otis Young.

despite the language and some of its depressing situations, making it not only palatable but actually fun.

At the first screening, the executives at Columbia, including Guber, hated everything about *Detail*, from its language to Ashby's nervous jump-cutting that to them seemed an odd mix of Godard stylistics and a kid with his first movie camera. They threatened not to release it at all, which Ayres countered by wrangling an invitation to exhibit it at the San Francisco Film Festival, where Jack's performance was so well received that Columbia had no choice but to commercially release the film. Later that year, after the Oscars, the film also played at the Cannes Film Festival, and Jack's performance was once again what everybody talked about.

Returning from Cannes, Jack stopped off in London, where director Ken Russell asked him to do a brief cameo in the film version of The Who's rock opera *Tommy*. Jack, eager to be reunited with Ann-Margret, agreed to play the doctor who examines the deaf, dumb, and blind boy. The $75,000 check for one day's work didn't hurt. Russell had originally wanted Christopher Lee for the part, but he was in Bangkok filming the James Bond flick *Man with the Golden Gun* and couldn't get away. Next on Russell's wish list was Peter Sellers, but when he turned him down, Jack stepped up, took the money, and ran, later claiming he did his own singing (demonstrating why the producers of *Clear Day* cut Jack's song).

To CELEBRATE JACK'S return to Los Angeles, Lou Adler took him to the Playboy mansion, where Jack got all the female comfort he could handle. He preferred Playmates dressed as nurses.

Adler then flew with Jack back east to do the New York scene—with all its beautiful and available, in Jackspeak, "moe-*dells*"—to Warhol's The Factory, Studio 54, and Regine's.

There he noticed a tall, dark-haired fashion model with a strong face and high-beam green eyes at a party thrown by Andy Warhol. She was Anjelica Huston, the younger child of legendary film director John Huston and Balanchine ballerina Enrica "Ricki" Soma, his fourth wife, and the granddaughter of actor Walter Huston.[5] Born in 1951 in Santa Monica, California, she spent an idyllic childhood living in a Georgian mansion in Galway, where horses roamed and sweet rhododendron bloomed everywhere. She attended school in Ireland and marveled at her father's charismatic presence whenever he was home, which was not all that often, as he was always off on one film project or another (or heavily involved with this woman or that).

She returned to Los Angeles in 1969, when she was eighteen years old, following the tragic death of her mother. She had blossomed into an imposingly tall, striking beauty, and her father cast his then shy and reluctant daughter as the lead in *A Walk with Love and Death*. The film was a disaster and Anjelica turned away from acting to what was, for her, an easier profession. Her good looks, lithe figure, and 5'10" height quickly made her a sought-after fashion model. She became a favorite of such top photographers as Helmut Newton, Guy Bourdin, and Bob Richardson, twenty-three years Angelica's senior when they started a blazing affair, during which time *Vogue* devoted thirty pages of a single issue to his photos of her.

But all the attention did nothing for her ego. "I loved the clothes, the champagne, the attention," she later recalled. "Everything but my own looks. Day after day I shared a mirror with the world's most beautiful women and stared at eyes that were bigger than mine, noses that were smaller. I cried and cried because I thought I was ugly . . ."

The camera, a lot of men, and some women disagreed. Still, she could not shake the feeling that she would need a strong man to rule her life. A man like her father.

Anjelica was a spike heel taller than Jack and, at twenty-two years old, fourteen years his junior; from the first moment she laid eyes on him at Warhol's, she couldn't get him out of her mind. She finally met him at a party at his house in Los Angeles. "I was invited by my then stepmother, Cici [Celeste Shane, her father's fifth wife]. The door

---

[5] John Huston was married five times. Enrica was killed in a car crash while still married to Huston. His other four marriages all ended in divorce. His other child with Enrica was Walter Anthony "Tony" Huston, who is today a lawyer and the father of actor Jack Huston.

opened and Jack's grinning face presented itself to me and I thought, 'Ah, I like you.'" . . . I was always attracted to bad boys, cool boys. Actors, musicians, those kind of guys."

She recognized in Jack a younger version of her wonderfully crazy, creative, live-life-to-the-fullest father. Jack had that same Irish stallion in him, and she knew right then and there they were going to be together: "When I was working in New York, it was very difficult to meet real men. It's so easy to become a fag hag if you're a successful model. Jack is very definitely a real man, one who gets your blood going."

She and Jack spent the night alone in his bedroom while the party took place throughout the rest of the house. The next day she returned to New York only long enough to pack whatever things she needed from the apartment she kept there, flew back to L.A., and moved into a small house near Jack's on Mulholland Drive.

For the next seventeen tumultuous years, strewn with affairs on both sides, they managed to stay involved, if not always together. She fell in love with him early on; he was handsome, he was manly, he was funny, he was cool. Perhaps most of all he gave her "a feeling that has something to do with fun and with family, a feeling like when you had a good time with your dad. It's a secure feeling, something like, 'Now we can relax: we're with Jack.'"

As for Jack, he loved the fun angle of their relationship, but the more she devoted herself to him, the more he felt smothered by her blanket of paternal need that reinforced his need for an escape clause, to feel free to be with any of those young, gorgeous, and willing moe-*dells* who were out there and just as sexually willing and adventurous as he was. Just as in his marriage, no matter how great the love, monogamy was just too monotonous.

CHAPTER 8

"Cocaine is in now because chicks dig it sexually . . . I guess it could be considered a sexual aid."

—Jack Nicholson

WITH HAL ASHBY AS HIS SUPPLIER AND ENTHUSIASTIC FELLOW user, Jack had gotten more heavily into cocaine during the making of *The Last Detail*. While psychedelics and pot were still his drugs of choice, coke was something he'd discovered sometimes helped delay the premature ejaculations that plagued him. By following what he'd heard about Errol Flynn, he learned that by putting a dab on the tip of his manhood, he could last longer, and, because of the way women reacted to that, he also believed it intensified the sensations for them.

Jack was by no means the only one in Hollywood to have come upon the so-called joys of the white Bolivian Marching Powder. When recreational drugs hit the film studios, it galloped through them like a white plague. Films ran wildly over budget, salaries skyrocketed, and contracts were torn up and rewritten, while nobody seemed to notice that fewer and fewer people were going to the movies they were making.

Columbia, on its last legs as a major studio, nearly shut down when its stock fell from a high of $30 a share in 1971 to a low of $2 a share in 1973. The culprit, or the scapegoat if you will, it was decided, was the rising cost of independent film studio pre-release guarantees. One of its biggest abusers, the board concluded, was BBS, which, under Bert Schneider, despite the success of *Easy Rider, Five Easy Pieces*, and *The Last Picture Show*, had helped the studio rack up an after-tax loss of

$50 million. Too many other BBS films, such as *Drive, He Said, A Safe Place*, and *The King of Marvin Gardens*, did not make any money.

Soon enough, heads rolled at Columbia. One of the first was Abe Schneider, Bert's father, eased out of the company after a few rounds of corporate musical chairs, leaving BBS and Bert Schneider in a precarious situation regarding his final film for BBS, the Vietnam documentary *Hearts and Minds*.

JACK AND ANJELICA were one of those couples that had never dated, just went from zero to sixty in no seconds. Jack gave Anjelica a welcome to L.A. gift, a Mercedes. After all, he told her, a girl needs a car to get around. Translation in Jackspeak: *Welcome to my world*. He began to call her "Toots" or "Tootsie" or "Tootman" or "Big," in Jackspeak. She in turn rather unsubtly nicknamed him "the hot pole."

In June 1973, Jack got word that Antonioni was at last ready to begin *The Passenger*, aka *Fatal Exit*, and that he should fly to Spain immediately to start filming. However, as he was preparing to leave, a bizarre series of circumstances began that would have a profound effect on Jack's life as they churned up the past and reached all the way back to make him question his parentage and therefore his actual identity. It all started innocently enough in 1973 when two enterprising students from a University of Southern California film class, Robert David Crane and Christopher Fryer, decided to write their graduate thesis together on Jack Nicholson. Their goal was to interview him and everybody associated with him. They sent out letters, assuring one and all this was not a personal investigation but one that would look at the films, with Jack's added commentary wherever possible.

It took them a year, during which time Jack made *The Passenger*. He asked Anjelica to accompany him to Europe for it, which made her extremely happy. To keep busy while Jack was filming, Anjelica was able to book a series of overseas modeling jobs. They were met at the airport by the paparazzi, where Jack teased both Anjelica and the press about being with Anjelica: "Since we've been together," he grinned, "she hasn't done a day's work. She hasn't given up her career completely. But she's not exactly what you would call ambitious . . . she gets perky around seven in the evening . . . we both love dressing up and going out at night. I love her in black! She could wear black both day and night as far as I'm concerned. But she is *always* beautiful." It was a riff she didn't especially appreciate, especially the part about her not working, followed by how beautiful she was. It hit a nerve, making her sound like she was one of his starlet hangers-on. As she said later, "Can you imagine what it was like living with Jack when the phones were always ringing and scripts were always coming in for him and there were deals to be made constantly and I couldn't even get a job."

The bad taste in her mouth stayed with her, and sooner rather than later, she returned to Los Angeles without him.

Jack was too busy to notice that they were having their first fight, preoccupied as he was with the long-awaited chance to work with Antonioni, although as filming went on he kept trying to figure out exactly what the film's isolated, quasi-existential story line was, what his character was all about, and what Antonioni was trying to say. Like Sergio Leone, another European director who aimed for an international audience, Antonioni understood that the less dialogue used the better, and that plot was less important than mood.

His co-star, Maria Schneider, of butter-up-the-butt fame after co-starring with Marlon Brando in Bernardo Bertolucci's 1972 *Last Tango in Paris*, seemed as disinterested in the film as she was in Jack. To one member of the press during production, Jack said, "Maria has a fantastic screen personality—the other personality I'm not nuts about."[1] To another, he was a little more forthright, confessing that theirs was

---

[1] Schneider, a lifelong druggie—during the middle of an interview for the film with the *New York Times* she rolled up a joint and smoked it—was plagued with mental problems, and was in and out of asylums her entire life. She made more movies, but none created the kind of stir either *Last Tango* or *The Passenger* did. She was knighted by the French Order of Arts and Letters in 2010. She died of cancer in February 2011.

more than just a friendship, although the details were left out. "Maria and I were old friends," Jack semiwhispered. "I'd been *out* with her [Jackspeak for slept with her]. I always think of her as a female James Dean—she's a great natural . . ."

The Passenger was shot mostly in Spain—Barcelona, Madrid, the Ramblas, Málaga, and Seville—and two weeks in Algeria at Fort Polignanc, which stood in for the African state of Chad. Everyone, including Jack, lived in tents in Algeria and suffered from the blistering heat. Then, after a brief stopover in Germany, it was off to England for five welcome weeks of postproduction in the luxury studios at Bloomsbury.

Even if he never entirely figured out what the film was about, Jack loved working with Antonioni. The plot, such as it was, had something to do with switched identities and a long train ride, leading some critics to compare it to Alfred Hitchcock's 1959 *North by Northwest* for its landscape screenplay and the idea of a character becoming an identity he assumes (as, in Hitchcock, Cary Grant's Roger O. Thornhill "becomes" George Kaplan).

Jack appreciated the film's air of mystery and ambiguity: "There are movies that you do where they don't look, on the face of them, certainly, mainline commercial. But you see and hope there's something in [*The Passenger*] that gives you a shot at that—an off-the-wall shot."

Years later, reflecting on the experience of making the film, Jack said, tellingly, "[Antonioni was] like a father figure to me. I worked with him because I wanted to be a film director and I thought I could learn from a master. He's one of the few people I know that I ever really listened to."

The Passenger was completed in September 1973, and the next day Jack boarded a nonstop flight from London to Los Angeles and reported to Paramount's wardrobe department at eight that morning to begin costume fittings for his next film, Roman Polanski's *Chinatown*.

Jack was eager to get home for two reasons: he wanted to begin preparations for *Chinatown*, and he wanted to be with Anjelica, who had gotten over her annoyance and was eagerly waiting to give him the most royal of welcomes.

The two students finally got to Jack in late 1974.[2] According to Crane and Fryer, "Having heard of the upcoming publication [of our interviews] a woman in New Jersey sent us a letter. She claimed to be married to Jack Nicholson's biological father . . . the letter described how Jack's mother was, in fact, the woman Jack thought was his much older sister, June. His 'Mom,' Ethel May, was really his grandmother and his older sister Lorraine was really his aunt. The woman writing the letter said that her husband, Jack's biological father [not John], was a wonderful man, not the hard-drinking deadbeat who had abandoned his wife and son [Ethel May and Jack]. The letter implored us not to repeat these false characterizations." In their pre-interview research the two had apparently uncovered some material that suggested, accurately, that John was thrown out of the house by Ethel May for drinking too much, and that he was, in fact, not her husband; they had never married. The letter writer did not identify herself or indicate who she believed Jack's real father was.

Crane and Fryer later claimed they brought the letter to Jack, who was shaken by it. He decided to call Lorraine. Now that all the senior players were gone, she decided to tell Jack the truth about who he really was, and who he wasn't.

These are the facts: His sister June was born in 1919, at home. By the time she was a teenager, she was dancing professionally with the bandleader Eddie King, whom she had first met when he was playing on the Jersey Shore. He briefly had a radio program, "Eddie King and His Radio Kiddies," and June appeared on it regularly as one of the "kiddies." In 1934, at the age of fifteen June dropped out of high school in search of a career on her own as a model, a singer, and a chorus girl.

For the next two years, until 1936, June was able to find work up and down the East Coast, from Florida all the way to New York City.

---

[2] There are two published editions of the interviews by Crane and Fryer. The first, *Face to Face*, is a compendium of interviews collected by them in the early seventies and published in 1975. The second, *Jack Nicholson: The Early Years* (2012), is essentially the same as the first, with the explanatory paragraph quoted here. See the bibliography for additional publication information.

During a brief stay back at the family house, she met Don Rose, who was also a performer and ten years her senior. The two began dating, and soon June fell in love with Rose, or Furcillo-Rose, as everybody who knew him away from the dance halls called him. On October 16, 1936, they married. The ceremony took place in Delaware, far enough away from Neptune so that no one would know. To further keep their secret, she signed the marriage certificate June Nilson—her stage name, a contraction of Nicholson, and he signed it Donald Furcillo. What she didn't know, but would soon find out, was that Furcillo-Rose was already married and had a child. When she found out, she abruptly dropped him and planned to get an annulment. But before she could, she became pregnant.

Early in 1937, June disappeared from Neptune. No one except Ethel May knew where or why. Ethel May had insisted that the baby not be born at home, or anywhere in New Jersey. Instead, she chose St. Vincent's Roman Catholic hospital in Manhattan's Greenwich Village, run at the time by the Sisters of Mercy, with June registered as "June Wilson," likely a misspelling of "Nilson." This was the reason Jack could never find his original birth certificate.

June gave birth April 22, 1937. Because Ethel May did not want Furcillo-Rose's name on the birth certificate, she listed the baby's name as John Joseph "Jack" Nicholson Jr., and her companion, John Nicholson, as the father. Ethel May, who was forty-four at the time, decided that she would act as the boy's mother, and John his father.

Two months after they all returned to Neptune, June took off once again, still determined to have a career in show business. This time she headed west but got only as far as Ohio, where, broke and hungry, she took a job at a Cleveland airfield. There, her good looks attracted a lot of men, and despite the fact she was technically still married to Furcillo-Rose, she wed one of them, a wealthy divorced test pilot by the name of Murray "Bob" Hawley. Not long after, Hawley relocated them to Southampton, New York. They had two children, and everything seemed to have settled in June's life—she even planned to reclaim Jack and make him part of her new family—until, one day in 1941 or 1942, Hawley abandoned June and the children for another woman. June, only twenty-three years old, then took the children with her to Los Angeles, hoping to make it big in the movies, leaving Jack behind at the Neptune house to be raised by Ethel May and John Nicholson.

All during this time, the forlorn Furcillo-Rose kept coming around, hoping to find June there. Ethel May hated him, but she knew he was the real father of the child, and couldn't just turn him away.

Who had really contacted the two students? Was it Furcillo-Rose himself, disguising his identity by claiming to be a woman, likely looking to cash in on Jack's celebrity and bankbook? Another possibility was Furcillo-Rose's mother, who always insisted her son was Jack's real father, even though they had never met.

Either way, Jack was devastated. He didn't want to believe it, especially the part about Fucillo-Rose being his real father, but the story had the ring of truth about it, as disturbing as it was.

Jack agreed to talk to the two boys for their thesis as long as they didn't ask him any questions about the letter in their work. They agreed.

A shaken Jack kept the terrible secret mostly to himself, except for a few friends, who insist he was deeply affected by both it and the near exposure of it. One close associate claims Jack was "devastated and shocked by the information." Peter Fonda said the possible publication caused "a deep hurt inside . . ." Michele Phillips, his ex-girlfriend who still kept in touch, said "The [possible publication of the news] was horrible for him. Over the weeks, the poor guy had a very very rough time adjusting to it. He'd been raised in this loving relationship . . . surrounded by women . . . now I think he felt all women were liars."

TWO MONTHS LATER, while Jack was immersed in the making of *Chinatown*, on December 12, 1973, *The Last Detail* was released to qualify for that year's Oscars, to mixed reviews but so-so box office. *Newsweek* loved Jack's bravura performance—"Nicholson dominates!" wrote Paul D. Zimmerman. Stanley Kauffmann later wrote, "Here [Jack] has a part exactly right for him . . . aside from the faint air of virtuoso occasion, he and the role are perfect for each other, and together they galvanize the film." Vincent Canby, in the *New York Times*, liked Jack better than he did the film: "The best thing about *The Last Detail* is the opportunity it provides Jack Nicholson to play the role of Signalman First Class Buddusky . . . his performance is big, intense, so full of gradations of mood that it becomes virtually a guide to a certain kind of muddled, well-meaning behavior." Andrew Sarris praised Ashby's auteuristic direction, while John Simon, the angriest uber-intellectual of his time, was not especially enamored of either the film or Jack's performance: "Nicholson gives what many consider a superlative performance, and what strikes me as yet another example of his customary turn."

Oscar talk began immediately. On a budget of $2.6 million, the film eventually grossed more than $10 million, a profitable ratio but in no way a blockbuster, and as expected went on to be nominated for a slew of awards for both Jack and the movie. The film was up for two Golden Globes—Jack for Best Motion Picture Actor in a Drama, and Randy Quaid for Best Supporting Actor in a Motion Picture—but neither actor won. Jack did win a BAFTA (British Academy of Film and Television Arts) award for his role in the film and Best Actor from the National Society of Film Critics and the New York Film Critics Circle.[3]

After this run of accolades, the studio sent Jack to New York to do publicity and drum up interest in a possible Oscar nomination for him. He took Anjelica with him and the two lived it up. In between promotional duties, they saw the Muhammad Ali–Joe Frazier fight at Madison Square Garden on January 28; two nights later it was Bob Dylan at the Garden. After the show, Jack and Anjelica stopped backstage to say hello. Bob was smiling and gracious when he met the couple. On February 5, they saw Joni Mitchell at Avery Fisher Hall. They capped off each night in New York at Elaine's, the Upper East Side nightspot that had become a must-stop for the writer/actor/newspaper columnist/celebrity set.

---

[3] Jack technically won the National Society of Film Critics and the New York Film Critics Circle awards the following year, 1975, for both *Chinatown* and *The Last Detail*.

◆ ◆ ◆

WHEN THE NOMINATIONS for that year's Oscars were announced, *The Last Detail* got three—Jack for Best Actor in a Leading Role, Randy Quaid for Best Actor in a Supporting Role, and Robert Towne for Best Writing for an Adapted Screenplay.

The 46th Annual Academy Awards were held on April 2, 1974, once again at the Dorothy Chandler Pavilion, this time hosted by David Niven, Burt Reynolds, Diana Ross, and Jack's girlfriend's father, John Huston.

Three years had passed since Jack had been nominated for an Oscar. His last appearance at the awards ceremony was in 1972, as a presenter. Despite some stated resistance—"Who wants to sit under 67 floodlights for four hours without even being able to go out to take a leak?"—Jack showed up looking resplendent in a tuxedo with a gray shirt underneath, and Anjelica gorgeous in black on his arm.[4]

He knew he was up against some formidable competition—most pointedly, to Jack, from Brando's second consecutive nomination (the year before he had been nominated and won for his role in *The Godfather*), for *Last Tango in Paris*, although after what Brando had pulled the previous year refusing to show up and sending Sacheen Littlefeather to pick up his award and make an acceptance speech that dealt with the rights of Native Americans, there was virtually no chance he would win. Al Pacino was nominated for Best Actor for his role in Sidney Lumet's *Serpico*, and the betting money was on Pacino for the win. Also nominated were Robert Redford for George Roy Hill's *The Sting* (but not Paul Newman for the same film, yet another role Jack had turned down) and Jack Lemmon's frankly weirdly edgy performance in John G. Avildsen's *Save the Tiger*.

The Oscar went, surprisingly, to Lemmon, even though *Save the Tiger* had been a box office disaster and the Academy usually doesn't

----

[4] Academy rules prohibit audience members from leaving their seats during the telecast, except during breaks. If one leaves and does not return in time, a "sitter" will take his or her place until the next break.

reward commercial failures. The Monday morning quarterbacks concluded that Lemmon had won by a process of elimination: Brando was a definite no-no, Redford without Newman was problematic, Pacino was still too young, and Lumet and his New York–based films were not well liked in L.A. (in those times, so-called New York pictures were rarely favored by the Academy), and *The Last Detail* had all those dirty words. Lemmon was an audience and Academy favorite but had last won an Oscar in 1955, for his supporting role in John Ford's, Mervyn LeRoy's, and Josh Logan's (uncredited) *Mister Roberts*. According to the Academy, he was due.

Jack was now a three-time loser at the Oscars. "I like the idea of winning at Cannes . . . but not getting our own Academy Award hurt real bad. I did it in that movie, that was my best role." It fell to Anjelica to comfort him as they made the Oscar afterparties. Later, back at the hotel, she did her best to convince him in the most delightful way that this night there were no losers.

BERT SCHNEIDER'S controversial anti-Vietnam documentary *Hearts and Minds* screened at Cannes in the spring of 1974. Rafelson couldn't care less about *Hearts and Minds* but was worried about what would happen to his own career without BBS behind him.

Rafelson was right to worry. After BBS was dissolved, he would not direct another feature film for four years. Studios found little to like about him; despite his early hits he was abrasive, arrogant, and, after *The King of Marvin Gardens*, considered a bad commercial risk.

Jack was aware of the split between Schneider and Rafelson and kept his distance from it. He was interested in making good movies, not political statements, playing characters consumed with the politics of romance rather than the romance of politics. He wanted to make good movies with great directors, and he no longer considered Rafelson in that league.

"I don't know why a guy goes to a hooker . . . [but] I'm Big Jack. I don't have to pay for it . . ."

—JACK NICHOLSON

WITH THE SUCCESS OF *THE GODFATHER*, BOB EVANS BECAME THE head of production at Paramount, charged with turning the troubled studio around. Part of Evans's new deal was the right to produce movies under his own name, with points (a percentage of the film's profits) above his salary. No sooner had the ink dried on his new contract than Evans signed up his first film, a screenplay written by Bob Towne called *Chinatown*. Towne was a big fan of Raymond Chandler and for a long time had wanted to write a screenplay that reflected Chandler's seamy-side-of-L.A. mystery style.

He first got the idea for the film from a police friend of his. "The one place I never really worked," the cop told Towne, "was Chinatown. They really run their own culture." It was that image of impenetrability, insularity, and inscrutability that he turned into the foundation of his story. Evans was at a loss as to why Towne wanted to write about Chinese people living in L.A. When he explained that the title was a metaphor, Evans agreed to give him $25,000 and 5 percent of the gross to write *Chinatown*.

Towne was writing at his usual snail's pace. After six months, by the early winter of 1973, Evans expressed his concern to Towne, who told him not to worry. He reminded Evans he was tailoring the lead role, Gittes, for Jack, whom Evans had originally offered $500,000 up front and a healthy piece of the net to do the film. It was a far cry from the $12,500 Jack had had to beg Evans for when he made *Clear Day*.

Sandy Bresler negotiated the deal to $750,000 up front and the same piece of the net. Jack made no apologies; his cost of living had skyrocketed. He now had a $12,000-a-month nut.

To direct, Evans wanted John Huston, who turned the project down, as did his other choice, Mike Nichols. After reading the first draft, neither thought the material was compelling enough. Evans's third choice was Roman Polanski.

Polanski had briefly been the prime suspect in the sensational murder of his wife, until he was able to prove he was in London during the time of the Manson massacre. When the trial started a year later, Polanski chose not to watch or take part in any of what he knew would be a media circus. Instead, he left L.A. in favor of world travel (carrying with him everywhere the saddest of talismans, a pair of Sharon's panties). Now, three years later, he had no desire to return to California, or anywhere in the States, to make a movie. He felt more at ease in Europe, where he was from. Evans caught up with him in Rome and approached him about returning to Hollywood to make *Chinatown*.

Polanski at first said no, that he did not want return to the scene of the crime, as it were. Besides, he insisted he had all but retired from filmmaking. Since the murders, he had directed a cathartic version of *Macbeth*, in which Macduff, while away, learns that his family has been murdered. Evans implored him to make the movie. Polanski's response was that he couldn't fit it in his schedule because he was going to Poland for Passover. Evans said he should instead come to his house for the biggest Seder he would ever see.

Polanski finally gave in and agreed to return to Los Angeles to make the movie, and Evans, true to his word, put together a massive Passover dinner that included such guests as Anne and Kirk Douglas; Carol and Walter Matthau and their son, Charlie; Warren Beatty; Jack and Anjelica. And Hugh Hefner, who had been one of the producers of *Macbeth*.

During all of this, Towne still hadn't finished his screenplay and had run out of money. Afraid to go to Evans, believing he would fire him, Towne went instead to Jack and pleaded poverty, saying he desperately needed cash. Jack gave him $10,000 with the proviso that Towne lock himself in his room until the script was finished.

Polanski, meanwhile, rented a small house, surprisingly, not far from the one on Cielo Drive where the Manson murders had taken place, and asked Towne to move in with him so he could help him with the script. For the next eight weeks, the two worked together day and night, and the further they got into it, the more their personal relationship deteriorated, mostly because of Towne's dog, who went with him everywhere and was always pissing on the floor, on all the furniture, even on Polanski's leg, and Towne kept interrupting their work sessions to walk him. Polanski also hated Towne's stinky, sloppy wet pipe that he smoked constantly and blew spit through that made an awful noise, like a perennially stuffed nose the owner refuses to blow. Towne constantly produced clouds of stale blue smoke that hung over the two as they worked. Polanski prided himself on being an outdoors man—skiing was one of his passions—and claimed the smoke was choking him, not just physically but creatively as well. When the monster that was *Chinatown*'s 180-page, three-hour script finally went into production, on the first day of shooting Polanski barred Towne, his dog, and his pipe from the set.

The plot of the film is largely a red herring about a detective who stumbles on a scheme to divert much-needed water to Los Angeles, at the expense of Owens Valley, which, deprived of its supply, eventually dries up. All of it had been written about before, and extensively—how the water created the orange groves, how the orange groves attracted the first movie moguls for their cheap and plentiful land. Involved in the mechanics of the deal were the city's mayor, Frederick Eaton; chief engineer, William Mulholland, who later had a street named after him (which Jack happened to live on); and the city's chamber of commerce—all of whom stood to benefit from a more water-accessible L.A.

However, the real story in the film belonged to Noah Cross, played by John Huston, who had agreed to be in it but not direct. It is one of family deception, sexual enslavement, incest, and murder, subjects Polanski could relate to far more easily than to the politics of water. And that was what made the film great. On the surface is a politically murky affair, below it an emotional volcano. Polanski turned Detective Gittes, played by Jack (named by Towne as a nod to their good friend Harry Gittes), into a thoughtful observer as he slowly uncovers the evil incarnate that is Noah Cross. There are long scenes in the desert (recalling James Dean's in the Texas oil fields in *Giant*) where Jack does nothing more than stare out into the vast space, trying to figure out the pieces of a puzzle that, like Towne's script, are too waterlogged for him to easily and neatly fit together.

By the time the film began production, Ali MacGraw, Evans's wife, who had first been cast in the female lead of Evelyn Mulwray, was out of the film because she had left Evans for Steve McQueen.

The part of Evelyn Mulwray was then offered to Jane Fonda, who passed, and eventually went to Faye Dunaway, whom Evans managed to get for $50,000. Dunaway had caused a sensation in her third film as Bonnie Parker in Arthur Penn's groundbreaking 1967 *Bonnie and Clyde*, but had since made some questionable career decisions. She did eleven films in five years, none of which were as big as *Bonnie and Clyde*, and her career was on a downslide. Dunaway was a difficult actress on some star trip all her own, and her peculiar aloofness infuriated Polanski, who was not used to treating actresses as anything but messengers in the service of his precious movies. One time Polanski went to fix something on one of her costumes, and she smacked him in the face, threatening to call the police and accuse him of attempted rape. Dunaway refused to continue unless Polanski was fired.

Evans, who had no use personally for Dunaway, stood behind Polanski and, if it came down to it, would replace Dunaway first. It took the promise from Evans of an enormous Oscar campaign that would surely result in at least a nomination for her, and, if it didn't, a Rolls-Royce Corniche, to get her to agree to let Polanski stay on the film. Evans made the same offer to Polanski, an Oscar buildup and a Rolls, if he let her stay. Polanski countered with a Bentley, Evans agreed, and the film resumed production.

The neo-noir film plods along as Gittes slowly begins to figure out the depths of the deceptions that have placed him in the middle of some sinister plot, underscored when his nose is nearly cut off (for being too nosy?) by a hit man played by Roman Polanski (the victim now the victimizer). Polanski needed no extra motivation to pluck off Jack's proboscis. In the midst of trying to film this labyrinthine script, Jack kept leaving rehearsals and missing takes to stay in his trailer, where he had set up a TV to watch the Lakers play. Occasionally, he would leave the set early to meet up with Lou Adler and drive over to the Fabulous Forum in Inglewood to watch the Lakers do their thing.

One time on set, Polanski needed Jack to come back and redo a shot, and Jack told him the Lakers were in the fourth quarter and he, Polanski, would have to wait. More than a little annoyed, Polanski wrapped the scene without the retake. Polanski then "ran into my dressing room, grabbed the television, and smashed it on the floor. I responded by storming out. . . ." Later they ran into each other at Gower and Sunset and laughed until they had tears in their eyes.

The plot of the film was so ambiguous that the original ending has Noah Cross killed by Mulwray, who, it turns out, is his daughter and his lover, and the mother of his child. It was changed by Polanski. He so hated the self-importance of his fading-star leading lady that instead he had her killed off, hoping the effect would drip over to her career. Unfortunately, that left Cross's granddaughter in his sole possession, further confusing the audience as the sordid facts of the film continued to unfold. To Jack, it all hit a little too close to home.

THE FIRST PREVIEW of *Chinatown* took place in San Luis Obispo, not that far from Los Angeles, and it was a disaster. Before the lights came up, half the audience had left. A panicky Polanski met with a calmer Evans, who suggested they put a new musical soundtrack on the film. Evans hired Jerry Goldsmith, who, in eight days, rescored the film, with music that was eerily in tune with the overall tone of the film. A few weeks later the reedited film was screened at the Directors Guild in Hollywood. The reaction was no better. Several luminaries came up to Evans and solemnly told him the film was unreleasable. Not to worry, he told them. Audiences will love Jack, and they will get what we're trying to do. To connect to his character, during filming Jack had all of Gittes's shirts monogrammed above the pocket, even though they were never seen in the film.

Chinatown opened in theaters on June 20, 1974, and, as Evans had predicted, proved an immediate hit with audiences and critics. Sensing that the film had Oscar potential, late that fall Paramount sent Jack on an international promotional tour, with Anjelica again accompanying him, this time to Stockholm, Hamburg, Munich, Paris, and Rome. In each city the film had already opened and was a smash hit. His next stop was Switzerland, where he was joined by Polanski, who had just finished the South American leg of the PR tour, for a couple of days of celebrity R and R, skiing. Polanski was not impressed with Jack's abilities on the slopes. "His style is like a guy who scratches his left ear with his right hand."

Eventually the tour came back to America. In New York Jack and Anjelica lived it up, squeezing in interviews mostly in the mornings to save the rest of the time for themselves (getting up early was the only problem for Jack). They also met up with Warren Beatty, David Geffen, and Mike Nichols. Wealthy now, Jack loved to play the glad-hander, dressing in gaudy clothes, lots of reds and yellows, and white-top loafers. His arrowhead eyebrows always shot up his scalp when he smiled, the lines of his forehead like the striated sides of an eight-layer cake, his dark hair slicked back and shiny like the side of a '58 Buick, his teeth shining. Jack reveled in reaching for every tab, proud to the point of near ostentation that he could take care of everybody.

Jack was agreeable to everything the studio asked him to do, except television. He had it written in his contract that he would not have to appear on the tube. All the talk shows wanted him, and they reached a huge audience, but he refused. Talk shows, he insisted, were not for Oscar contenders. "I have done radio interviews and stuff like that . . . but on a television show you're sort of captured in there." Later, he elaborated: "I think secrecy, and this is why I don't do television interviews, for instance—is a very important tool to the actor, both in the dynamic of playing a part and in the way it's perceived."

He preferred to wear the mask of character and believed that breaking the magic of the movie screen by crossing through it to the small screen of television, out of character, was ruinous to an actor.

FROM A BUDGET of $6 million, *Chinatown* grossed nearly $30 million in its 1974 initial domestic release. The film was hailed as Polanski's masterpiece. All the major reviews were positive and properly hailed Jack's performance. Charles Champlin, writing in the *Los Angeles Times*, declared, "*Chinatown* reminds you again—and thrillingly—that motion pictures are larger, not smaller, than life, they are not processed in drug stores and they are not television." *Newsweek* called it "a brilliant cinematic poem in the style of Poe, circa 1974," and *Saturday Review* said it was "superbly acted—especially by Jack Nicholson, who does everything so easily, casually, and appropriately that he hardly seems to be acting at all." Andrew Sarris best captured the essence of why *Chinatown* resonated, and still resonates, so powerfully with audiences: "Even Polanski's intense feeling for tragedy could never have been realized without the vision of tragedy expressed in Nicholson's star-crossed eyes . . ."

In the end it wasn't Polanski's film but Jack's, a fact that led everyone to believe he would finally walk away with his first Oscar, one of many *Chinatown* was expected to win. Evans, keeping his promise to heavily promote the film, had managed to get *Time* to agree to put Jack on the cover in August 1974 and intended to banner it with "THE STAR WITH THE KILLER SMILE." Jack was quite excited about it, until a *Time* reporter, preparing the story, asked him during an otherwise ordinary interview, one that Jack could have done in his sleep, if it was true that Ethel May was really his grandmother and Don Furcillo-Rose, not John Nicholson, his real father.

Jack was blown nearly off his sofa. *Again?* The first thing Jack wanted to know was where the reporter had heard that. It was *Time*'s policy not to reveal sources, and this reporter wouldn't, but Jack suspected it was the same source that had given the story to those two students. He had thought, or hoped, that it had gone away and he would never again have to deal with it. He had stuck his finger in the dam once and managed to plug it up; now he would have to try it again.

Jack later told Bogdanovich, "I was grateful I didn't have to deal with it with [any of] them. Show me any woman today who could keep a secret [like Ethel May], a confidence, or an intimacy to that degree. You got my kind of gal . . . They were all Irish warriors and powerful women . . . look, it's why in this instance I can't be my normally liberal self [and why I'm totally] pro-life. In today's world I wouldn't exist [if June had had an abortion] . . . June was only 16 . . . Finally finding out did clarify a lot of things. Because in either event my grandmother was a single parent . . . it verified certain very murmuring intuitions as deep as an 11-to-14-year-old mind can go."

Jack was horrified that this story would sooner or later be plastered all over the media, to have Ethel May's and June's and even John Nicholson's names dragged through the poisonous mud of gossip, or being called a bastard for the rest of his life. They were all gone and he wanted them to rest in peace. It was nobody's fucking business but his.

He decided to call *Time* and take his best shot. Turning on the Nicholson charm, he asked them not to run the material about his family, because he wanted to write about it himself. Incredibly, that was good enough for *Time*. No one at the magazine, Jack insisted, felt any journalistic urgency to write the true story. In return, he told them, he would give them any further access they might need for their piece on him. The cover story ran that August, with no mention of the skeletons in Jack's New Jersey family closet.

Another finger in the dike.

EARLY IN 1975, the Oscar nominations were announced, and *Chinatown* picked up eleven, including one for Jack for Best Performance by an Actor. The other favorite film, which would be *Chinatown*'s chief competition, was *The Godfather: Part II*, also nominated for eleven awards.

Jack was favored to win. He had already picked up the prestigious New York Film Critics Circle award as Best Actor, the same from the National Society of Film Critics (for *Chinatown* and *The Last Detail*), a BAFTA, and a Golden Globe.

THE AWARDS WERE held on the rainy night of April 8, 1975, once again at the Dorothy Chandler Pavilion, this time hosted by several members of the Rat Pack: Frank Sinatra, Sammy Davis Jr., Shirley MacLaine, and, out of a sense of loyalty to Oscar past, Bob Hope. Jack showed up in a tux, sunglasses, and a beret to hide his fast-thinning pate, with a resplendent Anjelica Huston proudly on his arm.

Jack's chances were improved by what was an especially weak pack of nominees, the softest grouping since he had first been nominated for Best Supporting Actor in *Easy Rider.* Art Carney, a well-liked TV actor best known for playing Ed Norton on Jackie Gleason's working-class sit-com *The Honeymooners,* for which he had won five Emmys, but whose résumé for feature films was slim, was nominated for Paul Mazursky's *Harry and Tonto.*[1] Albert Finney, the British actor, won a nomination for his appearance in Sidney Lumet's *Murder on the Orient Express.* Dustin Hoffman, disastrously miscast as the iconoclastic comedian Lenny Bruce in Bob Fosse's *Lenny,* received one, as did Al Pacino for Francis Coppola's *The Godfather: Part II,* a film that everyone agreed belonged to Robert De Niro, who was nominated as Best Actor in a Supporting Role for his superb performance. The smart money (six-to-five in Vegas) all went to Jack, who deserved to win not just for *Chinatown* but for his entire body of work, which had helped pull Hollywood kicking and screaming into the seventies.

Jaws dropped everywhere in the Dorothy Chandler Pavilion when the Best Actor Oscar went to . . . *Art Carney,* for a minor performance in a decidedly minor film, his road picture for geriatrics. It was felt that

---

[1] Carney won one Emmy for *The Honeymooners* and four for playing Norton on *The Jackie Gleason Show.*

the Oscar was a nod for a lifetime of work, mostly in vaudeville and on TV, and that this was surely the only time he would ever be nominated for an Oscar. The others would have many more chances.

Despite Evans's furious campaign, *Chinatown* lost Best Picture to *Godfather: Part II*; Ellen Burstyn, an actress everybody liked, won for Martin Scorsese's *Alice Doesn't Live Here Anymore*, over Faye Dunaway, whom nobody liked. Of the major players connected to *Chinatown*, Bob Towne, of all people, was the only winner, for Best Original Screenplay. Polanski lost Best Director to Coppola for *Godfather: Part II*.

The Oscar for Best Documentary feature of the year, presented by Lauren Hutton and Danny Thomas, went to Bert Schneider, for his controversial Vietnam film, and his swan song, *Hearts and Minds*, an award that infuriated many in the audience. Schneider fanned their flames when he read a congratulatory telegram from the Vietcong delegation at the Paris peace talks that began, "Greetings of friendship to all American people . . ." When he finished, to mixed applause, and left the stage, Frank Sinatra came on, glaring, looking like he was ready to kill anybody as long as his name was Bert Schneider, denounced the award and was, to his amazement, booed. Backstage everyone started arguing. MacLaine shook a finger in Sammy Davis Jr.'s face; John Wayne, outraged, made fists intended for but not thrown at the first face he ran into that he didn't like. The noise in the wings was so loud it could be heard throughout the auditorium.

In the midst of all the commotion, Schneider managed to slip away. He knew that Hollywood had seen the last of him, and he had seen the last of it. Holding his Oscar in his fist, he climbed into the back of his waiting limo and instructed the driver to take him home.

Jack watched the whole thing with bemusement. He wasn't a fan of *Hearts and Minds*, but he was happy it won. He only wished he'd had a chance to tell Bert how proud he was, but he couldn't get to him before he left. Jack never made any public comment about the film or the award.

◆ ◆ ◆

WHEN HE FINALLY arrived back at the house with Anjelica early the following morning, after putting on his game face and making all the requisite rounds, he found an envelope sticking in his fence. It was a bill. The IRS wanted $123,000 in back taxes they claimed Jack owed.

A month later *The Passenger* opened in theaters in America and disappeared in a week. The film grossed a paltry $620,000 in its initial release and received mixed-to-negative reviews about the lack of a cohesive plot. Andrew Sarris dubbed its director "Antonio-ennui."[2] After the film completed its initial theatrical run, because of issues dealing with the ownership of the negative, it was rarely seen in revival.[3]

---

[2] The film's reputation has grown with the passage of time. In 2005, on the occasion of the film's rerelease, *New York Times* critic Manohla Dargis called *The Passenger* "arguably Mr. Antonioni's greatest film."—*New York Times*, August 28, 2005.

[3] Jack settled with the studio for cash and all future distribution rights to *The Passenger*, a film he insisted was a work of art, and he wanted to add it to his permanent collection. The studio had no problem giving him *The Passenger*, as it believed it had run its course.

"To succeed—in order to become a Brando or a Bob Dylan, you can't just punch a time card, take a nap, and pick up your reviews and your money . . . your work is all consuming . . . whether you want to or not you do take your job home with you."

—JACK NICHOLSON

I N 1962, KEN KESEY PUBLISHED HIS GROUNDBREAKING NOVEL *ONE Flew over the Cuckoo's Nest,* which came out of his own experiences as a struggling writer. To pay the bills, he had worked the graveyard shift as an orderly at a mental health facility in Menlo Park, California. At the same time, he got heavily into peyote and LSD, became friendly with several patients, and witnessed some things that affected him deeply and he wouldn't forget. Eventually, his time at the institution became the basis for his semiautobiographical novel, *One Flew over the Cuckoo's Nest,* set in an Oregon state mental hospital in Salem, Oregon, which depicts the lives of several inmates and their supervisors, including one inmate, Randle Patrick McMurphy, whose rebellion against supervisor Nurse Ratched symbolizes the struggle of the rebel to be free in an ordered or controlled civilization. The novel and the subsequent play and feature film all ask the same question—are the inmates insane living in a sane world, or are they really sane in an insane world?

Faded granite-jawed golden boy Kirk Douglas hit his peak in 1960 playing the title role in Stanley Kubrick's *Spartacus,* another story of a rebel fighting against an unjust social order, after which Douglas's career began to slow down. He would never again achieve that level of popularity. Dissatisfied with the films he was now being offered, Kirk began to look for original properties as far away from sandals-swords-robes spectaculars as possible, and when he read a prepublication proof copy of *Cuckoo's Nest*, he believed that the story and especially the character of McMurphy were exactly what he needed to kick-start his career. He paid Kesey $47,000 for the rights and then, after failing to find backers for a movie version, decided to turn the story into a play and bring it to Broadway, proving the old adage that movie stars play the Great White Way on the way up and on the way down.[1]

Douglas had been a working Broadway actor before he was discovered by film producer Hal Wallis and brought to Hollywood, and now he wanted to return to Broadway with *Cuckoo's Nest*. If it was a success, he knew film producers would once again be lining up around the block for it and for him. Douglas partnered with well-known stage producer Dale Wasserman to produce it on Broadway. *Cuckoo's Nest* opened on November 13, 1963, to brisk business. Nine days later, JFK was assassinated in Dallas. Despite Kirk's best (and most stubborn efforts), nobody wanted to go to the theater to see a play about crazies and the show closed in January 1964.

For the better part of the next ten years, Kirk searched in vain for someone to pick up the play's movie option. At times he came close. In 1969, independent producer Joseph E. Levine's independent production company Avco Embassy, which had grossed over $100 million from Mike Nichols's offbeat 1967 *The Graduate*, briefly considered producing *Cuckoo's Nest* but ultimately passed.

A year later, Richard Rush, who had done three early films with Jack, thought it might be a good project to direct and Jack to star in. Kirk, who still controlled the rights, said no to Rush, believing he wasn't big enough, and the project lay dormant for two more years, until Kirk decided to conduct a fire sale and offer the rights to *Cuckoo's Nest* for

---

[1] Following the enormous success of *Spartacus*, Douglas made a series of less-than-blockbuster films, including Gottfried Reinhardt's 1961 *Town Without Pity* (shot in West Germany for United Artists); Robert Aldrich's 1961 *The Last Sunset*; David Miller's 1962 *Lonely Are the Brave*, made at Universal; and Vincente Minnelli's 1962 *Two Weeks in Another Town*, made at MGM. It was then that he discovered Kesey's novel and decided to acquire the rights.

$150,000 to anyone who wanted it. He got no takers. Kirk had not even a shadow of his former box office clout, and Ken Kesey was never a factor in Hollywood. Moreover, the original novel gave off an unpleasant whiff of 1950s sexism, especially when it came to its portrayal of Nurse Ratched.

Then, after a protracted legal battle over the film rights with Wasserman, a fed-up Kirk gave the whole package to his son, Michael Douglas. At the time, Michael was an up-and-coming actor appearing in a TV cop-chase show who desperately wanted to get into producing. As Michael remembers, "I said to my father, 'Why don't you let me take it over, and I promise that I'll at least make your original investment back for you.'"

With no other options, in 1972 Kirk agreed to have Michael run with it. As Michael put it, "My saga began—and it was a long one."

MICHAEL QUICKLY LEARNED the same thing his father had: that there was no interest in *Cuckoo's Nest*. He would have to start from scratch to get it produced. He went through all of Kirk's old files and found the name of Saul Zaentz, who, at one time, had wanted to partner with Kirk on the project. Zaentz was several years older than Michael, closer to Kirk's age, and had first made his name in the music business. When Michael caught up with Zaentz, both were living in San Francisco; Michael was shooting episodes of *The Streets of San Francisco*, and Zaentz was running his Fantasy Records. Zaentz had added rock and roll to his newly acquired label and signed several acts, including Creedence Clearwater Revival, fronted by John Fogerty. They became a hit machine and Fantasy's biggest moneymaker. Zaentz continued to diversify his business interests and wanted to get into film. After seeing a local San Francisco theatrical production of *Cuckoo's Nest*, he had tracked down the rights and got in touch with Kirk. The two didn't hit it off, and Zaentz went off to produce another movie that made no money.

Kirk had disliked Zaentz—his puffy, hippie veneer, his know-it-all attitude. But everything Kirk hated about Zaentz, Michael, a former hippie himself, loved. And Michael, busy with his TV series, was more than happy to let Zaentz be the up-front man. He offered Fantasy Films, Zaentz's film production company, a full partnership with Bigstick Productions, Michael's film production company, if Fantasy put up the film's entire $2 million budget.

Zaentz sat down and wrote a check.

ZAENTZ WANTED TO commission Kesey himself to write the screenplay, but Michael was hesitant about bringing the novelist into the deal. Michael had been around his father in Hollywood long enough to know that book writers didn't usually make good screenwriters, and besides, he knew, Kesey was known to be a bit of a head case.

Zaentz nevertheless set up a meeting with Kesey and offered him a generous deal, and he took it. Four months later he produced a script that both Michael and Zaentz agreed was useless. After a series of legal entanglements, they were able to buy out Kesey and hired the then relatively unknown and little experienced Bo Goldman to do a complete rewrite. While that was happening, Michael and Zaentz went in search of a director.

One of the first they considered was Hal Ashby. As it turned out, Ashby himself had long wanted to acquire the rights to *Cuckoo's Nest* but had neither the money nor the wherewithal to make the deal. Now that the film was moving forward, he wanted to direct it and bring Jack in to star.[2] By now, *Chinatown* had opened to great success, and he was eager to find a new project, and *Cuckoo's Nest* seemed perfect. It would take him out of himself and allow him to concentrate on the acting out of a complex character's personality; a character that would be remarkably close to who he really was.

Douglas and Zaentz, however, had other ideas. Their first choice to play McMurphy was Marlon Brando, who immediately said no, then

[2] Anjelica Huston later claimed that she had talked to Michael about *Cuckoo's Nest* before Ashby: "I don't know if I was the instrumental fact in that, but I mentioned to Jack that Michael wanted to see him about it."—Dennis McDougal, *Five Easy Decades*, p. 167.

Gene Hackman, who also turned them down. So did Burt Reynolds and James Caan.

Jack remained interested in playing McMurphy; he liked the script and also wanted to work with Ashby again, and the deal was made. Jack agreed to a million dollars up front and a piece of the gross.[3] Zaentz wanted Jack but not Ashby (Zaentz didn't like him), and still without a director, the film's projected start was delayed for another six months.

ON A RAINY June 17, 1974, at one o'clock in the afternoon, accompanied by his agent, Sandy Bresler; his daughter Jennifer, whom he had flown in for the occasion (one of the few times he got to see her without having to fly to Hawaii); Robert Towne; Lou Adler; Kathryn Holt (an artist friend of his); and Anjelica Huston, Jack was given the honor of becoming the 159th star to put his handprints in the courtyard of Mann's (Grauman's) Chinese Theater on Hollywood Boulevard. The once-prestigious honor was now little more than a publicity stunt to promote new movies, in this instance *Chinatown*. At the height of Hollywood Boulevard's popularity, in the 1930s, through the 1960s, 158 previous recipients had gone through the ritual. In the 1970s, Jack was the second of only seven honorees, one of them a droid (C-3PO)[4] (Darth Vader and R2-D2 also received the honor on C-3PO's big day).

Jack dutifully placed his hands and feet into the cool wet cement and used a pencil to sign his autograph in big block letters. Afterward, while Jack was having something to eat with Jennifer, Bresler, who had known all along but didn't want to put more of a damper on the day

[3] The latest estimate of Jack's earnings from *Cuckoo's Nest*, based on the film's gross, exceeds $20 million.

[4] The tradition dates back to 1927 when Norma Talmadge was the first to participate in what was, for Sid Grauman, the theater's original owner, a way to bring his Hollywood Boulevard Chinese-themed theater additional publicity. The venue changed hands frequently, and for a time it was called Mann's Chinese Theater. It has since been fully restored, complete to the original name. The handprint tradition then became a tourist attraction, paid for by the recipient or whatever film he or she was promoting. The last to place handprints in the cement as of this writing was Jane Fonda, in May 2013.

than the steady rain falling already had, quietly informed Jack of the delay in the start of production of *Cuckoo's Nest*.

THAT JULY, STILL under contract to Zaentz and Douglas, with a temporary option-out clause, Jack, eager to work, exercised it; after considering several offers, he signed on to do Mike Nichols's *The Fortune*, written by Jack's old friend Carole Eastman (as Adrien Joyce) and co-starring pal Warren Beatty.

Having the chance to work with Nichols again and being in a movie written by Eastman with his buddy Beatty were the reasons Jack agreed to do it over the many other offers, despite having not read the completed script. (Mike Nichols had signed on after reading only the half that Eastman had completed. She had given it to him on a flight to Warsaw, and by the time the plane landed he had made up his mind to do it.)[5] Nichols's career had floundered a bit after making *The Day of the Dolphin*, his disappointing first film following *Carnal Knowledge*. Jack's ex-roommate Don Devlin, who had since become close with Eastman, co-produced.

The Fortune, ostensibly a "caper" film minimally based on a real-life scam from the 1930s, in which a neo–Laurel and Hardy—Jack and Beatty—try to pull off a money-grabbing scam to separate a wealthy sanitary napkin heiress (ha ha) from her "fortune." As would soon become obvious to one and all, slapstick, or any style of comedy, for that matter, was not one of Beatty's fortes. *The Fortune*'s female lead was Stockard Channing, who could play broad comedy but whose talents were wasted here, and whose name had been way down Warren's wish list of co-stars, high among them Anjelica Huston, who wisely turned the pic-

[5] Hal Ashby, having been cut out of *Cuckoo's Nest*, offered Jack the role of Woody Guthrie in the biopic *Bound for Glory*, but he turned it down, as did Bob Dylan. The role eventually went to David Carradine. Bernardo Bertolucci wanted Jack to play Dashiell Hammett's Continental Op in a film version of *Red Harvest*. Jack was interested, but the film was never made. Tony Richardson offered him the lead in *The Bodyguard*, and after Jack turned it down it was reconceived for Steve McQueen and Diana Ross. It eventually was made in 1992 with Kevin Costner and Whitney Houston.

ture down to keep her relationship with Jack on solid ground. Anjelica later said, "I don't think Jack really wanted to be with an actress, because he had been with them before and it hadn't been successful . . ."

Nichols had originally sought Bette Midler to play the female lead. Midler was far better known than Channing but committed a fatal error when she met Nichols and, in her familiar out-of-the-side-of-her-mouth manner, aggressively quizzed him on what other movies he had made. Midler was out, Channing was in.

Jack often took Jennifer with him on set. She was staying with Jack while she was on summer vacation. One day during a break he had a conversation with Jennifer and asked his ten-year-old daughter, who would sometimes hum softly to herself, if she liked to sing. She nodded. Well, then, had she had ever heard of the song "I Found a Million-Dollar Baby (in a Five and Ten Cent Store)"? She replied, "What's a five-and-ten-cent store?"

WHEN *THE FORTUNE* came out, one or two critics cited Jack's performance as better than the others', but that was like saying cyanide was better than arsenic. The film's tried and true conceit—put together stars and let their charisma do the acting—this time did not work. What came across to audiences was a tiresome, ill-paced noncomedy that unintentionally reeked of homoerotic bonding, as do most male-male films where the female lead is only minimally involved and is not a sexually desirable character. If anything, the film proved the difference between Beatty as an actor with star power and Jack as a star who could act. As Henry Jaglom pointed out, "Jack was more than of his time. He was not just another hippie, temporary break-out indie star (like Bruce Dern). Jack could legitimately act, and write, and produce and direct. He was not conventionally handsome, especially after he lost most of his youthful appeal—he was fast approaching forty—but he was a superb character actor. Beatty was a traditional movie star, more like a gorgeous woman, whose run at the top was going to be limited to how long his looks lasted."

♦ ♦ ♦

MICHAEL DOUGLAS AND Saul Zaentz were still searching for a director. Michael once more returned to his father's files, where this time he came up with the name of Miloš Forman, the Czech director whose career had begun while his native country was still in the Soviet sphere. Kirk had been visiting Russia and Prague as a goodwill ambassador for the U.S. State Department in the sixties and for the first time met Forman. Kirk had loved his 1965 *Loves of a Blonde*, which would eventually be nominated for a 1967 Golden Globe for Best Foreign-Language Foreign Film and an Academy Award for Best Foreign Film (it lost both to Claude Lelouch's *A Man and a Woman*). Kirk promised to send Forman a copy of Kesey's book and asked if he would consider making a film out of it. When Kirk returned to the States and did not hear back from Forman, the famous Douglas temper showed its fangs, and Kirk swore he would have nothing more to do with the director.

Forman's international reputation continued to grow, and after the 1968 Prague Spring, he came to America in 1971 to make his first American film, *Taking Off,* which he co-wrote with John Guare, Jean-Claude Carrière, and John Klein—a late-to-the-table sixties generation-gap film. Forman was right at home with the notion of an anti-hero. Everyone in his country who was involved in helping to gain its freedom was an anti-hero fighting against the system. In America he was an outsider of a different sort, new to the ways and mores of the country. In every way, then, he saw some of himself in the rebel McMurphy and knew what he wanted to do with the film. After Forman left a meeting with Michael and Zaentz agreeing to direct, they were so happy they turned to each other and started crying.

With Forman aboard and Jack's schedule cleared, the film was finally ready to go into production.

It fell to Michael to do the job no one else had wanted. Kirk was still laboring under the fantasy that if the film got made he was going to play McMurphy, that he was still the wild young man he had been eleven years earlier on Broadway. When Michael told him that Jack was playing McMurphy, Kirk's response was "almost incomprehensible. They wanted someone else for McMurphy? Why? That was *my* part. I'd found him. I could create him, make him breathe. But after ten [*sic*] years of telling everybody what a great role it is . . . now I'm too old? . . . I could *still* play that part."

Michael listened, empathized, and comforted. But Kirk was out and Jack was in, and that was the way it was going to be.

In Miloš Forman's 1975 *One Flew over the Cuckoo's Nest,* Jack's macho man McMurphy takes on Nurse Ratched, an older martinet of a woman who hides behind and uses the authority of her position to destroy his sense of rebellion. McMurphy fights against an authority he believes is sicker and more corrupt than the prisoners over whom Ratched rules. She is in charge, their Mother Superior, and also, perhaps, the mother they never had. She represents to the inmates the moment in their lives when everything first started to go wrong.

Douglas and Zaentz were still looking to cast this crucial role. After several well-known actresses had already turned the role down, including Anne Bancroft, Faye Dunaway, Jane Fonda, and Ellen Burstyn, because of the original novel's lingering sexist reputation, they signed the relatively unknown Louise Fletcher. Forman had seen her in Robert Altman's just-released *Thieves Like Us* and thought she would make a great Ratched. Douglas, Zaentz, and Forman called her in to read, and agreed she was perfect for the part. What followed next was a week of nine hundred auditions for the ensemble cast (some no more than a pass-by). Douglas insisted that his good friend Danny DeVito play Martini, one of the inmates. Most of the rest who were chosen were relative unknowns. Many would go on to successful careers in the theater, movies, or TV, including William Redfield, Brad Dourif, Sydney Lassick, Christopher Lloyd, Dean R. Brooks, William Duell, Vincent Schiavelli, Delos V. Smith Jr., Michael Berryman, Nathan George, Mews Small, Scatman Crothers, and Louisa Moritz.

To GET PERMISSION to film inside the institution, Michael had personally prevailed upon the hospital's current superintendent, Dean R.

Brooks, who happened to have loved the book; he felt the system was so much more enlightened now, and believed the film could provide a historical look back at how far mental treatment had come (it didn't hurt that Michael gave Brooks a small part in the film as the superintendent, in effect allowing him to play himself). In return, Brooks allowed Forman to spend six weeks working on the final script while actually living in the institution and let two cast members, DeVito and Lloyd (who would both later work together on the sitcom *Taxi*) sit in on actual therapy sessions.

Because of *Chinatown* promotion commitments and some post-production on *The Fortune*, Jack actually arrived a week after filming began in January 1975, on location at Oregon State Hospital in Salem, where the events that had formed the nucleus of Kesey's novel had actually taken place. When he finally did show, Jack persuaded Brooks to let him mingle with the most disturbed patients, eat with them in the mess hall, and be allowed to watch the administration of shock treatments, in those years a regular practice at Oregon State Hospital. He gained relatively free rein among the 582 patients: arsonists, mass murderers, a rapist, and a stone-cold killer. He went up to one patient and asked him what he was in for, and as casually as telling the time, he said he had blown someone away. When Jack asked why, the patient said he didn't know; the guy was one of his closest friends. "He told me just the way I'm telling you. No emotion, nothing. Just 'Jeeze, I can see they can't let me out of here 'cause I don't know why I did it . . . I guess I'm here forever.'"

"They tell me I'm getting crazier every day," Jack said, alluding to his Method approach to McMurphy, a part that was more challenging than any he had done so far. "Crazier than usual that is. But it is difficult to hold on to reality when you're playing a psychopath every day. Usually I don't have trouble slipping out of a film role, but here I don't go home from a movie studio. I go home from a mental institution. And there's nothing in between. I haven't even been out to the town of Salem yet."

Anjelica, who had come along with Jack and originally intended to spend the entire shoot with him, couldn't take the level of his intensity and concentration and, despite having been given a small nonspeaking role, packed her bags and returned to wait it out in L.A. Jack was so immersed in McMurphy, he had no time to pay any attention to Anjelica. And once again, she felt she received no encouragement from Jack about her wanting to act.

And there were problems of a different sort, including Jack's Method acting, staying in character even when not in front of the camera, caught on with the other cast members, and all the actors began to do it, leading to a peculiar doubling between the real inmates and the actor-inmates. The actors never broke character, even at meals. Adding to this was that, except for one boating sequence, Forman had chosen to shoot the film in sequence.

Jack, ever the basketball junkie, a game he called "the classical music of sports," rented an apartment near the hospital so he could spend evenings and weekends watching college basketball at Corvallis or Eugene or go to a Blazers game in Portland if he could get up and back in time, and even managed to work basketball into a sequence in the film, where he tries to teach one of the key characters, the mute giant (Will Sampson), how to play.

That February, Jack won his BAFTA award for *Chinatown*. Because he was still filming *Cuckoo's Nest*, he couldn't fly to London to be there in person, so he filmed his acceptance speech in the mental hospital in Salem. As the cameras rolled he stood behind a glass wall, then smashed his fist through fake, breakaway glass, smiled, and said, "It is really smashing of you to give me this award." Jack loved a good joke.

But as the production crawled on, his and everybody's sense of humor began to fade; it became more difficult to tell whether they were *playing* inmates or *were* inmates. He told *Newsday* that during much of the filming he felt more like a prisoner than an actor: Except for his few escapes to watch basketball games, "for more than four months, I spent the days there and would come out only at night, walking down this little path in which my footprints were indelibly marked by the almost constant rain, to the place where I was living. I'd have dinner in bed and go to sleep and then get up the next morning—still in the dark—and go back to the maximum security ward. It was basically being an inmate, with dinner privileges out." To another reporter, he said, jokingly, that the mental institute was "a nice place just to visit," and added, referring to the long shoot, "What saved the day for me was to see how much good it did for the patients to work in the film. One of our extras improved so much he was discharged when the shooting ended."

And to still another, he was even more personal and revelatory, bringing sex into the mix, offering how women played into his version of the Method: "The secret to *Cuckoo's Nest*—and it's not in the book— was that this guy's a scamp who knows he's irresistible to women and in reality he expects Nurse Ratched to be seduced by him. This is his tragic flaw. This is why he ultimately fails. I discussed this with Louise, and only with her. That's what I felt was actually happening with that character—it was one long unsuccessful seduction which the guy was pathologically sure of."

ONLY A FEW weeks passed between the ending of production on *Cuckoo's Nest* and Jack's arrival in Montana to begin work on Arthur Penn's *The Missouri Breaks*. *Breaks* was Penn's third western, following 1958's Method oater *The Left Handed Gun* starring Paul Newman at his Actors Studio level of intensity, and 1970s *Little Big Man*, a post-*Graduate* showcase for a young Dustin Hoffman.

One of the reasons Jack wanted to be in the film, besides working with Marlon Brando, was the chance to act with some good friends, including Harry Dean Stanton, who had landed a role, and Randy Quaid, from *The Last Detail*. Another was how much the script appealed to him. A quick read showed that his character, Tom Logan, is a rustler who falls on hard times and into a feud with local land baron and neighbor John McLiam (David Braxton), who in turn hires professional "enforcer" Robert E. Lee Clayton (Marlon Brando) to deal with Logan. The fact that for him the character was a roll off a log after the intensity of making *Cuckoo's Nest* was another thing that appealed to Jack, as was the relatively short shooting schedule and the fact that Sandra had once again agreed to let eleven-year-old Jennifer stay with him on location the entire shoot (where he would have to constantly keep Jennifer away from the crew's ongoing poker games she kept wanting to join). But the real deal-maker, of course, was the chance to play opposite Brando.

He still considered Brando the greatest movie actor of all time. They had never gotten close, despite the fact that they were neighbors. Brando never came over to schmooze or hang out, and he had let himself go to an alarming degree. About the only thing they had in common was a housekeeper, Angela Borlaza. Still, it was Brando.

By the time Jack arrived on set, he was told that the acting legend had forced Penn to expand Jack's role. There was nothing generous about this. Brando had become lazy after his 1972 double dip of *The Godfather* and *Last Tango* and didn't want to work that hard (and wouldn't ever again). He wanted all the weight of the film put on Jack's shoulders. According to Brando, "Poor Nicholson was stuck in the center of it all, cranking the damned thing out, while I whipped in and out of scenes like greased lightning." Jack: "I was very hurt. The picture was terribly out of balance, and I said so . . . Arthur Penn doesn't talk to me anymore because I told him I didn't like his picture. The movie could've been saved in the cutting room, but nobody listened."

It was a depressing reality check for Jack. His idol from *The Wild One* and *On the Waterfront* showed up to film this horse opera weighing in at 250 pounds; walked around the set in a yellow bathrobe; threw temper tantrums regularly, one at the unions because a young Chinese girl whom he had invited to the set was not allowed to watch the day's shoot; played his role reading off cue cards; and used an earpiece to have his lines fed to him as he said them. Inexplicably, Marlon spoke his lines in an Irish accent. And one time Brando argued with Penn for five hours without a break over the validity of a single scene. The estimated cost of those five hours was $10,000. Brando didn't even phone in his performance; it was more like he used two soup cans and a string, causing Jack to wonder, "Marlon's still the greatest actor in the world, so why does he need those goddamn cue cards?" It didn't help that Brando was acutely aware that Nicholson was routinely referred to as the Marlon Brando of his generation.

To do the film, Jack received a $1.25 million salary up front for his 47½ days' work, plus 10 percent of the gross. Brando took less of a salary, an even million, but 11 percent of the gross. Each earned about $15 million.[6]

Brando did it only for the money. He believed he was finished as a serious actor and didn't give a damn. He had bought an island near Tahiti and it was costing him multiple millions to develop it as a potential resort.

For Jack, however, Brando's on set over-the-hill quirkiness was less bewildering than it was foreboding, a wake-up call to Jack of what happens to actors who get eaten alive by the voraciousness of the monster fame.

ONE FLEW OVER THE CUCKOO'S NEST premiered on November 19, 1975, to overwhelming box office. Even as audiences packed into movie theaters to see it, critics were, for the most part, up and down about the film. Roger Ebert, writing for the *Chicago Sun-Times*, called it "a film so good in so many of its parts that there's a temptation to forgive it when it goes wrong. But it does go wrong, insisting on making larger points than its story can really carry, so that at the end, the human qualities of the characters get lost in the significance of it all. And yet there are moments of brilliance." Ebert would eventually revise his opinion upward.

Vincent Canby, in the *New York Times*, liked it less: "Even granting the artist his license, America is much too big and various to be satisfactorily reduced to the dimensions of one mental ward in a movie like this."

In the *New Yorker* Pauline Kael called *Cuckoo's Nest* "a powerful,

---

[6] Here, because of cost overruns, advertising, and other costs, the agreed-upon break-even number was $12.5 million. According to court records, before the film opened, Jack filed a breach-of-contract suit against Proteus Films and Kastner's EK Corporation. He had exercised an option to sell back to Kastner 5 percent of his share of the movie's gross for $1 million. When Kastner failed to pay up, Jack sued. Eventually the case was settled out of court.

smashing, effective movie—one that will probably stir audiences' emotions and join the ranks of such pop-mythology films as *The Wild One*, *Rebel without a Cause* and *Easy Rider*, the three most iconic, culture-shifting films of the '50s and '60s." One might differ with Kael, but to Jack her comparisons couldn't have been better, putting him in the company of both Brando and Dean.

Cuckoo's Nest went on to gross an astonishing $108,981,275, the bulk of that in 1975 dollars (before additional sources of revenue became available, including video, cable, Netflix, and streaming). It ranks eighty-fourth on the list of highest-grossing movies of all time.[7] It played to packed houses all over the world; in Sweden it reportedly played in one theater continuously for eleven years, and it is ranked thirty-three in the American Film Institute's listing *One Hundred Years . . . One Hundred Movies*.

JUST BEFORE THE heavy promotion for the film kicked in, Jack was asked by Sam Spiegel to join a number of other major stars and do a cameo in Elia Kazan's filmed version of F. Scott Fitzgerald's *The Last Tycoon*, with a script by Harold Pinter, loosely (*very* loosely) based on the life of MGM boy-genius producer Irving Thalberg, who died at the age of thirty-seven. Jack could not say no to the chance to work for one of his idols, Elia Kazan, the only director to have worked with both Brando and James Dean (and who was widely reviled throughout the industry as having given testimony and named names to the House Un-American Activities Committee in the 1950s, a move that all but ruined the rest of his career). Jack had no problems working with Kazan because of politics. "I'm the first friendly Communist in the history of American movies," Jack jokingly told Andy Warhol.

Joining him in the roster of cameos were Tony Curtis, Robert Mitchum, Donald Pleasence, Ray Milland, Dana Andrews, John Carradine, Jack's once-blacklisted acting teacher Jeff Corey, and Anjelica.

---

[7] Victor Fleming's *Gone with the Wind* (1939) is number one; and number eighty-five is Robert Altman's *M*A*S*H* (1970).

Robert De Niro was cast in the lead as Monroe Stahr, the character Fitzgerald had based on Thalberg, but it soon became apparent during production that Kazan's heart wasn't in it. He later confessed that he had done the film (which would be the last he directed) for the money. He was broke, his mother was sick, and his career was moribund. His direction seemed stagy and slow, and despite the stellar roster of performers, the film, which opened in November 1976, bombed at the box office.

JACK KNEW IT was time to pay some real attention to Anjelica, whom he had rarely seen since she left the filming of *Cuckoo's Nest*. He sensed that she was upset about his not being around. Because of conflicting schedules their paths hadn't crossed even once during the filming of *Tycoon*. To celebrate her birthday, he took a rare detour from his standard daily fare of larded Mexican food—he loved the local L.A. establishments that served the real thing over any of the chains or fast-food joints, and the Mexican sidewalk carts along the streets of Western Avenue.

For the occasion, Jack arranged a special dinner for the two of them at Chasen's restaurant, the storied white building with green trim on Doheny just south of Santa Monica Boulevard, the preferred dining establishment of the Alfred Hitchcocks, the Ronald Reagans, the Jimmy Stewarts, the Dale Wassermans. It was a place Jack rarely frequented, but he knew that Anjelica had been there many times with her father and liked the atmosphere, so he thought it would be a good place to have her party. To join in the celebration, Jack invited Warren Beatty, Bob Evans, David Geffen, Marlo Thomas, Dustin Hoffman, and superagent Sue Mengers, the cream of new Hollywood.

After dinner, Jack took Anjelica for one more course—a fistful of street chimichangas.

THREE MONTHS AFTER *Cuckoo's Nest's* huge U.S. opening, United Artists decided to send Michael Douglas and Jack out on a worldwide publicity tour, during which time the two became even closer than they had been during production. They shared a lot of the same tastes in food, drink (Michael liked alcohol more than Jack), drugs, cigarettes, cigars, and, of course, beautiful young women. They stripped and devoured them like peeling shrimp as they romped through England, Sweden, Denmark, France, Germany, Italy, Japan, and Australia. According to Jack, tongue firmly planted in cheek (and elsewhere), the tour was all about politics, social behavior, and religion. "The Italian interviews were the most lively. I'm a genius at encountering the Marxist dialectic."

Wherever they went the film opened big, and on those nights they found themselves swarmed by hordes of pot-smoking hot young women willing to audition for anything the two wished. Paris was one long party where Jack took to wearing a beret wherever he went. He was swarmed by paparazzi in Rome; one asked Jack to remove the beret and his dark sunglasses for the sake of a better shot. "Oh no," Jack said, flashing his signature grin. "I never take the hat off. I even sleep with it on." He then explained that he was "resodding" his balding hairline with transplants and had to wear the beret to protect the freshly injected follicles. Nor would he remove his Wayfarers. "With my sunglasses on I'm *Jack Nicholson . . .*"

The party finally ended when Jack had to return to America to promote *The Missouri Breaks* and prepare for the Oscars, where he hoped this time he would get what he deserved.

While Jack was away, Anjelica, fed up with Jack's philandering, wasn't content with sitting home waiting for the phone to ring. She decided to fly to England, to South Kensington, to visit her ex-lover Ryan O'Neal. They had been together briefly between his first two marriages, to Joanna Moore and Leigh Taylor-Young, and before she had hooked up with Bob Richardson. They stayed in the same luxury hotel suite and never left it the entire time she was there. They ate, slept, and made love all in the same luxurious king-size bed. When Jack found out, from a paparazzo, which may have been the whole point, he said, rather grimly, "I don't want to be mentioned in the same sentence as

O'Neal. We [once were] but are no longer friends. But I don't want to talk about why."

As it happened, O'Neal had been Bob Evans's fair-haired boy during the filming of *Love Story* when Evans had been head of production at Paramount, and Jack had gotten to know O'Neal a little because Jack got to know everybody. He could run all around Europe with Michael Douglas screwing anything that moved, but when he found out about Anjelica and O'Neal, he was hurt; it was indicative of how he saw their relationship. She was, in some ways, supposed to be the patient mother so he could be the eternal bad boy. She wasn't going to play that game.

When she and Jack returned separately to Los Angeles, Anjelica gave him an ultimatum of sorts. She said she wanted to be married, and he said he had already been down that road and it didn't work for him, but if she gave him a little time he would try to get there. She said she would give him some time, not a lot, and if he didn't marry her then that would be it.

It was where their relationship stood on the night of the Academy Awards ceremony, held once again at the Dorothy Chandler Pavilion, this year on March 29, 1976. The hosting duties were divided between Goldie Hawn, representing "new" Hollywood, and veteran song-and-dance man Gene Kelly holding up the rear. Additional individual segments were given to actors Walter Matthau, George Segal, and Robert Shaw. *One Flew over the Cuckoo's Nest* had been nominated for nine Oscars, including Best Actor for Jack Nicholson. The film that early on had been considered its biggest competition was Hal Ashby's *Shampoo*, Warren Beatty's film about a sex-crazed hairdresser that was loosely based on the wild life of Jay Sebring, one of the guests killed at Sharon Tate's house the night of the Manson murders. *Shampoo* was nominated for four Oscars—Best Actor in a Supporting Role (Jack Warden), Best Actress in a Supporting Role (Lee Grant), Best Original Screenplay (Robert Towne and Warren Beatty), and Best Art Direction (Richard Sylbert, W. Stewart Campbell, and George Gaines). Beatty was not nominated for Best Actor.

Jack showed up that night wearing a tuxedo, and something new—a hairpiece, to cover the still-visible transplants—and his requisite Way-farers. He had Anjelica on one arm, looking beautiful, and as always his daughter, Jennifer, on the other, now twelve and an increasingly frequent visitor at Jack's house, as she was old enough now to be able to fly by herself nonstop from Hawaii to Hollywood with relative ease. Sandra, who had since remarried, having met a spiritual leader she'd fallen in love with, was fine with it.

Jack and company were seated so that he was next to Michael Doug-las, who was there with Brenda Vaccaro (his soon-to-be ex; Charles Champlin, in the *Los Angeles Times*, reported that Vaccaro's relation-ship with Michael was now officially in the "friend" stage and she was shopping for a house of her own). She was also nominated, for Best Supporting Actress for her work in Guy Greene's *Once Is Not Enough*, which starred Kirk Douglas in a soapy adaptation of Jacqueline Su-sann's novel of the same name.

Things did not begin auspiciously for Jack and his team. *Cuckoo's Nest* lost its first four nominations.

With each successive loss, Jack slid lower in his seat. He was sure now that the Nicholson Oscar curse was operating on schedule and was going to spell doom for *Cuckoo's Nest*. At one point, he put his fingers up to cover his lips from the TV cameras and whispered to Michael, "I told you!" After the first four losses, Jack was sure he had no chance of winning. "The people who vote for these things don't like me much," he rationalized to one interviewer prior to the ceremony. "You see, I don't spend my time doing charity. And that's very important to the Academy, the image you create. It's not that I've got anything against charitable work. It's just that I don't have the time."[8]

And then the tide turned, and *Cuckoo's Nest* began its legendary

---

[8] The January before the awards were due to be given out, according to Alan Warren, there was another reason Jack couldn't win. The Academy thought Jack was too young. "Industry wags say Nicholson won't receive one until he passes forty, at which time he'll become eligible because of his age, just as Gig Young, Jack Lemmon and Art Carney did, all of whom beat out Nicholson in the past." —Alan Warren, *Film Buff*, January 1976.

run for glory. The nominations for Best Screenplay Adapted from Other Material were Stanley Kubrick, for *Barry Lyndon*; John Huston and Gladys Hill, for *The Man Who Would Be King*; Ruggero Maccari and Dino Risi, for *Scent of a Woman*; Neil Simon, for *The Sunshine Boys*; and Laurence Hauben and Bo Goldman, for *Cuckoo's Nest* (but not Ken Kesey, who was not approved by the Writers Guild to be listed as one of the screenwriters). There was a pause as Gore Vidal read the winning names. "Laurence Hauben and Bo Goldman!" The two men rushed to the stage and Hauben took over the microphone to thank the Academy and his fellow workers on the film by telling them, "They are some of the most finest people I've ever known!"

Louise Fletcher, the forty-one-year-old actress, then pulled one of the great upsets in Academy history when she won Best Performance by an Actress, despite the less-than-spectacular competition that year: Ann-Margret in *Tommy*, whose chances were hurt by her comparison to her role in *Carnal Knowledge*, the film she should have won for; Isabelle Adjani in François Truffaut's *The Story of Adele H.*, about French national hero Victor Hugo's daughter's relationship with a soldier, a film almost nobody in America saw; Glenda Jackson in Trevor Nunn's *Hedda*, his film version of Ibsen's *Hedda Gabler* that even fewer people saw; and Carol Kane in Joan Micklin Silver's also little-seen *Hester Street*. When Fletcher's name was announced, she smiled, went up to the stage, thanked everybody, and ended her short speech by simultaneously speaking and signing in American Sign Language so that her deaf mother could "hear" her. Translated into words, she said, "I want to say thank you for teaching me to have a dream. You are seeing my dream come true." The Chandler Pavilion erupted.

Now it was time for Best Director. To present, Diane Keaton appeared with director William Wyler. The nominees included Miloš Forman, now the odds-on favorite; Robert Altman, for his hugely entertaining ensemble film *Nashville*; Federico Fellini, for *Amarcord*, a great movie few in America saw but those who did liked; Stanley Kubrick, for *Barry Lyndon*, a film that a lot of people saw and few liked; and Sidney Lumet, for *Dog Day Afternoon*. And the winner was . . . Miloš Forman, for *Cuckoo's Nest.* The audience that night loved his enthusiastic adrenaline-driven acceptance speech.

Best Actor came next. The nominees were Walter Matthau, for *The Sunshine Boys;* Al Pacino, for *Dog Day Afternoon;* Maximilian Schell, for *The Man in the Glass Booth,* a film based on a play inspired by the trial of Adolf Eichmann, written by Harold Pinter; James Whitmore as Harry Truman in Steve Binder's blah *Give 'Em Hell, Harry!,* which had no chance, Harry; and Jack Nicholson for his astonishing immersion-therapy performance.

When presenter Art Carney called out Jack's name, the audience stood and applauded as he flashed them a million-dollar grin, yanked off his Wayfarers, sprinted down the aisle as if he were dribbling in for a layup, and strode onto the majestic stage of the Chandler Pavilion. (The TV camera picked up Walter Matthau in close-up, clearly mouthing to his wife, "It's about time.")

As Jack accepted the Oscar, in a bit of poetic justice handed to him by Carney, he said into the mike, "I guess this proves there are as many nuts in the Academy as anywhere else!" The audience roared. Because he was fully expecting to go home a five-time loser, smiling Jack had no victory speech prepared, so he started off thanking, of all people, the legendary Mary Pickford, who just minutes earlier had been honored with a special Academy Honorary Award she accepted at Pickfair, telecast live via the then complicated remote pickup. After a few more mandatory thank-yous, Jack ended his short speech by saying, "Last but not least, [I'd like to thank] my agent who, about ten years ago, advised me that I had no business being an actor." Another round of spirited applause, and Jack happily exited the stage accompanied on either side by two gorgeous starlets, both nearly a head taller than him, with Carney picking up the rear.

Audrey Hepburn was given the honor of announcing the winner of the last award of the evening, Best Picture, but it almost didn't have to be called. There wasn't a person in the house who didn't now know that *Cuckoo's Nest* was going to beat *Barry Lyndon, Dog Day Afternoon, Nashville,* and the super-successful summer horror flick *Jaws.*

Even before the word *One* left her mouth, Michael jumped up as if someone had put an electric charge in his seat. When he got to the stage he excitedly told the audience that this was "the first time since *It Happened One Night* in 1937! [*sic*]."[9] To banging applause, Michael left the stage with Zaentz. For the paparazzi, they hugged and kissed their Oscars and held them in the air like the trophies of triumph that they were. Michael joked, "It's all downhill from here."

Kirk Douglas didn't bother to attend. Although afterward, Michael told reporters that Kirk was in Palm Springs and didn't want to distract from his son's big night, Kirk was at home in Beverly Hills, simmering as he watched the whole thing on TV.

For Louise Fletcher, who had been nobody's first choice for the role of Nurse Ratched—far from it; she was not pretty enough to be a leading lady, not unattractive enough to be a character actress, and too old to play ingénues—this was the highlight of her career. She would make more than fifty movies in her career and do good TV work, but name-above-the-title star status ultimately eluded her. For Forman, the win propelled him to the A-list of Hollywood studio directors, and a few years later he would win another Oscar for *Amadeus*, produced by Saul Zaentz (without Michael Douglas). After the excitement died down, when Forman asked his two young sons what they wanted to do to celebrate, they said they wanted to meet Columbo (Peter Falk) and see *Jaws*.

Ken Kesey, still smarting over having his novel taken away from him, also did not attend the awards. A few days later he told a reporter he'd wished those envelopes had contained subpoenas instead of the names of winners. "Oscar night should have been one of the great days of my life, like my wedding. I really love movies. When they can be turned around to break your heart like this, well, it's like something you never thought would happen." Kesey's feelings were somewhat assuaged by yet another settlement from Michael and Zaentz to Kesey's amended lawsuit that would keep him well-off for the rest of his life.

But for Jack, it was a night filled with nothing but pure joy. Back-

---

[9] It was 1935, for the 1934 Capra film that had won the four major awards—Best Actor, Best Actress, Best Director, Best Film.

stage, for the press, he stepped to the mike and blurted out, "God, isn't it fantastic?" One reporter asked, "When you were doing *Little Shop of Horrors* did you ever think it would lead to this?"

Still smiling, he took off his Wayfarers with one hand and wiped his damp eyes with the other and said, "Yes, I did," and everyone in the room laughed good-naturedly. "And I have one more ambition, that is to don a gray chauffeur's livery uniform and drive Forman into Prague in a Rolls-Royce."

Michael, Anjelica, Jack, and Brenda went to every Oscar party together that night, and when Anjelica and Brenda couldn't take any more, they were sent home, while Jack and Michael continued to do the town. He never let go of his Oscar, not even when he went to the bathroom, until he got home sometime before dawn. Anjelica was there, sleeping in his bed. He got cleaned up and later told at least one close friend that he took Oscar with him when he got in next to Anjelica—the threesome to end all threesomes.

The next day a stream of friends dropped by to congratulate him. Jack's habit of keeping his front door unlocked provided unannounced entrée for Mike Nichols, Art Garfunkel, Candice Bergen, Warren Beatty, and at least a dozen others. Jack and Anjelica together thanked them all for coming.

He was thirty-eight years old; *Cuckoo's Nest* was his *The Wild One, On the Waterfront, East of Eden,* and *Rebel without a Cause* all rolled into one. He had reached the top of his profession. The only question now was, could he stay there.

Part III

The

Good

Life

PREVIOUS PAGE: Lou Adler and Jack attending a Lakers' game, sitting in the front row at the Staples Center. *Courtesy of Getty Images*

"I'm from that late '50s, '60s underground American film movement that honestly believes you can make any movie on any subject for any price. What's hard to do is change what is formally acceptable to a movie audience."

—JACK NICHOLSON

JACK WAS EXHAUSTED. HAVING MADE SIX PICTURES ON THREE CONtinents and five countries in two years culminating in winning one Oscar,[1] he purchased a little two-bedroom farmhouse vacation spot in Aspen, the hip hideaway for 1970s superstars, and became a member of the wake-up-at-the-crack-of-noon celebrity set. He called it "my little red house" and packed it with Picassos and Matisses. It sat at the base of a cliff a thousand feet high, with a mountain river running beneath his terrace.

Lou Adler had a place nearby, so did Bob Rafelson. It was through them that Jack first became familiar with Aspen, and when this relatively modest house, at least by superstar standards, became available, he grabbed it. He wanted to be, for a time, "basically alone. Me and my cook. When you ski all day, you go home and eat and go to bed . . ."

In Aspen, there were the rockers, among them Don Henley and Glenn Frey of the Eagles, and John Denver. There were the actors,

---

[1] These are the release dates: *Chinatown* (U.S. release dates), 1974; *The Passenger* (U.S.–Italy), Spain, England, Germany, Algeria, 1974; *Tommy* (England), 1975; *The Fortune* (U.S.), 1975; *One Flew over the Cuckoo's Nest* (U.S.), 1975; *The Missouri Breaks* (U.S.), 1976; *The Last Tycoon*. All six films were made from 1974 to 1976.

like Michael Douglas and Jack; the politicians, including Gary Hart; and always the beautiful starlets and the divorcées who lived off their generous settlements and alimony. Andy Williams's ex, actress Claudine Longet, was one of those. On March 21, 1976, while in Aspen, she killed her boyfriend in his home, former Olympic skier Vladimir "Spider" Sabich, in a jealous rage.

She stood trial ten months later, in January 1977, during which she claimed the gun that had killed Sabich had discharged accidentally while he was showing her how to use it. The trial became the talk of Aspen and Los Angeles, and Jack attended almost every day, fascinated by it the same way he had been with the Manson trial. He always sat in the first row of spectators, usually next to Williams, mystified by the lovely face of a woman driven to kill.

She eventually got off with a thirty-day sentence for criminal negligence and then married her lawyer.

Besides watching the trial, Jack's plan was to kick back and spend the entire winter in Aspen, do some skiing, take some advanced lessons, and get back into writing by working on the script of a western he had been playing with for a while called *Moontrap* (aka *Moon Trap*), set in Oregon in 1850. The plot involves a white mountain man who has been living with an Indian tribe and has an Indian wife but wants to make it in the white world. Jack hoped winning the Oscar would make it easier to get the film produced. It didn't. His best hope, moneyman Lester Persky, whom Jack had first met at Jimmy Carter's inaugural gala, was initially enthusiastic about the project but cooled on it when Jack decided he also wanted to direct it and have Lee Marvin play the lead rather than himself (in 1990 Kevin Costner would direct and star in a somewhat similar film called *Dances with Wolves*). Without Jack committing to being onscreen, Persky quickly lost interest, and *Moontrap* went nowhere.

In August 1977, the story of his heritage that he dreaded would one day come out, finally did. It was casually dropped by the normally staid, scandal-free, Sunday morning supplement *Parade,* in a piece by columnist Walter Scott, who told the whole Ethel/June story, and added

that his source was Jack's real father, Don Furcillo-Rose. Jack immediately tracked down his number and placed a phone call directly to
Furcillo-Rose.

When they connected, Jack asked if he was his real father, he said
yes, and added that he had been part of a love triangle between June
and Ethel May, which was the real reason why Ethel May let him occasionally stay at the house after June left.

Jack was understandably shocked. He refused to accept that
Furcillo-Rose was his father.

It didn't take long after the article was published for the phone to
start ringing. Some time later, Jack told his agent to redirect all calls to
his lawyers, who prepared a public statement that was also sent by registered mail to Furcillo-Rose. It said, "Our client [Jack Nicholson] refutes
and repudiates as without foundation the statements by [Furcillo-Rose]
alleging he is Mr. Nicholson's father. Such statements are false and
defamatory." For the longest time, Jack would not discuss any of it with
anybody, and he never again talked to Furcillo-Rose. [2]

JACK'S FRIENDS KNEW that his door was always open to them, even
when he wasn't home. Even when he wasn't in California. Even when
he wasn't in the country. One day early in March, while Jack was in
Aspen, Roman Polanski helped himself to the use of Jack's Mulholland
Drive home and Jacuzzi. In February 1977, seven years after his wife's
murder, Polanski met and was intensely attracted to thirteen-year-old
Samantha Gailey. He was taken by the young girl's beauty and traveled
with her to her home in Woodland Hills, an expensive neighborhood
in the valley, to ask her mother for permission to photograph Samantha for the French edition of *Vogue*. Gailey's mother was not offended;
she was a TV actress, model, and friend of Polanski, and at the time

---

[2] What complicated things further was that when Jack's legal team contacted
Furcillo-Rose and asked him to submit to a blood test that would clear up once
and for all if he was Jack's father, he refused.

nothing seemed out of the ordinary. She agreed, and Polanski took the young Gailey to a nearby outdoor secluded area, where, after taking several photos of her, he persuaded the young girl to pose topless for him, which she did.

A month later, on March 10, 1977, Polanski scheduled another photo session, and this time he took Gailey to Jack's house, knowing Jack was away; he gave her half a Quaalude and a glass of champagne to wash it down—he took the other half—and then had the girl take off all of her clothes and get into the hot tub. He did the same. Afterward, he instructed Gailey to go into the bedroom. Reluctantly, she later told a grand jury, when he joined her, she let him have sex with her.

Their lovemaking was interrupted by a persistent knock at the front door.

That same afternoon, as it happened, knowing Jack was in Aspen, Anjelica had given up on believing in anything that had the words *marriage* and *Jack* in the same sentence. She made their split official when she began moving the things she kept at Jack's Hollywood Hills place to Ryan O'Neal's Malibu beach house.

She thought it might be a good time to go over to his house to get the last of her stuff. As she drove up the left fork, she noticed Polanski's car in the driveway. She didn't think much about it. She knew that Polanski often came over to Jack's, even when he wasn't there. She opened the unlocked front door and called out Polanski's name to let him know it was her. After a few moments, he opened the door to Jack's upstairs bedroom and shouted that he was in there, finishing up a photo shoot.

Anjelica was still in the house when Gailey came out of the bedroom, her clothes and hair disheveled and not looking at all like she was doing a high-fashion modeling session. She talked briefly with Anjelica and then went by herself to Polanski's car, to wait for him to drive her home. A few minutes later Polanski came out of the bedroom, looking similarly unkempt. He mumbled a few words to Anjelica, then left the house, got into his car, and drove away. Anjelica didn't think too much about it; Polanski was a regular visitor to the house, and more than one time she had seen him stoned, and she knew that he liked young-looking women.

Almost immediately after Polanski dropped her off, Gailey called her boyfriend to fill him in on the details of what had just happened: that, according to later grand jury transcripts, Polanski had performed oral, vaginal, and anal sex on her; that they had drunk champagne while nude in the hot tub; and that they had shared a Quaalude. She also claimed none of it happened in Jack Nicholson's house, that when they arrived they heard other voices and Polanski took her instead to a house about a half mile away (this was eventually proven not to be true). It is not clear from the transcripts (and has never been) whether she was disturbed by what had happened or just bragging about it to her boyfriend, especially since she didn't choose to tell her mother. Her sister overheard that phone conversation and told their mother, who then called the police. The next day, both mother and daughter were questioned for several hours, during which the young Gailey insisted that Polanski had forced himself on her. The LAPD then went after Polanski. They apprehended him in the lobby of the Beverly Wilshire Hotel. He did not deny the incident but kept telling the police the sex had been consensual. He claimed that he was the victim of entrapment, that Gailey was the true aggressor, looking to advance her career through him.

Deputy District Attorneys Jim Grodin and David Wells took Polanski back to Jack's house to search for evidence. When they arrived, Anjelica was there, still removing her things. They decided to search her purse, found a half gram of cocaine in it, and arrested her on the spot. They also found some hashish in a container in a bureau in the upstairs master bedroom. (Fortunately, for him, the rest of Jack's ample stash of drugs was so well hidden, in fake shaving cream containers and the like, that the police missed it.)

Polanski was taken to jail and arraigned on six felony charges, including suspicion of raping a thirteen-year-old girl by use of drugs, sodomy, lewd and lascivious acts upon a child under fourteen, and feeding a controlled substance to a minor. He posted $2,500 bail and was released. Anjelica was also charged with illegal possession of cocaine and released on $1,500 bail. The police told reporters that so far they had no reason to believe at the present time that either Jack or Anjelica had any connection to the alleged rape.

When the news reached him in Aspen, Jack booked the next flight back to Los Angeles. Anjelica met him at the airport and she asked if she could stay with him until everything was straightened out. She was frightened and upset. Jack said of course.

On Wednesday, March 23, after four hours of deliberation, Polanski was formally charged by the Los Angeles County Grand Jury, indicted on the same six felony counts, and ordered to surrender to police no later than the following Tuesday. His lawyer managed to get the surrender postponed several times. Anjelica's case, the police said, was now being handled as a separate incident, and her charges were left pending.

Two months later, the district attorney's office dropped all charges against Anjelica. Her lawyer had successfully argued that the amount of cocaine was insufficient for a felony charge and that in any case the police had no right to search her purse that day without a separate warrant.[3]

THREE DAYS AFTER his arrest, Polanski, looking completely unperturbed, was spotted at a Beverly Hills restaurant with another girl who appeared to be little more than a teenager.

ON APRIL 1, despite Jack's ironclad alibi that he was in Aspen when the incident happened, the police wanted him to let them take a set of

---

[3] It remains unclear if Anjelica had agreed to testify against Polanski, as no trial ever took place. She has always vehemently denied that she struck any deal to get her charges dropped, but according to David Thomson, she "gave evidence when Roman Polanski's trouble with the law occurred in Jack's house." Thomson gives no source for his information. The quote is from "Jack Nicholson, King of Mulholland: He Just Wants to Make Nice," *Playgirl*, April 1981.

his fingerprints to see if they matched those found on the container of hashish. Jack refused and insisted he had no idea where that hashish had come from. A few days later, the LAPD was then somehow able to obtain a set of Jack's prints from the Aspen, Colorado, police department (why they had them is not clear), and when they didn't match the prints lifted from the hashish container, they issued a warrant for Jack's arrest and took him into custody so they could get a set of his prints. He was fingerprinted at the station and let go without being charged with anything. The prints matched the set from Aspen, but not those on the hashish box. Whose it was remains a mystery to this day.

The police stayed close to him for weeks after, and let him know it. He found himself on the periphery of one of those major Hollywood scandals that was sure to lead to a media circus, the kind that often hurts everyone pulled into it, even though he was three thousand miles away when the alleged incident had occurred.[4]

To STAY OUT of any more trouble, Jack sequestered himself at his Hollywood home with his art—"my pictures," as he called them. His collection had grown formidable: Tamayo, Modigliani, Botero, Soutine, Matisse, Picasso, a sculpture by Rodin. A hundred million dollars' worth of art leaning against the walls of his simple, half-million-dollar house that was furnished with the same-as-the-day-he-bought-them well-worn armchairs, sink-into sofas, and large soft ottomans.

He was still in no hurry to go back to work, especially after this latest round of controversy, despite the deluge of offers and continual in-depth praise from think-piece critics like Alan Warren, who anointed him as the Bogart of the seventies, having, "the feral energy lurking

---

[4] In August, a still-free Polanski avoided standing trial by copping a plea and being admitted to California's state prison at Chino for a forty-two-day psychiatric evaluation. After his release, the night before he was to be sentenced, he learned the judge was going to break the plea bargain and sentence him to up to twenty years behind bars. Polanski then fled the country and to date has not returned; he remains a criminal fugitive in the eyes of the law. Polanski has never directed another movie in Hollywood.

just beneath the easygoing, almost lazy-appearing exterior, which re-sembles that of Henry or Peter Fonda. He seems laconic, but this is only part of his technique—words do come forth, and when they do they seem always too few and too late, so that they are supercharged with a violent intensity. They seem to come from directly within Nich-olson, not from Nicholson the actor or from Nicholson the scriptwriter. They seem improvised on the spot, just as Brando's lines always do . . ."

Talk of a sequel to *Chinatown* surfaced. Towne had already finished a draft, but after thinking it over Jack said no, preferring to try to get his stalled *Moontrap* project off the ground.

Louis Malle wanted him for *Pretty Baby* opposite Brooke Shields. Jack said no to that too (Keith Carradine eventually got the part). Hal Ashby had landed the plum directing assignment for *Coming Home*, a film about the harsh realities of the Vietnam War, and wanted Jack to star in it. It was a great part, but Jack turned it down as well and sug-gested to Ashby he give the role instead to Dern. Ashby did, only not for the part he wanted Jack for, opposite Jane Fonda as the paraplegic veteran, but as her unsympathetic military husband. The other part went to Jon Voight (who won an Oscar for his performance, as did Fonda for hers).

Andy Warhol had wanted Jack for a film he wanted to direct about Jackson Pollock. And he wanted Anjelica to play Pollock's girlfriend, Ruth Kligman. Jack turned Warhol down too. Even Polanski had a script he somehow thought was perfect for Jack—*Pirates*, a swashbuck-ler. Jack turned it down because it was going to be filmed in Tunisia (it was eventually made in 1986, with Walter Matthau in the role Polanski wanted Jack for, and it bombed badly).

Producer Ron Clark wanted him for a remake of Jack Arnold's 1957 sci-fi classic *The Incredible Shrinking Man*. It was tempting, but Jack said no to that as well. Henry Jaglom was trying to help Orson Welles film what would be his final original script, *The Big Brass Ring*, and asked Jack to be in it, but when he declined, the project stalled. Welles's movie never got made in his lifetime. Steven Spielberg wanted Jack to star in *Close Encounters of the Third Kind*, but Jack said he didn't want to make a flying saucer film. That role went to Richard Dreyfuss.

Michael Douglas had a script that he thought Jack would be great in. Jack said no. The film eventually became 1979's *The China Syndrome* and the part went to Jack Lemmon, whose performance in it earned him an Oscar nomination.

The only offer he was interested in was from Stanley Kubrick, a director whose work Jack greatly admired. Kubrick had called Jack asking if he would be interested in starring in the film version of Stephen King's *The Shining* (to collaborate, really; Kubrick admired Jack's ability as a scriptwriter and was eager for his input in bringing this difficult novel to the screen). Jack said yes immediately. He had missed the chance once before to work with Kubrick on the Napoleon project that never happened; he wasn't going to let another one get away.[5]

Kubrick's career-making films included 1957's neo-Wellesian *Paths of Glory*, produced by and starring Kirk Douglas; 1962's erotically suggestive *Lolita*; 1964's darkly satirical *Dr. Strangelove, or How I Learned to Stop Worrying and Love the Bomb*; 1968's stoney *2001: A Space Odyssey*; 1971's furious *A Clockwork Orange*, based on Anthony Burgess's dark satirical novel; and 1975's period-piece-gone-wrong *Barry Lyndon*. His work had earned him a reputation as a filmmaker who made high-quality movies but worked very slowly. Then, when *The Shining* initially failed to come together, a disappointed Jack said he would always be available to Kubrick to make that film.

Jack flew to New York for a few days prior to his commitment to appear at the April 3, 1978, Oscars to present Best Picture. He wanted to give himself a little sprucing up. He planned to fly back to L.A. the day of the Awards, hand one out, and then try to spend some time with Anjelica. He hadn't seen much of her since the Polanski incident.

Exhausted and alone, Anjelica wouldn't see him after the Oscars, and Jack decided instead to fly to St. Tropez, on the French Riviera, where he was soon seen all over with a young, lithe beauty named Winny-Loo Hardley. When the local paparazzi got wind, he retreated

---

[5] In March 2013 it was announced that the Kubrick estate had made an agreement with Steven Spielberg to film Kubrick's *Napoleon* script. Jack is not involved at this point and not likely to be.

with her to the privacy and protection of producer Sam Spiegel's yacht, where, upon boarding, he dropped his pants and mooned the mob of paparazzi camped on the shore.

A few weeks later, he flew to London and checked into the Connaught Hotel to attend a party that Donald Sutherland was throwing in Jack's honor. There he met up with Mick Jagger and the two spent some time with racehorse owner Nelson Seabra, who had a reputation for being the best gin rummy player in all of Europe. Racing horses and card playing were both things Jack was very familiar with.

From London he flew back to New York, where he slept most of the time during the day, and at night he hung out with Diana Vreeland and the Andy Warhol clique doing the club scene, where cocaine flowed so heavily it seemed as if a permanent blizzard had hit the city. John Phillips, the former husband of Jack's ex-girlfriend Michelle, and one of the most successful singer-songwriters of the sixties, had been caught in the snowstorm and reduced to begging for coke money. Jack later told friends he felt sorry for him.

Back at the hotel Jack took a long hard look at himself in the mirror to find out why Diana hadn't fallen on her knees for him. What he saw was a man who was forty and fat, and nearly bald.

The next day he began another series of painful hair transplants that ultimately didn't take. Youth remained stubbornly elusive.

ANJELICA, MEANWHILE, was having a long talk with her father about her career. Huston was blunt. He told her that at twenty-seven she was a little too old to think about a real career in film, despite the few parts she had done. "I didn't have much confidence at that time in my life, and that comment made a big impact. It hadn't occurred to me that I might be too old."

She was lost in thought driving home after that discussion. She thought her father had been too harsh and not encouraging enough. "Shortly after my chat with my father, I was driving down Coldwater Canyon at dusk when a BMW came very, very fast from up ahead and clipped the bumper of the car in front of me. I watched the whole thing in slow motion. My next memory is headlights, and then I felt a tremendous impact. These were the days before we all wore seat belts, so I smashed against the steering wheel or the windshield. When I reached up to wipe the blood from my face, I had no nose.

"I made it to Cedars-Sinai, where I had a long operation to remove the bone shards from my forehead and skull and reconstruct my nose. When I opened my eyes, Jack was standing there with flowers."

Seeing him did something to her. She felt the love that had faded between them suddenly return. As did her desire to make it as an actress despite what her father had said and how she knew Jack felt. "After that, my thinking turned around. I felt much more capable, receptive, and energized—for the first time, I could see myself as a conqueror. Instead of feeling defensive about my lack of experience, I sought out an acting teacher and started to deepen my knowledge. It was like I'd woken up." She decided she wasn't going to ever live with Jack again, that it was not good for her ego, and she bought a small house for herself, a statement of independence and determination. Reflecting on the move-out further, Anjelica said, "Living with Jack [had become] impossible for me."

JACK HAD BEEN turned on by the thought of working with Kubrick, and when it didn't happen, he accepted the next offer that came his way, to star in and also direct Paramount Pictures' comic western called *Goin' South*. It was scheduled to start shooting immediately on location in Mexico (substituting for Texas). He had waited a long time to step back into his director's shoes and was looking forward to proving he could do it.

The film was co-produced by Jack's old friend Harry Gittes and Harold Schneider, and directed by John Herman Shaner, and it had a boatload of writers, including Shaner, Al Ramrus, Charles Shyer, and Alan Mandel. (That many writers usually means the script is not very strong.) Jack had wanted to do another western, a genre he was familiar with, and thought *Goin' South* might be a good follow-up to *Missouri Breaks*. This time his co-stars would be John Belushi, a comic actor who had made it big on TV's *Saturday Night Live*. He believed Belushi was perfect for the small role of a sleazy sheriff. A completely unknown, the plain-looking Mary Steenburgen, who had studied acting at the Neighborhood Playhouse in New York, was discovered by Jack in Paramount's reception area. He had been looking for an actress who could play the dour but dominating frontierswoman Julie Tate, who saves the life of Henry Lloyd Moon (Jack), a doomed-to-die-by-hanging horse and cattle thief and bank robber. Just before the execution, Julie takes advantage of a little-known Civil War ordinance that allows a woman to save the life of a condemned man by marrying him and taking responsibility for his behavior. It amounts to a form of sexual slavery, without any of the balancing benefit of sexual favors. It was supposed to be funny.

Goin' South, with its tongue in cheek and other places (the title is a slang expression for oral sex), suggests a submissive role for Moon in what amounts to a soft-core S&M relationship, the real theme of the film. Steenburgen, who had previously been a waitress at the Magic Pan, was plucked out of obscurity by Jack for her "quiet, ingenuous aura." Without being beautiful, he said, she was totally seductive.

Before being tested for the film, she had never even been on a soundstage. As she remembered, "I did a screen test and when I hadn't heard anything five days later, I was going to go back to New York. I went to Paramount to get the money they owed me for my hotel bill, and Jack was sitting there, smoking a big cigar and he said, 'Don't worry about it, you're on the payroll.' He stood up for me in so many ways because I was so naïve and so inexperienced about film. He tried to teach me things it had taken him years to learn. He's very generous that way; he takes great delight in other actors doing well."

Whatever feelings of atonement Jack may have had for the way he had treated women in Hollywood in the past (and the way they had treated him), *Goin' South* was equal parts self-victimization and self-atonement, as well as what he saw as the entrapment and ongoing victimization of Polanski. It was rich material, and right in Jack's wheelhouse. Because he had been compared to Bogart for so many years,

Publicity photo of June Nicholson, circa late 1930s to early 1940s. She performed as a dancer under the name June Nilson, an abbreviation of "Nicholson."

Early publicity photo of Don Furcillo, who performed under the name of Don Rose and was the primary love interest of the eighteen-year-old June Nilson.

Ethel May Rhoades, the matriarch of the Nicholson household, and her boyfriend (they never married) and Jack's namesake, John Joseph Nicholson Sr.

The previously undiscovered marriage certificate of Don Furcillo and "Rose Nilson." They married in Maryland, far away from Neptune, to keep the secret from the rest of the family.

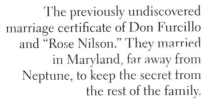

NEW JERSEY STATE DEPARTMENT OF HEALTH
TRENTON, N.J.

September 2, 1987
(Date)

NOTE: If this is a copy of a birth record, any agreement of or differences between the child's surname and the surname of its father does not imply legitimacy or illegitimacy. This is merely a copy of the information supplied for production of the original birth certificate.

THIS IS TO CERTIFY THAT THE FOLLOWING IS A TRUE COPY OF A RECORD FILED IN THIS DEPARTMENT.

Charles A. Harbut
State Registrar of Vital Statistics

WARNING. DO NOT ACCEPT THIS COPY UNLESS THE RAISED SEAL OF THE STATE DEPARTMENT OF HEALTH IS AFFIXED HEREON.

The delayed registration and completely false certificate of birth for Jack Nicholson.

Jack Nicholson, age five.

Jack Nicholson's senior-year high school yearbook photo, Manasquan High School, 1954.

Roger Corman, young
and eager and searching
for his future in film.
Courtesy of Getty Images

An early publicity photo of Sandra
Knight, circa late '50s, before she
became Jack Nicholson's first and
only wife, in 1962.

Promotional poster for Irving
Lerner's 1960 *Studs Lonigan*,
one of Jack's first leading
roles. At twenty-three years
old, he was a handsome, lean,
self-styled Brando-to-be.
Courtesy of Rebel Road Archives

Jack and the Monkees at the Valley Music Hall in Salt Lake City, Utah, May 17, 1968. The Monkees's performance of "Circle Sky" was used in Bob Rafelson's *Head*, released November that same year. *Courtesy of Henry Diltz*

Jack, Davy Jones, and an extremely rare photo of Bob Rafelson. This was taken the same night as above. *Courtesy of Henry Diltz*

A miscast Jack Nicholson in Vincente Minnelli's *On a Clear Day You Can See Forever*, released in 1970 and made before *Easy Rider*.
Courtesy of Getty Images

The iconic image of Jack Nicholson as Bobby Dupea in Bob Rafelson's *Five Easy Pieces. Courtesy of Getty Images*

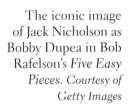

Jack Nicholson and Karen Black in *Five Easy Pieces. Courtesy of Rebel Road Archives*

A scene from Jack's directorial debut, the unsuccessful 1971 *Drive, He Said.*
Courtesy of Rebel Road Archives

Jack and Michelle Phillips, with the love light in her eyes, at the Governor's
Ball following the April 1971 Academy Awards ceremony, just after Jack lost
Best Actor for *Five Easy Pieces* to George C. Scott for his performance in the
title role of Franklin J. Schaffner's *Patton. Courtesy of WireImage*

Lobby card for Mike Nichols's 1971 *Carnal Knowledge*, with Art Garfunkel and Jack. *Courtesy of Rebel Road Archives*

Candice Bergen and Jack in a scene from *Carnal Knowledge*.
Courtesy of Rebel Road Archives

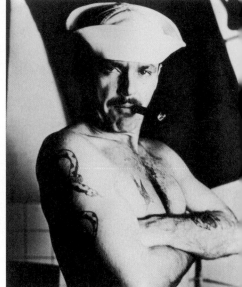

Jack as "Badass" Buddusky in
Hal Ashby's 1973 *The Last Detail.*
Courtesy of Rebel Road Archives

Jack and "Dernsie" in
Bob Rafelson's 1972
*The King of Marvin
Gardens. Courtesy of
Getty Images*

Jack signing his name
at Grauman's Chinese
Theater, June 1974.
Courtesy of Getty Images

Co-star, father figure, and potential father-in-law John Huston with Jack Nicholson in Roman Polanski's 1974 *Chinatown. Courtesy of Getty Images*

Chinatown.
Courtesy of Rebel Road Archives

Jack by the pool in the only house he ever owned, on Mulholland Drive near the top of the Hollywood Hills. In the background is his daughter, Jennifer (mother Sandra), July 1974. *Courtesy of Getty Images*

The highlight of Jack's 1975 run, Miloš Forman's *One Flew Over the Cuckoo's Nest*. The film was the first in forty-one years to win all four major Oscars. The recipients, left to right: producer Michael Douglas, director Miloš Forman, actress Louise Fletcher, Jack, producer Saul Zaentz. *Courtesy of Rebel Road Archives*

Jack and Stockard Channing in Mike Nichols's 1975 misfire *The Fortune. Courtesy of Rebel Road Archives*

Jack and Maria Schneider in Michelangelo Antonioni's 1975 release, *The Passenger*, about a neo-Hitchcockian hero in search of his own identity. *Courtesy of Rebel Road Archives*

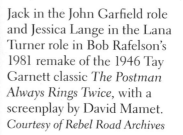

Jack in the John Garfield role and Jessica Lange in the Lana Turner role in Bob Rafelson's 1981 remake of the 1946 Tay Garnett classic *The Postman Always Rings Twice*, with a screenplay by David Mamet. *Courtesy of Rebel Road Archives*

Jack as Eugene O'Neill in Warren Beatty's epic 1981 *Reds*, for which he was nominated for Best Supporting Actor. *Courtesy of Rebel Road Archives*

Jack, Shirley MacLaine, and James L. Brooks posing with their Oscars for Brooks's 1983 *Terms of Endearment*. *Courtesy of WireImage*

Jack and Anjelica Huston, his longest and most meaningful romantic relationship, pictured here in 1985. *Courtesy of Time Life Pictures/Getty Images*

Kathleen Turner and Jack Nicholson as loving killers killing lovers in John Huston's endlessly entertaining *Prizzi's Honor*. *Courtesy of Rebel Road Archives*

Jack and director Rob Reiner, 1992's *A Few Good Men*.
Courtesy of Rebel Road Archives

Jack in character to play the title role of 1992's *Hoffa*, directed by his good friend Danny DeVito. Two TV actors and two dark characters in one year.
Courtesy of Rebel Road Archives

Jack and Rebecca Broussard, the mother of two of his children. Although she wanted to, they were never married to each other. *Courtesy of Time/Life Pictures/Getty Images*

Jack Nicholson with Kellita Smith (left) and Priscilla Barnes in Sean Penn's 1995 *The Crossing Guard. Courtesy of Rebel Road Archives*

Jack with Lara Flynn Boyle attending the premiere of Alexander Payne's *About Schmidt*. *Courtesy of WireImage*

Three stars and one director—Jack, Mark Wahlberg, and Martin Scorsese at the Warner Bros. premiere of *The Departed*, September 26, 2006, at the Ziegfeld Theater in Manhattan, New York. Jack appears to still be in character. *Courtesy of Getty Images*

here was his chance to emulate not just the great actor but the great actor's role in Huston's 1951 *The African Queen,* a film *Goin' South* resembled in some ways. Along the way Julie reforms Henry by teaching him true Christian values. Jack filled out *Goin' South* with a lot of his pals in cameo roles—many from the *Cuckoo's Nest* ensemble, including Danny DeVito and Christopher Lloyd.

Despite his training at the feet of Corman and the BBS boys, where brevity was king and a second take was thought of as extraneous, while directing this film Jack reshot almost every scene, and if an actor was not happy with a take, he would gladly shoot the whole thing again.

Jack was energized by holding the director's stick, the first time since 1971's *Drive, He Said.* At two every morning, when the rest of the cast and crew were exhausted from the heat and bitten to distraction by bugs, Jack was rarin' to go. He often stayed up all night marking out scenes, camera angles, lighting, and so forth. It was Gittes who finally tried to put the brakes on Jack, for the sake of the film's budget and to get this thing done before Paramount, unhappy with the slow pace of progress, pulled the plug. Discussing the next day's shoot, Gittes told him, "All we can hope for is that next year, this picture won't just be another faded T-shirt."

If Jack was excited about the film, he was also nervous, and for good reason. On the other side of forty, he appears for the first time as a middle-aged character actor, without a trace of the lean and hungry good-looking rebel that defined so many of his earlier roles. He comes off in the film as quirky, goofy, and weirdly off-pace, which may be partly attributed to lingering injuries to his left hand and several ribs after being thrown from a horse and partly because of the excessive heat, the militant mosquitoes, and an extremely dry throat he kept trying to quench with tequila rather than water. Worse, John Belushi was in the throes of a drug addiction that kept him from showing up on time, and his erratic behavior started to get to Jack. One day when Belushi failed to show, Jack found him sleeping and threatened to fire him, or kill him, or both.

Paramount, meanwhile, after seeing the first round of rushes, wanted Jack to hurry up and finish it. Nobody in the screening room liked his frankly weird performance, Steenburgen's lack of sex appeal, and Belushi's bizarre acting. In his own defense, Jack tried to explain, rather sheepishly, that "actually, I was trying to do a kind of Clark Gable spin on the character."

SHORTLY AFTER he finished *Goin' South*, Jack received word from Kubrick that he was to arrive in London the last week in June 1978 to begin work on *The Shining*. After two years, Kubrick's screen adaptation of the Stephen King novel was finally going into production with a scheduled twenty-five-week shoot.

THE FILM WAS shot between May 1978 and February 1979 on the soundstages of London's EMI-Elstree Studios in Borehamwood, Hertfordshire. When Jack first arrived, he was put up at the Dorchester but was moved at his request by the film's distributor, Warner Bros., to a little house on the Thames, which Jack greatly preferred to a hotel swarming with paparazzi.

No sooner did he arrive than a parade of friends stopped by to visit. Harry Dean Stanton was in town shooting Ridley Scott's ten-little-Indians-in-outer-space sci-fi thriller *Alien* and became a frequent visitor, usually with a couple of girls. Bob Dylan always came alone. Mick Jagger, like Harry Dean, brought girls instead of flowers. George Harrison and John Lennon came by at various times to hang out, sing, eat, and joke around, turning Jack's London dwelling into an informal, ongoing salon-on-the-Thames.

Early on during his stay in London, Jack met Margaret Trudeau, the estranged wife of Canada's prime minister, fresh from her dalliance with Mick Jagger (who made the introduction). They fell into a hot and heavy affair that ended when Jack took up with Christina Onassis, the wealthy, overweight daughter of the Greek shipping magnate. There were also affairs with Melanie Griffith and Jill St. John, all of which kept him going during the long production and contributed to his back problems exacerbated by an on-set accident that at times left him unable to get out of bed and caused him to miss a couple of days' work on the film. Jack's happyland carousel reconvened when Bianca Jagger eagerly took over nursing duties.

The shoot proved long and difficult for everyone except Kubrick. The screenplay, co-written by Diane Johnson, took so long to film that they had to share studio space with two other films scheduled to be in that studio space after *The Shining*—Irvin Kersher's *The Empire Strikes Back* and Mike Hodges's *Flash Gordon*.

Kubrick, the perfectionist, wanted everything onscreen to look and sound perfect. That was why he often did forty or more takes of a single shot, sometimes one hundred, which Jack found tedious and unnecessary, despite the fact that he had done precisely the same thing on *Goin' South*. As a director, Jack understood the quest for perfection, but as an actor he felt his best stuff came in the first few takes, after which he lost the intensity and the reality of the moment.

Seen through Kubrick's creative lens, *The Shining* looked like what it was, a weird horror story, cut with moments of high humor, like Jack's memorable "Heerrrrre's Johnny!" punch line, a 1970s reference to TV talk show host Johnny Carson (Jack later said it was his comment on television, which he still felt was a nightmare medium).

As SHOOTING WOUND down, Kubrick said he needed a few days off to figure out how to use the newly developed Steadicam—a camera that could be handheld without showing visible shaking on the screen—to frame some key tracking shots. Jack took the opportunity to fly to New York for the October 6, 1978, opening of *Goin' South*. Seen from the distance of time, it was now clear to Jack that the film was a dud, a conclusion shared by all the critics after its official opening. Pauline Kael, sharpening her knives, was particularly outraged by Jack's character's "working his mouth with tongue darting out and dangling lewdly. He's like an advertisement for a porno film." The next part of her review eviscerated his directing: "Wasn't there anybody on the set who'd tell Nicholson to give it a rest? An actor-director who prances about the screen maniacally can easily fool himself into thinking that his film is jumping. Nicholson jumps in *Goin' South*, all right, but *Goin' South* is inert." The film opened and closed quickly. The only good reviews it received were for Steenburgen's performance, but she did not have the kind of star power needed to save the film. Made for $6 million, it grossed less than $8 million in its initial domestic release.

Jack was more upset about the film's commercial failure as a director than he was as an actor. He had yet to direct a film that the public accepted. He was determined to keep trying until he got it right.

He returned to London after Christmas, delaying his departure so he could celebrate the holidays in the States, which may have been at least partly an excuse not to have to go back to work on *The Shining*. He had, by now, lost all enthusiasm for the film and Kubrick's wearying perfectionism. When he did finally return in January, he wasn't there very long before a fire gutted one of *The Shining*'s major sets, further delaying the production. What had originally been a scheduled December 1979 opening was pushed back until Easter 1980, and then only if Kubrick could finish the film in time.

Kubrick finally completed *The Shining* late in February, and Jack immediately returned to L.A., where he was met with a flood of new offers. Hal Ashby wanted him to co-star with Clint Eastwood in a filmed version of Richard Brautigan's Gothic western novel *The Hawkline Monster*, but Jack turned Ashby down to work with Warren Beatty, who was producing, directing, and starring in an epic based on the life of John Reed called *Reds*, co-starring Beatty's then real-life girlfriend, Diane Keaton ("Special K" in Jackspeak) as Reed's real-life girlfriend, Louise Bryant. Beatty wanted Jack to play the small but important role of Eugene O'Neill but didn't tell him so right away. They were great pals, but women, not filmmaking, was their most shared obsession, which sometimes got between them. Michelle Phillips, Jack's former live-in, had taken up with Beatty after she left Jack. Warren didn't want to lose him for the film over the Phillips affair, so he came up with a scheme straight out of Tom Sawyer; he wouldn't ask Jack to play O'Neill, he would get Jack to ask him.

He invited Jack to a casting session, ostensibly to find the right actor to play O'Neill. During it, Beatty told Jack, "I've got to get an actor to play Eugene O'Neill and it's got to be somebody who leaves not a shadow of a doubt that he could take Diane away from me," to which Jack replied, grinning, "Well, you have no choice. There's only one person—me!"

According to reports in the press, *Playgirl*, and other such bastions of journalism, Jack really believed he could take Keaton away from Beatty, payback for Beatty's having gone with Phillips. The result was that Warren played opposite Keaton onscreen and in real life, with Jack trying to steal her onscreen *and* in real life.

If Beatty knew what Jack was up to, it didn't bother him. He was so deeply involved with the making of the film that if he did know, he likely thought it added to the level of dramatic tension and conflict between Reed and Bryant, Beatty and Keaton, O'Neill and Bryant, Jack and Keaton, Reed and O'Neill, and Jack and Warren. To complicate matters further, Jack developed a real-life crush on Keaton, although he always maintained that nothing ever happened between them, and that the attraction was a product of his Method-immersion style of creating a character.

Jack tried to make light of all of it. "I get such a bang out of Warren, I mean he's so funny I can't sit still . . . I was meant to be in love with Miss Keaton, which isn't hard. I had 'The Pro' there as my boss and I was playing a real fascinating character so I had a good time."

Jack returned to London to film his scenes for *Reds* during the summer of 1979; Beatty had sets built there to stand in for Provincetown. He threw himself into the part of O'Neill with a quiet intensity that he had not put on display since *Five Easy Pieces*. He was nearly a decade older now than he was when he played Bobby Dupea, which gave both his face and his body the gravitas that he hadn't had before.

To prepare for the role, he met with Oona O'Neill, the playwright's daughter, who was married to Charlie Chaplin. To arrange it, Jack went to Bert Schneider, who made the connection. Schneider had been the one who'd heralded Chaplin's triumphant return to America in 1972 to receive an honorary Oscar after being exiled during the blacklisting era. Oona was happy to do whatever Bert asked, including meeting with Jack. He later hinted that he also based at least part of his mustachioed character on his early memories of John Nicholson Sr.[6]

DURING BREAKS IN filming, Jack made several visits to Paris to visit Polanski, now living there. Jack volunteered to escort the fugitive director back to the States, something Polanski had suggested he might agree to at the Cannes Film Festival in May that year if he got a guarantee of either probation or minimal jail time. Without it, Polanski said, he had to remain, at least for the time being, a fugitive.

He didn't get it and he didn't go back.

Also while in London, Jack visited Kubrick to discuss *The Shining*'s rescheduled May 1980 release. Despite their artistic differences, Jack and Kubrick remained good friends, so much so that afterward, Jack regularly sent tapes of Lakers games to the expat director, who, because of working with Jack, had become a basketball fanatic.

As the seventies cross-faded into the eighties, Jack was now firmly a part of the Hollywood mainstream, a champion driver in its fabulous fast lane, reckless and daring and unafraid of anyone or anything. When Jack was asked by a fan at an airport what made him a superstar, without breaking stride, Jack smiled and said, "I'm not a superstar. I'm a *Mega*-star!"

---

[6] Oona loved Jack's portrayal and wrote Jack a note to tell him so: "After a lifetime of acquired indifference the inevitable finally happened. Thanks to you, dear Jack, I fell in love with my father." Jack called it "the greatest compliment I ever got."—Both the letter and Jack's reply are from Chris Chase, "At the Movies," *New York Times*, February 5, 1982.

"I'm not much for birthdays . . . In 1972 I eliminated all years from my life. I don't keep track of anything by years or weeks. I call it my living experiment . . . I'm unemployed with no irons in the fire . . . the good ones don't make a movie a year . . . they wait . . ."

—JACK NICHOLSON

J ACK WAS NOTHING IF NOT LOYAL. HE NEVER FORGOT HIS FRIENDS, especially those who struggled with him in the early days and those who helped him get to where he was. That was why when Bob Rafelson again asked Jack to play the John Garfield role in a 1980s remake of Tay Garnett's 1946 film adaptation for MGM of James M. Cain's tale of sexual betrayal and brutal murder, *The Postman Always Rings Twice*, he still couldn't say no.

As it happened, Jack had been looking for a role that would allow him to bring a more complex, adult sexual aspect to the screen than his recent films. Except for Eugene O'Neill in *Reds*, which wasn't a leading role, he hadn't played a sexual character in a feature film since Jonathan in *Carnal Knowledge*. "I hadn't done a lot of sexual acting— for lack of a better word—and it's something I always felt I did well, in classes and workshops . . . in life, as in films, it's a relatively unexplored area that's extremely ritualized with convention." Frank Chambers was a twisted sexual being, morally decrepit and stuffed with lust. Jack shared certain sexual interests with the character, who had a weakness for young and beautiful women and sex on top of kitchen tables. Jack could connect to Chambers as an actor and as a man.

This was his fourth film with Rafelson, who was desperately in need of a hit. Things had not gone well for him since Schneider had dissolved BBS and become something of a recluse. Rafelson, on the other hand, wanted to keep making movies, but his style of small, personal early 1970s filmmaking had fallen out of fashion in Hollywood. Rafelson made only one film in the seven years after the commercial failure of *Marvin Gardens.* He was never that well liked even at the height of his success. He was rough-hewn, quick-tempered, and confrontational. Henry Jaglom thinks he remembers seeing Rafelson throw somebody he was arguing with down a flight of stairs during the making of a film.

There were other reasons for his absence from the industry. In 1973, a year after he directed *The King of Marvin Gardens,* Rafelson's daughter died in a gas explosion accident at his Aspen home. Shortly thereafter, his wife, Toby, was diagnosed with cancer. She eventually recovered, but her brush with death made her rethink her marriage strewn with the years of infidelity she had endured. She decided to legally separate from Rafelson. Three years passed before he made another movie, *Stay Hungry,* starring Jeff Bridges, Sally Field, Arnold Schwarzenegger, and Scatman Crothers. During filming, Rafelson had an affair with Field, and when Toby found out, she filed for divorce. The film did only moderately well, and four more years passed before he got another shot to direct. That film was *Brubaker,* starring Robert Redford. Rafelson was fired after ten days. Word was that Redford didn't like Rafelson's manner and had him replaced by the far less demonstrative Stuart Rosenberg, a journeyman director and former film editor who was content to let Redford call the shots.

Rafelson's next, possibly last chance to direct was this remake of *Postman,* for Paramount (Lorimar Productions). Jack was one of the few actors in the industry willing to work with Rafelson; most thought he was too tough and his style dated. Jack knew he held the balance of power and Rafelson couldn't pull his bully tactics with him. If he did, his star would simply walk out and never return. Jack asked for and got $3 million, fully one-third of the film's relatively modest $9 million budget, all that Paramount was willing to risk on Rafelson. There was loyalty and there was loyalty. If he was going to do a favor for Rafelson, Rafelson was going to have to show his appreciation. He agreed to Jack's price because he had no choice. and on December 4, 1979, the completed deal was announced in the trades. In typical boastful fashion, Rafelson declared in print that *Postman* would be "the most erotic movie I've ever conceived!"[1]

Jack's co-star was Jessica Lange, but she wasn't the studio's first choice. They were pushing for Raquel Welch until Jack said no. He didn't think she projected any heat. He preferred Meryl Streep, and she almost signed on, until she learned she was pregnant and had to bow out. Diane Keaton and Debra Winger, at the peak of their careers, were both turned down by Jack. When he again suggested Lange, this time the studio said yes.

The chance to work with Jack had almost happened once before, when Lange auditioned for *Goin' South*, and while Jack didn't give her the role, believing she was too glamorous, he did want her this time for the role of Cora Smith, played by Lana Turner in the 1946 version of the film.[2] Jack wanted her for the "terrific farm girl-goes-to-the-city aura about her; she's solid and substantial with a kind of rolling femaleness."

Jack's salary was announced in the trades; Lange's too and was considerably less. She was fairly new to movies, a blond beauty who had made only three films, beginning with the unfortunate 1976 remake of *King Kong*, directed by John Guillermin. Despite winning a Golden Globe for New Star of the Year for a role made famous in the original by Fay Wray, Lange did not see herself as a mindless bimbo and turned down so many of those roles that she didn't make another film for three years. Lange returned to the big screen in Bob Fosse's sensational 1979 autobiographical *All That Jazz,* in which she played Angelique, the gorgeous Angel of Death. The film was an Oscar-winning hit, but the next year she took a step back, appearing in Robert Scheerer's forgettably lowbrow female caper film *How to Beat the High Co$t of Living.* When the opportunity to do *Postman* came along, Lange jumped at it, believ-

---

[1] The film had a censorship battle prior to release. In order to receive an R rating, some of the hottest scenes—and there were several—were cut out of the theatrical version and restored for the videocassette and DVD versions.

[2] The original 1934 novel was remade three times: Luchino Visconte's 1942 Italian *Obsessione,* Tay Garnett's 1946 *The Postman Always Rings Twice,* and Rafelson's 1981 version, starring Jack Nicholson and Jessica Lange.

ing that playing opposite Jack Nicholson could be her breakout film as a leading lady.

Rafelson wanted Jim Harrison to write the screenplay but he had a three-picture contract with Paramount and was unavailable. Jack then suggested the edgy, tough-writing David Mamet, winner of the New York Drama Critics Circle and Obie awards for his play *American Buffalo* (a future Pulitzer Prize recipient for 1984's stage version of *Glengarry Glen Ross*). Mamet took the assignment and finished his script in January 1980.

At Jack's urging, Rafelson gave the cast an unusually long five-month rehearsal time. Jack was after the same sense of intensity and continuity that shooting in sequence had given *Five Easy Pieces*. The flow of the script's locations made that impossible, and Jack suggested to Rafelson that he use long single takes and fewer takes wherever possible. Rafelson acquiesced. He may have been the official director of the film, but Jack was obviously pulling all the strings. Rafelson gave Jack his head to get the film made.

The director hired Sven Nykvist, Ingmar Bergman's favorite cinematographer, to help create moody dark-and-light, faded-color neo-noir atmospherics. All the while Jack pushed Mamet to emphasize the film's sexual theme in his script.

The story takes place some time during the Great Depression and begins when a drifter, Frank Chambers (Jack), stops at a California roadside diner somewhere off the beaten track, operated by a luscious young woman, Cora Smith (Lange), unhappily (and inexplicably) married to a much older, unattractive man, Nick Papadakis (John Colicos). The age difference between Nick and Cora explains why she is sexually unfulfilled, like a widow with a living dead husband, longing to be reheated, and soon is, by the blackest of cards. She hires Frank to help out around the diner.

Cora has designs on improving the place as a way of upgrading her own life, while Frank has designs on her. Nick, a bitter man with no ambition just looking to get by, wants to keep it the way it is. In a highly erotic scene, while Nick is upstairs half drunk, Frank seduces Cora (or Cora seduces him). They make passionate love, fully clothed but highly suggestive, over a kitchen table.

They are soon plotting to kill Nick. They pull it off and are quickly arrested and put on trial. The clumsy DA loses the case to a clever lawyer, and the two go free. Not long after, celebrating their victory, they get in a car accident. Cora is killed, leaving Frank free but alone.

Mamet's script is seamy and lowlife, but it left out a vital part of the original novel and the 1946 film version, and by doing so took the power out of the story. In those versions, after the fatal car crash, Frank is arrested for the murder of Cora, although this time, ironically, he is innocent. Nonetheless, he is tried, found guilty, and sentenced to death. Frank's last lines as he is going to his death are "You forget that the postman always rings twice. Yeah. He rang twice for Cora and now he's ringing twice for me," the memorable metaphorical title phrase.[3] The novel (as the Garnett version does, but not Rafelson's) begins on death row, with Frank recalling the events that led him there. One thinks immediately of the other great seduction/husband killer/weak male/strong woman movie of the 1940s, Billy Wilder's brilliant adaptation of James M. Cain's 1944 novella, the remarkably similar and far superior, both on the page and screen, *Double Indemnity*.[4]

Mamet and Rafelson may have felt Garnett's final sequence too preachy and unambivalent (one could see Cora's death as punishment enough). Rafelson's version only has the sound of sirens in the background as Frank realizes Cora is dead, and it is a stretch to believe audiences could, or would, fill in that many blanks. In Rafelson's version, Nick's hysterical, weakly out-of-character self-pity, weeping at the side

---

[3] The film's title originally had nothing to do with the plot of the novel. According to Cain, the title came from his anxiety waiting for the postman to bring him news of whether he had sold a manuscript. He knew when the postman arrived because it was his habit to always ring twice, in two short pushes on the doorbell.

[4] *Double Indemnity* was written nine years after *The Postman Always Rings Twice*. It is essentially an updated version of *Postman*, filmed two years before Garnett's 1946 adaptation. The decision to film *Postman* was based, in part, on the enormous success of *Double Indemnity*.

of Cora's corpse, reflects on the loss of her hot body, not the mourning for her lost soul.

The emphasis with Rafelson was on sex, but Mamet's script, as directed by Rafelson, didn't have any of the sadomasochistic elements of the original 1934 novel. Because the sex is explicit but unconvincing in the Rafelson film, all of that is lost. One great touch in Jack's film: they celebrate Nick's murder with a candlelit dinner. Their cold-bloodedness is striking enough; the dinner is startlingly romantic and represents the restaurant Cora hopes she will realize from the murder.

Jack not only was well aware of what the film required emotionally but welcomed an attempt to reclaim some of his own fading onscreen sex appeal. "I did *Postman* because I hadn't come down the middle with the fastball about sex in a movie. The whole reason for [making it] is sex, and that's why I wanted to do it . . . the obligatory scene in *Postman* happens when the two kill her husband and she gets so hot she has to fuck right then and there . . . I like the idea that there is not a speck of nudity in *Postman* . . ."

Perhaps to keep his very real attraction for Lange in check, or maybe just to help Anjelica's career, and his relationship with her, improve, Jack insisted that Rafelson cast her in the role of Madge, a whip-cracking lion-taming German temptress, of all things, a small but highly suggestive role, intimating that Jack's character (if not Jack himself) was into showing off a little of his freak side, the only time in the film he does.

Anjelica jumped at the chance to be in the film, even if the role had nothng to do with the plot, and its sheer bizzareness broke the mood of the film. Five years had passed since her last onscreen appearance.

Soon after filming ended, Jack described their on-and-off relationship this way: "I've always viewed [us] as Jean-Paul Sartre and Simone de Beauvoir . . . I respect her more than I do other women and there's something about the way she is that I just adore . . . [but] if you told me twenty years ago that some woman could go off and fuck one of my best friends [Ryan O'Neal] and I'd end up reading about it in newspapers, and that four years later I wouldn't even give a shit, I'd say, 'You're talking to the wrong guy here. That's not the way I am. I might want to be that guy, but I'm not.' Now, I am."

During a break in filming, Jack flew alone to New York for the highly anticipated May 23, 1980, Memorial Day weekend opening of *The Shining*. He was seen around town with Diane Keaton and took her to an advance screening of the film while Beatty was off in Spain, still shooting a few remaining scenes for *Reds*. On the way to the screening, Jack and Diane got stuck in an elevator with TV talk show host Dick Cavett. After they were finally freed, they all went to the screening, and afterward Jack and Diane did the town, hitting, among other places, the then-popular disco Xenon, where it was certain they would be seen by the paparazzi. Jack gleefully smiled for every photographer, always with his arm around Keaton, knowing that Beatty would surely see these photos.

The next day, Jack underwent yet another round of hair transplants. Not only was his hair still receding, but his weight problem had gotten out of hand. He was not into exercise and all those enchiladas had added up. He had starved himself to look believable as a lover in *Postman*, but nonetheless, at forty-three, he had a belly the size of a basketball that, despite all his efforts, was getting bigger. And he needed his first pair of reading glasses.

WARNER BROS., *The Shining*'s distributor, had hoped the film, the first major release of the summer season, would bring the studio a big take at the box office. The night of the gala holiday weekend opening, Jack skipped out of the premiere once the film started to attend a party thrown by Mick Jagger. Shortly after arriving, Jack laid eyes on Playmate model Bebe Buell, one of the hottest and most notorious rock groupies of the day. Her major talent for driving famous men crazy worked perfectly on Jack. Elvis Costello was among the many performers who had once fallen for Buell, and after she left him he wrote some of his best, most bitter songs about her.[5] Jack wanted her badly that night, and could have had her, except he also found himself attracted

---

[5] Many believe "Alison" and "Party Girl" were written about Buell, but Costello has always denied this.

to sultry actress Rachel Ward. They retired to one of the bedrooms in Jagger's hotel suite and didn't come out until the next morning.

Jack then decided he still wanted Buell and sent her roses every hour on the hour to try to persuade her to hook up. Not surprisingly, word of Jack's pursuit hit the trades, and by the time he returned to L.A. to finish *Postman*, Anjelica was furious, not about his dalliance with Buell, but Jack's being the secret father of Susan Anspach's love child. Anspach had revealed it to the press in terms that were quite convincing. Despite the fact that Jack and Anspach's affair had ended with the completion of production on *Pieces* and she had married someone else (whom she later divorced), Anjelica, who wanted a child more than anything, was out of her mind with anger.

After Anspach's announcement, Jack was asked by the press where his relationship stood with Anjelica, and he was unusually frank with them, if not entirely honest, perhaps in an attempt to mend some fences and soothe some wounds. Of their seven-year-on-and-off and at times tumultuous relationship, he declared, "I certainly would say she's the love of my life . . . we've striven for a straightforward, honest, yet mature relationship . . . she has had to do the hardest work in that area because I'm the one who is so easily gossiped about . . . there are other women in my life who are simply friends of mine. Most of the credit for our wonderfully successful relationship has to do with her flexibility. I ask her to marry me all the time. Sometimes she turns me down, sometimes she says yes. We don't get around to it . . ."

Despite *The Shining*'s disappointing reviews—Pauline Kael in the *New Yorker* described Jack's performance as "cramped, slightly robotized," and David Denby in *New York Magazine* called the film "stiff and pompous"—only Andrew Sarris, a critic not overly fond of Kubrick, liked the film enough to place it at number twenty on his best-films-of-the-year column in the *Village Voice*. *The Shining* earned $44 million in its initial domestic release, from the studio's original investment of $19 million. Good, not great. It was the fourteenth-highest-grossing film of the year (Irvin Kershner's *The Empire Strikes Back* was the highest, with a $209 million gross), but not the blockbuster that Warners,

Kubrick, or Jack had hoped for. That put even more importance on *Postman* to be the big hit he needed it to be.

BACK IN L.A. to finish filming and his scenes, Jack, still smarting over his reviews for *The Shining*, and trying to adjust to his latest clash with Anjelica, was contacted by director Tony Richardson about being in *The Border*, to be filmed in El Paso and Guatemala that summer, co-starring Harvey Keitel and Warren Oates. Jack said yes, making it his fifth film in three years following his vow to take it easy after he won the Oscar. He chose *The Border* over an offer by Miloš Forman to be in his *Ragtime*. Although he had loved working with Forman on *Cuckoo's Nest*, he didn't want to be in another large-cast ensemble movie. Because Forman was a friend, Jack did agree to make an unbilled appearance in the film as a pirate at the beach. But his focus was on *The Border*.

Jack had never worked with the British-born Richardson before but loved *The Border*'s script, which was why he wanted to star in it. It was Richardson's twenty-second film, on a résumé sprinkled with a fair number of jewels that included the 1959 movie version of John Osborne's *Look Back in Anger*, *The Entertainer* (1960—another Osborne adaptation), *A Taste of Honey* (1961), and *Tom Jones* (1963).

The Border, with its modest budget of $4.5 million (that escalated to a whopping $22 million before the film was finished), was originally conceived as a small film about the personal and professional problems of INS patrolman Charlie Smith, a part (and a film) originally written for actor Robert Blake, Jack's onetime love rival. Blake, however, had a habit of always seeming to alienate the money people, part of his bizarre personality that for most of his career made him his own worst enemy. When he said the wrong thing to one of the executives at Universal during preproduction (reportedly "Go fuck yourself") and then angrily criticized the studio during an outburst on *The Tonight Show with Johnny Carson*, not only was he summarily fired from the film, but Carson, then the most powerful entertainer on TV, who abhorred anyone who brought controversy to his show, barred him from ever again appearing on it. Richardson then called Jack, who had had no love for Blake and agreed to do the film if its budget was increased to include his asking salary of $6 million. Universal agreed, believing, correctly, that Jack was a much more bankable star than Blake.

With the delay caused by Blake's firing and Jack's hiring, the producers tried to rush into production so that filming could begin two weeks before a threatened July 1980 Screen Actors Guild (SAG) strike. Any film that went into production before the strike started was allowed to finish. Unfortunately, they didn't make the deadline and the film was delayed.

Jack welcomed the break. The back injury he had suffered during the making of *The Shining* was bothering him again. The day after the work stoppage, he flew to St. Tropez and spent the remainder of the summer recuperating in France on Sam Spiegel's yacht.

While there, Jack was contacted by John Huston, who wanted him to play Rooster Hannigan in the film version of the musical *Annie*. Jack liked the idea and a deal was in the making until Carol Burnett, the film's Miss Hannigan, a well-known anti-drug crusader, rejected him because of his casual dismissal about all the concern over drugs in an interview that appeared in the July 28, 1980, issue of *People*, where he was quoted as having said they were no big thing. In its August 18 issue, the magazine published an open letter to Jack from Burnett: "Dear Jack, Drugs 'Ain't no big thing?' Maybe not in your home. With love and hope, Carol Burnett." His part went instead to Tim Curry.

That fall, with the strike settled, Jack returned to Mexico to shoot *The Border*. As production proceeded, Jack became increasingly convinced *The Border* was not going to be the film he had hoped it would be.

By the March 20, 1981, New York premiere of *Postman*, Jack had lost twenty pounds by enlisting the services of Judy Mazel, of *The Beverly Hills Diet* book fame; she was known throughout Hollywood as the "dietrix to the stars." She told W magazine that she did most of her work with Jack by phone, talking to him as often as eight times a day. She said she had uncovered his biggest problem: "He can go only so many days without enchiladas."

Still, the weight came off, his latest round of transplants were taking, and he looked and felt better than he had in years. He began to recover his old swagger, until *Postman* opened to mixed-to-poor reviews that were particularly hard on his portrayal of Frank. Richard Corliss wrote in *Time*: "Nicholson's performance as Frank is studied . . . the dashing star of a decade ago has dared to inhabit the molting seediness of the character actor . . ." *Newsweek*'s David Ansen wrote: "The [film's] problems may be traced to the miscasting of Jack Nicholson . . . [who] is a bit too old for the part . . ." Stanley Kauffmann wrote in *Commentary*: "[Jack] looks a good deal of the time as if he hadn't recovered from the *Cuckoo's Nest* lobotomy." And this came from Pauline Kael: "[Jack's] performance could have been given by a Nicholson impersonator." Others attacked what they claimed were Jack's overly imitative 1940s Bogart style of acting. The consensus: in this version, the postman only rang once.

The film earned only $12 million in its initial domestic release, less than its negative cost, a blow to Jack's desire to remain relevant in a business where he had once been king of the hill. Only six years after his bravura performance and Oscar win for *Cuckoo's Nest*, the hard truth was that Jack's name was no longer enough to automatically guarantee the financing of a big-budget film. He signed on for something called *Roadshow* that would reunite him with Mary Steenburgen, but when several directors passed, including Martin Britt and Richard Brooks, MGM, despite Jack's commitment, canceled the project.[6]

JACK WAS LOSING it and he knew it. He went to see John Huston for a heart-to-heart. Huston and Jack had remained close, despite Jack's bumpy ride with Anjelica. Huston told Jack to stop making films for a while and try to do a little rose-smelling. The last thing he wanted

---

[6] Jack would make six out of seven unsuccessful films after *Cuckoo's Nest: The Missouri Breaks, The Last Tycoon, Goin' South, The Shining* (which underperformed but managed a small profit), *The Postman Always Rings Twice* (also eventually produced a minimal profit), the forth coming *Reds* (which would be a modest hit), and *The Border*, the latter yet to be released.

to do, Huston warned, was to turn into an actor whose films didn't matter.

THAT JUNE, THREE months after the disastrous opening of *Postman*, Jack boarded a plane bound for Hawaii to visit his daughter, Jennifer, now seventeen and graduating from Punahou High School with plans to attend USC. Jack wanted to be there to see it. He had missed so much of her childhood in the years when traveling back and forth from Hawaii was prohibitive.

When he returned to Los Angeles, he was determined to crawl out from underneath the weight of Jack the movie star and try to rediscover Jack the man. To do so, he took another extended hiatus and didn't make a movie for two years. Between 1981 and 1983, whenever Jack was asked why, his stock answer was that he simply hadn't found anything good enough, or that he was holed up in Aspen working on a screenplay.

In January 1982, Jack briefly emerged from his self-imposed semi-isolation to do some minimal contractual promotion for *The Border*, a fruitless task he hadn't wanted to do but he was committed to when he signed on. The film received mostly negative reviews, which, like those of *Postman*, once again centered on Jack's performance more than they did on the movie as a whole. Typical was David Ehrenstein's piece in the *L.A. Reader*: "Even if we were given an explanation [to the film's Clint Eastwood–like shoot-'em-up denouement] that washed, and the film were a success from start to finish, it wouldn't alter one basic fact—with *The Border*, Jack Nicholson's career has come to an impasse."

The month before, Beatty's *Reds* had finally opened to rave reviews but disappointing box office.[7] *Reds* was nominated for twelve Oscars, in-

---

7 In the byzantine shadow world of Hollywood finance, although *Reds* took in between $40 million and $50 million in its initial domestic run, because of its huge cost ($35 million) and excessive length (194 minutes) that made multiple nightly screenings impossible, the film did not make significant profits. The final accounting is still taking place.

cluding Best Actor (Beatty), Best Actress (Keaton), Best Picture (Beatty, producer), Best Actress in a Supporting Role (Maureen Stapleton), a nomination for Jack as Best Actor in a Supporting Role, and several additional technical awards. Jack's nomination signaled a possible uptick in the direction of his career. When he learned of it, he told friends he was sure he wouldn't win and retreated once more, this time to Colorado, taking along only his personal cook. He spent his days skiing, eating, biking, and sleeping late. His typewriter sat there quiet and still. As much as he wanted to, whenever he tried to write, nothing came out of him and instead, he put food in.

All too soon, much of the weight he had worked so hard to lose came back, as it usually does with crash dieting. He allowed only a few friends to visit, among them Bert Schneider, Harry Dean Stanton, Bob Rafelson, Hunter S. Thompson, and Lou Adler. Adler watched Lakers games with Jack via cable hookup. One of Jack's few forays to Los Angeles was to attend the single most important event in Hollywood, one of superagent Sue Mengers's ultralavish affairs in her Beverly Hills home. Jack, one of her "Twinkles"—her name for her pet movie stars—arrived more than two hours late, a no-no at a Mengers bash, which, in her time, was considered the most difficult invite to get. He'd figured as long as he was in L.A. he would attend a Lakers game first with Adler. His priorities were crystal clear.

Also, in January 1982, Anjelica, very possibly at the urging of her father, who had always hoped she and Jack would wind up together, and despite her anger over the Anspach baby, simply couldn't stay away from him. She began flying back and forth from L.A. to Aspen, to make sure he was okay and had everything he needed. At first she wasn't sure what his reaction would be, but when he said how happy he was to see her, she decided to stay through Christmas and see what happened.

Aspen during the holidays is one long party, and to get Jack out of his house and his own self-imposed isolation and funk, Anjelica dragged him to as many as she could. At one of them they ran into Andy Warhol, who flaunted Margaret Trudeau's just-published memoir to both of them, pointing out in typical Warholian deadpan what she had written about her affairs with Ryan O'Neal and actor Tom Sullivan. Jack bristled at Warhol but said nothing. Everyone knew that Warhol loved gossip. Jack hoped Warhol wouldn't ask him in front of Anjelica about his affair with actress Winnie Hollman. The big talk in Hollywood, unproven, was that she had recently given birth to a daughter fathered by Jack.[8] Warhol didn't, and for the moment, Jack dodged another bullet.

In March 1982, Jack flew back to Hollywood to attend the Academy Awards, held on the twenty-ninth, at the Dorothy Chandler Pavilion, hosted that year by Johnny Carson. Jack was certain he was not going to win for *Reds*, but he wanted to support Warren in what looked as if it could be the biggest night of his life. Beatty showed up with Keaton on his arm (although word was their relationship had cooled during the making of the film), and Jack arrived with Anjelica. The four sat together in the same row. When Beatty won for Best Director, the camera caught a shot of Jack, his eyes covered with sunglasses, looking quite satisfied.

Jack kept smiling even when he lost Best Supporting Actor in an upset to Sir John Gielgud for his performance in Steve Gordon's decidedly minor comedy *Arthur.*

---

[8] She had, but nobody at the time could prove it. The baby was the result of a secret five-year relationship between Jack and Winnie Hollman. Honey Hollman finally confirmed that Jack was her father when she turned twenty-five in 2006. She had been raised in Copenhagen by her mother, who never kept the secret from her. Jack had little or no involvement in Honey Hollman's life.

Part IV

Return

of

the

Joker

PREVIOUS PAGE: The Joker. *Courtesy of Rebel Road Archives*

"After Cuckoo's Nest, I had been so lucky for so long as an actor that I felt overly praised. Well, I said that for two pictures and they got up my ass for five years in a row . . . the result was that people started applying a different standard to me and thinking, 'Yeah, this fucking guy is over praised. Let's attack the living shit out of him.' And they did . . ."

—JACK NICHOLSON

I N MARCH 1983 JACK ANNOUNCED HIS NEXT FILM WOULD BE *TERMS of Endearment*, written, produced, and directed by TV sitcom veteran James L. Brooks, set to begin production at the end of the month. When he first read the script he loved it, believing it was the vehicle that could repair his broken career: "I can think of only a couple of other pictures where I've read the part and said, 'Oh shit, I'll be great in this.'" He was not at all bothered by taking a supporting role. He had done it before, in *Reds*, with much success. "My whole career strategy has been to build a base so that I could take the roles I want to play. I'd hate to think that a shorter part might not be available because I was worried about my billing." Jack wanted the role so much that despite Paramount's nervous $10 million budget that left no room for Jack's $3 million salary, he agreed to do it for nothing up front and a healthy slice of the back end.

He flew to Houston, Texas, where much of the film was to be shot, while Anjelica stayed behind in Los Angeles to continue the pursuit of her own career. He spent most of his down time at a luxurious spa, the cost of which was paid by the production.

Jack received third billing above the title, after reincarnationist/

actress Shirley MacLaine and super-hot Debra Winger, coming off two big hits in a row, playing Sissy opposite John Travolta in James Bridges's 1980 *Urban Cowboy* and Paula opposite Richard Gere in Taylor Hackford's 1982 *An Officer and a Gentleman,* for which she was nominated for a Best Actress Oscar (she lost to Meryl Streep for *Sophie's Choice*).

Brooks was a singular talent. He had begun TV's second Golden Age of situation comedy in 1970 with the arrival of *The Mary Tyler Moore Show,* starring Moore as a single, career-minded independent woman, at the time a role unthinkable on television (as it still was to a large degree in real life). The show was a smash hit and ran for seven seasons, making stars out of Moore and her supporting cast of characters, and established its creators, James L. Brooks and Allan Burns, as major TV sitcom players. Burns formed a partnership with Brooks when they were approached by Grant Tinker to create a show for his wife, actress Mary Tyler Moore.

Two years after *The Mary Tyler Moore Show* ended, in 1979, Brooks, without Burns, broke into film producing with *Starting Over,* from his own script (co-written with Dan Wakefield, adapted from his novel) directed by Alan J. Pakula. The film, starring Burt Reynolds and Jill Clayburgh, did well enough to get Brooks a deal to produce, direct, and write *Terms of Endearment,* based on the Larry McMurtry novel of the same name. Despite Brooks's stellar credentials in TV, the leap to the big screen proved harder than he thought and he had difficulty getting *Terms* funded. Jennifer Jones, one of the biggest stars of the 1940s and 1950s, had bought the film rights to the novel, seeing the middle-aged character of Aurora Greenway as the perfect comeback role for her. Jones then approached Brooks about producing. He read it and liked it, but not for Jones. He asked Paramount to buy the rights from her and give it to him. Jones resisted but eventually agreed, as no studio was willing to touch the project with her attached to it. Then, in classic Hollywood form, Paramount got cold feet, telling Brooks it was too different, too unlike anything else out there that was making money. That much was true. Hollywood films had fallen into the grip of big, hollow spectacles, the Spielberg/Lucas style of filmmaking that had overtaken the more personal movies of the early seventies.

Brooks confronted Paramount by saying, "You mean, we're in danger of doing some original work?" He shamed the studio into funding the film, but only for $9 million; he picked up another million from MTM, bringing him to the $10 million he needed to go ahead.[1]

According to Brooks, after an early draft of the script, he realized "you needed a male star, but you couldn't get a male star to do it because the part [of Breedlove] was short and because the actor had to give up his vanity." Burt Reynolds was Brooks's first choice to play him, because he had worked previously with Burt in *Starting Over* and believed he was perfect for this role. He might have actually been great, but turned down the role because Brooks wouldn't let him do it with his toupee or allow his always-held-in potbelly to be seen, two key characteristics—balding and sagging—the role called for. A disappointed Brooks next approached Paul Newman. When he said no, Debra Winger suggested Jack might make a great Breedlove. "Jack was always too much to hope for," Brooks said. "The first feature I ever wrote was *Starting Over*, and I wrote that with him in mind, but we never got him." That was the role that instead went to Reynolds.

MacLaine also hadn't been Brooks's first choice to play Greenway. He had wanted Anne Bancroft or Louise Fletcher, but when he showed them an early version of the script, neither thought it was funny. The only one who "got it" was MacLaine. She thought it was a riot, even with the tragic turn of the third act. And because of it, she won the part. She modeled her character, she said later, on Martha Mitchell.[2]

Also cast were Jeff Daniels and Jack's good friend Danny DeVito.

◆ ◆ ◆

---

[1] Mary Tyler Moore Enterprises, run at the time by Grant Tinker.

[2] The two female stars reportedly battled over billing. The problem was resolved by giving MacLaine first position in the credits, and Winger first position in the advertising. James Brooks said it was done to make sure that the two female leads got first billing someplace. Mort Viner, MacLaine's agent, said she accepted the arrangement "gracefully." Doug Taylor, Winger's publicity agent, was less gracious—he called it a case of "age before beauty."—From an article that appeared in the *Wall Street Journal*, January 25, 1984.

BREEDLOVE WAS A perfect name for Jack's character, one in which he recognized a lot of himself. He is a retired astronaut who lives in a beach house by himself and loves getting drunk and making love with women. The film's primary focus is on a mother and a daughter who live near Breedlove and spend their lives looking for love with men who, for one reason or another, don't want to look back. Breedlove and the mother, Aurora Greenway (Shirley MacLaine), develop a brief but intense romance, filled with unexpected warmth and humor from Jack.

Production began March 14, 1983, and resulted in one of those magical moments in cinema, when all the pieces mesh perfectly into one beautiful whole, like one of those reverse shots of an automobile blown to bits that, when projected on a screen, all seem to magically fly back together and become whole. Brooks's script, littered as it was with TV sitcom one-liners (which Jack hated and, he believed, kept the film from being truly great), gave him the opportunity to introduce a new shade of character to his repertoire, one that would remain with him, in one form or another, for the rest of his career. This Jack was soft-spoken, slow-paced, hefty, balding, slightly tipsy, chasing skirts (that part wasn't new), and letting problems roll off his back (that part was). He would never be a film comic like Jerry Lewis, who essentially played himself his entire career. Jack had developed into an actor who could do comedy rather than a comic actor.

He found a bathrobe in wardrobe that he adopted as his uniform and wore when he was shooting and off-camera. It became the connective tissue that allowed him to meld his character in the film with who he was in real life. According to Brooks, "He lived in that robe!" He also wore an expensive astronaut's watch throughout the shoot.

In *Terms*, sporting a huge gut, Jack falls into an unlikely relationship with Aurora and slowly finds a way to open her up (sexually and emotionally). He shows her another, better way to live. He takes her for drives along the beach in a convertible, sitting high on the seat and driving with his toe. Everything seems to be going great (so great that one begins to wonder where else the film can go), when Brooks pulls out one of the great clichés of romantic films, and transforms a middle-aged love story into a middle-aged version of *Love Story.* Halfway through the film, as Aurora is coping with the travails of the troubled marriage of her daughter Emma (Debra Winger), Emma comes down with terminal cancer.

This plot twist almost never works. *Love Story* got around it by not showing a lot of hospital rooms and keeping Ali MacGraw's character looking bright and healthy almost to the end. Brooks managed to pull it off by making the cartoonish characters of the first half of the film have to adjust to family tragedy in the second, to act like real adults with real responsibilities and emotions. It elevated the picture out of the level of TV sitcom and into legitimate big-screen cinematic melodrama.

TERMS OF ENDEARMENT opened in limited release on November 23, 1983, and nationwide two weeks later. Critics loved the film and especially Jack's performance in it. Richard Schickel, writing in *Time,* called Jack's performance "a joyously comic display of just the kind of wrong stuff that appalls and attracts . . ." David Ansen, in *Newsweek,* noted that "Nicholson may be unique for a star of his stature; he hasn't the usual leading man's vanity; indeed, he seems to revel in playing the slob, exhibiting his paunch." Pauline Kael, in the *New Yorker,* wrote: "The years have given Jack an impressive, broader face, and his comedy has never been more alert, more polished. He isn't getting laughs because of his lines; he's getting them because of his insinuating delivery . . . it isn't just the flab hanging out that makes him funny—it's that he stands like a dirty-minded little kid who hasn't yet learned to suck in his gut, an old sex warrior who can't be bothered." *Daily Variety* decided that the "teaming of Shirley MacLaine and Jack Nicholson at their best makes *Terms of Endearment* an enormously enjoyable offering for Christmas." And Andrew Sarris, writing in the *Village Voice,* summed up the whole of the film's parts this way: "There is real talent at work in *Terms of Endearment,* notably that of Nicholson . . . even more than that of MacLaine and Winger . . . To win an Oscar, actresses must be suffering and submissive creatures with excessively messy lives.

This is both the message and the mechanism of *Terms of Endearment* as the most widely admired tearjerker of the year. Its expertise makes it nonetheless the Cabbage Patch doll of Christmas movies."

Audiences loved it too. It earned $4.5 million, half its production costs, on Thanksgiving weekend, and $25 million in two months, when most other holiday movies had disappeared from the big screen, and it would go on to gross just under $109 million in its initial domestic release (Jack's eventual earnings were reportedly $9 million). It was the second-highest-grossing film of 1983 (1983–1984 grosses combined). Only Richard Marquand's *Return of the Jedi*, of George Lucas's bottomless money-pit franchise, beat it at the box office, earning more than $250 million.[3]

Paramount had been right, there was nothing else like it out there. And so was Brooks, who had correctly predicted that this was the reason audiences would flock to see it.

TERMS OF ENDEARMENT earned eleven Oscar nominations, including one for Best Performance in a Supporting Role for Jack, which thrust him right back onto Hollywood's A-list of hottest and most desirable actors.[4] Once again, everyone in the press wanted to know what Jack thought about everything, and, basking in his latest resurrection, he was only too happy to clue everyone in on what was on his mind. To Stephen Farber, in the *New York Times*, about his performance in *Terms*, he said, "I'm in my forties, and if I'm going to continue to grow

---

[3] The other eight top ten grossers of 1983 were, in descending order, Adrian Lyne's *Flashdance* ($93 million); John Landis's *Trading Places* ($90 million); John Badham's *WarGames* ($79.5 million); John Glen's *Octopussy* ($68 million); Clint Eastwood's *Sudden Impact* ($67.6 million); Sylvester Stallone's *Stayin' Alive* ($64.8 million); Stan Dragoti's *Mr. Mom* ($64.7 million); and Paul Brickman's *Risky Business* ($63.5 million).

[4] The other nominations for Best Actor in a Supporting Role were Charles Durning in Alan Johnson's *To Be or Not to Be*, John Lithgow in *Terms of Endearment*, Sam Shepard in Philip Kaufman's *The Right Stuff*, and Rip Torn in Martin Ritt's *Cross Creek*.

as a person and an artist, I can't keep playing 35-year-old ideas of romance. This is a transition that I'm interested in making and it's an area which I think has been explored in sullen, lime-green tracts about the midlife crisis, or in situation comedy . . . I got very interested in the idea of how to age a character . . . pushing the old tummy out, not disguising certain things photographically. The other thing that's fun about doing short parts is you know you're going to get done before everyone else."

Mike Nichols said about Jack's performance in the film, "Look at what he did in *Terms of Endearment* with that stomach hanging out." Jack agreed. "One of the things that motivated me with that character is that everyone was starting to make a total cliché out of middle age . . . I just went against the grain of the cliché . . ."

AFTER *TERMS OF ENDEARMENT*'S enormous box office success, Jack decided to celebrate in Aspen. He invited Anjelica, but she said she couldn't go because she was tied up with too many things in L.A. Jack didn't appear to mind. He was having too much fun being the oldest kid in Hollywood to think about anything so unfunny as growing up. He may have learned how to play more mature onscreen, but in real life he was still the same old arrested adolescent, at least when it came to women.

Andy Warhol came to Aspen for a visit and, with the understated directness of his manner and his flat vocal style, told Jack how fat he had gotten. This time it didn't bother him at all. His weight just might win him an Oscar. Jack took off for Europe for some R and R with super-*moe-dell* Veruschka by his side. He basked in the flashing cameras pointed his way that shot off tiny bolts of fame as they walked together through London's Heathrow—his smile, and his waist, wider than ever.

While in London, Jack's tolerance of the gossip press was tested when *The Sun* printed a story claiming that Jack had suffered "a string" of drug busts and that he loved getting high at least four days out of any given week. None of it was true. Jack was trying to lay off drugs to help his increasingly tender stomach, one of the by-products of a big belly.

He sued for defamation and the paper quickly gave in, retreating and apologizing and reportedly settling out of court. Jack used the occasion to put in a good word for the legalization of drugs.

Back in the States, he returned once more to Aspen, intending to stay there for the rest of the winter, or forever if he felt like it, or at least until April and the Academy Awards, where the limelight and the Awards gods would once more shine down upon him.

THAT YEAR'S ANNUAL Oscar ceremonies were held on April 9, 1984, at the Dorothy Chandler Pavilion in downtown Los Angeles with Johnny Carson back at the helm. Jack arrived, Wayfarers in place, smile clicked to high beam, and Anjelica back on his arm to walk the red carpet. They drew the loudest ovation from the outdoor onlookers.

In typical Oscar fashion, it took a full half hour for the first winner to be announced, Best Actor in a Supporting Role. Mary Tyler Moore and Timothy Hutton took the stage and read the names of the nominations. The cameras caught the nominees' faces in simultaneous close-ups, to catch their reactions when the winning name was announced (all except Sam Shepard, who was not there; a photo of him was substituted). When Moore opened the envelope and read Jack's name, his eyebrows shot to the sky and he actually pulled off his Wayfarers, looking surprised and delighted as he walked up to the stage. Once there he kissed Mary on the hand and replaced his glasses.

After respectfully, if playfully, thanking the other nominees, Jack murmured, "I was going to say a lot about how Shirley and Debra inspired me, but I understand they're planning an interpretive dance later right after the Best Actress Award to explain everything about life." That brought a roar of laughter from the audience. When it died down, Jack thanked the L.A. rock scene and the Aspen congregation, inexplicably leaving out the Los Angeles Lakers and Anjelica: "All you rock people down at the Roxy and up in the Rockies, rock on!"

Jack's Oscar win, his first in eight years, was the icing on the cake that served to officially mark his return to the top of his game.

He was Hollywood's Prince again. He could do whatever he wanted, and with whom, and whenever he felt like it. He could gorge on the best street-side Mexican food in L.A. and his favorite dessert, chocolate mousse and whipped cream at the Carlyle Hotel in New York. Weight? Fuck it. Work? Fuck that too. Writing? Ditto fuck. He was *Jack Nicholson*, with two Oscars he could hang like double six-guns from his belt. *Look out, ol' Jackie was back!*

"I've been overweight since I was four years old. Of course, I have all the normal defenses against it. But it's always bugged me. I don't want to overinflate my role and my job, but isn't there more to me than what I weigh?"

—JACK NICHOLSON

TWO MONTHS LATER, IN JUNE 1984, JACK'S ONGOING OSCAR CELebration was interrupted when *Wired: The Short Life and Fast Times of John Belushi,* Bob Woodward's Watergate-style book-length reporting of the drug death of the comic actor, was published. A year earlier, the corpulent performer had died of a lethal injection of a "speedball," a combination of heroin and cocaine. Woodward was able to reach a lot of people and get them to talk, celebrities who otherwise never spoke to the press about these types of tragedies. At the time, Hollywood was supercharged; cocaine ran through it like a virus. With a reporter like Woodward nipping at everyone's heels, the same Woodward whose reporting had helped push a president to resign, Hollywood's pervasive guilt and fear were brought into the spotlight. Everyone was afraid *not* to talk to him.

Even Jack, who had sworn off interviews in general and had experienced firsthand the demonized Belushi, to whom he'd given his first film role in *Goin' South,* tried to make some kind of a deal with Woodward. Trade-off with journalists had become Jack's specialty. He would cooperate if the writer would not sensationalize those aspects of Hollywood the public didn't need to know that much about.

What was he thinking?

Woodward was a highly praised, award-winning investigative journalist who took no prisoners. He wrote a detailed, if sensationalistic account of the last days of Belushi's life that spared no one and was really a fire-and-brimstone indictment of a social scene among the pampered celebrity set. As for Jack, Woodward had somehow found out about his habit of "upstairs" drugs—the cocaine he kept in the bedroom just for himself—the VIP stash reserved for best friends and especially beautiful women, and the "downstairs" drugs for the rest of the crowd at party time. In a not-so-subtle way, Woodward implied that cocaine had taken over the rhythm of Hollywood life and that Jack was living in the American capital of high-grade powder, one of the so-called perks of being a Hollywood movie star, where the rules for the rest of the citizenry didn't always apply.

When the book came out, Jack was furious that Woodward included all the drug stuff about him, and publicly referred to Woodward as a "ghoul and an exploiter of emotionally disturbed widows" for profiting off the death of Belushi, and predicted the book would end Woodward's career as a serious journalist.

Jack's and Hollywood's rage at Woodward was, to say the least, misplaced. Woodward hadn't pulled back the shades of some secret window into Hollywood; he was holding up a cautionary mirror to its face. Instead of recognizing that, in classic form, Jack and everybody else in Hollywood blamed the messenger, worse, an outsider, for pulling back the curtains on their private and privileged ways.

But Jack didn't sue Woodward, as he had *The Sun*. Woodward had nailed the story and any court would clearly see that. Up until the publication of the book, Jack had always disdained cocaine. Now, if he went to court, the results could be disastrous. Woodward had correctly described Hollywood's cinematic social set for what it was, a section of society dangerously out of control—obsessed with money, sex, fame, and drugs—and that didn't take care of its own, even as fellow actors, producers, and directors were dropping dead everywhere from overdoses and from a new disease that some saw as a scourge on those who exceeded the bounds of morality. It was called AIDS and it would irrevocably change Hollywood's cultural landscape. Nobody knew how you got it, and there was no cure if you did. At first, it was called the gay disease, and even though more men and women in Hollywood were gay than the public might imagine, nobody seemed to care because it couldn't possibly happen to them. They were too careful, they were too successful, they were too young, they were too invincible. Rock Hudson's very public death from complications as a result of the disease in 1985 would change all that. As much as Jack and everyone else in Hollywood railed against it, they knew Woodward had gotten the story dead right.

SCRIPTS CONTINUED TO come Jack's way. He was sought after to play Ernest Hemingway in a biopic, the thinking in Hollywood being, as it usually is, logically loose-limbed—if Jack could play Eugene O'Neill in *Reds*, why not that other great Lost Generation writer? He said he wasn't interested (the part went instead to Clive Owen and eventually wound up as a TV movie co-starring Nicole Kidman). He was also offered the role of Eliot Ness by Brian De Palma for his big-screen version of the TV series *The Untouchables*, with a script by *Postman's* David Mamet; he said no (he didn't want to make another movie with Mamet). The part went instead to Kevin Costner. Jack's instinct to pass was the right one. The film would belong to Robert De Niro as Al Capone, and the only thing anybody remembers from it is Capone bashing in the skull of another gangster with a baseball bat.

He had recently read Saul Bellow's novel *Henderson the Rain King*, which he bought the film rights to, with the intention of adapting it for himself and possibly directing it as well, but the project went nowhere. Even though he was sure it could be huge, he couldn't get anyone interested, either the studios or an independent producer who could make it and bring it to them for distribution. Bellow, he was told by everyone, was unfilmable.

There had also been talk of a sequel to *Terms of Endearment*, but Jack had made it clear he had no intention of going there again. Besides, there was talk that the long-overdue sequel to *Chinatown*, already postponed numerous times because of the continuing unavailability of Roman Polanski, was back in development. If he was going to do a sequel to any film, it would be this one. And if they wanted him, it would have to be with Polanski directing, which was always the holdup. Jack didn't want anybody else to direct the film and hoped that Polanski's situation had progressed to the point where the sequel was active again with him involved.

Not that he was all that eager to get back to work. He was seen frequently around New York with Debra Winger, before jetting off to San Francisco to buy six more paintings by Russell Chatham, after attending the artist's one-man show at the Maxwell Galleries. Jack gave *Rolling Stone* an interview in which he discussed his negative thoughts about monogamy and the inherent problems of being in a long-term relationship with Anjelica, specifically her desire to someday have children and his desire not to have any more. To Jack it was *been there, done that.* To Anjelica it was *need to do it, with or without Jack.*

The day after his newest art purchases, he flew to London with Anjelica, having managed to look the other way to avoid her cold stares. He spent his free time playing tennis, a game he'd enjoyed intermittently through the years, less so when he was heavy like he was now and playing made his ankles hurt. They then flew to New York so that Jack could pursue his ongoing hunt for the work of new artists, then to Phoenix for a Lakers game, and when they got home, Anjelica, as usual, went her own way and he dove into the always-high pile of scripts waiting for him to read that had been passed on to him by Bresler.

It was from this pile, unexpectedly, that he found a script he totally fell in love with. He knew he wasn't going to be able to turn it down, even though he had no idea what it was supposed to be about. He just loved the writing so much. "In the beginning," he recalled later, "I didn't even realize the movie was a comedy . . . an action-comedy like *Beverly Hills Cop* and *Henry V.* It's got girls, adventure, interesting talk, very black humor . . . I'd never done anything like it." Here was a tectonic career shift, away from the sitcom-jokiness-meets-Camille that was *Terms of Endearment* to something darker and more complex. The character's name was Charley Partanna. The movie, based on the novel by Richard Condon, was *Prizzi's Honor.*

"Mob" movies, which were popular in the thirties—when Warner

Bros. had a lock on them—were back in style after Francis Ford Coppola's 1973 *The Godfather*, at Parramount, made them relevant again, using the Corleones to explicate the story of American capitalism. Mobs were merely corporations involved in the big and dirty business of making money. *It's not personal, Sonny! It's strictly business!"* Dozens of films followed, all trying to imitate the look and message of *The Godfather*, but none came close to duplicating Coppola's expansive vision, or his dream cast of Brando, Caan, Keaton, Pacino, Duvall, Cazale, and in the first sequel, De Niro. Many initially thought *Prizzi's Honor* was, in some ways, a satire on *The Godfather*, minus the cannolis.

What cinched making it for Jack was that John Huston had signed on to direct, someone he had always thought of as his adult father figure. "He's been my idol since childhood and we've gotten to know each other pretty well over the last 15 years. I'm kind of a Johnny-come-lately in Johnny's life . . . like—this guy was a legend when I was in grammar school. The way he relates to actors and the way he watches a scene."

The timing was a bit awkward as the long-awaited *Chinatown* sequel, now called *The Two Jakes*, had indeed moved back into active preproduction, the snail-paced Towne having at long last finished an acceptable script; Bob Evans was in place to produce, and with Polanski not coming back anytime soon, Evans offered Towne the chance to direct, which he grabbed. Like all good screenwriters, many of whom are frustrated directors, Towne, who had never directed before, believed he could do a better job helming his own scripts than anybody else. Evans assured Jack that Towne could do it, and Jack reluctantly gave the project his personal green light. They already had a start date that couldn't be postponed. That left relatively little time for him to do *Prizzi's Honor*, but Jack promised Huston he would get the film made, on time and within the bounds of its relatively modest budget. Huston was a one-take, two-take director, something Jack appreciated. As far as Huston was concerned, they were a perfect match. "Jack's a virtuoso. He can do the acting scales on one hand."

And then came the real-life twist, as good as, if not better than, anything in the film. Huston cast Anjelica to play Maerose Prizzi, Charley Partanna's (Jack's) forsaken girlfriend. Huston decided to give her the key female role in what would be the biggest break of her career to date and a chance to kill Jack off, at least on screen.

Partanna is the Prizzi family's official hit man (one of the jokes of the film is that nobody in the family has any honor) and romantically involved with Maerose. In the film's opening sequence, a mob wedding (a satirical reference to *The Godfather*), Charley sees and immediately falls for the gorgeous Irene Walker (Kathleen Turner), who, as it turns out, is also a hit "man." They meet, fall in lust, and then, in short order, decide to get married. The senior Prizzi, superbly played by William Hickey, the head of the mob side of the family and the father of Maerose, orders a hit on Charley for "ruining" his daughter's honor when Maerose lies to him about how Charley had "forced himself" on her, after he's left her for Walker. And Prizzi also wants Walker killed for taking part in a Las Vegas money scam without the family's permission. He orders Charley to carry out the hit.

In the film, the spidery Anjelica is determined to either win Charley back from Irene Walker or have him killed for jilting her in favor of the ravishing blonde. How it must have tickled the seventy-eight-year-old Huston to have his daughter act out a fantasy revenge on her real-life boyfriend for all the misery he had heaped upon her during their more than decade-long relationship. Huston, like Jack, had done his share of womanizing, with five marriages and numerous affairs under his belt, and he had a fair measure of directorial wisdom when it came to getting personally involved while directing other high-wire couples such as Bogie and Bacall (*Key Largo*, 1948).

The results showed up in the film's splendid mirror-perfect image of the ins and outs of the couple's real-life relationship. Offscreen Jack could laugh about their misadventures. Onscreen the audience would do the laughing for him. Jack explained the duality of their movie chemistry in *Prizzi's Honor* with an ironic Shakespearean reference. "Mainly [Anjelica and I] just ran down what the motivations were of the people in different scenes. We arrived at the answer that she's like

Lady Macbeth. She's going to be the queen of this realm, and I'm going to be the king of it . . ."

Jack especially loved the "doubling" aspect of the film's plot, while not letting the darker aspects of it get too close to him emotionally. Throughout production he kept busy continuing to satisfy an apparently insatiable desire to chase and bed gorgeous and willing young starlets. He was now into the newest "hip" thing in Hollywood, dating porn stars. He called it research.

Which was why, during the filming of *Prizzi's Honor*, Jack and Anjelica stayed in separate suites at the Carlyle Hotel. Most evenings Anjelica stayed in, by herself, while Jack went out and partied it up in his favorite night-side town.

To GET A handle on how best to play Partanna, during production Jack slipped into several of Brooklyn's most infamous outer-borough bars and beaneries. In one of these dingy, beer-soaked hangs, where stale cigarette smoke weaved through the air in layers of visible blue, fog to the eyes and a killer to the lungs, and where ordering a martini or a margarita instead of a shot of Irish whiskey and a brew could get one heaved out the door, Jack made pals with a couple of local wannabe Corleones, mostly tribute collectors who controlled their fiefdom's local trash pickup, or ran numbers, or loan-sharked to those who couldn't otherwise make the rent. It was at these neighborhood drowneries that Jack also learned the two-bit hoodlum walk of the small-timer who prances elbows-first to make him feel like a big man. But it was the lip thing that most fascinated Jack and provided a pathway to the character of Charley Partanna. All the local boys never moved their upper lip. By stuffing a wad of Kleenex under his own he was able to freeze it, which turned out to be key to his character's kingdom. He added a choked Brooklyn accent that made every sentence sound as if the last word pounded its fist on the table. Dialect specialist and actress Julie Bovasso, best remembered for her role as John Travolta's mother in *Saturday Night Fever*, helped him put the final touches on his Brooklyn accent—"*Ey, Charley*"—so different from his natural Jersey Shore intonation. "Let's face it," he told one writer, "certain parts of the character needed un–Jack Nicholsoning."

The rest was easy. Rheumy eyes (helped along by a little squirt of glycerin), Vaseline slicked-back hair, broken nose via actor's putty, and thirty extra pounds of heft, put on by downing bowls of garlic-drenched tomato-paste pasta personally prepared for him by one of his advisors on the film, Tommy Baratta. (After production ended, Jack kept him on as his part-time cook for every movie he made.) The icing for Jack was the wardrobe, yellow jackets and dark turtlenecks, and it was a done deal.

JUST AS THE final prints of *Prizzi's Honor* were being shipped to the-aters for a June 13, 1985, opening, *The Two Jakes* was ready to go into production. Bob Evans had made a negative pickup deal with Para-mount, which meant the studio would finance the film and then make its money as its distributor.

Jack was ready to bring J. J. Gittes back to life. To slim down for the role, after packing on the weight for *Prizzi*, Jack went on one of his "crash" health-food-and-exercise diets. He wanted to resemble the earlier Gittes as much as possible.

Kelly McGillis, an up-and-coming actress who would play opposite Tom Cruise in Tony Scott's 1985 *Top Gun*, and Cathy Moriarty, of *Raging Bull* fame, De Niro's and Scorsese's tour-de-force 1980 film bio of Jake LaMotta, were cast for the film's two female leads. Also plugged in were Dennis Hopper, whose career had fallen into decline but to whom Jack felt loyal and gave him a part in the film; Joe Pesci, like Mo-riarty, from *Raging Bull*; Perry Lopez; and Scott Wilson. Robert Towne also wanted Bob Evans to return to acting in *The Two Jakes*, something he had never been very good at, to play the other Jake, real-estate de-veloper and overall rat Jake Berman. Evans hadn't been in front of a camera since 1959 but agreed, and for the occasion treated himself to an extensive facelift and a visit to a Tahitian weight-loss spa.

And then just four days before production was scheduled to begin, Towne, the director, fired Evans the actor. His screen tests demonstrated what everyone else in the business already knew, that the best that could be said of him as an actor was that he was a great producer. Jack was visibly angered by Towne's move and let him know it. Evans was a good friend and Jack believed he should be treated with more respect than that. Paramount then stepped in, demanding that Evans remain in the film. Shooting was delayed while what seemed like endless meetings took place, with neither side willing to budge. Finally, Towne, feeling that the studio had challenged and compromised his authority, quit the film. Paramount, believing the production was now in free-fall even before a foot of film had been shot, pulled out of its commitment. Jack then frantically tried to save the production by asking Warren Beatty to step in and replace Towne. Beatty said no. Jack then went to Huston to try to persuade him to take over directing *Two Jakes*. Huston, who was already having health problems during *Prizzi's Honor*, regretfully declined the offer.

And just like that *The Two Jakes* turned into no Jakes; the picture was dead in the water, to the tune of a $3 million preproduction cost that Paramount had to pay. The aborted picture also cost Towne Jack's friendship.

THE SAME WEEK *The Two Jakes* shut down, Jack's beloved Lakers won the NBA championship, four games to two, against the hated Boston Celtics, the first time L.A. had ever beaten Boston in the finals. Despite all that was going on, Jack managed to be at every home game.

Prizzi's Honor opened and received mixed reviews from the critics—Pauline Kael in the *New Yorker* said of Jack's performance, "It is a virtuoso set of variations on your basic double take and traditional slow burns . . . Nicholson doesn't overdo his blurred expressions or his uncomprehending stare; he's a witty actor who keeps you eager for what he'll do next." Richard Schickel, writing in *Time*, called it "one of [Jack's] boldest performances." David Ansen, in *Newsweek*, was less impressed: "Nicholson takes wild chances: assuming a deceptively dumb Brooklyn accent, he plays this hilarious anti-hero as if he were a schizo who couldn't decide if his role in life was Bogart's or Elisha Cook's [in John Huston's 1941 *The Maltese Falcon*]."

Audiences were less ambivalent. From a $16 million budget, *Prizzi's Honor* grossed $26 million in its initial domestic release (more than $4 million on opening weekend), and nearly twice that overseas. And almost from the beginning, there was Oscar buzz for Jack, Anjelica, Kathleen Turner, and John Huston.

Just as Jack was basking in the glow of Charley Partanna and bemoaning the fate of J. J. Gittes, he was asked by Mike Nichols to step in to replace Mandy Patinkin, playing Mark Forman, in the film adaptation of Nora Ephron's *Heartburn*, her thinly disguised evisceration of Carl Bernstein, to whom she had been briefly married before Bernstein's womanizing ended their union.[1] On paper, Patinkin had seemed the perfect actor to play Forman, but it quickly became evident to Nichols on the first day of shooting that paper and film were not the same, and Patinkin was utterly wrong for the part. Patinkin couldn't wait to leave.

To replace him, Nichols wanted Jack, not that he looked especially Jewish (or Jewish at all), but he could act. Because it was so important to Nichols, one of his closest friends, Jack took over the role. (The $4 million up-front paycheck may have had something to do with it as well.)

When Jack came aboard, Bernstein met with him at the Russian Tea Room—they were casual, not close, friends, and Jack still considered Woodward, Bernstein's onetime reporting partner, a lowlife. Over lunch, Bernstein tried to persuade Jack not to do the film. Jack managed to ease Bernstein's fears by telling him it was better to have a friend play him than a stranger. Jack assured him he would do right by both the part and Bernstein.

When it came to shooting, Jack came off so affable that audiences

---

[1] Their seemingly perfect marriage—two Jewish journalists enjoying fame during the day and pizza in bed at night watching old movies—ended when Ephron discovered that Bernstein was having an affair with Margaret Jay, wife of the British ambassador to Washington.

wondered why Rachel (Streep/Ephron) would ever leave such a great guy. Later on, Jack told *Rolling Stone*, "I was specifically hired *not* to play [Bernstein]. Mike and Nora and Meryl were very anxious to move the film into fiction. And since I had no desire on a couple of days' notice to do a biographical portrait, that suited me just fine."

Jack and Meryl Streep began filming in Manhattan in August. Jack first met Streep the first day he was on set. Nichols had wanted to keep some tension between them before the cameras rolled. According to Streep, "It was like meeting Mick Jagger or Bob Dylan. He was a big deal . . ." To break that tension, just before their first scene together, Nicholson knocked on Streep's trailer door and asked if he could use her toilet. She said sure. End of tension.[2]

According to an appreciative Nichols, "Jack is the guy who takes parts others have turned down . . . and explodes them into something nobody could have conceived of . . . all his brilliance at character and gesture is consumed and made invisible by the expanse of his nature . . . you can't see any technique. It just appears to be life."

Jack's late arrival gave him little time to prepare for a role that he somehow managed to pull off. Filming was completed that October, and Jack immediately headed to Aspen for some R and R. For the rest of the year he took it easy in the mountains, without Anjelica, until early in 1986, while skiing, Jack took a bad turn on a slope, fell, broke his elbow, and hurt several ligaments in his thumb. The injuries were serious enough to require surgery. When Anjelica heard about it, she flew immediately to his side to take care of him. They were never closer than when he was injured and immobile and she could be in control.

They showed up together at the Oscar ceremonies, held on March 24, 1986, at the Dorothy Chandler Pavilion, hosted by the unlikely triumvirate of Jane Fonda, Alan Alda, and Robin Williams.

---

[2] Whatever friendship or relationship they might have had ended in September, when Streep reportedly threw him out of her hotel room and vowed never to make another movie with him. The story was widely reported in the British press, and Streep denied it happened, but sources said the reason was Jack's relentless sexual overtures.

Anjelica looked resplendent in a green gown designed by Tzetzi Ganev, while a still banged-up Jack walked tenderly along beside her. He had been nominated for Best Performance by an Actor for his role as Charley Partanna, and Anjelica for Best Performance in a Supporting Role by an Actress for Maerose, and the film received six more nominations—Best Supporting Actor, William Hickey; Best Costume Design, Donfeld; Best Director, John Huston; Best Film Editing, Rudi Fehr and Kaja Fehr; Best Picture, John Foreman, producer; and Best Screenplay Based on Material from Another Medium, Richard Condon and Janet Roach.

But this was not to be Jack's year, or the film's, although it started out well when Anjelica won her Oscar over an especially weak crowd of nominees, Margaret Avery in Steven Spielberg's *The Color Purple*, Oprah Winfrey in the same film, Meg Tilly in Norman Jewison's *Agnes of God*, and Amy Madigan in Bud Yorkin's *Twice in a Lifetime*. When Marsha Mason and Richard Dreyfuss announced Anjelica's win, the TV cameras caught Jack's and John Huston's reactions.[3] Both had tears streaming down their faces.

Anjelica strode to the stage, tall and proud. This was her first nomination and her first win. As the applause curved down, she spoke into the microphone: "This means a lot to me, since it comes from a role in which I was directed by my father. And I know it means a lot to him."

It was intended as a public thank-you to her father, who was terminally ill. It was also intended as a different type of message to Jack, whom she never mentioned.

Considered the favorite in his category, Jack was upset by an actor not particularly well liked in Hollywood, William Hurt, in a film that was even less well liked, Héctor Babenco's *Kiss of the Spider Woman*. Jack's face was captured by TV cameras as Hurt's name was announced. It remained frozen in a smile.

---

[3] This made her the third generation of Hustons to win Oscars. Both Walter and John won Oscars for *The Treasure of the Sierra Madre*, in which Walter acted and John directed. John also won an Oscar for *Treasure*'s screenplay.

Her winning and his losing were apparently fine with Jack. He was a big star; she'd always wanted to be one. Now their emotional playing field might be at least a bit more level.

After the long show ended, they agreed to skip the formal festivities in favor of going back to his place to celebrate—with a bottle of wine and a bag of cheeseburgers and French fries from In-N-Out, Jack's favorite non-Mexican L.A. fast food.

And each other.

"I hate being one of the older people in films. Fifty was the first time I paid any attention to age. God, fifty brought me crashing to my knees. I'm very conversant with the fear of death. I've only been aware of it for the last, oh, thirty years or so . . . interviewing the [actresses] on The Two Jakes *I suddenly realized, I'm not going to fall for a nineteen-year-old. I'm too old for this girl . . . for all these girls . . ."*

—JACK NICHOLSON

JACK WAS FAST APPROACHING THE MIDCENTURY MARK, AND AS IT does for everybody, it felt like it came too fast. He knew that quality roles would become increasingly difficult to find, with most of the juiciest parts going to the new kids in town—Eddie Murphy, Michael J. Fox, Paul Hogan (from Australia, with his *Crocodile Dundee* and "Throw one more on the barbie" television commercials); Mel Gibson, and a host of others. Jack and his generation were slowly and irrevocably being consigned to geezer duty.

To push that time back as long as possible, Jack the shining superstar had also become Jack the savvy survivor. He still had his long-term agent, Sandy Bresler, who took all the offers that came in, screened them, and passed them on to Jack, with advice on what to take and what to pass on; but it was Jack who always made the final decisions. He could still afford to accept or turn down any role. And he did.

Paul Mazursky, the actor-turned-director—he was in Richard Brooks's iconic 1955 juvenile delinquent drama *Blackboard Jungle* playing one of the rebellious teenagers in Glenn Ford's classroom and hit the box office jackpot directing 1978's *An Unmarried Woman*—wanted Jack to star opposite Bette Midler in an American remake of Jean Renoir's 1932

French classic *Boudu sauvé des eaux, Down and Out in Beverly Hills.*
Mazursky personally made the pilgrimage to Jack's house on Mulholland on New Year's Day 1986 to sell him on the script and persuade him to star in it. According to Mazursky, he had trouble dealing with Jack during the visit because he was completely stoned on pot, immersed in the broadcast of the Rose Bowl, and couldn't be bothered.

The part went instead to Nick Nolte.

Barry Levinson then offered Jack the brother in *Rain Man,* and again Jack said no, understanding that whoever played the mentally challenged brother would walk away with the picture. Jack's role went to Tom Cruise, who did indeed play the foil to one of Dustin Hoffman's bravura performances.

Jack didn't pass on an offer from Warner Bros. and Peter Guber to the tune of $6 million, plus back-end gross percentages, to play the horniest devil in the world (Daryl) in *The Witches of Eastwick* about ten times what he would have made up front had he gone with Mazursky. He considered Guber a friend but also someone who knew how to get big movies made, and for Jack, the friendship and the savvy were the deciding factors in taking the film. At the same time Jack also signed an agreement to star in *Ironweed,* based on the William Kennedy novel, something he wanted to do after *Witches* simply because he loved Kennedy's book.

According to Peter Guber, "We had bought the rights to *Witches* from John Updike, developed the screenplay with Michael Cristofer, signed the three female leads, and then were stuck for a long time. How do we get someone to play the devil, we wondered? And then I got it, three women trying to conjure Jack Nicholson for a relationship was the perfect fix! After all, at that time he definitely had part of the devil in him. He had done *The Shining* a few years earlier, a part that also had some of the devil in it. I knew he could be great in *Witches* because the character had to have that Machiavellian aspect to it, along with some intellectual gravitas, and I felt that Jack certainly had both and the special magic that a star of his magnitude brings to any picture. Finally, this film is really all about sexual politics, something Jack knew a little about."

The Witches of Eastwick, directed by Australian native George Miller, who had done the *Mad Max* trilogy that made Mel Gibson an international star, was adapted from the satirical pro-feminist novel by John Updike, and proved a hard film to define. Even Miller seemed at first not to get it; he had wanted Robert De Niro, who, unfortunately (or fortunately) for Miller, was busy with his own "devil" movie, Alan Parker's *Angel Heart,* decidedly darker and much more suited for De Niro than *Witches.* Eventually, with Guber's encouragement, Miller made the connection between Jack the actor and Jack the womanizer.

In *Witches,* three horny women (Cher, Susan Sarandon, and Michelle Pfeiffer) make a deal with the devil to get impregnated and then banish him from their lives forever (a kind of inverse satire on Polanski's *Rosemary's Baby*). For Jack, the role of the seducer wasn't much of a stretch.

Anjelica had auditioned to play one of the witches, but despite her recent Oscar triumph and Jack's influence and power (or perhaps because of it), Miller turned her down. Miffed, she accepted instead a part in Francis Coppola's *Gardens of Stone* and flew to D.C. for some location filming. To try to cool things out, Jack flew to Washington on Anjelica's birthday to give her a bracelet. They spent the night together and then he flew back to continue working on *Witches.*

The film, with a budget set at $20 million, was shot south of Boston and in Little Compton, Rhode Island, and from the beginning was fraught with problems, not the least of which was the collision of female star egos among Cher, Sarandon, and Pfeiffer, working together without much chemistry in a script that touched upon misogynistically driven revenge. They weren't good sharers.

Because Jack was playing a character who thrived on excess and gluttony, he was not at all embarrassed when called upon by Miller to do a seminude scene. Rather than complain and try to have it cut out, or demand the use of a double, he seemed to devilishly revel in his obesity.

When the clash among the female stars grew worse and threatened to shut down the production, Miller's lack of familiarity with how to handle Hollywood divas frustrated Jack, as did Guber's holding Miller's feet to the fire for expense overruns in a film that called for so many special effects. Guber considered releasing him, until Jack stepped in and threatened to walk if he did. Guber then prevailed upon Jack to assist his Aussie helmer to get the picture done without going over budget. And, if there were any problems, Jack should be the one to bring them to Guber, not Miller. "In fact," according to Guber, "Jack was the glue that held the entire production together."

Fortunately, he had an idea how to stop all the problems. Recalls Miller: "Early on in our shoot, Jack had 4½ minutes of dialogue. It was the ironing board scene—a big key scene. We had a particularly noisy crew. Jack walked into the marble hall, took his screenplay and threw it down with a thundering whack on the marble table, and gave this ranting performance about how he hated getting up in the morning and learning lines and how he was a night person. He went on and on at the top of his voice. The whole place went silent. He gave me a wink. He was almost doing my job for me, working the crew for me. They were totally reverent after that and we got the concentration we needed."

If Jack wasn't overly concerned with any of it—the kitten scratching, the crew, Anjelica's absence, or the budget—it was because during production he had become preoccupied with actress Veronica Cartwright, who was in the film, resuming an affair with her that had begun during the filming of *Goin' South*, and that, despite his relationship with Anjelica, had never really completely ended. It was likely the reason Jack didn't fight harder to get Anjelica into the movie.

JUST AS PRODUCTION was winding down on *The Witches of Eastwick*, *Heartburn* opened on July 25, 1986, pushed back to cinema Siberia, after the first rush of the big summer films had opened and before that fall's scheduled favorites. It received mixed-to-poor reviews and did just all right at the box office, about $25 million in its initial domestic release, a few million short of break-even. Audiences couldn't connect to the two leads, or them to each other. (The film did have a second life in video, where it found an audience and eventually turned a profit.)

♦ ♦ ♦

EARLY IN 1987, strictly for a lark, Jack, encouraged by U2's Bono, decided to make a talking children's album, with Bobby McFerrin supplying the musical background. They did their version of Kipling's "Elephant's Child," his first professional job after *Witches*. By all accounts, Jack had a ball. The recording was part of Jack's narration for a half-hour PBS special by the same name, produced by Mark Sottnick.

Then, during several delays before the start of production on his next film, *Ironweed*, having to do with studio issues, as a favor for James L. Brooks, Jack agreed to do a noncredited cameo as a TV newscaster for Brooks's satire on TV journalism, *Broadcast News*, as long as he wasn't given any billing or mentioned in any prepublicity. He didn't want to upset the balance of the ensemble cast or mislead the public into thinking this was a "Jack Nicholson" picture.

In *Ironweed*, Héctor Babenco's film adaption of William Kennedy's Pulitzer Prize–winning, Albany-based novel, Jack was cast as Francis Phelan, a washed-up baseball player looking to find atonement for accidentally killing his infant son after dropping him. The film was dark, humorless, and ponderous, the kind of thing Hollywood normally shuns, but Jack wanted to do it, so it got made. Why? "I would like playing an Irish bum." He had plenty of role models from his early days to choose from, beginning with John Nicholson. *Ironweed* was made that fall on location in Albany over a seventeen-week period. And as soon as it began, rumors exploded like wild mushrooms that something was going on between Jack and his co-star, I'll-never-work-with-him-again Meryl Streep. There had been talk that the two had grown unusually close, but both denied it. Jack was in a bit of a bind, as he was actively, if secretly, still seeing Cartwright.

However, once filming began on *Ironweed*, everyone on the set, and those who heard about it, were talking not about the film's script, or direction, or scenic design, but about Jack and Meryl. Often during shooting, his Winnebago seemed to be balanced on four overworked Slinkys. One unnamed source told Mitchell Fink, of the *Los Angeles Herald*

Examiner, that "whatever is going on inside that Winnebago it's starting to get out of hand, to the point where it's embarrassing a lot of people on the set." The story appeared on April 22, 1987, Jack's fiftieth birthday.

AFTER PRODUCTION ENDED on *Ironweed,* Jack flew back to L.A., and a few days later he showed up backstage at the Los Angeles Coliseum to watch U2 perform a holiday set complete with a fireworks show after the concert. According to Bono, "I turned around and there was this really disheveled looking guy. All he said was 'I liked the fireworks, guys,' and then asked us if we wanted hot dogs." Bono didn't learn until later it was Jack, still in costume and character from *Ironweed,* seeing if anybody would recognize him. And still later, he learned that Jack was thinking of having U2 do the soundtrack of *The Two Jakes,* if it ever happened.[1]

Comfortably back on the West Coast, Jack resumed his obsessive attachment to watching the Lakers from courtside and enjoying the box office bonanza that continued to roll in from the recently opened *The Witches of Eastwick,* on its way to a $64 million take in its initial domestic release, placing it in the top ten earners in Hollywood that year. Nothing could relieve heartburn like a hit.

He was spotted at Morton's restaurant in L.A., dining with Streep, which helped fuel the speculation that they were a couple; Morton's was not exactly on Jack's list of preferred food establishments. After dinner, to avoid the paparazzi, the two sneaked away together.

In July 1987, word reached Jack that John Huston had collapsed on set while his son Danny, Anjelica's brother, was directing him in a film for TV, *Mister Corbett's Ghost.* Huston had recently completed what would be his last directorial effort, *The Dead,* an appropriately

---

[1] The film happened; the soundtrack didn't. Jack and Bono were both represented by the same PR agency, Mahoney/Wasserman, which was how Jack was connected to and became friendly with Bono.

elegiac film based on a James Joyce short story about love and loss, written by his son Tony and starring Anjelica. It would be released posthumously.

Jack immediately flew to the hospital in Middleton, Rhode Island, to be with Huston, staying by his side until, on August 28, 1987, at age eighty-one, the great director passed. It was reported that Jack had promised Huston on his deathbed that he would look after Anjelica, and he accompanied her to the funeral. "For a certain period of my life," Jack said afterward, "I knew the greatest guy alive . . . certain guys like John, they're father figures to me. I was mad for John Huston . . ."

However, he didn't spend that night with Anjelica, when she probably needed him more than most others, because he simply couldn't fit her into his busy social calendar. As Jack moved into his fifties, it was as if he was becoming more desperate. The late bloomer had come into his own in Hollywood, and in his younger days women were everywhere, even before he became "Jack Nicholson." Now, though, it seemed as if he had something to prove, that he could still get them, that he could still satisfy them sexually. Whether he did, or whether they satisfied him, may not have even mattered. Women were no longer purely objects of desire but a form of self-affirmation. After all these years, Anjelica, with her strong maternal streak and desires, didn't exactly ring his bells, if in fact she ever had. What kept them together was an "I'll be there when you need me" kind of attachment, something deeper and in the long run perhaps more meaningful than purely romantic.

He had recently become involved with a nineteen-year-old British actress he had met in L.A. named Karen Mayo-Chandler and begun an intensely sexual affair, even while juggling Anjelica, Cartwright, the occasional Lakers cheerleader, and possibly Streep. He especially loved Mayo-Chandler's wild sexual streak. Mayo-Chandler then accepted *Playboy*'s offer of $150,000 to pose naked and spill the beans about her recent affair with Jack. She smiled happily through it all. At one point in her interview, she referred to Jack as "that horny little devil . . . he has this image of being like Bogart, a lovable rogue, a naughty little boy . . ." She intimated that he was into playful S&M—"A guaranteed non-stop sex machine into fun and games, like spankings, handcuffs, whips and Polaroid pictures . . . ," described her sex life with "Spanking Jack" as "mad, wild, and wonderful," and pointed out almost matter-of-factly that Jack was about the same age as her mother. She also claimed that he had given her his blessing to do the layout and interview. He later denied knowing anything about it.[2]

And then there was golden blond-haired actress Rebecca Broussard, who happened to be a dead ringer for Mimi Machu and the same age, twenty-four, as Jack's daughter, Jennifer. Jack had no problem with the fact that Broussard was so much younger. Just the opposite. He claimed Broussard's youth, like Mayo-Chandler's, was a sexual elixir. He went after Broussard and got her. "She's what I like. She's wild. Everything. Just, she's wild. Wild's *it*."

Broussard, a Kentucky-bred blonde, left college to come to New York and become a model; she was married for almost two years to record producer Richard Perry. After they divorced, Broussard moved to Hollywood and got a job as a waitress in Helena Kallianiotes's new hot-spot Hollywood night club, Helena's, which was where she first met Jack. He had some medicine of his own she seemed to like. "The first time Jack Nicholson touched my hand, I almost blacked out. I saw flashes of light. The minute I was introduced to him [by Helena] I knew something was there."

She was soon openly going with him to Aspen, and auditioning for Jack for the role of J. J. Gittes's secretary in the perennially stalled *The Two Jakes*. No gratitude is sweeter or more intense than from a pretty young girl promised a role in a big Hollywood movie.

Jack felt rejuvenated by Broussard, and Anjelica felt fed up. She decided she was finally through with Jack, once and for all, and as if to

----

[2] Mayo-Chandler gleefully chronicled her brief but intense romance with Jack in a *Playboy* spread that left little to the imagination, in print or in photos. Jack stopped seeing her after that. Mayo-Chandler died in July 2006 of breast cancer.

prove it, perhaps to herself as much as to Jack, put her Beverly Glen house for sale and moved to Benedict Canyon, far enough away from Mulholland so as to not have to worry about Jack ever wanting to come over to borrow a cup of sugar. And she signed on to act in the upcoming TV miniseries *Lonesome Dove.* Jack, meanwhile, leased a big house for Broussard, a sugar bowl away from Mulholland.

PETER GUBER HAD been after Jack since the start of *The Witches of Eastwick* to play the Joker in the upcoming big-screen version of *Batman,* and Jack had continually said no. Guber persisted, saying it would be the biggest picture of his career. Then he signed Tim Burton to direct. Burton, who began, like Jack did, in animation (on far different levels), worked his way through the ranks, and in 1987 he earned the right to direct *Beetlejuice.* Even before it was released, Burton signed with Warner Bros. to do one of the studio's biggest new productions, its highly anticipated *Batman.*

Guber: "It was always about capturing Jack's natural personality and using it in different ways. Kind of like getting Arnold Schwarzenegger to do a romantic comedy. Now, this was going to be the next big superhero picture, done a little differently from *Superman,* mainly because of the addition of Tim Burton, who was going to transform this into something that had never been seen before. Everybody scoffed, saying we wouldn't get anybody over seven to come and see it. But I knew the key to turning this into a franchise was to get an iconic adult actor to play the most important role, the villain.

"But Nicholson was playing hard-to-get. I knew that and figured the best thing to do was to take Tim Burton to Aspen, where Nicholson was, let them meet and help convince Jack to take the part. Tim said fine, we flew up there, to Jack's ranch, they met and Jack said, 'Let's go riding.' All the color drained from Tim's face. He turned to me and said, 'I don't ride.' 'You do now,' I said and threw him on a horse. Along the way Tim convinced Jack that they could make real magic in the film, that it would open up a whole new, younger audience to him, and that's when Jack said okay, let's do it. For five million up front and a hefty percentage of the gross."[3] Jack smelled a big film here and had packed his back end of the deal. Batman may have gotten all the press, but Jack was intent on getting all the money.

Jack's nose was right. As Guber had promised, it made him a household name all over again, as Batman became the biggest box office film of the year, with the fiftieth best opening (adjusted) gross of any American film ever made.[4]

Never the fool when it came to money, Jack thought Burton was on to something when he talked about opening a new audience. I talked to Tim about keeping the movie bright.[5]

"We had him for a three-week shoot [in England at the end of October]," Guber remembered, "which, predictably, stretched into six, and Jack was furious. 'I'm missing all my goddamn Lakers games,' he kept grousing to everybody. All we did was laugh. Jack was completely professional and finished the film without another word about basketball and wound up making a fortune doing it." To prepare for the role, Jack immersed himself in Nietzsche.

---

[3] Estimates put Jack's final earnings from the film in the $90 million range. Rumors persist that Jack sold his back-end points for a flat $50 million. This has been denied by Sandy Bresler.

[4] *Batman* led the pack with a whopping $251 million gross, followed by Spielberg's *Indiana Jones and the Last Crusade*, $198 million; Richard Donner's *Lethal Weapon 2*, $147 million; Amy Heckerling's *Look Who's Talking*, $140 million; Joe Johnston's *Honey, I Shrunk the Kids*, $131 million; Robert Zemeckis's *Back to the Future Part II*, $118 million; Ivan Reitman's *Ghostbusters II*, $112 million; Bruce Beresford's *Driving Miss Daisy*, $107 million; Ron Howard's *Parenthood*, $100 million; and Peter Weir's *Dead Poets Society*, $96 million. *Batman* would be, according to *Variety*, the highest domestic-grossing film of Jack's career, post-1989, followed by *A Few Good Men* ($41.3 million), *Hoffa* ($24.8 million), *The Two Jakes* ($10 million), and *Man Trouble* ($4 million).

[5] Early on, while still a boy living in New Jersey, Jack had once met TV's future iconic Joker, Cesar Romero, from the campy *Batman* TV series. Nicholson had met Romero when he, Jack, was a lifeguard in New Jersey and Romero was in the Coast Guard; Jack recalled Romero as "one of the greatest looking men in the business." Romero told Jack the day they met, "Hollywood is the lousiest town in the world when you're not working." Jack said he never forgot that.—Information and quotes from *Variety*, August 29, 1988.

In addition to using his paycheck from *Batman* to add several paint-ings by Picasso, Matisse, Magritte, de Lempicka, and Bouguereau to his wall-leaning collection of art, there were other reasons Jack had agreed to do the role. Besides leching after co-star Kim Basinger (who later described Jack as "crazy, nasty, and the most highly sexed human I've ever known"), he told Bogdanovich, "I considered it an artistic commitment . . . I had worked in what actors call 'en masque'—you're wearing a mask, acting in a mask feels very liberating. You're not quite as exposed. One of the few books Jeff Corey recommended to us was *Masks or Faces.*" His best line in the film, the one that made audiences hysterical, was delivered in full Joker mask and garb: *"Can somebody tell me what kind of world we live in when a man dressed up as a bat gets all of my press!"*

Jack loved his green hair wig, red mouth, and electrified purple clown outfit so much that he paid the production $70,000 to take them home. He thought they might come in handy, someday. After all, green was a good color for Jack.

Part V

A Few

Good

Roles

Previous page: Jack Nicholson plays Col. Nathan R. Jessup, USMC, and Col. Jessup plays God, in Rob Reiner's *A Few Good Men*, from a screenplay by Aaron Sorkin. *Courtesy of Getty Images*

"The actor is Camus's ideal existential hero because life is absurd . . . the man who lives more lives is in a better position than the guy who lives just one."

—JACK NICHOLSON

A YEAR AFTER JOHN HUSTON'S 1987 DEATH, HAL ASHBY PASSED. HE was only fifty-nine years old. If Huston's body was preserved by alcohol, Ashby's was rotted by coke. Both had memorials held at the Director's Guild Theater on Sunset. Huston's was standing room only; Ashby's was half full. That same year, Andy Warhol died at age fifty-eight in a New York hospital recovering from minor surgery.

These three deaths deeply depressed Jack. They were important people in his life, and their loss left him in no mood to go back to work. He flatly turned down Peter Guber's offer of $7.5 million, plus a generous piece of the back end, to do a *Batman* sequel that would have given the Joker a much larger part. He was both amused and relieved when the trades announced that his friend Danny DeVito was going to play the Penguin in the eventual sequel, *Batman Returns*, scheduled for release in 1992. Let Robin have a turn at some big-bucks comic book glory. [1]

Jonathan Demme, meanwhile, tried to persuade Jack to take the role

---

[1] But not all of it. According to the *Los Angeles Times* (June 28, 1991), Jack had cut an extraordinary merchandising deal to play the Joker that included all Batman merchandise, present and future, regardless if it was the Joker or not. It was estimated at the time he stood to make $15 million from the deal. Rumors spread that along with John McEnroe and Johnny Carson, he might buy a piece of the Lakers with the money. That deal never happened.

of Hannibal Lecter in *The Silence of the Lambs* (1991), which would pair him once more with Michelle Pfeiffer, one of his co-stars from *The Witches of Eastwick*. He was tempted, but said no. Those two roles eventually went to Anthony Hopkins and Jodie Foster, and the film became the first picture to win all five major Oscars since *One Flew over the Cuckoo's Nest* twenty-six years earlier. Hopkins won Best Actor, Foster won Best Actress, the film's producers won Best Picture, Demme won Best Director, and Ted Tally won for Best (Adapted) Screenplay.

Next came director John Badham, who wanted Jack to play a New York City detective in something called *The Hard Way* (1991). He said no, and the part went instead to James Woods. Tony Scott followed with an offer to Jack to star in *The Last Boy Scout* (1991), but again Jack said no, and that part went to Bruce Willis.

The one role he did say yes to was one he had waited what seemed like forever to get to play: J. J. Gittes. The *Chinatown* sequel had once again been resurrected, again without Polanski, who was still in self-imposed exile; but there was one director he believed could do the job better than anyone else.

Jack Nicholson.

He had not directed anything since *Goin' South*, which proved as much of a bomb as his only other directorial effort, *Drive, He Said*. Although he had vowed never to direct again, the desire to prove he could do it was strong enough to make him change his mind.

Bob Evans, who had somehow found a way to bring the project back to life, this time offered Jack $11 million to star in and direct the sequel, which Evans envisioned as the second part of a *Godfather*-like trilogy. His new production partner was Harold Schneider, who had worked with Jack for *Goin' South*. At Jack's directive Evans and Schneider hired Jack's daughter, Jennifer, now twenty-five, to be their assistant. She was interested in getting into movies. Evans once again hired Towne to rewrite his own script, despite Jack's making it clear he would have nothing to do with Towne directly. Right from the beginning there was trouble. Jack kept rejecting each revision and made Towne do several until he was finally satisfied.

Filming on *The Two Jakes* began August 18, 1989, in Los Angeles. The story jumps ahead ten years and one World War later from the original. In 1948, private detective Gittes is hired by a client, Julius "Jake" Berman, a real estate developer (Harvey Keitel), to find out if his wife, Kitty (Meg Tilly), is committing adultery. Before Gittes can prove anything is going on, Berman kills the man he thinks has been bedding his wife, who turns out to be Jake's business partner. Jake is pulled into both the new murder and memories of the murder of Evelyn Mulwray (Faye Dunaway allowed only her voice to be used for the remake). Missing yet vivid in their absence were John Huston, who had added just the right amount of mystery and trepidation to the original, and, of course, Polanski, who, at one point, suggested the film be shot in Paris so he could direct it, an idea that Jack liked, but for financial reasons, was rejected.

Production wasn't going well, and the mood of the cast and crew grew decidedly darker the day Anjelica showed up, unannounced, at the same Valencia, California, studio twenty-five miles north of Paramount where her father had shot his last film, 1987's *The Dead*. She had recently returned from New York, where she had just finished Paul Mazursky's *Enemies: A Love Story*. The night before, Jack had told Anjelica that Broussard, who was in the movie, playing Jake's secretary, was pregnant with his child, and Anjelica blew a gasket. The next morning she headed straight for the set where *The Two Jakes* was being filmed, brushed aside crew members who tried to stop her, stepped into the action shot, and physically mauled Jack with both fists and feet, letting out her fury for every wrong that Jack had done to her. Jack put his head down and his hands up to protect himself while letting Anjelica get it out of her system.

On April 16, 1990, Broussard delivered Lorraine Nicholson, seven pounds, fourteen ounces, at Cedars-Sinai Medical Center in Los Angeles (the baby girl was named after his sister/aunt). Fifty-two-year-old Jack happily agreed to support both mother and child, his third. The night before Broussard gave birth, Jack left her alone to attend a Lakers game with Don Devlin, and on the way home he stopped at Bob

Evans's house to watch the screening of a film. When he got back to Mulholland it was around two in the morning, just in time to rush Broussard, who had gone into labor, to the hospital. Four hours later, she gave birth.

Jack was there to catch baby Lorraine when she came into the world. "We had everybody helping us and a beautiful room and the clouds—she came at dawn. Only four hours of labor." He looked at the doctors, smiled, and said, "She's rich, too."

Jack then bought Broussard a $2 million home in Beverly Hills and set up an ample trust fund for Lorraine, claiming he still preferred to live alone. He needed his privacy, he told Broussard, who was a bit surprised by Jack's decision. "I'm very moody," he told a magazine interviewer, "and I shouldn't be around anyone when I think the world is too awful to tolerate. I need to have a place where no one gets into. Rebecca understands that, and it's fantastic for our relationship," he insisted. "It's my office—not my harem."

EVERYBODY INVOLVED WITH *The Two Jakes* knew the film was not very good. On set it had been dubbed by one crew member as "Jack's sex pen." It was not going to be a hit, probably not even make back its negative cost. Once again, Jack was overwhelmed and, as he had in *Goin' South*, discovered that doing double duty as director and actor was something he couldn't handle; one canceled out the concentration on the other. "You got any idea what it's like to direct a movie and star in it too? I'll tell ya. You're up at six and on the set at eight. You shoot all morning—settin' up shots, directin' the actors, playin' your own part all at the same time. Then you miss lunch 'cause you're thrashin' out production problems. In the afternoon you shoot till dark. The actors go home—*you* don't. You got two hours of conferences *before* you look at what you shot the day before. Suddenly it's midnight and you haven't had supper . . . so you go eat, and if you manage to get home by two a.m. you're lucky. You're dead beat, but you can't go to bed yet. You're also an actor. You got to study your lines for the next day. So you put out the lights at three, and three hours later the alarm goes off. That's the *normal* routine. However, Bob Towne and I had to rewrite the script *while* we were shooting; and the only time I could write was in the wee hours. So for about three months, I got one, two hours of sleep a night . . . *The Two Jakes* is the hardest work I've ever done." Because Towne and Jack were still not talking to each other, Jack had to take Towne's notes and work from them by himself.

Vilmos Zsigmond, the film's director of photography, added another side of what was so difficult about making the movie: "Filming Jack wasn't easy. I had to cover up all that weight and use tricks to hide the red in his eyes."

Evans, who had not produced a decent film in years—his last major effort, 1984's *The Cotton Club,* a pathetic attempt to make an African American version of *The Godfather* that made no money and was mired in a scandal that included a real-life murder and more—was now broke and had to sell his French Regency house at the foot of tony Coldwater Canyon, which he had owned for twenty-three years, complete with pool, tennis court, and separate projection house. Jack couldn't stand the thought of that; Evans had cast him while still an unknown actor in *On a Clear Day,* and Jack never forgot it. As ever with Jack, loyalty took precedence over everything. Now Evans, who had reached the heights of filmmaking and had taken advantage of all the perks, including women and drugs, was paying the piper. Reluctantly and tearfully he sold his house to wealthy international entrepreneur Tony Murray for just under $5 million, although the house was easily worth ten. He desperately needed cash.

After Jack and Beatty did what amounted to an unofficial drug intervention with Evans, Jack flew to Monte Carlo and, invoking a technical clause in the escrow account, returned the $5 million (plus buyback penalties) from his own pocket to Murray and gave the house back to Evans.

AND NOW HE had to deal with Anjelica, or try to; she had made it plain through the media, after their on-set brouhaha, that after seventeen stormy years with him, with the arrival of Broussard's baby, she was finally and forever finished with Jack. To one reporter, she said, "It never feels good to have been left and to have been left for a younger woman . . . I was very devastated by our having to separate, but there was no choice. There was no way I could go on being with Jack, who was fathering a child by another woman. I'm not that kind of woman."

Jack's reaction was to blame the press for invading his privacy. "Do you know what it was like to pick up *Vanity Fair* and see the headline on the Anjelica story [in which Anjelica was interviewed—"Anjelica Huston Hots Up—Life after Jack"]? It hurt. It wasn't realistic. She knew there was another woman and a baby, and then it was just all out there in the public eye and the privacy and the intimacy were gone . . ." That was all he had. He knew he had hurt Anjelica and feared now she was never coming back. He was right to be afraid.

On May 23, 1991, two years after her slap-him-upside-the-head breakup with Jack, Anjelica married well-regarded sculptor Robert Graham. The couple lived in Venice, California, and stayed married until his death at age ninety on December 27, 2008. They had no children.

Don Devlin observed this about Jack's sexual soap operas, including his relationship with Anjelica: "[His sexual] relationships were very strong and filled with huge emotional ups and downs. Every one of them fell into an identical pattern. Jack is such an overwhelming character that girls were always madly in love with him. Then he starts to behave fairly, then he starts to lose the girl, then he goes chasing after her again, then the relationship changes—the girl usually gets the upper hand. Then he becomes a little boy . . . Jack started his sexual career later than most of his friends . . . he was a very good boy, and behaved himself extremely well in his early years. Once he got into his seductive mode, he really went after it with a vengeance." Devlin hit upon something very insightful. Neither Anjelica nor Jack was inherently wrong, or right. Theirs wasn't a moral failure. The inability to either leave each other for good or make a real mutual commitment was the disease that killed their relationship.

◆ ◆ ◆

THE TWO JAKES opened on August 10, 1990, nine months after its originally scheduled Christmas 1989 holiday slot, a decision made after Paramount execs viewed the film in its rough-cut form of two hours and
forty-eight minutes, and decided it was too long to release in its current
form. To try to save its original place in the schedule, Jack personally
cut the negative to 2:24, in a small cutting room at Paramount, wearing
a tie-dyed Hawaiian shirt, white jeans, and white saddle shoes, an outfit
he didn't change once during these sessions. Paramount held firm on
the August release, despite Jack's and Evans's furious resistance, insisting that nobody goes to the movies in August.

Paramount proved prescient in dumping *The Two Jakes*. Not surprisingly, to them, it opened to mostly negative reviews. From a budget
of $19 million the film grossed only $10 million and quickly disappeared, despite valiant last-minute attempts by Jack to promote the film
in the press. No matter how hard he tried, he couldn't change the essential truth—that the passage of time, the loss of its original director,
Polanski, and original cast members Huston and Dunaway, had fatally
diminished *The Two Jakes*. Paramount quickly canceled Evans's plan
for the third film in his proposed trilogy, thus putting an end to Jack's
directing career.

On December 25, 1989, *People* named Jack one of the "25 Most In-
triguing People of the Year" and put his face on the cover, in costume
and mask as the Joker, along with Michelle Pfeiffer, Madonna, Billy
Crystal, John Goodman, and Mr. and Mrs. George H. W. Bush.

At the end of 1990, the *New York Times* wrote an assessment of
where the money was in the film industry and declared Jack Nicholson the wealthiest actor in Hollywood. *Batman* alone made him $60
million and counting. He later told the same paper that nearly all his
post-Corman films had turned a profit (except for *The Border* and *The
Fortune*), and that he had received back-end money for every film since
Easy Rider.

His biggest indulgence remained the acquisition of new art and he
took great pleasure from his two (acknowledged) children. He continued to search for a new project to star in, which was not all that easy,
as the younger moviegoing generation knew him only as the Joker.

He could do dozens of those types of roles if he wanted. He didn't. What Jack was looking for was a script that would give him what all the money in the world and colorful makeup couldn't—the return of his relevance as a serious actor.

And then, as if on cue, Bob Rafelson came knocking with a script by Carole Eastman called *Man Trouble* that was tailor-made, Rafelson insisted, for Jack and Meryl Streep. The script had gone nowhere with the studios, but before Jack could make up his mind, Streep pulled out of whatever commitment she may have made to the project and was replaced by Ellen Barkin. The project lay dormant until Jack decided to do the film anyway. Rafelson had made only two movies after 1981's *The Postman Always Rings Twice*—1987's *Black Widow*, a modest box office hit, and 1990's critically well-received but little-seen *Mountains of the Moon*. What helped Jack make up his mind was that the film was written by Eastman, who, after a long hiatus, had started writing under her own name again. She hadn't had a script of hers produced in sixteen years, since the failure of *The Fortune*. Either she couldn't get work because of it, or it had unsettled her to the point where she didn't want to or couldn't write anymore. Rafelson, who at the time was considered nonfundable by the studios, had somehow found Penta Pictures, a small Italian company that agreed to back the film to the tune of $30 million, but only if Jack agreed to be in it.

The plot of *Man Trouble* revolves around the misadventures of the ironically named Harry Bliss (Jack, sporting a 'stache). He is the operator of a professional guard dog service and is going through marriage counseling in a last-ditch effort to save his failing marriage to Adele (Lauren Tom). A beautiful married opera singer, Joan Spruance (Barkin, in real life fifteen years younger than Jack), begins to receive death threats, and hires Harry's service. All too soon they become romantically involved and all the inevitable (and predictable) problems ensue.

Jack made sure the film was packed with friends, grateful for the work—Harry Dean Stanton, who was always looking for acting jobs, and not one but *two* girlfriends: Veronica Cartwright, and, in a small role as a hospital administrator, Rebecca Broussard.

Little more need be said of the film beyond what Stanley Kauff-mann wrote about it in the *New Republic*: "Jack's appearance in this scrawny turkey can be seen as an act of loyalty to old friends." *Man Trouble* grossed just $4 million and all but ended the careers of East-man and Rafelson, and marked the last time Jack would attempt to play a leading man in film.

"I've only borrowed money once in my life and I have a very fearfully conservative idea about when I'm fine. One of my early quotes in this area was I don't care how many zeros are on the check, if you're working for the check, you're living at subsistence level . . ."

—JACK NICHOLSON

I N 1989, A SYRACUSE GRADUATE WHO HAD STRUGGLED FOR A COU-ple of years trying to make it as an actor wrote a play for Broadway that got produced and became a huge hit. His name was Aaron Sorkin and his play was *A Few Good Men.* After graduating with a BFA in musical theater, he then moved to Manhattan hoping to break into the business.

His sister, an attorney for the U.S. Navy's Judge Advocate General Corps, or JAGC, had been assigned to defend a group of Marines accused of participating in a hazing incident. It was through conversations with her that Sorkin came up with the idea of writing a play that tested the logic and the morality of those in charge of the military-industrial complex.

When he finished his courtroom drama, he sent it to producer David Brown, whom he had met during the production of a one-acter Sorkin had written that impressed Brown and inspired him to ask to see some more of his work.

Brown read *A Few Good Men* and wanted to make it into a movie but acquiesced to Sorkin's demand that it be done first as a play on Broadway. After a successful run, Brown took it to Hollywood, showed the film script version to several production companies, and

was turned down by all of them. He then went to Rob Reiner, a pro-
ducer/director at Castle Rock Entertainment, a film production con-
sortium of which Reiner was one of the partners. Reiner optioned
the script with the proviso that he would also direct. The son of
famed comic writer and performer Carl Reiner, Rob had directed
a slew of hit movies, including 1984's *This Is Spinal Tap* (which he
also partially wrote and appeared in), 1986's *Stand by Me*, 1987's
The Princess Bride (written by one of Sorkin's idols, William Goldman), 1989's *When Harry Met Sally* . . . ; considered a lightweight,
he longed to be taken seriously as a director, which, in Hollywood,
means directing important films about big subjects. Reiner was certain that *A Few Good Men* was the one. (He reportedly hired an
uncredited William Goldman to work with Sorkin to "open up" the
stagy courtroom drama for film by expanding the role of the pros-
ecutor, LTJG Daniel Alistair Kaffee, JAGC, USN, for Tom Cruise to
take the role, which he did.) Demi Moore was cast as LCDR JoAnne
Galloway, JAGC, USN, a more experienced lawyer to help Kaffee,
thereby adding some hoped-for sexual heat to a story involving the
trial of two Marines accused of inadvertently killing a third Marine
who died while being hazed by them. Unfortunately that heat never
emerged.

The key role in the film, that of Colonel Jessup, was originally
played on Broadway by Stephen Lang, who hoped to repeat his performance on film, but too many bigger names wanted it, among them De
Niro, James Woods, and Pacino, but Reiner wanted Jack, even when
his asking price for the four scenes Jessup was in, which amounted to
ten days' work, was $5 million, or $500,000 a day. Cruise received $12.5
million for a much larger part.

During production, the word on the set was that Cruise and Jack
did not get along, mirroring the tension between the two characters
that heightened the level of both performances. Colonel Jessup's
character is more than a little reminiscent of *The Caine Mutiny*'s infamous Captain Queeg, the flawed commander of the *Caine*, right
down to a self-incriminating loss of temper, wit, and ultimately, san-

ity that was the climax of both Edward Dmytryk's film and Reiner's *A Few Good Men*. Jack's German shepherd performance as Colonel Jessup, right down to his teeth-baring monster of a breakdown on the stand—"*YOU CAN'T HANDLE THE TRUTH!*"—is the film's memorable highlight.

ON FEBRUARY 20, 1992, twenty-two months after the arrival of their first baby, Broussard gave birth to a second, an eight-pound, six-ounce boy they named Raymond. A beaming Jack told *Variety* he was "sky high" and that "the baby looks like Rebecca—thank goodness. But he's got my big dick!" Continuing on that theme, Jack told *Us* that "the only trouble Ray will have with women is an over-abundance!"

That made five offspring for Jack: his daughter from his first and only marriage, twenty-eight-year-old Jennifer, whom he had become close to since she moved to Los Angeles; Caleb, twenty-one, whom he had never met; Lorraine and Raymond, his two children with Rebecca Broussard; and the child he had with Hollman.

In April, Jack was photographed by Annie Leibovitz for the April 1992 issue of *Vanity Fair*, with Jack on the cover holding his and Broussard's twenty-two-month-old daughter and two-month-old son. He was fifty-five years old. Inside the magazine, Jack gushed about fatherhood, and how great it was to have someone around to take care of the kids and him, that Broussard wanted to be a mother and loved being with Jack. On the surface they seemed idyllic. Below, it was going to be difficult to sustain this children-enduced euphoria.

According to one friend, "Rebecca's number one, but they live in separate houses in L.A. and he does see other women." According to another, "Jack really loves [Rebecca] a lot. How could he not? But Jack can't give himself to one woman. He loves them all. I'm sure he still loves Anjelica, and always will . . . it hurts Anjelica to deal with Jack now . . . and it's hard on Jack too. I don't think they speak privately, not even on the phone . . ."

"It's an unusual arrangement," Jack conceded, "but the last twenty-five years or so have shown me that I'm not good at cohabitation . . . [With Rebecca] I look at it as a two-bedroom apartment—[my] house and her house."

As for Rebecca, when asked about Jack's well-known inability to remain monogamous, which he freely admitted, she said, "I'd really rather not talk about my relationship with Jack. I think that should be private."

MAN TROUBLE OPENED that summer, 1992; it was made for $30 million, but crashed and burned to the tune of a $4 million gross. It was another costly setback for Rafelson, who would not make a feature film again for four more years. Eastman would write only one more movie in her lifetime, and that would be for TV. Jack felt bad for them, but by now he was used to Rafelson films failing. He knew he was a better actor than Rafelson was a director, so the blame wouldn't be put on him for anything except trying to help a couple of friends.

After spending the summer on the Mediterranean with Rebecca and their two children, Jack began to itch to get back in front of the cameras. A Few Good Men had been a happy experience. Here he was drowning in fatherhood, and decided the best thing to do was to get back to land and make a new movie.

Although Jack wasn't crazy about the playwright David Mamet after Postman, a new Mamet screenplay came along about the life of Jimmy Hoffa that he really liked. Plus, his good friend Danny DeVito was set to direct. He had heard DeVito was having trouble casting the lead and thought it might be interesting to escape his own reality for a while by playing a gangster who couldn't escape his. Jack offered his services, and DeVito instantly accepted.

As DeVito began filming, Hoffa quickly found itself mired in budget trouble. The distribution studio, Warner Bros., had set it at $35 million, including Jack's salary. It soon escalated above $45 million, with no end in sight.

Jack filmed on location in Pittsburgh for four grueling months, and the result was one of his least interesting portrayals. Mamet's script never came to life. As a result, Jack's acting came off as generic, a central casting bad guy with a bulldog face. Despite all the cost overruns, DeVito believed they were justified because he was making a film about someone he perceived as a national hero—another major problem with *Hoffa*, a character description that was similarly unexplored, leaving Jack's performance on the cardboard side of character.

Jack spent his off time in a $1,500-a-night hotel suite, paid for by the production, where, whenever Lakers games were broadcast, Jack stopped any scenes he was in or stayed awake deep into the night to watch the West Coast satellite feed of the Lakers, something he was far more interested in than the movie he was making. The poor script, the slow pace, and the production's consistent money problems forced DeVito to rethink his schedule, and the general boredom of the excessive downtimes managed to kill Jack's interest in the film.

Immediately after shooting ended, he was off to the Berlin Film Festival, where *Hoffa* was set to be screened. While there, he had a chance to meet up with Roman Polanski and his wife, Emmanuelle. The Polanskis had also recently welcomed a baby daughter, Morgane, and Jack and Roman spent a few hours together talking about the joys of fatherhood. Jack made a halfhearted plea to persuade Polanski to come back with him, but with *The Two Jakes* history, Jack could only muster up that one half.

BACK IN THE STATES, Jack had two films released in December 1992. On the twelfth, *A Few Good Men* opened to rave reviews and was the number one film for three straight weeks. It grossed $243 million, worldwide, off a budget of $43 million, and a slew of Oscar nominations, including one for Jack, that reconfirmed his status as the premier character actor in Hollywood.

Hoffa opened on Christmas Day and, off a final budget somewhere around $35 million, the film grossed $25 million domestically and another $5 million overseas. It was ignored by the Academy but nominated for a Razzie (Golden Raspberry), given annually to an actor who holds the distinction of giving the worst performance of the year. That year, Jack was nominated twice—for *Hoffa* and *Man Trouble*. He lost to Sylvester Stallone for *Stop! Or My Mom Will Shoot!*

Jack could laugh off the Razzie, but not the affair that Broussard started soon afterward with a much younger, good-looking man, even as Jack found himself in a brief but intense affair with the blond French actress Julie Delpy. If he was going to do his thing, then she was going to do hers. But his romance with Delpy fizzled, and Jack took the blame for its failure. In a bizarre interview with the *Mail Online*, Jack said: "I'm still wild at heart. But I've struck bio-gravity. I can't hit on women in public anymore. I didn't decide this; it just doesn't feel right at my age . . . If men are honest, everything they do and everywhere they go is for a chance to see women. There were points in my life where I felt oddly irresistible to women. I'm not in that state now and that makes me sad . . ." The combination mea culpa was half apology, half warning, not just to Rebecca but for his own, personal Miss America pageant: "I've been in love in my life, but it always starts with obsession that lasts exactly 18 months and then it changes. If I'd known and been prepared for that, I may have been able to orchestrate the whole relationship thing better . . . The reality was that I was annihilated emotionally by [this last separation] from Anjelica. That was probably the toughest period of my life." Nicholson went on to say that his heart remained broken by Huston. It was not something Broussard wanted to hear.

Jack tried to get Broussard back, and for a while it seemed to work, but their reconciliation did not hold. She would no longer tolerate Jack's inability to emotionally commit, or his chronic roving eye. Broussard decided after four years, two children, and no wedding ring that she really had had enough. It was time to liberate herself from Jack, and that was exactly what she did. He fell apart over it and begged her to come back, but Broussard was unmovable. She sold the house he had given her, and a few years later wed music producer Alex Kelly, to whom she remains married.

Jack went back to his paintings.

THE OSCAR AWARDS ceremony took place on March 29, 1993, at the Dorothy Chandler Pavilion, hosted by Billy Crystal.

This was Jack's fourth nomination for Best Performance by a Supporting Actor, for A Few Good Men, with Terms of Endearment his only previous win in this category, and his tenth nomination in the combined categories of supporting and leading actor roles, which he had won only once, for One Flew over the Cuckoo's Nest. But everyone's focus was on Clint Eastwood, who, in all his years on TV and in movies, had never won anything in his long career, despite a number of notable film roles, including the creation of the iconic Dirty Harry and the Man with No Name. This year he was being lauded for his eulogistic western, the powerful Unforgiven, in which he produced, directed, and starred. The Academy nominated him for Best Picture (producer), Best Director, and Best Actor. Gene Hackman, who gave a bravura performance in the film as the personification of Old West evil, was nominated for Best Supporting Actor.[1]

Unforgiven received a total of nine Oscar nominations, A Few Good Men four. The other unlikely film that year that had any real heat was Martin Brest's Scent of a Woman, with Al Pacino's over-the-top but audience-pleasing performance as a blind curmudgeon who turns out to be a good guy, a film notable for Pacino's tango with the beautiful Gabrielle Anwar and the introduction of "HOO-WAH" to the American book of classic movie contributions to the English language, right up there that same year with "You can't handle the truth!"

Jack showed up in tux and tails and his signature Wayfarers. His

---

[1] Besides Jack and Hackman, the other nominees for Best Performance by a Supporting Actor were Jaye Davidson in Neil Jordan's The Crying Game; Al Pacino, nominated for Best Actor in Martin Brest's Scent of a Woman and Best Supporting Actor in James Foley's Glengarry Glen Ross; and David Paymer in Billy Crystal's Mr. Saturday Night.

category was announced early in the evening. When Gene Hackman's name was called, he stood to rousing applause. It was Hackman's second Oscar. He had won in 1972 for Best Performance by an Actor for his role in William Friedkin's 1971 *The French Connection.*

The rest of the evening was long and laborious for Jack, and by the end of the ceremony, his last Oscar win seemed a million years ago.

CHAPTER 18

"I'm one of the very few actors who can do what he wants . . ."

—JACK NICHOLSON

COMING OFF HIS OSCAR LOSS, THE FIFTY-SIX-YEAR-OLD JACK WAS fed up with making movies and told friends he wanted to quit the business once and for all, take it easy, go to Lakers games, and just veg out after quietly traveling to New York for another round of hair transplants. They never really took, but he kept coming back for more.

The films he turned down during this period included Lee Tamahori's *Mulholland Falls,* which Jack felt was a bit too similar to *Chinatown.* The role Tamahori wanted him for eventually went to Nick Nolte. Warner Bros. asked him to star opposite the then-hot Jodie Foster in Robert Zemeckis's sci-fi film *Contact.* Jack turned it down, saying he didn't do sci-fi, and the role went instead to Matthew McConaughey. He was also offered the starring role in the remake of *Diabolique* with Sharon Stone and Isabelle Adjani. He turned it down and his role went to Chazz Palminteri. He also turned down *The Fan,* and that role went instead to Robert De Niro.

Soon enough, he grew bored with doing nothing and started looking around for something new to occupy his time. He tried getting into the nightclub business. Helena Kallianiotes had recently closed her Hollywood club, which was one of his favorite after-hours hangouts, and when Alan Finkelstein, one of Jack's night-side friends from the Studio 54/Warhol days in New York, came to him with an offer to partner up and buy out a former gay club in West Hollywood and transform it into something called the Monkey Bar, Jack jumped at it. Opening night he was sure Helena's "regulars," including Bob Evans,

Mick Jagger, Nick Nolte, and Don Henley, would all be there and sure enough they were. Jack was there every night, enjoying his own little private-room celebrity fiefdom, with no cameras allowed in to catch his alarming weight gain.

However, his presence there lasted only a few weeks, before he got bored playing nightclub impresario. This time when a new film offer came in, he took it, and just like that his film retirement was over. This was a remake and reimagined version of the classic *The Wolfman*.

"Wolfman" pictures were once one of Hollywood's favorite genres, part of the horror cycle made famous by James Whale's 1931 *Franken-stein*. In 1933 Whale made a film version of H. G. Wells's *The Invisible Man*, with a script partly doctored by the great Preston Sturges, that made its star Claude Rains, barely seen in the film as he played the gauze-wrapped title role, Hollywood newest sensation, and helped temporarily move horror from the basement of B-movies to the ballroom of the A's. George Waggner's 1941 *The Wolf Man* gave the title role to Lon Chaney Jr., and he repeated it in sequels for years.

After another few years and dozens more films, the genre lost its audience and was for the most part relegated to the Hollywood junk bin until director John Landis reconfigured and updated the wolfman in his 1981 campy *An American Werewolf in London*. The film proved a hit ($61 million gross in its initial domestic release, off a $10 million budget), and Hollywood began looking for ways to revive the genre. A year after *American Werewolf* was released, paperback writer Jim Harrison claimed he had had a werewolf-like experience while he was alone in a Michigan cabin. Years later, he turned his "experience" into a screenplay.

Harrison ran into Jack one day in Paris, where he'd gone to relax, and over drinks he vividly re-created the night of the occurrence and left his script of the experience. Jack read it and loved it and wanted to make it into a movie. He brought it to Columbia and they offered a finance/distribution deal worth $40 million, with Jack playing the werewolf. He said he would, for a $13 million fee up front, and only if one of five directors he chose would make it with him. His list included Peter Weir, who said no; Kubrick, who showed no interest in the project; Bertolucci, also a no; Polanski, still in exile, and Columbia wouldn't make it overseas—too expensive; and Mike Nichols. It was Nichols who said yes to produce, Nichols wanted Douglas Wick, who had worked with Nichols on the successful 1988 comedy *Working Girl*. Jack approved Wick, and Nichols postponed what would have been his next project, *The Remains of the Day*, to start *Wolf* (he would never make *Remains*; it was eventually directed in 1993 by James Ivory).

In the film, Jack's character, Will Randall, works in publishing, and to prepare for the role Jack patterned his character on the well-known Random House editorial director Jason Epstein, whom he knew socially. He copied Epstein's walk and his style of talking. Jack even began to use tar-reducing cigarette filters like Epstein did. And once again he yo-yo'd down his body weight—he felt he needed to lose fifty pounds to play Randall. To do so, he hired his old friend Tommy Baratta, now chef and owner of Marylou's, a small seafood restaurant on West 9th Street in Greenwich Village, one of the places where Jack liked to eat and drink when he was in New York. At Jack's request and his own expense, Baratta had a separate, private smoking room built, so Jack could puff on his cigars and cigarettes while eating without annoying any of the other diners.

Baratta put Jack on a stringent diet and exercise program. Soon enough, he was, if not slim—that would never happen again—trim enough to play Randall; a little heft made sense for a man who also happens to be a wolf.

Production began, and soon enough things started to go off track. In the beginning, it appeared to be a love affair between Harrison and Jack until they began to disagree about what the film was really all about. Jack believed the roots of the story were not in environmentalism, as Harrison had written it, but in Native American mysticism, which he somehow was convinced could be communicated by Randall's transformation from man to wolf. And when he couldn't pull it off as written, he complained to Nichols, who agreed that Jack's character should be making a comment about the taming aspects of American civilization. They both went to Harrison to fix the script. Harrison not only hated these interpretations, he felt they seriously dumbed down the screenplay he had written. After five additional rewrites, Harrison declared that "[Nichols] took my wolf and made it into a Chihuahua." He not only quit the picture, he left the industry, ending his twenty-year career as a writer in Hollywood.

Wesley Strick, who had written Scorsese's 1991 remake of *Cape Fear*, took over and rewrote the screenplay, aided by Nichols's onetime performing partner, Elaine May, uncredited for her work on the film (though by all inside accounts, much of her script was what ended up on the screen). Her version turned the wolf from some kind of Indian ghost to an out-of-control womanizer, a turn Jack liked). Here is how he told May he wanted to express the mystic in the wolfman: "I wanted to get involved in some kissing and then pull back in a very subtle silhouette from it with a hungry and longer tongue. I thought that would be a very interesting cinematic image, just have this great wolf tongue down her throat."

The film co-starred Michelle Pfeiffer (twenty-one years younger than Jack) as the victim/victimizer (with Jack more a seductive Dracula than a hairy werewolf) and also featured his daughter Jennifer in a small role. Shooting was finished by July 1993, and after an early screening proved disastrous, Columbia pulled it from its scheduled Christmas release. The film needed additional work, and the budget escalated to a whopping $70 million with no release date in sight.

INTO THE NEW YEAR, Jack was without a steady girlfriend. He always operated better when he was with a young, beautiful woman who professed to love him. With Broussard gone, Anjelica gone, and no one there to make him feel right, his temper, which he managed to keep in check most of the time, may have escaped its safety valve after all the intensity making *Wolf*—or it may simply have been Jack having a bad day. Jack had taken up golf during the making of *The Two Jakes*, because Gittes was a golfer. On February 8, 1994, on the way to play a round of golf in the Valley, he was driving along Moorpark leading up to the intersection of Riverside when he thought he'd been cut off by a big-ass Mercedes. The driver stopped at the next light, and Jack grabbed a graphite two-iron from his golf bag, which was in his trunk, and proceeded to smash the windshield and roof of the Mercedes.[1] The owner of the car, thirty-eight-year-old Robert Scott Blank of Hollywood, claimed he never got out of his car, a sensible decision. When Jack was satisfied he had gotten justice, his road rage spent, he got back into his car and continued driving on.

Blank recognized his attacker immediately and took down Jack's license plate number during the assault. There were two eyewitnesses to the bizarre event, and one of them also wrote down Jack's number. After Jack left, Blank called the police, who interviewed Blank and the two witnesses and showed up at Jack's house to arrest him. He was taken to the police station in Van Nuys, charged with two misdemeanors, one count of assault against Blank, and one count of assault against his car. He was released on his own recognizance.

A week later, Blank filed a civil suit, claiming that he had been hurt by some of the flying windshield glass and, during the attack, was in fear for his life.

On March 3, three weeks before he was to be arraigned, on the advice of his lawyers, Jack settled with Blank by publicly apologizing and paying him an unknown sum to drop the charges.[2] After the case was settled, Jack answered all questions but essentially gave the same answers to everyone. He told *Us* and others that he was upset because a friend of his had recently died, and that he was deeply embroiled with the making of a movie, immersed in his character.[3]

While all of this was going on, Jack was named the recipient of 1994's AFI Lifetime Achievement Award, in a ceremony held on March 3 at the famed Beverly Hilton Hotel ballroom. It was a bit of a hollow prize, one more self-serving industry ceremony, this one established in

---

[1] *Golf Digest* reported that it may have been a three- or five-iron.

[2] Sources claim the amount was $500,000.

[3] There is an interesting postscript to the incident. That November, several months after the incident, Blank sent a letter of apology for cutting Jack off but gave no explanation for it. Jack felt vindicated by this belated confession. Everyone in his circle agreed that Blank had made a purposeful killing off Jack's temper tantrum, and that Jack was right that he had, indeed, been cut off.

1973 by the AFI board of directors to honor a single individual for his or her lifetime contribution to enriching American culture by advancing the art of film through motion pictures and television. John Ford was the first recipient, Jack the twenty-second. But to Jack, it meant more than even the Oscars. This night was all about him, his the only award handed out. Everybody who spoke talked about him. The audience was full of friends and co-workers. It was the kind of attention and recognition from the industry that Jack savored.

On the night of the event, taped for later cable broadcast, he and Rebecca Broussard (they had agreed to remain public friends for the sake of the children) were brought to their table as the band played Steppenwolf's *Born to Be Wild*, the unofficial theme song of *Easy Rider* and a tongue-in-cheek description of Jack's life.

Among the guests were a table filled with his co-stars, including Shelley Duvall, Mary Steenburgen, Louise Fletcher, Ellen Barkin, Kathleen Turner, Candice Bergen, Faye Dunaway, Madeline Stowe, Cher, and Broussard. Among the female no-shows were Anjelica Huston, Susan Anspach, Mimi Machu, Carole Eastman, Michelle Phillips, and Sandra Knight. The more notable male attendees were Warren Beatty, Bob Rafelson, Kareem Abdul-Jabbar, Michael Douglas, Dustin Hoffman, Bob Rafelson (but not Bert Schneider), and Bob Dylan, with whom Jack had become friendly while Dylan was hanging out with Jagger when Jack was in London making *The Shining* and remained so after filming ended.

After a number of speakers, all telling stories about their experiences with Jack, it was, finally, his time to accept the award. Mike Nichols introduced him, at one point referring to him directly as Nick, and that no one deserved the award more. He also said that if you ask any kid, "He'll tell you that Jack is the hippest place in the universe, coolest place in America, the Independent Republic of Jack. The hardest thing to do is wear a gift well, and Jack wears it with a killer smile and a pair of shades." The audience applauded, Nichols stepped back, and Jack came to the podium. He walked from his table to a standing ovation.

"I'm touched," he said, adding, self-deprecatingly, "Unfortunately I'm not drunk and lucky to be at large." His reference to the golf in-

cident brought a healthy round of laughter and applause. He then acknowledged a rare public appearance by his sister Lorraine, who had
come all the way from New Jersey, and his daughter Jennifer. He also
singled out Broussard, the mother of his children: "She changed her
mind a lot of times, she said let's take the babies but I said they were
too young to drink." Broussard didn't find it at all funny. He went on to
acknowledge all his friends, especially the female ones. He then said
the Buddhists had asked him if anybody had ever won it twice. Huge
laugh. He then skipped over most of his speech: "Yeah yeah . . . I'm a
late blooming success . . . all of that . . . just a hick actor . . ." And then
he choked up. "You know I love you all . . . My work motto is 'Everything counts' . . . My life motto is 'More good times.' . . . I guess the
only really danger here is after this I'll fall in love with myself . . ." For
the first time ever in public he mentioned his mother and his sister, not
differentiating one from the other, and Shorty too, thanking them for
all they had done for him: "So, Mud, June, Shorty, who had an enormous nose. I may be Godless, I may be faithless, I still pray that they
can hear me. I started out to please them and had a ball." He made no
mention of Furcillo-Rose. He then smiled, and as if to respond to the
many past-tense speeches that had been given earlier that night about
his work, he said, "All these things about age and time. *You ain't seen
nothing yet!*"

He received a standing ovation as he wiped away a tear and, holding the award, made his way back to his table, blowing air through his
cheeks like he was glad he got through it, and took his seat between
Broussard and Candice Bergen.

JACK WANTED TO find a role that would somehow reinvigorate his relevance, the way Clint Eastwood had with *Unforgiven*. He needed fresh
creative blood. A commercial producer offered him $10 million to do
an unseen voice-over that would last all of ten seconds. He said no in
a single breath's time. That was not where he was going to wind up,
hawking garbage on TV.

He thought he found his future in actor/writer/director Sean Penn, who reminded Jack of himself twenty years prior: talented, young, intense, excessive, and consumed with the notion of being an artist. The difference between the two was star power: Jack had it, Penn didn't, perhaps one of the reasons why Penn, too, had publicly stated that he was giving up acting in favor of directing his own scripts because acting was no longer pleasurable. Would Penn benefit commercially from Jack's star power, or would Jack find creative reinvigoration working with Hollywood's baddest boy?

And would anybody care?

Part Six

Sunset on the Boulevard

PREVIOUS PAGE: Diane Keaton and Jack Nicholson walking on the beach in
Nancy Meyers's 2003 *Something's Got to Give. Courtesy of Rebel Road Archives*

"I'd like to take the middle-aged actor into real steaming sensuality..."
—JACK NICHOLSON

WOLF FINALLY OPENED IN JUNE 1994 TO A SERIES OF POOR RE-views and was expected to quickly disappear. However, no one counted on Jack's resilient star power and Nichols's strong fan base, which, combined, drove the film to become a $131 million box office smash.

He went out and promoted the film in the States and then in England and Europe, treating himself to a good time on the studio's nickel. While Jack was hawking the film in London, a reporter for the *Observer* noted, "Since the day he arrived from New York by private plane two weeks ago, Nicholson has been partying with beautiful women . . . one looked young enough to be the 57-year-old actor's daughter [she wasn't]. Others appeared considerably younger . . . for the past fortnight he danced nightly in the pale moonlight, not returning to the Connaught Hotel until close to dawn."

At the Venice Film Festival, Jack was asked by a reporter why he wanted to play a wolf, and how he researched the role. Jack smiled and said, "The thing I like best about wolves is that one guy fucks all the women." A roomful of reporters, mostly male, cheered.[1]

Anthony Lane, the articulate new-blood film critic for the *New Yorker*, gave the best summation of all the critics who reviewed the

---

[1] While doing promotion for the film, Jack was interviewed by a comely French journalist. Later, he told *Spy* that he told the woman after the interview, "I would have tried to have intimate knowledge of you." The woman replied, "Twenty years ago you tried to fuck my mother."

film: "Will Randall is the part that Jack was born to play . . . He was a wolf man long before this picture was ever conceived. *Wolf* is like a one-movie retrospective of [his] schizoid career."

Stars like to work with stars. Most of the time, big ones are sought out by lesser ones, but occasionally big ones do seek out lesser ones. Sean Penn, whose heroes were Bob Dylan, Phil Ochs, and Dennis Hopper, sought greater mainstream film validation by working with a hip powerhouse like Jack Nicholson, a mainstream actor with more than a little independent film cred. The opportunity to go out on those creative limbs lessens as stars like Jack get older, and the roles they are offered are, logically, meant for middle-aged actors. Middle age is not the time for rebellion. It's the time to play jokers and werewolves.

Penn approached Jack in the summer of 1994 about being in *The Crossing Guard*, a script Penn had written and intended to direct. Penn may have been discovered by audiences after his turn in Amy Heckerling's 1982 *Fast Times at Ridgemont High*, and then played the Hollywood game for a while, was not this Penn, the darker, self-styled rebel artist. His 1985 marriage to pop star Madonna (who had been a girl twirl for Jack reportedly both before and after her marriage to Sean) and his subsequent arrest and jail time in 1987 for punching a paparazzo were elements that helped change him, and in some ways take him, whether by choice or action, out of the mainstream.

After his arrest, Penn was no long considered as bankable by the studios, and he reached out to Jack first in 1992 and again early in 1994, to get him to agree to appear in *The Crossing Guard*. This was the second film written, produced, and directed by Penn; 1991's *The Indian Runner* was the first. *The Crossing Guard* was also going to co-star, of all people, a now happily married Anjelica Huston. Jack waived his normal fee to be in the film. When Anjelica found out Jack was going to be her co-star, she agreed to stay with it as long as Jack remained strictly professional throughout the shoot. If Jack had other ideas, consciously or otherwise, he didn't give any indication of it. One unnamed member of the crew who worked on the film said he saw nothing but politeness and courtesy between them. They stayed in opposite corners for most of the shoot. If he had any ulterior motives, she did not. She was happily married. She still loved Jack, she would always love him, but she had put their romantic relationship behind her.

To make things even more interesting, the other female lead was Penn's second wife-to-be, Robin Wright. (Penn and Madonna were divorced in 1989, and he then had two children with Wright—a girl named Dylan and a boy they named Hopper Jack Penn, after Dennis Hopper and Jack.)

The film, shot mostly at night to give it a noir feeling, is about two men linked by the accidental murder of the daughter of one and the revenge sought by the other. Freddy Gale (Jack) is obsessed with revenge; he wants to kill the tellingly named John Booth (David Morse, whose off-beat performance in *The Indian Runner* Penn especially liked so much he used the actor again). While drunk, Booth accidentally runs over Gale's four-year-old daughter and spends four years in prison for it. Upon his release, Gale intends to kill Booth to exact his full revenge.

The premise is good, the execution less so, with a climax that is at once hokey and unbelievable. Somewhere beneath the film's mountain of self-loathing and Method posturing was an allegory for the meaninglessness of war and the necessity of peace, a favorite subject of Penn's (who not only went to jail for punching a photographer, but allegedly hung another one out a window by his ankles, and allegedly was said to have hit Madonna with a baseball bat).

However, despite its hollow foundation, Jack loved the character Gale's mixture of rage, sadness, and obsessive desire for redemption. "It was kind of like working without a net," Jack later recalled. "First-person acting—because there's not a lot of character to hide behind, so to speak. No makeup, no wardrobe, no haircut, no limp, no accent, no voice, no nothing. Just emotion . . ."

The Crossing Guard was released on November 16, 1995, and received mostly good reviews but had a limited distribution and did not draw a significant audience. *The Crossing Guard* had been financed by the up-and-coming Weinstein brothers' production company Miramax, in exchange for international distribution rights. It was made on a budget of $9 million but grossed only $869,000 in its initial domestic release. Ironically, the film, and Penn's writing and directing career, might have been better off without the distraction of Jack's fame and charisma in a project that required a character that had absolutely no redemptive qualities and therefore generated no sympathy from the other characters in the film or from the audience.

Several months after the film's brief run, fifty-seven-year-old Jack decided to settle (or heal) a lot of old scores. First, he made good on his long-standing threat to foreclose on the house he had bought for Susan Anspach. He didn't need the money; it was something he felt he had to do after Anspach sent a chiding letter to *Vanity Fair* about that April 1994 interview with Jack, in which he had raved about fatherhood but failed to mention or acknowledge his son Caleb. Anspach's letter appeared in the June issue, noting that Caleb was Jack's child, too.

Jack exploded when he saw it. "I told Ms. Anspach that this is a catastrophic approach to life, making protestations and all that. I don't think it accomplishes anything." What especially got Jack so angry was that he had continued to help Anspach financially, even after her second marriage had ended and she had difficulty getting work in an increasingly youth-obsessed Hollywood, right up until the publication of her letter, which he took as an act of disrespect, after which he stopped all assistance and foreclosed.

Anspach then showed up at his front door with Caleb, to let Jack see his son for only the second time. He had never publicly admitted he was the boy's father. After an awkward moment between them, Jack embraced the now twenty-five-year-old CNN employee. He and Caleb became friends, if not exactly bosom buddies. Caleb wanted to get to know his real father better, and Jack had no problem with that.

But Jack's relationship with Anspach remained hostile and the foreclosure stood, on top of which he added a lawsuit for unpaid loans he had made to her through the years, totaling $600,000. In response, the fifty-three-year-old Anspach filed a countersuit against Jack, claiming through her lawyers that Jack had fraudulently led her to believe that she would not have to repay the loans, including the money for the house. Anspach also claimed to have kept seeing Jack secretly into the 1980s, all during her marriage and his involvement with Huston and Broussard.

As she bitterly told the *Los Angeles Times*, following the filing of her countersuit: "I could have sold the house in 1989, paid off Jack in full and walked away with a million-dollar profit" if she'd known he was one day going to foreclose. Jack's response, through his lawyers, was, "Unfortunately for Anspach, the law is straightforward. When you borrow money, eventually you have to pay it back." But it wasn't the money that had gotten him so angry, it was the public humiliation, the embarrassment, especially the letter Anspach wrote to *Vanity Fair.* There were some things that didn't belong to the public, he believed, and he wanted to teach her a lesson not to try to push him around. Depositions for Jack's lawsuit went ahead that August. Shortly afterward, a Superior Court judge ordered a trial to begin the following March. While all this was going on, he had quietly donated sixty acres of deer-inhabited land in the hills above Santa Monica to a California conservancy dedicated to preventing overdevelopment of that part of Los Angeles, as if to underscore that none of this was about the money; at least not for him.

JACK WANTED TO work again, and sooner rather than later. His next film would see him try to move forward by retreating, by returning to the directorial realm of none other than Bob Rafelson, whose own career was on the brink of extinction. Rafelson hadn't made a feature film since the disastrous *Man Trouble,* and after extensive trips to Tibet and the Amazon he wanted to make one more film and rightly believed he could get Jack to be in it.

Rafelson's new picture was *Blood and Wine,* which Rafelson described as an erotic Oedipal film noir (it was neither Oedipal nor noir), scripted by Nick Villiers and Alison Cross. It was financed by Majestic Films, a London-based company Rafelson found that was willing to put up $15 million for the foreign rights. Majestic was Rafelson's miracle; no U.S. studio or independent group would go near him. The film was necessarily shot fast and cheap, with little money left after Jack's $10 million up-front fee. He also got a piece of the back end. Rafelson agreed. His co-star in the film was Jennifer Lopez (thirty-two years younger than Jack).

Rafelson played the completed film in noncompetition at the San Sebastian Film Festival in September 1996. Fox Searchlight Pictures then picked it up for American theatrical distribution. The film also starred Judy Davis, Michael Caine, and Stephen Dorff.

Jack also agreed to do a cameo in Robert Harling's *The Evening Star,* co-written by Harling and Larry McMurtry, the sequel to *Terms of Endearment* that James Brooks was not involved with. Jack did the four-day part as a favor to his friend Shirley MacLaine, who reprised her Academy Award–winning role of Aurora Greenway, after which he received a script by Mark Andrus and James Brooks that Brooks would direct called *Old Friends*, at once hilarious and heartbreaking, and far superior to anything Jack had read or done in recent years. It was about a character named Melvin Udall, a middle-aged misanthropic, homophobic, obsessive-compulsive writer who works at home and slowly gets drawn into the lives of his gay next-door neighbor and a waitress at the breakfast shop where he eats the same meal every day, and manages to alienate everyone he interacts with. He counts the edges of sidewalk cement blocks to make sure he doesn't, God forbid, step on any cracks.[2]

Various names had declined the chance to play Udall in the movie, including Kevin Kline, before Jack took it on. In September 1996, *Old Friends*, retitled *As Good as It Gets,* finally went before the cameras. Getting the casting just right had caused part of the delay; everybody was working somewhere else at the time. Brooks desperately wanted but couldn't get Holly Hunter to play the female lead as waitress Carol Connelly. The role went instead to Helen Hunt (twenty-six years younger than Jack). He got Greg Kinnear for Jack's gay neighbor after Ralph Fiennes turned down the role, and Cuba Gooding Jr. to play Kinnear's rough-and-tough agent.

The challenge for Jack was how to turn Udall from a cartoon character into a three-dimensional human being, capable of caring and

---

[2] Rumors abounded as to whom Udall was based on. The name heard most often by some was Hollywood writer/director/producer Dennis Klein, an acquaintance of Brooks.

being cared about. It wasn't easy, and more than once Jack thought about giving up the part entirely. He struggled to find a way into the character without hating who he was. In the beginning, Udall comes off as a complete jerk, but gradually, as the film progresses, he turns into a decent, if not exactly likable human being. Jack the actor may have known what was going to happen to him later on, but Jack the character couldn't. He had to play what he knew in the present tense, and that pulled him through without letting his performance either go overboard or turn into a parody of someone suffering from OCD. What made the connection for him was the realization that in real life he was claustrophobic in restaurants and always sought the seat closest to the exit. It wasn't a terminal disease, but it was a bit quirky, and it got his foot in the door of Udall's psyche. What came out of it was a walk on a performance tightrope, and Jack pulled it off flawlessly, easily his best performance since *Prizzi's Honor.*

Sometime just after production ended, Jack had sufficiently cooled off and, perhaps because he liked Caleb so much, decided to settle things with Anspach. He deeded the property to Caleb and stipulated that Anspach could continue to live in the house, and all the land would eventually go to their son. Caleb sold it a few years later, with Anspach's permission, in a deal that benefited both of them.

JACK ALSO AGREED to make an appearance in his friend Tim Burton's goofball comedy based on a series of trading cards, *Mars Attacks!*, in multiple roles reminiscent of what Peter Sellers did in Stanley Kubrick's 1964 *Dr. Strangelove,* including one as the president of the United States and one as a Vegas hustler. The film co-starred Sarah Jessica Parker, Pierce Brosnan, and Lukas Haas.

Production ended on November 11, a relatively brief shoot, after which Jack was sued for $10 million by Catherine Sheehan, a self-admitted prostitute who claimed that on October 12, he had hired her and another unnamed woman to show up at his L.A. home wearing little black dresses. According to them, he proceeded to rough them up and then, apparently dissatisfied, refused to pay their agreed-upon $1,000. In her lawsuit, she claimed that her injuries prevented her from working, that Jack had grabbed her by the hair and dragged her several feet before slamming her head on the floor, and when she and her friend tried to leave he threatened to kill her if she called the police. She did anyway, they investigated, and she filed a criminal complaint that went nowhere. She settled for $32,000. Then she sued again, for an additional $60,000 for doctor bills, claiming one of her breast implants had been ruptured that night. Jack settled that as well. No one believed he had done any of the things he was accused of. Celebrities run the risk of being sued by opportunists, and in the end the episode seemed a combination of Jack indulging himself for fun and a hooker indulging herself for money.

ON DECEMBER 12, 1996, *Mars Attacks!* opened to dismal reviews and proved a box office loser, earning $37 million (domestic) off a $101 million budget, despite an expensive promotional campaign and a red carpet opening at Hollywood's Chinese Theater. It broke even with the foreign box office but did not go into significant profit. A week before, as part of the promotional campaign for the film, Jack received his long-overdue star on Hollywood's Walk of Fame, the 2,077th in the industry's publicity ritual, in which the personality "buys" the space where the star is to be put. Jack had long rejected the idea, acting a little like Melvin Udall, not liking the idea of everyone walking all over him every day, people spitting on it, and dogs using it to relieve themselves, but this time he let his agent convince him it was a good thing to do. A reasonably sized crowd showed up that included Rebecca Broussard and their four-year-old son, Raymond.

The Evening Star opened Christmas day and laid another bomb, grossing $12 million.

In February 1997, Jennifer, who had given birth a year and a half earlier to Sean Knight Nicholson (named, in part, for Sean Penn), decided to marry the father, Mark Norfleet, whom she had first met while both attended Panahou School. The reception was held at the Bel-Air

Hotel, where Jack's "date" was friend and director James L. Brooks. Over drinks they discussed a project Jack had in mind, hinting that he was interested in directing one more picture, which Brooks would write and produce. Brooks said he would think about it, and nothing more was said for the time being.[3]

A FEW DAYS after, fifty-nine-year-old Jack took a quick PR trip to London. While there he saw a West End sex revue that included such charming bits as sex toys being used woman-to-woman and a feigned gang rape of a virgin. It was called *Voyeurz*. Jack wound up taking one of its female stars, Christine Salata, back to his suite with him at the Connaught Hotel. Their affair lasted two days. Jack instructed the girls to call him by his first name. "I can't help but notice that women, especially, when they're in any sort of amorous mood, don't say my name that much, so I like it when they do. I like being called 'Jack.' I like being identified by my name. At that moment." When he left the morning of the third day, he left Salata a note saying he would try to keep in touch. He signed it "Jack."

---

[3] They divorced in 2003, as Jennifer insisted on pursuing an acting career.

"We wanted to create a kind of really bad man, basically a villain who was pretty flamboyant and somebody who you wanted them to get pretty bad. I thought it would bring out the best in Marty . . ."
—JACK NICHOLSON

BLOOD AND WINE OPENED ON FEBRUARY 21, 1997, TO OKAY REviews, and grossed just over $1 million in its initial release, but it made back most of its money overseas and eventually became a staple of international cable and DVD. It was especially popular in Hong Kong, where virtually every film Jack made that was released there was a huge hit. The Chinese loved Jack. He was comically candid about the film's lack of immediate success in America, good-naturedly criticizing the director and the lack of distribution. He couldn't be too critical. He knew the film wasn't well done.

ON JULY 27, 1997, Don Furcillo-Rose, still trying to sell his story that he was Jack's real father, passed away. He was buried in New Jersey. Lorraine then called Jack to tell him the news. Jack sent no condolences, no flowers; he did not pay for the funeral and never mentioned Furcillo-Rose's name in public again.

BUT THEN AS GOOD AS IT GETS opened on Christmas Day, 1997, to solid reviews and tremendous box office and all was okay again, as Jack knew it would be. Sean Mitchell in the *Los Angeles Times* called it "As Funny as It Gets." Jack was singled out by several other critics for his wonderful performance, especially how he was able to balance the humor and the pathos of his character. The film would go on to gross $314 million internationally, making it the second-best-grossing film of his career, after *Batman*.

Oscar buzz began for Jack immediately.

He went along with it as much as he could take, keeping magazine interviews to a minimum—they had caused him enough trouble—and continued to refuse to appear on any television shows to promote the film. The studio pushed him, but there was nothing they could do. It was in his contract that he didn't have to do promotion if he didn't want to. And he didn't want to.

Despite the lack of Jack, there was also talk of a Golden Globe for his performance, and the *New York Times* used it to take a hard look at sexism and ageism in Hollywood, with Jack, unfortunately for him, sitting in the bull's-eye. The article that caused all the water-cooler talk was by feminist-auterist critic and film historian Molly Haskell. It appeared that February under the heading "Where the Old Boy Always Gets the Girl." In it, she pointed out that the sight of sixty-year-old Jack as a grouchily desirable mate in *As Good as It Gets* to Helen Hunt, thirty-four in real life, had elicited "a range of incensed women's comments from 'Repulsive' to 'Yuck' to 'Puhleeze!'" Haskell acknowledged that some things had improved, but throughout the history of Hollywood aging stars like Cary Grant and Fred Astaire consistently played opposite ever-younger girls.

Jack was made aware of Haskell's *Times* article that singled him out as one of Hollywood's new dirty old men when Fred Schruers, interviewing him for *Rolling Stone*, asked him to comment on it. Jack's answer left smoke trailing off the pages of the magazine: "Well, Molly could answer her own questions if she did even close to what I'm sure is the responsible research she does in other areas. These people continually try to socialize and intellectualize these issues. Nature doesn't care about that . . ."

Haskell had made a good point, but Jack, even in anger, made a better one. With few exceptions, his films were not meant to be sociological statements or documentaries. He was, simply, a very popular movie

star. Audiences loved him. And who complained when he played opposite Shirley MacLaine in *Terms of Endearment*? MacLaine was three
years older than him. Jack was not a flag waver for any causes but good
acting. Haskell's sociological weapons were, in fact, just the opposite of
what her husband, the legendary Andrew Sarris, had warned against—
when studying films one should be careful not to miss the forest for the
trees. Sarris was eleven years older than Haskell.

As *Good as It Gets* received nine Oscar nominations, including one
for Jack, his eleventh, matching Laurence Olivier's long-standing record. (Jack didn't bother to wake up for the live dawn broadcast of the
announcement of the nominees from the Academy, or for Jim Brooks
when he called to break the good news.)

Around this time Jack had begun seeing the divorced Rebecca
Broussard again. One friend of Jack's said about his old/new relationship with Broussard, "They're the closest they've ever been . . . they are
finally talking about getting married . . ."

To celebrate his Oscar nomination, the completion of five films in
two and a half years, and Broussard's thirty-fifth birthday that January,
and he had missed, he threw a big party up in Aspen, during which he
announced to everyone present how happy he was.

Broussard was less so. No ring came that night from Jack and no
proposal of marriage.

From there he took her to Rome for the European opening to do
some promotion of *As Good as It Gets*. Everywhere the two went he
was asked by reporters about the possibility of wedding bells in his future. Jack just smiled and said things like "I'm on a constant honeymoon with Rebecca Broussard, the mother of my children." Whenever
he said things like that, Broussard bristled but said nothing.

THE OSCAR AWARDS were handed out on March 23, 1998, at the
Shrine Auditorium, hosted by Billy Crystal. It had been one of Hollywood's better years, both critically and commercially. *Titanic*'s spec-

tacular coming attractions had brought audiences to see the film in droves, while *As Good as It Gets* showed off both Jack and Brooks in top form, with Helen Hunt, Hollywood's new favorite leading lady, giving a perfectly nuanced performance as Jack's "sort of" girlfriend, and it propelled the good-looking Greg Kinnear, a former cable TV show host with a few small movie roles under his belt, into the big screen forefront with his anti-cliché portrayal of a young gay artist. Peter Cattaneo's *The Full Monty* was the sleeper in the pack, a "small" picture that gave new meaning to that word. *Good Will Hunting* introduced the writing duo of Matt Damon, who also appeared in it, and Ben Affleck and allowed Robin Williams to turn in a performance that, for once, wasn't too manic. Curtis Hanson's *L.A. Confidential* was a high-quality neo-noir film about corruption in the Los Angeles Police Department (set safely in the 1950s).

The Best Actor category that Oscar season was especially competitive. A few days earlier, Jack had told *Variety* that he wished the contest could wind up in a five-way tie, but no one ever believes the across-the-board false modesty that precedes the night of the Oscars. His competition this time was Matt Damon (*Good Will Hunting*); Robert Duvall in *The Apostle*, a small film about a flawed evangelist that he had also directed, written, and produced; old friend Peter Fonda in Victor Nuñez's *Ulee's Gold*; and Dustin Hoffman in Barry Levinson's *Wag the Dog*.

When Frances McDormand, the previous winner for Best Actress (for *Fargo*), opened the envelope to announce who had won Best Performance by an Actor, Jack, sitting next to Rebecca, grinned and later said of the moment, "I dropped about three quarts of water the minute they said my name!"

He trotted to the stage smiling and looking just the slightest bit overwhelmed. It was his third Oscar, one less than the all-time champ, Katharine Hepburn, and tied him with Walter Brennan, Ingrid Bergman, and, as of 2013, with Meryl Streep and Daniel Day-Lewis.

The next day he sounded as if he was celebrating his longevity when he told *Variety*, "I have a career that covers three decades . . . I won one in the '70s. I won one in the '80s, and now I won one in the '90s!"

◆ ◆ ◆

IN JULY, JACK was invited personally by one of his admirers, Fidel Castro, to attend the Cuban Film Festival. Jack was excited about being able to travel to Cuba and again took Broussard with him for the week-long stay. He met personally with Castro for three hours, after which he publicly declared that "Castro is a genius!" The Cuban leader, in return, gave Jack a large box of Cuban cigars, which, unfortunately, he couldn't take with him out of the country. Not long after his return to the States, Jack, one of the least vocal political figures in Hollywood, urged President Clinton to resume diplomatic relations with Cuba.

He and Broussard continued their honeymoon-without-a-wedding, traveling on to Ireland so Jack could get in some golf. Then it was on to Wimbledon, and then to France to watch the last game of the World Cup, where he met up with Dennis Hopper, who had painted his face the colors of the French flag. Then to Spain, for the opening there of *As Good as It Gets* and to visit Michael "Mikey" Douglas at his home there. He had always wanted to make another picture with Douglas producing, but it had never happened. As Douglas's acting career grew ever more successful, his desire to produce receded, especially after he won Best Performance by an Actor for Oliver Stone's 1987 *Wall Street*. Douglas had found out the hard way that acting was so much easier than producing. Jack had known it all the time, which was why he rarely got involved in that end of making movies.

IN NOVEMBER, it was announced that Jack would be receiving the Hollywood Foreign Press Association's 1999 Cecil B. DeMille award at January's Golden Globes presentations "for his outstanding contribution to the world of entertainment." It was Jack's fiftieth industry-wide award for acting. According to the organization's president, Helmut Voss, "We picked him because of his amazing body of work and his worldwide appeal . . ." The association, which always operated in secret, had let it slip that giving Jack the award was a good way to guarantee his presence and, in turn, higher ratings for the TV show that was broadcast around the world.

A week later, Jack put the five-bedroom Beverly Hills house he had bought for Broussard in 1989 up for sale. To many, this signaled the last step before the two would get married. They were wrong. Jack was veering away from the one-time marriage-seeking missile that was Broussard, who put up no argument about the house. She had cooled down, having had enough of Jack's stalling and was more than ready to move on. Broussard, whose marriage had lasted less than two years, was certain now she and Jack would never marry, and soon began dating a young actor named Al Corley, best known for his role in the original *Dynasty* TV series. Their relationship didn't last, and Broussard eventually married Alex Kelly in 2001.

Jack wished them all well.

TWO YEARS HAD slipped by since he had wrapped production on *As Good as It Gets*, and the only meaningful thing (to him) that he had done, besides attending every Lakers home game and presenting at the Oscars in March 1999, his tenth appearance, to hand out the Best Performance by an Actress Oscar to Gwyneth Paltrow, was to get hot and heavy with a flaming redheaded actress by the name of Lara Flynn Boyle.

Boyle was thirty-three years Jack's junior, and hot, both professionally and personally. She had made a name for herself on David Lynch's TV series *Twin Peaks* and followed that with a starring role in ABC's legal drama *The Practice*. She also had a reputation for walking on the wild side that matched Jack's in its hedonistic fervor. Flynn had just broken up with actor/comedian David Spade and met Jack in, of all places, the men's room at a Hollywood party, where he'd gone off to sneak a smoke. She'd followed him in, lit up as well, and began to chat. It didn't take the time to smoke a filter tip for the lithe twenty-eight-year-old to arouse the interest of the roundish, balding sixty-one-year-old. They started dating, and soon they were inseparable. According to Jack's daughter Jennifer, his first child with Broussard, Boyle was just another in a long line of beautiful women her father dated, older at first, then the same age, then younger.

Boyle was Jack's kind of girl—she could drink and party with the best of them, and she had a female edge the type of which Jack always liked to cut himself on. She had "dare me" written all over, and Jack wanted to dare the everything out of her. So much so that within a month Boyle, who liked to refer to her new man as "Jack Pot Belly," had accomplished the seemingly impossible by moving into his man cave.

That summer, while living with Boyle, Jack invited Broussard to go to Wimbledon with him, and she accepted his offer.

In August, his daughter Jennifer gave birth to her second child. For the occasion, Jack bought her a $2.75 million house in Brentwood and sent over several pieces from his art collection to help dress it up. By this time she had given up a stalled film career for one in interior decorating that catered to the stars.

IN THE FALL of 1999, Jack turned down a new series of film offers. Harry Gittes had a screenplay set up at Universal, *American Caesar,* a modern retelling of Shakespeare's *Julius Caesar.* Jack didn't want to do it. Nor was he interested in a sequel to *Goin' South* that was in development. Jack wanted no part of that. Good friend Fred Roos wanted him for something called *Him and Her.* Jack said no. He even turned down the never-say-no-to Clint Eastwood when he asked Jack to be in his senior-citizens astronaut comedy *Space Cowboys.* Jack liked Clint well enough but was just not interested in making a comedy about men getting older.

However, when Sean Penn put together enough funding for a third film, *The Pledge,* Jack said yes. He loved working with Sean, but this time there would be no financial breaks. Jack demanded and got his full $10 million fee up front and his normal piece of the back end. Penn couldn't say no; he needed Jack's name on the dotted line to seal the financial $30 million distribution deal he had managed to put together with Warner Bros. No doubt Jack's name was more important to Warners than Penn's. Production began early in 2000 and, except for one or two scenes filmed in Reno, Nevada, it was shot entirely in British Columbia to take advantage of Canada's generous tax breaks.

The Pledge is a curious little film. Set in the 1950s, it nonetheless focused on an unsolved murder that resembled the sensational 1996 Jon-Benét-Ramsay case. In the film, the culprit is a mysterious dark character called "the Wizard," played by the up-and-coming Benicio Del Toro. Jack played Jerry Black, a retired cop who dedicates the rest of his life to finding the child's killer (in a way, this film's plot was not that far afield from *The Crossing Guard*). The mother was played by Patricia Clarkson. Also in the film were Aaron Eckhart, Robin Wright Penn (she and Sean had since married), Helen Mirren, Vanessa Redgrave, and Sam Shepard.

With a good script by Jerzt and Mary Olson-Komolowski that suffered only from an overly ambiguous ending, the film opened in January 2001 and did moderately well, grossing $29 million. It represented an enormous leap for Penn, but it was still not enough. When the film had gone $15 million over budget and the studio refused to make it up, Penn had had to put in his own money to finish it.

WHEN JACK RETURNED to the States, he and Boyle entered a new phase of their highly public affair, one familiar to Jack, the break-up/make-up seesaw. Friends of the couple agreed among themselves (according to one of them who wishes to remain anonymous) that Boyle had the upper hand with Jack and "liked to crack the sexual whip."

Jack, meanwhile, signed on to Harry Gittes's new project, a dramedy called *About Schmidt* loosely based on a 1995 novel by Louis Begley. Perhaps feeling he owed Gittes, Jack agreed to a pay cut (moving some of his up-front money to the back end) to get the $32-million-budget film made. Gittes, having given up on his *American Caesar* script, had *About Schmidt* tailored to Jack. The film concerned the plight of an older man who retires and plans how he is going to spend his time when his wife suddenly dies. He then sets out on a "life-learning" journey alone in the Winnebago he had just bought. The script is an affecting one about the problems of aging that Jack highly preferred to the *Space Cowboys* view of older men reverting to the behavior of little boys. The cast also included Kathy Bates as the mother of Schmidt's daughter's fiancé, and Jeannie, his daughter (played by Hope Davis, "Hopie" in Jackspeak). When he shows up alone for Jeannie's wedding, Roberta (Bates) makes a pass at him. After the wedding, Jack leaves the festivities by himself. Stripped of his career, his wife, and now his daughter, Schmidt must face the rest of his life lonely and alone. It was a gentle tour de force for which Jack gained weight and adapted a comb-over hairstyle—"I couldn't look at myself in the mirror the whole three months I was doing this picture, the most miserable role I ever had in my life," he told one reporter. To another, he said, "I looked at him as the man I might have become if I wasn't lucky enough to wind up in show business."

With a script by Alexander Payne and Jim Taylor, the film was produced by New Line Cinema, which guaranteed distribution and was willing to green-light the relative newcomer Payne to direct as well as co-write the film. Payne had had a moderate hit with *Election* at Paramount and taken home a slew of non-Oscar awards for it.

Filming went well, and after production ended, Jack took off with Boyle for the south of France, even as the buzz that ripped through Hollywood was that she had also started seeing Bruce Willis.

On December 2, 2001, sixty-four-year-old Jack, who had been named by President George W. Bush as a Kennedy Center honoree, along with Julie Andrews, Van Cliburn, Quincy Jones, and Luciano Pavarotti, had flown with Warren Beatty and his wife, Annette Bening, to attend the next-day's ceremonies. Jack went without an escort. Jack and Boyle had split up when they returned from France. No one was surprised.[1]

During the ceremonies at the Kennedy Center, the president proclaimed that Jack Nicholson "was one of the true greats of this or any other generation of actors. America cannot resist the mystery, the hint of menace, and of course, that killer smile."

---

[1] Jack later told *People* that he had first learned he was being honored while in bed, "where I usually am," and received a call from Quincy Jones to tell him the good news. He told the magazine he was honored that it was Bush who had nominated him, but that he remained "a big Democrat."

♦ ♦ ♦

ABOUT SCHMIDT WAS considered so good that it was held back by New Line until December 13, 2002, to cash in on the holiday moviegoing season and capture the attention of the Academy. Both the film and Jack received rave reviews, and it did extremely well at the box office. Off its $30 million budget, it grossed more than $105 million internationally. In February 2003, Jack and Kathy Bates were both nominated for Oscars, Jack for Best Performance by an Actor, Bates for Best Supporting Actress.[2] For Jack, it was his twelfth nomination.

Also, Jack appeared to be ready to talk publicly about why for the first time in a very long time he was without a steady female companion and how happy it made him feel to stop relentlessly pursuing young women. To *Newsweek* he said, "There are a lot of crazy nitwit things I can't do anymore . . . I don't have the same libido. It used to be that I didn't think I could go to sleep if I wasn't involved in some kind of amorous contact or another. Well, I spend a lot of time sleeping alone these days. That's different and it's very liberating . . . my fear is that I'm beginning to prefer it . . ."

Later, Jack continued his public self-contemplation/confession in *People:* "A younger woman is not necessarily for me. I'm pretty old, so almost everyone is younger. I won't pretend that I haven't been a rogue most of my life, because I have and would still be if I had the energy. I sat in a restaurant recently, and I could've knocked off 2,000 of them—every age, and their mothers too. Right now, though, I just can't do the dance. And if I bother, they've got to be a good dancer."[3]

♦ ♦ ♦

---

[2] Jack was also nominated for and won a 2003 Golden Globe as Best Actor in a Drama. When he received the award he shook his head and said, "I thought we made a comedy," which got a huge laugh from the audience at the Beverly Hilton Hotel, where the Globes ceremony was held every year.

[3] Jack later told another reporter in London that the secret to his former seven-night-a-week lovemaking sessions was "peanut butter sandwiches in bed."—Jack Malvern, *The Times* (London), February 2, 2004.

IN MARCH 2003, the Academy Awards were held in a spiffy, brand-new venue, the Kodak Theatre on Hollywood Boulevard. As part of the movie industry's attempt to rescue the boulevard from the brink of drug and porn oblivion, the strip from the Roosevelt Hotel to Highland had been fast-tracked for the comeback trail. Since its post–World War II decline, millions of tourist dollars had been lost because of the degradation of what was once the most famous film site in the world. The first phase of Hollywood Boulevard's renovation was completed with the emergence of the Kodak Theatre on Hollywood and Highland, built to be the permanent home of the Oscars and the occasional red-carpet event.[4]

All the heat that night wasn't only Oscar's new digs but also the kiss that Adrien Brody, dark-horse winner of Best Performance by an Actor for *The Pianist*, planted on presenter Halle Berry. *The Pianist* was a French, German, Polish, and U.K. production directed by Jack's old friend Roman Polanski, who won for Best Director, which thrilled Jack. Polanski was unable to accept, still living in self-imposed exile overseas. The win was intended to send a strong message that it forgave Polanski and wanted him back in Hollywood where they believed he belonged.

Jack, his co-star Bates, and the movie were shut out. Despite his strong performance in *About Schmidt*, it was not his year for Oscar.

Nor was it for Jack's next outing, Peter Segal's *Anger Management* (2003), a star vehicle for Adam Sandler. The film was completed before *About Schmidt* was released, and it too did well at the box office, with an opening Easter week take of $44.5 million. Jack's role as an anger-management therapist is little more than a foil to Sandler and is one of his least interesting or memorable roles.

SIXTY-FIVE-YEAR-OLD JACK NEXT signed on with Columbia to co-star with Diane Keaton in his fifty-ninth movie, *Something's Gotta Give*, written and directed by Nancy Meyers, whose previous film, *What*

---

[4] Kodak went bankrupt and the theater's name was changed in 2012 to the Dolby Theatre.

Women Want, starred Mel Gibson and Helen Hunt in an ill-fated stab by Gibson at comedy.

The new screenplay was originally titled *Love Me or Leave Me*, but because that was the name of a 1950s James Cagney–Doris Day pic, the title was changed to *Something's Gotta Give*. The gist of the story is that a middle-aged writer (Keaton) becomes involved with a sixty-three-year-old playboy-mogul, Harry Sanborn (Jack), even though he is already involved with her much younger daughter (Amanda Peet). Sanborn learns his life lessons from strong women—Diane Keaton, Frances McDormand, and Amanda Peet. As Meyers recalled, "Jack's character really unfolds as the movie progresses, so you get to see the Jack that breaks your heart . . . there was always a fuss being made over Jack. He enjoyed it. His mom was a hairdresser. 'I grew up in a beauty parlor' is an expression he used quite often. I think we provided the beauty parlor for him again."

On the surface, the role appeared to be, at first glance, an extension of his character from *As Good as It Gets*, but soon enough we find he is far less neurotic, far more narcissistic. In *Something*, Harry Sanborn (Jack), plagued with heart attack scares and other self-diagnosed early warning signs of doom, "comes to his senses" and winds up with Keaton. Harry is, in a way, more a reflection of the new Jack, no longer in need of chasing young, nubile girls. The film ends on an upbeat note with Jack in Paris singing Édith Piaf's "La Vie en Rose" (over the credits in movie theaters, onscreen in the DVD).

The question was, Would the audience buy this Jack? The answer was yes. The film, shot that summer, opened on December 12, 2003, and proved a smash, on a budget of $66 million (a large piece of it going to the salaries of Keaton and Jack); it grossed more than $266 million in its initial international run.

Perhaps buoyed by the film's big hit, Jack wanted one last steak after all these salads to properly say farewell to the film business and the audiences that had kept him in it for half a century. In December 2003, just as *Something's Gotta Give* was opening, Jack played with the notion of making a film about his own life (perhaps a version of the memoir he had told *Time* he wanted to write), but ultimately he decided that artistic truth, not chronological fact, was his forte; he would continue to deliver his story through the characters he played in other people's movies and forget about writing his memoirs.

IT WASN'T UNTIL February 2005 that sixty-seven-year old Jack believed he had finally found the perfect vehicle for what might very well be his fond farewell—the right script, the right director, the right producer, the right studio, and the right co-stars. If his recent crowd pleasers had been lightweights, this was one ton of a movie. Jack may have wanted to make it more than just for the obvious reasons. He had spilled the beans to the public about what was most likely a drop in his testosterone levels. Now he needed to prove to himself that he hadn't lost his bite. He had to know if his supercharged sex life was also what made his acting so potent.

The opportunity to make this test came with Martin Scorsese's offer to Jack to star in a cop/mafia remake of a popular 2002 Chinese (Hong Kong) movie about undercover mob infiltration (the Chinese version was about an aging mobster, called *Infernal Affairs*—*Moo Gaan Dou*—literally translated as "The Nonstop Way," the lowest level of hell in Buddhism, directed by Wai-keung Lau and Alan Mak).[5]

Jack's co-stars in the American undercover cat-and-mouse version, *The Departed*, were the post-*Titanic*, grown-up, and super-hot Leonardo DiCaprio, Matt Damon, and Mark Wahlberg, the latter two bringing a whiff of authentic Boston street life to the Beantown tale.[6] It was produced by Brad Pitt, Brad Grey, and Graham King (King also co-executive-produced Scorsese's 2002 *Gangs of New York* and was a producer on 2004's *The Aviator*, both starring DiCaprio). Jack enthusiastically signed up for the ride.

---

[5] The film, credited with reviving Hong Kong cinema's international popularity, received only limited distribution in the United States.

[6] During production, Jack banned all Boston Celtics T-shirts from the set. That rule went for both cast and crew, and, to put a cap on it, he wore a Yankees hat whenever he went out on the streets of Boston.

The Departed had a solid budget of $90 million, with distribution guaranteed by Warner Bros. Jack's character's part, originally a small one in the Chinese version, was expanded and made into one of the prime focal points of the film. "We built this character layer by layer, until we had something that fit inside a great genre film, but also pushed the envelope until the movie becomes almost operatic," Jack said, putting his finger on Scorsese's love for the dramatic, the ethnic, and the lyrical grandiose, all meshed into a single flow of events put into motion with Scorsese's speedball rhythm of encouraged on-set improvisation. "There's a scene in a bar where I'm scaring the shit out of Leo's character with a gun," Jack said. "There wasn't any gun in the script. We had shot the scene the night before but Marty said he had a light schedule the next day and I wanted to try a few more takes. I wanted to come up with something different, so I asked the prop master to hide a gun on the set, and to bring a fire extinguisher as well. The look on his face when I asked for that fire extinguisher was priceless."

Scorsese remembers the moment this way: "The first thing Jack did was sniff his glass and say, 'I smell a rat' . . . and then he pulled a gun on [Leo]. He didn't tell me he had a gun. It was great . . . I still get the chills . . ." Later, Jack added, "I was going to set the table on fire with bourbon out of my mouth . . ." That sequence made it into the film.

In another scene, Jack powdered the bottom of one actress with cocaine, strapped on a dildo, and chased after Matt Damon. That sequence did not make it into the film.

In *The Departed*, Jack plays Frank Costello, a Boston mob boss of an Irish gang that has been infiltrated by two opposing undercover cops. When each discovers there is a second mole, he tries to expose the other so as not to be killed first. Jack was thrilled by the notion of playing a tough guy in Scorsese's cinematic idiom and molded his character after the notorious Boston organized crime mobster James "Whitey" Bulger Jr., as bad as they get. The story of his earlier, violent years when he ran his mob and the attempt by competing undercover agents to infiltrate his gang was the basis of the American version of the film.

Costello is killed in a dark back alley in a final, typically Scorsesian resolution, death coming in a hail of bullets, the dead body left in the mouth of a bulldozer.[7]

THE DEPARTED PREMIERED on September 26, 2006, to mixed-to-positive reviews, and grossed $290 million in its initial domestic release, reconfirming Jack's preeminence as America's favorite movie everything: rebel, Joker, middle-aged pot-bellied lover, OCD curmudgeon, old man alone, and terrifying gangster. His performance in *The Departed* exploded off the screen.

Despite the reservations of some critics—the *New York Times'* Manohla Dargis, in her review of the film, complained that "Mr. Nicholson begins to mix too much Jack into his characterization" and that "Mr. Scorsese . . . spends a lot of time vying for attention with his famous star" (isn't that why they're stars?)—it took American film's auteurist champion, Andrew Sarris, writing in the *New York Observer*, to recognize the film's proper sociological and stylistic perspectives: "*The Departed* strikes unexpectedly deep chords of tragic poignancy with the emotional fallout from an atmosphere of perpetual paranoia so characteristic of our post-9/11 world. No one can completely trust anyone else . . . an electrifying entertainment . . . it is truly an occasion for rejoicing."

The Departed, so dark and powerful it burns itself into one's sensibilities, ultimately may be the film for which the post-Joker Jack will be most remembered.

Even before *The Departed* wrapped, a reenergized Jack quickly signed on to star with Morgan Freeman (who suggested him for the film) in Rob Reiner's *The Bucket List*, a smell-the-roses, meaning-of-life morality tale about two terminal cancer patients who wish to fulfill a "bucket list" of things before they—kick the bucket. Having just come

---

[7] According to Graham King, Jack worked on the script to increase the size of his part but King prefers to call it a collaborative effort. King also denies that the original Costello character was based on Bulger.—David Carr, "A Screen First: Scorsese and Jaaack," *New York Times*, January 1, 2006.

out of the lowest depths of hell for Scorsese, a trip to heaven sounded more than right to Jack. His shaved head sent rumors flying that he was seriously ill when he showed up without explanation for it as a presenter at the Oscars the following February 25, 2007. The false word ripped through Hollywood that he was dying of cancer. Jack loved it.

The Bucket List opened on January 11, 2008, and, to the surprise of many of the tracking geniuses in the film business who gave it no chance. Despite some scathing reviews, especially that of Roger Ebert, who was suffering at the time from thyroid cancer: *"The Bucket List* thinks dying of cancer is a laugh riot followed by a dime-store epiphany." Directed by Rob Reiner, who had worked before with Jack on *A Few Good Men* to the mutual satisfaction of both, the film feels like an expanded sitcom, with a new destination every week. It proved a smash at the box office. *The Bucket List* grossed $290 million in its initial domestic and international release, proving that Jack's star power was intact, as was that of the other senior citizen star of the film, Morgan Freeman.

As soon as the film was released, Jack took himself to Cap-Ferrat, France, where the seventy-two-year-old teenager found a young, pretty girl in a short dress willing to dance the night away with him.

HE WAS IN no hurry to return to the States, until James L. Brooks once again came calling. He had a script for Jack, something called *How Do You Know*, a romantic comedy with all the right ingredients, including a stellar cast—Jack, Reese Witherspoon, Paul Rudd, Owen Wilson, and a solid supporting cast. The problem was the story and Jack's part in it. In there somewhere is a triangulated love story among Witherspoon, Rudd, and Wilson, with Jack as Rudd's father, in what feels like a different picture. The entanglements become increasingly unfunny, and as the film ends it remains unclear who's with whom and if one, two, or three of them are going to jail. Brooks should have realized after five years of trying to put the film together (or maybe because it took five years he may have lost his perspective) that its pieces didn't fit. Jack did the movie for Brooks anyway. The net production cost (after tax breaks) for the film was $100 million. When it finally did open on December 17, 2010, expectations were high but the film bombed badly, earning barely half of what it cost.

WHEN HE TURNED seventy-four, Jack began to consolidate his holdings, selling off pieces of land or complete homes meant for his children, his ex-wife, or himself, for which he no longer had any use.

He still smoked three packs a day but got into yoga, as much as he could tolerate, his personal compromise to working out every day. He also concentrated on getting his college-age children into the best schools. He still went to every Lakers home game and became an everyday golfer. He spent an increasing number of nights accepting awards, medals, and commendations, like the one Governor Arnold Schwarzenegger gave to Jack as he was inducted into the California Hall of Fame in December 2008.

And burying his peers. It was the one role that never ran out of sequels. "One of the toughest parts of aging," Jack said recently, "is losing your friends. At first it starts quietly, then pretty soon it's every month, and you can't help but think, 'when is that bell going to go off for me?' . . . At this time of life, you feel just a sword's point from death. It's frightening; who wants to face God and the clear white light?"

Carole Eastman had died relatively young in February 2004. Jack had known her since he first arrived in Hollywood and began taking acting classes. He loved her style of creativity as much as her beauty; to Jack her style of creativity *was* her beauty, and he always felt she understood better than anybody else what he needed on a page to help him bring a character to life.

Five months later, in July 2004, Marlon Brando died. Marlon and Jack had never been close friends, but Marlon was Jack's first idol—he had worshipped Brando from his days as an usher during his first summer job at the Neptune local movie house. It was there he watched *The Wild One* over and over again. How could Jack ever have known that one day they would act together and that he would be called the next Marlon Brando? When Brando passed, Jack bought his house and adjoining property to ensure that no one else would move into it and evict the memory or the spirit of his legendary neighbor.

In May 2010, Dennis Hopper died at seventy-four after a life hard-lived and a long bout with prostate cancer. At Hopper's funeral in Taos, New Mexico, standing alongside Peter Fonda, Jack told the Associated Press, "It was a very singular relationship I had with him. We were soul mates in a way. I really miss him."

December 12, 2012 brought the passing of Bert Schneider after a long illness; although by now Bert was practically forgotten in Hollywood, at least in part because of his own reclusiveness, Peter Biskind rightly remembered him as someone who "played a key role in the birth of the so-called New Hollywood of the late '60s and early '70s." It was no secret in Hollywood that Schneider and Jack had had a falling-out and had not been close for years, and that Schneider had fallen on hard times, but when Jack heard that Schneider was ill, he made sure that his friend wanted for nothing.

After Schneider's death, Jack became less visible around town. The faces at the usual haunts had become unfamiliar to him, and Aspen seemed hardly worth the trouble. He no longer wanted to take the long flights to New York, or the longer ones to London and Paris. He became something of a love seat philosopher rather than a philosophical lover. His biggest pleasures these days was smoking a pack a day of cigarettes and his Cohibas.

Also, in 2012, in New York, he went to look at some new art to add to his $100 million collection, and he went to a party hosted by Keith Richards. He stayed at it only long enough to see Richards, and after granted a rare, nonpromotional interview to the press, reminiscing about the old days. As Jack said later, "Keith would stay up seven nights in a row. I stayed up late, but I slept in late, too. I always believed in taking care of myself. There was always a discipline within my partying structure. I've never kept a camera waiting and in all my career I only missed one day of work, on *The Shining*, when I put my back out. . . . There were these wild guys over there. I wanted to show them what Jack the Waggle could do . . .

"The last three times I've been in New York filming, I didn't leave my hotel room for one single night."

He had everything a man could ask for but a peaceful, workable relationship. "The reality was that I was annihilated by the separation from Anjelica [after I told her Broussard was pregnant and she beat me up]. That was probably the toughest period of my life."

Meanwhile, sixty-one-year-old Anjelica's career had taken a major upturn when she joined the TV show *Smash*, which opened her up to a new, younger audience. Ironically, while Jack sat home, she was the one surrounded by beautiful young girls as she continued her own successful career.

When she talks about Jack now, she does so with warmth and affection, and just a touch of recognition about what might have been. "Jack is someone I've adored in my life and will continue to love forever. I don't take him lightly . . . That's a real relationship. Real relationships have continuity, and Jack and I have a deep, abiding love and affection for each other. I'm proud that we've gotten through some very tough times together."

JACK MADE AN appearance at the 2013 Academy Awards. He was asked to present the Best Picture of the Year Oscar and to share the duties with a beamed-in Michelle Obama. The crowd greeted both affectionately. After the ceremonies finally ended, the winners had to walk the gauntlet of morning-show booths looking to nab a sound bite for the next morning's broadcasts. Undoubtedly the hottest winner of the night (in every way) was Jennifer Lawrence. When George Stephanopoulos's producers saw her, they pulled her over to his ABC network booth. As they talked the mindless gibberish that Oscar winners' heads are full of—who I should have thanked, who I *shouldn't* have thanked, I love my husband even though I didn't mention his name, do we have to share everything, things like that—someone lurked in the unsure background of the live TV camera. A hand came out and touched Lawrence's shoulder. Ignoring Stephanopoulos, the voice of the man it belonged to said to her, "You did such a beautiful job! I don't mean to crash your interview." It was Jack Nicholson, Wayfarers in place, drink in hand, eyebrows reaching for the sky.

Lawrence laughed and said, "Yeah, you're being really rude." She was only half kidding. This was *her* moment.

Jack started to walk away, then came back. "Enjoy the night. I loved you in the movie. It was great. You look like an old girlfriend of mine."

Lawrence didn't miss a beat. "Oh really? Do I look like a new girlfriend?"

Once again Jack started to leave, but came back. "I thought about it."

Lawrence buried her head in her hands. To Stephanopoulos she whispered, "Oh, my God! Is he still here?"

Jack: "I'll be waiting . . ."

Lawrence: "Oh, my God! I need a rearview mirror!"

Jennifer Lawrence was twenty-two years old. Jack finally gave up. His own description of this stage of his life had come embarrassingly alive.

It was the only thing about that year's Oscars anyone would remember.

Not long afterward he found his way home. The next day when he woke he called Anjelica, just to see how she was doing. She was the only one who could make everything all right again. At least for now.

FILMOGRAPHY

FEATURE FILMS—YEAR OF RELEASE

The Cry Baby Killer, 1958. Allied Artists. Director: Joe Addis. Producer: Roger Corman, David Kramarsky, David March. Screenplay: Leo Gordon, Melvin Levy. With Harry Lauter, Jack Nicholson, Carolyn Mitchell.

The Wild Ride, 1960. Filmgroup. Director: Harvey Berman. Producer: Harvey Berman, Kinte Kertuch. Screenplay: Ann Porter, Marion Rothman. With Jack Nicholson, Georgianna Carter, Robert Bean.

The Little Shop of Horrors, 1960. Filmgroup. Director: Roger Corman. Producer: Roger Corman. Screenplay: Charles B. Griffith. With Jonathan Haze, Jackie Joseph, Mel Welles, Dick Miller, Jack Nicholson.

Studs Lonigan, 1960. MGM. Director: Irving Lerner. Producer: Philip Yordan. Screenplay: Philip Yordan. With Christopher Knight, Frank Gorshin, Jack Nicholson.

The Broken Land, 1962. Associated Producers, Inc. (API). Director: John Bushelman. Producer: Leonard A. Schwartz, Roger Corman. Screenwriter: Edward J. Lakso. With Kent Taylor, Jack Nicholson, Diana Darrin.

The Raven, 1963. American International Pictures (AIP). Director: Roger Corman. Producer: Roger Corman. Screenplay: Richard Matheson. With Vincent Price, Peter Lorre, Boris Karloff, Hazel Court, Olive Sturgess, Jack Nicholson.

The Terror, 1963. Filmgroup. Director: Roger Corman (uncredited: Francis Ford Coppola, Monte Hellman, Jack Hill, Jack Nicholson). Producer: Roger Corman. Screenplay: Leo Gordon, Jack Hill (uncredited: Roger Corman). With Boris Karloff, Jack Nicholson, Sandra Knight, Dick Miller, Jonathan Haze.

Ensign Pulver, 1964. Warner Bros. Director: John Logan. Producer: Josh Logan. Screenplay: Josh Logan, Peter S. Fiehleman. With Robert Walker Jr., Burl Ives, Walter Matthau, Larry Hagman, Jack Nicholson.

Flight to Fury, 1964. Feature Film Corp. of America. Director: Monte Hellman.

Producer: Eddie Romero. Screenplay: Monte Hellman, Jack Nicholson, Fred Roos. With Jack Nicholson, Dewey Martin.

Back Door to Hell, 1964. Twentieth Century-Fox. Director: Monte Hellman. Producer: Fred Roos. Screenplay: John Hackett. With Jimmie Rodgers, John Hackett, Jack Nicholson.

Ride in the Whirlwind, 1965. Walter Reade Organization (for television; unreleased commercially in theaters). Director: Monte Hellman. Producer: Monte Hellman, Jack Nicholson. Screenplay: Jack Nicholson. With Jack Nicholson, Millie Perkins, Cameron Mitchell, Harry Dean Stanton.

The Shooting, 1966. Walter Reade Organization (for television; unreleased commercially in theaters). Director: Monte Hellman. Producer: Jack Nicholson, Monte Hellman. Screenplay: Carole Eastman (writing as Adrien Joyce). With Jack Nicholson, Warren Oates, Millie Perkins, Will Hutchins.

Hells Angels on Wheels, 1967. Fanfare Films. Director: Roger Corman. Producer: Joe Solomon. Screenplay: R. Wright Campbell. With Jack Nicholson, Adam Roarke, Sabina Scharf, Jack Starrett.

The St. Valentine's Day Massacre, 1967. Twentieth Century-Fox. Director: Roger Corman. Producer: Roger Corman. Screenplay: Howard Browne. With George Segal, Jason Robards, Ralph Meeker (uncredited: Jack Nicholson).

The Trip, 1967. AIP. Director: Roger Corman. Producer: Roger Corman. Screenplay: Jack Nicholson. With Peter Fonda, Dennis Hopper, Bruce Dern, Susan Strasberg.

Psych-Out, 1968. AIP. Director: Richard Rush. Producer: Dick Clark, Norman T. Herman. Screenplay: Betty Tusher, E. Hunter Willett, Betsy Ulius. With Susan Sarandon, Dean Stockwell, Jack Nicholson, Bruce Dern, Max Julien.

Head, 1968. Columbia Pictures. Director: Bob Rafelson. Producer: Bert Schneider, Bob Rafelson, Jack Nicholson. Screenplay: Bob Rafelson, Jack Nicholson. With the Monkees: Davy Jones, Mickey Dolenz, Peter Tork, Michael Nesmith.

Easy Rider, 1969. Columbia Pictures, Raybert Productions. Director: Dennis Hopper. Producer: Peter Fonda. Screenplay: Peter Fonda, Dennis Hopper, Terry Southern. With Peter Fonda, Dennis Hopper, Jack Nicholson, Karen Black.

The Rebel Rousers, 1970. Four Star Excelsior. Director: Martin B. Cohen. Producer: Martin B. Cohen. Screenplay: Michael Kars, Abe Polsky, Martin B. Cohen. With Cameron Mitchell, Bruce Dern, Jack Nicholson, Diane Ladd.

On a Clear Day You Can See Forever, 1970. Paramount. Director: Vincente Minnelli. Producer: Howard W. Koch. Screenplay: Alan Jay Lerner. With Barbra Streisand, Yves Montand, Jack Nicholson.

Five Easy Pieces, 1970. BBS Productions. Director: Bob Rafelson. Producer: Bob Rafelson, Richard Wechsler. Screenwriter: Bob Rafelson, Adrien Joyce (Carole Eastman). With Jack Nicholson, Karen Black, Susan Anspach, Helena Kallianiotes.

Carnal Knowledge, 1971. Avco Embassy Pictures. Director: Mike Nichols. Producer: Mike Nichols. Screenplay: Jules Feiffer. With Jack Nicholson, Art Garfunkel, Ann-Margret, Candice Bergen, Rita Moreno, Carol Kane.

Drive, He Said, 1971. Columbia Pictures, BBS Productions. Director: Jack Nicholson. Producer: Jack Nicholson, Steve Blauner. Screenplay: Jeremy Larner, Jack Nicholson, Terrence Malick (uncredited). With William Tepper, Karen Black, Bruce Dern, Robert Towne, Henry Jaglom.

A Safe Place, 1971. Columbia Pictures, BBS Productions. Director: Henry Jaglom. Producer: Bert Schneider. Screenplay: Henry Jaglom. With Tuesday Weld, Orson Welles, Jack Nicholson.

The King of Marvin Gardens, 1972. Columbia Pictures, BBS Productions. Director: Bob Rafelson. Producer: Steve Blauner, Bob Rafelson, Harold Schneider. Screenplay: Jacob Brackman, Bob Rafelson. With Jack Nicholson, Bruce Dern, Ellen Burstyn.

The Last Detail, 1973. Columbia Pictures. Director: Hal Ashby. Producer: Gerald Ayres. Screenplay: Robert Towne, based on an original novel by Darryl Ponicsan. With Jack Nicholson, Randy Quaid, Otis Young.

Chinatown, 1974. Paramount Pictures. Director: Roman Polanski. Producer: Robert Evans. Screenplay: Robert Towne. With Jack Nicholson, Faye Dunaway, John Huston.

The Passenger, 1975. MGM. Director: Michelangelo Antonioni. Producer: Carlo Ponti. Screenplay: Mark Peploe, Michelangelo Antonioni, Peter Wollen. With Jack Nicholson, Maria Schneider, Steven Berkoff, Ian Hendry, Jenny Runacre.

Tommy, 1975. Columbia Pictures. Director: Ken Russell. Producer: Ken Russell, Roger Stigwood. Screenplay: Ken Russell, Pete Townshend. With Roger Daltrey, Ann-Margret, Oliver Reed, Tina Turner, Elton John, Eric Clapton, Keith Moon, Paul Nicholas, Jack Nicholson, Robert Powell.

The Fortune, 1975. Columbia Pictures. Director: Mike Nichols. Producer: Don Devlin, Mike Nichols. Screenplay: Adrien Joyce. With Warren Beatty, Jack Nicholson, Stockard Channing.

One Flew over the Cuckoo's Nest, 1975. United Artists. Director: Miloš Forman. Producer: Michael Douglas, Saul Zaentz. Screenplay: Lawrence Hauben, Bo Goldman. With Jack Nicholson, Louise Fletcher, William Redfield, Brad Dourif, Danny DeVito, Sydney Lassick, Christopher Lloyd, Will Sampson.

The Missouri Breaks, 1976. United Artists. Director: Arthur Penn. Producer: Elliott Kastner, Robert M. Sherman. Screenplay: Thomas McGuane. With Jack Nicholson, Marlon Brando, Randy Quaid, Kathleen Lloyd, Frederic Forrest, Harry Dean Stanton.

The Last Tycoon, 1976. Paramount Pictures. Director: Elia Kazan. Producer: Sam Spiegel. Screenplay: Harold Pinter, based on the novel by F. Scott Fitzgerald. With Robert De Niro, Tony Curtis, Robert Mitchum, Jack Nicholson, Donald Pleasance, Jeanne Moreau.

Goin' South, 1978. Paramount Pictures. Director: Jack Nicholson. Producer: Harry Gittes, Harold Schneider. Screenplay: John Herman Shaner, Al Ramus, Charles Shyer, Alan Mandel. With Jack Nicholson, Mary Steenburgen, Christopher Lloyd, John Belushi.

The Shining, 1980. Warner Bros. (distributor). Director: Stanley Kubrick. Producer: Stanley Kubrick. Screenplay: Stanley Kubrick, Diane Johnson, based on the novel by Stephen King. With Jack Nicholson, Shelley Duvall, Danny Lloyd, Scatman Crothers.

The Postman Always Rings Twice, 1981. Paramount Pictures (distributor for Lorimar Productions). Director: Bob Rafelson. Producer: Bob Rafelson, Charles Mulvehill. Screenplay: David Mamet. With Jack Nicholson, Jessica Lange.

Ragtime, 1981. Paramount Pictures (distributor). Director: Miloš Forman. Producer: Dino De Laurentiis. Screenwriter: Michael Weller, Bo Goldman (uncredited), based on the novel by E. L. Doctorow. With James Cagney, Brad Dourif, Moses Gunn, Elizabeth McGovern, Kenneth McMillan, Howard E. Rollins Jr., Mary Steenburgen, Samuel L. Jackson, Fran Drescher, Debbie Allen, Jack Nicholson (uncredited).

Reds, 1981. Paramount Pictures. Director: Warren Beatty. Producer: Warren Beatty. Screenplay: Warren Beatty, Trevor Griffiths. With Warren Beatty, Diane Keaton, Jack Nicholson, Paul Sorvino, Maureen Stapleton, Gene Hackman, Edward Herrmann, Jerzy Kosinski.

The Border, 1982. Universal Pictures (distributor), Universal Pictures, RKO Pictures. Director: Tony Richardson. Producer: Edgar Bronfman Jr. Screenplay: David Freeman, Walon Green, Deric Washburn. With Jack Nicholson, Harvey Keitel, Valerie Perrine, Warren Oates.

Terms of Endearment, 1983. Paramount Pictures. Director: James L. Brooks. Producer: James L. Brooks. Screenplay: James L. Brooks, based on the novel by Larry McMurtry. With Shirley MacLaine, Debra Winger, Jack Nicholson, Danny DeVito, Jeff Daniels, John Lithgow.

Terror in the Aisles, 1984. Universal Pictures (distributor). Documentary. Jack appears only briefly, in clips, mostly from his Corman period.

Prizzi's Honor, 1985. Twentieth Century-Fox (U.S. distributor). Director: John Huston. Producer: John Foreman. Screenplay: Richard Condon, Janet Roach. With Jack Nicholson, Kathleen Turner, Robert Loggia, Anjelica Huston, William Hickey.

Heartburn, 1986. Paramount Pictures. Director: Mike Nichols. Producer: Roger Greenhut, Mike Nichols. Screenplay: Nora Ephron. With Jack Nicholson, Meryl Streep.

The Witches of Eastwick, 1987. Warner Bros. (distributor), The Guber-Peters Company. Director: George Miller. Producer: Neil Canton, Peter Guber, Jon Peters. Screenplay: Michael Cristofer, based on the novel by John Updike. With Jack Nicholson, Cher, Susan Sarandon, Michelle Pfeiffer.

Broadcast News, 1987. Twentieth Century-Fox. Director: James L. Brooks. Producer: James L. Brooks. Screenplay: James L. Brooks. With William Hurt, Albert Brooks, Holly Hunter, Robert Prosky, Lois Chiles, Joan Cusack, Jack Nicholson.

Ironweed, 1987. TriStar Pictures. Director: Héctor Babenco. Producer: Keith Barish, Marcia Nasatir. Screenplay: William Kennedy, based on his novel of the same name. With Jack Nicholson, Meryl Streep, Carroll Baker, Michael O'Keefe, Diane Venora, Fred Gwynne, Margaret Whitton, Tom Waits.

Batman, 1989. Warner Bros. (distributor), The Guber-Peters Company, Poly-Gram Filmed Entertainment. Director: Tim Burton. Producer: Peter Guber, Jon Peters, Benjamin Melniker, Michael Uslin. Screenplay: Sam Hamm, Warren Skaaren, based on characters created by Bob Kane. With Jack Nicholson, Michael Keaton, Kim Basinger, Robert Wuhl, Pat Hingle, Billy Dee Williams, Michael Gough, Jack Palance.

The Two Jakes, 1990. Paramount Pictures. Director: Jack Nicholson. Producer: Robert Evans, Harold Schneider, Jack Nicholson. Screenplay: Robert Towne. With Jack Nicholson, Harvey Keitel, Meg Tilly, Madeline Stowe.

Man Trouble, 1992. Twentieth Century-Fox. Director: Bob Rafelson. Producer: Vittorio Cecchi Gori, Carole Eastman, Bruce Gilbert. Screenwriter: Carole Eastman. With Jack Nicholson, Ellen Barkin, Harry Dean Stanton, Beverly D'Angelo.

A Few Good Men, 1992. Columbia Pictures (distributor), Castle Rock Entertainment. Director: Rob Reiner. Producer: David Brown, Rob Reiner, Andrew Scheinman. Screenplay: Aaron Sorkin. With Jack Nicholson, Tom Cruise, Demi Moore, Kevin Pollack, Kevin Bacon, J. T. Walsh, Keifer Sutherland.

Hoffa, 1992. Twentieth Century-Fox. Director: Danny DeVito. Producer: Caldecott Chubb, Danny DeVito, Edward R. Pressman. Screenplay: David Mamet. With Jack Nicholson, Danny DeVito, Armand Assante, J. T. Walsh, John Reilly.

Wolf, 1994. Columbia Pictures. Director: Mike Nichols. Producer: Douglas Wick, Neal A. Machlis. Screenplay: Jim Harrison, Wesley Strick, Elaine May (uncredited). With Jack Nicholson, Michelle Pfeiffer.

The Crossing Guard, 1995. Miramax (distributor). Director: Sean Penn. Producer: Sean Penn, David S. Hamburger. Screenplay: Sean Penn. With Jack Nicholson, David Morse, Robin Wright, Anjelica Huston.

Blood and Wine, 1996. Fox Searchlight Pictures. Director: Bob Rafelson. Producer: Jeremy Thomas. Screenplay: Alison Cross, Nick Villers. With Jack Nicholson, Stephen Dorff, Jennifer Lopez, Judy Davis, Michael Caine.

The Evening Star, 1996. Paramount Pictures. Director: Robert Harling. Producer: David Kirkpatrick, Polly Platt. Screenplay: Larry McMurtry, Robert Harling. With Shirley MacLaine, Bill Paxton, Juliette Lewis, Miranda Richardson, Jack Nicholson.

Mars Attacks!, 1996. Warner Bros. (distributor), Tim Burton Productions. Director: Tim Burton. Producer: Tim Burton, Larry J. Franco. Screenplay: Jonathan Gems. With Jack Nicholson, Glenn Close, Annette Bening, Pierce Brosnan, Danny DeVito.

As Good as It Gets, 1997. TriStar Pictures (distributor), Gracie Films. Director: James L. Brooks. Producer: James L. Brooks, Bridget Johnson, Kristi Zea. Screenplay: Mark Andrus, James L. Brooks. With Jack Nicholson, Helen Hunt, Greg Kinnear, Cuba Gooding Jr.

The Pledge, 2001. Warner Bros. (distributor). Director: Sean Penn. Producer: Andrew Stevens. Screenplay: Jerzy Kromolowski, Mary Olson-Kromolowski. With Jack Nicholson, Aaron Eckhart, Helen Mirren, Robin Wright Penn, Vanessa Redgrave, Sam Shepard.

About Schmidt, 2002. New Line Cinema (distributor). Director: Alexander Payne. Producer: Michael Bresman, Harry Gittes, Rachel Horovitz. With Jack Nicholson, Hope Davis, Dermot Mulroney, Kathy Bates.

Anger Management, 2003. Columbia Pictures (distributor). Director: Peter Segal. Producer: Adam Sandler (executive), Allen Covet, Jack Giaraputo, Tim Herlihy. Screenplay: David S. Dorfman. With Adam Sandler, Jack Nicholson, Marisa Tomei, Luis Guzmán, Allen Covert, Lynne Thigpen, Kurt Fuller, Jonathan Loughran, Krista Allen, January Jones, Woody Harrelson, John Turturro.

Something's Gotta Give, 2003. Columbia Pictures (U.S. distributor), Warner

Bros. (non-U.S.. distributor). Director: Nancy Meyers. Producer: Nancy Meyers. Screenplay: Nancy Meyers. With Jack Nicholson, Diane Keaton, Keanu Reeves, Frances McDormand, Amanda Peet, Jon Favreau.

The Departed, 2006. Warner Bros. (distributor), Plan B Entertainment, GK Films, Vertigo Entertainment, Media Asia Films. Director: Martin Scorsese. Producer: Brad Pitt, Brad Grey, Graham King. Screenplay: William Monahan (based on *Infernal Affairs* by Alan Mak and Felix Chong). With Jack Nicholson, Leonardo DiCaprio, Matt Damon, Mark Wahlberg.

The Bucket List, 2007. Warner Bros. (distributor). Director: Rob Reiner. Producer: Craig Zadan, Neil Meron, Alan Greisman, Rob Reiner. Screenplay: Justin Zackham. With Jack Nicholson, Morgan Freeman, Sean Hayes, Rob Morrow.

How Do You Know, 2010. Columbia Pictures (distributor), Gracie Films. Director: James L. Brooks. Producer: Julie Ansell, James L. Brooks, Paula Weinstein. Screenplay: James L. Brooks. With Jack Nicholson, Reese Witherspoon, Paul Rudd, Owen Wilson.

TV SHOWS (EXCLUDING ENTERTAINMENT/NEWS PROGRAMS)

Matinee Theatre (1 episode)
"Are You Listening?" (September 3, 1956)—Actor
Mr. Lucky (1 episode)
"Operation Fortuna" (May 21, 1960)—Martin
The Barbara Stanwyck Show (1 episode)
"The Mink Coat" (September 19, 1960)—Bud
Tales of Wells Fargo (1 episode)
"That Washburn Girl" (February 13, 1961)—Tom Washburn
Sea Hunt (1 episode)
"Round Up" (September 23, 1961)—John Stark
Bronco (1 episode)
"The Equalizer" (December 18, 1961)—Bob Doolin
Hawaiian Eye (1 episode)
"Total Eclipse" (February 21, 1962)—Tony Morgan
Dr. Kildare (4 episodes)
  —*"A Patient Lost"* (February 22, 1966)—Jaime Angel
  —*"What Happened to All the Sunshine and Roses?"* (February 28, 1966)—Jaime Angel
  —*"The Taste of Crow"* (March 7, 1966)—Jaime Angel
  —*"Out of a Concrete Tower"* (March 8, 1966)—Jaime Angel

The Andy Griffith Show (2 episodes)
  —*"Aunt Bee, the Juror"* (October 23, 1967)—Marvin Jenkins
  —*"Opie Finds a Baby"* (November 21, 1966)—Mr. Garland
Voyage to the Bottom of the Sea (1 episode)
"The Lost Bomb" (December 11, 1966)—Crewman (uncredited)
The Guns of Will Sonnett (1 episode)
"A Son for a Son" (October 20, 1967)—Tom Murdock

AWARDS

ACADEMY AWARDS

2003
NOMINATED: Best Actor in a Leading Role: *About Schmidt* (2002)

1998
WON: Best Actor in a Leading Role: *As Good as It Gets* (1997)

1993
NOMINATED: Best Actor in a Supporting Role: *A Few Good Men* (1992)

1988
NOMINATED: Best Actor in a Leading Role: *Ironweed* (1987)

1986
NOMINATED: Best Actor in a Leading Role: *Prizzi's Honor* (1985)

1984
WON: Best Actor in a Supporting Role: *Terms of Endearment* (1983)

1982
NOMINATED: Best Actor in a Supporting Role: *Reds* (1981)

1976
WON: Best Actor in a Leading Role: *One Flew over the Cuckoo's Nest* (1975)

1975
NOMINATED: Best Actor in a Leading Role: *Chinatown* (1974)

1974
NOMINATED: Best Actor in a Leading Role: *The Last Detail* (1973)

1971
NOMINATED: Best Actor in a Leading Role: *Five Easy Pieces* (1970)

1970
NOMINATED: Best Actor in a Supporting Role: *Easy Rider* (1969)

ACADEMY OF SCIENCE FICTION, FANTASY & HORROR FILMS (SATURN AWARDS)

1995
NOMINATED: Best Actor: *Wolf* (1994)

1991
NOMINATED: Best Actor: *Batman* (1989)

1988
WON: Best Actor: *The Witches of Eastwick* (1987)

AMERICAN COMEDY AWARDS

1998
WON: Funniest Actor in a Motion Picture (Leading Role): *As Good as It Gets* (1997)

AMERICAN FILM INSTITUTE

1994
WON: Life Achievement Award

AUSTIN FILM CRITICS ASSOCIATION

2006
WON: Best Supporting Actor: *The Departed* (2006)

BAFTA FILM AWARDS

2007
NOMINATED: Best Performance by an Actor in a Supporting Role: *The Departed* (2006)

2003
NOMINATED: Best Performance by an Actor in a Leading Role: *About Schmidt* (2002)

1990
NOMINATED: Best Actor in a Supporting Role: *Batman* (1989)

1983
WON: Best Supporting Actor: *Reds* (1981)

1977
WON: Best Actor: *One Flew over the Cuckoo's Nest* (1975)

1975
WON: Best Actor: *Chinatown* (1974)

1974
WON: Best Actor: *The Last Detail* (1973)

1970
NOMINATED: Best Supporting Actor: *Easy Rider* (1969)

BLOCKBUSTER ENTERTAINMENT AWARDS

1999
NOMINATED: Favorite Actor (Video): *As Good as It Gets* (1997)

BOSTON SOCIETY OF FILM CRITICS AWARDS

1986
WON: Best Actor: *Prizzi's Honor* (1985)

1984
WON: Best Supporting Actor: *Terms of Endearment* (1983)

1982
WON: Best Supporting Actor: *Reds* (1981)

BROADCAST FILM CRITICS ASSOCIATION AWARDS

2007
NOMINATED: Best Supporting Actor: *The Departed* (2006)

2003
WON: Best Actor: *About Schmidt* (2002)

1998
WON: Best Actor: *As Good as It Gets* (1997)

CANNES FILM FESTIVAL

1974
WON: Best Actor: *The Last Detail* (1973)

1971
NOMINATED: Golden Palm: *Drive, He Said* (1971)

CHICAGO FILM CRITICS ASSOCIATION AWARDS

2006
NOMINATED: Best Supporting Actor: *The Departed* (2006)
2002
NOMINATED: Best Actor: *About Schmidt* (2002)

CINE VEGAS INTERNATIONAL FILM FESTIVAL

2004
WON: Marquee Award

DALLAS–FORT WORTH FILM CRITICS ASSOCIATION AWARDS

2003
WON: Best Actor: *About Schmidt* (2002)

DAVID DI DONATELLO AWARDS

1976
WON: Best Foreign Actor: *One Flew over the Cuckoo's Nest* (1975)

FOTOGRAMAS DE PLATA

1975
WON: Best Foreign Movie Performer

GOLDEN GLOBES

2007
NOMINATED: Best Performance by an Actor in a Supporting Role in a Motion
    Picture: *The Departed* (2006)
2004
NOMINATED: Best Performance by an Actor in a Motion Picture—Musical or
    Comedy: *Something's Gotta Give* (2003)
2003
WON: Best Performance by an Actor in a Motion Picture—Drama: *About
    Schmidt* (2002)

1999

WON: Cecil B. DeMille Award for outstanding contribution to the entertainment field.

1998

WON: Best Performance by an Actor in a Motion Picture—Comedy/Musical: *As Good as It Gets* (1997)

1993

NOMINATED: Best Performance by an Actor in a Motion Picture—Drama: *Hoffa* (1992)

1993

NOMINATED: Best Performance by an Actor in a Supporting Role in a Motion Picture: *A Few Good Men* (1992)

1990

NOMINATED: Best Performance by an Actor in a Motion Picture—Comedy/Musical: *Batman* (1989)

1988

NOMINATED: Best Performance by an Actor in a Motion Picture—Drama: *Ironweed* (1987)

1986

WON: Best Performance by an Actor in a Motion Picture—Comedy/Musical: *Prizzi's Honor* (1985)

1984

WON: Best Performance by an Actor in a Supporting Role in a Motion Picture: *Terms of Endearment* (1983)

1982

NOMINATED: Best Motion Picture Actor in a Supporting Role: *Reds* (1981)

1976

WON: Best Motion Picture Actor—Drama, *One Flew over the Cuckoo's Nest* (1975)

1975

WON: Best Motion Picture Actor—Drama: *Chinatown* (1974)

1974

NOMINATED: Best Motion Picture Actor—Drama: *The Last Detail* (1973)

1972

NOMINATED: Best Motion Picture Actor—Drama: *Carnal Knowledge* (1971)

1971

NOMINATED: Best Motion Picture Actor—Drama: *Five Easy Pieces* (1970)

1970

NOMINATED: Best Supporting Actor: *Easy Rider* (1969)

GOLDENE KAMERA

2004
WON: Goldene Kamera, Film International

KANSAS CITY FILM CRITICS CIRCLE AWARDS

1984
WON: Best Supporting Actor: *Terms of Endearment* (1983)
1982
WON: Best Supporting Actor: *Reds* (1981)
1975
WON: Best Actor: *Chinatown* (1974)
1970
WON: Best Supporting Actor: *Easy Rider* (1969)

LAUREL AWARDS

1971
WON: Golden Laurel, Best Dramatic Performance, Male (2nd place): *Five Easy Pieces* (1970)
1971
NOMINATED: Golden Laurel Star, Male (9th place)
1970
WON: Golden Laurel, Male Supporting Performance: *Easy Rider* (1969)

LONDON CRITICS CIRCLE FILM AWARDS

1999
WON: Actor of the Year: *As Good as It Gets* (1997)

LOS ANGELES FILM CRITICS ASSOCIATION AWARDS

2002
WON: Best Actor: *About Schmidt* (2002)
1987
WON: Best Actor: *Ironweed* (1987)
1983
WON: Best Supporting Actor: *Terms of Endearment* (1983)

MOSCOW INTERNATIONAL FILM FESTIVAL

2001
WON: Stanislavsky Prize

MTV MOVIE AWARDS

2007
WON: Best Villain: *The Departed* (2006)

1993
NOMINATED: Best Male Performance: *A Few Good Men* (1992)

1993
NOMINATED: Best Villain: *A Few Good Men* (1992)

NATIONAL BOARD OF REVIEW

2006
WON: Best Ensemble: *The Departed* (2006) (shared with Leonardo DiCaprio, Matt Damon, Mark Wahlberg)

1997
WON: Best Actor: *As Good as It Gets* (1997)

1992
WON: Best Supporting Actor: *A Few Good Men* (1992)

1983
WON: Best Supporting Actor: *Terms of Endearment* (1983)

1981
WON: Best Supporting Actor: *Reds* (1981)

1975
WON: Best Actor: *One Flew over the Cuckoo's Nest* (1975)

NATIONAL SOCIETY OF FILM CRITICS AWARDS

1986
WON: Best Actor: *Prizzi's Honor* (1985)

1984
WON: Best Supporting Actor: *Terms of Endearment* (1983)

1975
WON: Best Actor: *One Flew over the Cuckoo's Nest* (1975)

1975
WON: Best Actor: *Chinatown* (1974)
1970
WON: Best Supporting Actor: *Easy Rider* (1969)

NEW YORK FILM CRITICS CIRCLE AWARDS

1987
WON: Best Actor: *The Witches of Eastwick* (1987)
1985
WON: Best Actor: *Prizzi's Honor* (1985)
1983
WON: Best Supporting Actor: *Terms of Endearment* (1983)
1975
WON: Best Actor: *One Flew over the Cuckoo's Nest* (1975)
1974
WON: Best Actor: *Chinatown* (1974)
1969
WON: Best Supporting Actor: *Easy Rider* (1969)

ONLINE FILM CRITICS SOCIETY AWARDS

2007
NOMINATED: Best Supporting Actor: *The Departed* (2006)
2003
NOMINATED: Best Actor: *About Schmidt* (2002)
1998
WON: Best Actor: *As Good as It Gets* (1997)

PEOPLE'S CHOICE AWARDS

2007
NOMINATED: Favorite On-Screen Match-Up, *The Departed* (2006) (shared with Matt Damon, Leonardo DiCaprio)

PHOENIX FILM CRITICS SOCIETY AWARDS

2006
WON: Best Performance by an Actor in a Supporting Role: *The Departed* (2006)

2003
NOMINATED: Best Actor in a Leading Role: *About Schmidt* (2002)

RAZZIE AWARDS

1993
NOMINATED: Worst Actor: *Hoffa* (1992)

SANT JORDI AWARDS

1977
WON: Best Foreign Actor (*Mejor Actor Extranjero*): *One Flew over the Cuckoo's Nest* (1975)

GOLDEN SATELLITE AWARDS

2006
NOMINATED: Best Actor in a Supporting Role: *The Departed* (2006)

2003
NOMINATED: Best Performance by an Actor in a Motion Picture, Drama: *About Schmidt* (2002)

1998
WON: Best Performance by an Actor in a Motion Picture—Comedy or Musical: *As Good as It Gets* (1997)

1997
NOMINATED: Best Performance by an Actor in a Motion Picture—Comedy or Musical: *Mars Attacks!* (1996)

SCREEN ACTORS GUILD AWARDS

2007
NOMINATED: Outstanding Performance by a Cast in a Motion Picture: *The Departed* (2006) (shared with Leonardo DiCaprio, Matt Damon, Mark Wahlberg)

2003
NOMINATED: Outstanding Performance by a Male Actor in a Leading Role: *About Schmidt* (2002)

1998
WON: Outstanding Performance by a Male Actor in a Leading Role: *As Good as It Gets* (1997)

SOUTHEASTERN FILM CRITICS ASSOCIATION AWARDS

1993
WON: Best Supporting Actor: *A Few Good Men* (1992)

TEEN CHOICE AWARDS

2003
NOMINATED: Choice Movie Hissy Fit: *Anger Management* (2003)

WALK OF FAME

1997
STAR on Walk of Fame: Located at 6925 Hollywood Boulevard

WASHINGTON DC AREA FILM CRITICS ASSOCIATION AWARDS

2002
WON: Best Actor: *About Schmidt* (2002)

NOTES AND SOURCES

BOOKS AND VIDEOS

Bergen, Candice. *Knock Wood*. New York: Simon and Schuster, 1984.

Biskind, Peter. *Easy Riders, Raging Bulls: How the Sex-Drugs-and-Rock-'n'-Roll Generation Saved Hollywood*. New York: Simon and Schuster, 1998.

———. *Star*. New York: Simon and Schuster, 2010.

Brode, Douglas. *The Films of Jack Nicholson* (3rd ed.). Secaucus, NJ: Carol, 1996.

Corman, Roger. *The Nurses Collection* (DVD). Shout DVD #SF 13149, rereleased 2012.

Crane, Robert David, and Christopher Fryer. *Jack Nicholson: Face to Face*. Philadelphia: Lippincott, 1975.

———. *Jack Nicholson: The Early Years*. Lexington: University Press of Kentucky, 2012.

Douglas, Kirk. *The Ragman's Son: An Autobiography*. New York: Simon and Schuster, 1988.

Kinn, Gail, and Jim Piazza. *The Academy Awards*. New York: Black Dog and Leventhal, 2002.

Lim, Dennis, ed. *The* Village Voice *Film Guide*. Hoboken, NJ: Wiley, 2007.

McDougal, Dennis. *Five Easy Decades: How Jack Nicholson Became the Biggest Movie Star in Modern Times*. Hoboken, NJ: Wiley, 2008.

Phillips, John, and Jim Jerome. *Papa John: An Autobiography*. New York: Dolphin Books, 1986.

Phillips, Michelle. *California Dreamin'*. New York: Warner Books, 1986.

Sarris, Andrew. *The American Cinema: Directors and Directions, 1929–1968*. New York: Dutton, 1968.

———. *Confessions of a Cultist*. New York: Simon and Schuster, 1971.

———. *You Ain't Heard Nothin' Yet*. New York: Oxford University Press, 1998.

Schickel, Richard. *Conversations with Scorsese*. New York: Knopf, 2011.

Sellers, Robert. *Hollywood Hellraisers: The Wild Lives and Fast Times of Marlon Brando, Dennis Hopper, Warren Beatty, and Jack Nicholson*. New York: Skyline, 2010.

Stapleton, Alex (dir.). *Corman's World: Exploits of a Hollywood Rebel*. DVD. A&E IndieFilms, 2011.

Stevens, George Jr. *Conversations at the American Film Institute with the Great Moviemakers: The Next Generation from the 1950s to Hollywood Today*. New York: Knopf, 2012.

Wiley, Mason, and Damien Bona. *Inside Oscar* (rev. ed.). New York: Ballantine, 1996.

Winkler, Peter L. *Dennis Hopper: The Wild Ride of a Hollywood Rebel*. Fort Lee, NJ: Barricade Books, 2011.

OPENING QUOTES

xi: "There is James Cagney . . ." Mike Nichols, to Ron Rosenbaum, *New York Times Magazine*, July 13, 1986.

xi: "Marlon Brando influenced me . . ." Jack Nicholson, quoted in *Hollywood Reporter*, August 10, 2004.

xi: "He's our Bogart . . ." Henry Jaglom, quoted in *People*, December 6, 2002.

xi: "When I started off . . ." Jack Nicholson, quoted in "Cries & Whispers," August 22, 2002.

xi: "He has a great deal of respect . . ." Bruce Dern, to Robert Crane and Christopher Fryer, *Jack Nicholson: The Early Years*, p. 72.

xi: "What would it be like . . ." Jack Nicholson, to Mike Sager, *Esquire*, January 2004.

INTRODUCTION

1: "One never really recovers from his own birth . . ." Jack Nicholson, quoted in the *Playboy* interview by Richard Warren Lewis, *Playboy*, April 1972.

2: "I had Shorty . . ." Jack Nicholson, quoted by Dennis McDougal, *Five Easy Decades*, p. 12.

CHAPTER 1

9: "I have the blood of kings . . ." Jack Nicholson, quoted by Neal Weaver, *After Dark*, October 1969.

9: "It's a miracle . . ." Jack Nicholson, to Bill Davidson, "The Conquering Antihero," *New York Times Magazine*, October 12, 1975.

10: "rocked the house . . ." Lorraine, quoted by Robert Sellers, *Hollywood Hellraisers*, p. 17.

10: The anecdote about lying on the floor kicking and screaming is from Mimi Machu, who also noted that Jack would lose his wallet and keys several times a week during their relationship. Quoted by Leo Janos, *Cosmopolitan*, December 1976.

10: "Later on . . ." Jack Nicholson, quoted in *Playboy*, April 1972.

10: because of his extended human skills rather than superhuman skills or supernatural powers . . . Jack Nicholson, quoted in *New York Times*, June 18, 1989.

10: "I was very driven . . ." Jack Nicholson, quoted in *Rolling Stone*, October 5, 2006.

11: "I never felt poor . . ." Jack Nicholson, to Martin Torgoff, *Interview*, August 1984.

12: "He wanted to be an athlete . . ." Classmate Hoop Keith, quoted by Dennis McDougal, *Five Easy Decades*, p. 17.

13: "He would hang around . . ." Sandra Hawes, quoted ibid., p. 19.

CHAPTER 2

15: "I got into acting by being a fan . . ." Jack Nicholson, quoted by Neal Weaver, *After Dark*, October 1969.

15: "[When I was old enough] I headed west . . ." Jack Nicholson, to Peter Bogdanovich, *Suddeutsche Zeitung Magazin*, 2006.

18: "There were certain things . . ." Jack Nicholson, to David Sheff, *Playboy*, January 2004.

18: "I was part of a generation . . ." Jack Nicholson, quoted in *Playboy*, April 1972.

19: "I had no [real or meaningful] friends . . ." Jack Nicholson, to Martin Torgoff, *Interview*, August 1984.

19: "I had [already] bought a [plane] ticket . . ." Jack Nicholson, to Peter Bogdanovich, *Suddeutsche Zeitung Magazin*, 2006.

20: "I saw everybody . . ." Ibid.

22: "I think I knew . . ." Jack Nicholson, quoted by Dennis McDougal, *Five Easy Decades*, p. 13.

24: "When an actor . . ." Jeff Corey, quoted by Jack Nicholson in *Los Angeles Times*, November 3, 2002.

25: "I liked him a lot . . ." Georgianna Carter, quoted by Dennis McDougal, *Five Easy Decades*.

CHAPTER 3

26: "Early on, I would say . . ." Jack Nicholson, to Robert Crane and Christopher Fryer, *Genesis Magazine*, February 1975.

26: "Corman was one of those guys . . ." Mike Medavoy, interview by author, April 19, 2012.

27: "One of the things . . ." David Thomson, commentary for Criterion collection of BBS films, 2010.

27: "Corman provided everyone . . ." Peter Biskind, interview by author, June 18, 2012.

27: "It was difficult . . ." Roger Corman, interview by author.

28: "I began work on Monday . . ." Roger Corman, quoted in Michael Ned Holte, "Value Engineering: Roger Corman Within His Own Context," *East of Borneo*, October 10, 2010.

28: "The only job . . ." Roger Corman, interview by author.

28: "The idea was to save money . . ." Mike Medavoy, interview by author.

29: "I could see the problem . . ." Roger Corman, interview by author.

29: "I had learned the use . . ." Ibid.

29: "[Corman] came into the class" and "show me some poetry" and "Maybe, Jeff . . ." Jack Nicholson to Jay Cocks, *Time*, August 12, 1974.

29: "I was absolutely certain . . ." Roger Corman, interview by author.

30: "Times were changing . . ." Ibid.

30: "I hadn't really worked before . . ." Jack Nicholson, speaking in the documentary film *Corman's World: Exploits of a Hollywood Rebel*, directed by Alex Stapleton, DVD, A&E IndieFilms, 2011.

32: "the wildest house in Hollywood . . ." Douglas Brode, *The Films of Jack Nicholson*, p. 18.

32: "Whenever I think of Jack . . ." Harry Dean Stanton, quoted ibid.

33: "I had met this other . . ." Roger Corman, interview by author.

33: "I think in all my movies . . ." Ibid.

34: "very wry . . . but very cynical . . ." Monte Hellman, quoted by Mary Blume, *Los Angeles Times*, April 4, 1971.

34: "Jack already had a reputation . . ." Monte Hellman, interview by author.

36: "It was actually shot in two days . . ." Roger Corman, interview by author.

36: "The reason I got it . . ." Jack Nicholson, quoted by Neal Weaver, *After Dark*, October 1969.

38: "All of your conceptual reality . . ." Jack Nicholson, quoted in *Playboy*, April 1972.

38: "While the ceremony . . ." Jack Nicholson, quoted in *Newsweek*, December 9, 2002.

38: "I said, look, Roger . . ." Jack Nicholson, *Corman's World* DVD, A&E Indie-Films, 2011.

39: "as [the magnificent sets . . ." Boris Karloff, quoted by Douglas Brode, *The Films of Jack Nicholson*, p. 52.

CHAPTER 4

40: "I never dug [being in Corman's films] . . ." Jack Nicholson, quoted by Douglas Brode, *The Films of Jack Nicholson*, pp. 42–43.

44: "in those days . . ." Monte Hellman, interview by author.

44: "Three weeks for one . . ." Ibid.

45: "McLuhan mystery . . ." Jack Nicholson, quoted by Neal Weaver, *After Dark*, October 1969.

45: "lots of tomahawks and ketchup . . ." Roger Corman, quoted by Dennis McDougal, *Five Easy Decades*, p. 57.

45: "I agreed to let them . . ." Roger Corman, interview by author.

46: "existential western . . ." Jack Nicholson, quoted by Neal Weaver, *After Dark*, October 1969.

46: "a horror picture . . ." Monte Hellman, interview by author.

47: "As a young Turk . . ." Jack Nicholson, to Gene Siskel, *Chicago Tribune*, June 16, 1985.

47: "That was the first time . . ." Jack Nicholson, to Peter Bogdanovich, *Suddeutsche Zeitung Magazin*, 2006.

48: "That year was the most . . ." Monte Hellman, interview by author.

48: "Monte was a real talent . . ." Mike Medavoy, interview by author.

50: "The Hells Angels . . ." Roger Corman, interview by author.

52: "She fell in love with God and Jack couldn't compete . . ." Helena Kallianiotes, quoted by Dennis McDougal, *Five Easy Decades*, p. 70.

52: "My marriage broke up . . ." Jack Nicholson, quoted in *Playboy*, April 1972.

53: "Bruce was *one* of my favorite actors . . ." Roger Corman, interview by author.

53: "By now, Roger and I . . ." Jack Nicholson, speaking in the documentary film. *Corman's World: Exploits of a Hollywood Rebel*, directed by Alex Stapleton, DVD, A&E IndieFilms, 2011.

53: "I had known Jack and Peter . . ." Dennis Hopper, to Michael Rechtshaffen, *Hollywood Reporter*, January 19, 1999.

56: "Our eyes met . . ." Karen Black, interview by author.

56: "I was with her . . ." Jack Nicholson, quoted by Jacoba Atlas and Marni Butterfield, *Show Magazine*, May 1971.

58: "I always sort of stunk on television . . ." Jack Nicholson, to Martin Torgoff, *Interview*, August 1984.

CHAPTER 5

59: "Being stoned . . ." Jack Nicholson, to Robert Crane and Christopher Fryer, *Genesis*, February 1975.

60: "I want to make . . ." Bert Schneider, quoted by Peter Biskind, *Easy Riders, Raging Bulls*, p. 57.

60: "When I liked a picture . . ." Bob Rafelson, to Louise France, *The Times*, (London), May 15, 1998.

61: "I'm a New Wave baby . . ." Jack Nicholson, to Julian Schnabel, *Interview*, April 2003.

63: "We all agreed . . ." Micky Dolenz, interview by author.

63: "I can write any movie about anything . . ." Jack Nicholson, to Peter Bogdanovich, *Suddeutsche Zeitung Magazin*, 2006.

64: "Jack used to act out all the parts . . ." Bob Rafelson, to Michael Rechtshaffen, *Hollywood Reporter*, January 19, 1999.

64: "He just started hanging . . ." Micky Dolenz, interview by author.

64: "Bob knew me . . ." Toni Basil, interview by author.

64: "They were looking to deconstruct . . ." Micky Dolenz, interview by author.

65: "I hope nobody ever likes it . . ." Jack Nicholson, quoted by Neal Weaver, *After Dark*, October 1969.

66: "I was sure . . ." Roger Corman, interview by author.

67: "How's your bike movie coming? . . ." Bob Rafelson, quoted by Peter Biskind, *Easy Riders, Raging Bulls*, p. 61.

68: "We were all . . ." Karen Black, interview by author.

68: "In the first scene . . ." Toni Basil, interview by author.

70: "I'll wait for you in the street . . ." Rip Torn, quoted by Peter Biskind, *Easy Riders, Raging Bulls*.

70: "Almost everyone wanted me out of acting . . ." Jack Nicholson, quoted by Ross, *Movie Digest*, January 1972.

71: "There hasn't been a motorcycle picture . . ." Jack Nicholson, quoted by Les Wedman, *Los Angeles Times*, January 11, 1970.

71: "That long scene . . ." Jack Nicholson, quoted by Neal Weaver, *After Dark*, October 1969.

73: "I set up a meeting . . ." Bob Evans, "Advertising and Film."

73: "I don't know a movie . . ." Jack Nicholson, quoted by Harry Clein, *Entertainment World*, November 7, 1969.

74: "I feel Dennis . . ." Karen Black, interview by author.

74: "[Schneider] told me . . ." Henry Jaglom, to Nicholas Freud Jones, BBC2, 1995. Reissued on DVD as part of a five-disc 2010 retrospective of BBS, *America Lost and Found: The BBS Story*.

75: "I edited . . ." Dennis Hopper, to Nicholas Freud Jones, BBC2, 1995.

75: "*His* movie . . ." Peter Fonda, to Nicholas Freud Jones BBC2, 1995.

76: Jane Fonda and Bruce Dern anecdote . . . With minor edits here, this anecdote appears in Peter Biskind, *Easy Riders, Raging Bulls*, p. 73.

76: "I had just become . . ." Peter Guber, interview by author.

76 "John Wayne of biker films . . ." Jack Nicholson, quoted in *Playboy*, April 1972.

CHAPTER 6

78: "Since my overnight stardom . . ." Jack Nicholson, quoted in *Playboy*, April 1972.

79: "We were two maniacs. . . ." Mimi Machu, quoted in Dennis McDougal, *Five Easy Decades*, p. 122.

79: "I'm interested in sex . . ." Jack Nicholson, to Chris Chase, *Cosmopolitan*, February 1983.

79: "Nobody ever noticed him . . ." Rex Reed, "The Man Who Walked Off with *Easy Rider*," *New York Times*, March 1, 1970.

80: "Any man who insists . . ." Henry Fonda, quoted by Mason Wiley and Damien Bona, *Inside Oscar*, p. 440.

81: "I've always wanted to be a movie actor . . ." Jack Nicholson, quoted by Deac Rossell, *Philadelphia After Dark*, September 24, 1969.

81: "I liked the part . . ." Jack Nicholson, quoted by Mary Blume, *Los Angeles Times*, April 4, 1971.

83: "I had the address . . ." This and the rest of the anecdote, including Brando and the roses, and the Légers leaning against the wall, are from Peter Guber, interview by author.

84: "I've taken all the drugs . . ." Jack Nicholson, quoted in *Newsweek*.

85: "Jack started the scene . . ." Helen Kallianotes, interview by author.

85: "My character was written . . ." Jack Nicholson, quoted by Gene Siskel, *Chicago Tribune*, quoted by Douglas Brode, *The Films of Jack Nicholson*, p. 117.

86: "*On the Road* gone wrong . . ." Douglas Brinkley, quoted in *Newsweek*, reprinted in *Show Magazine*, May 1971.

87: "ecstasy . . ." Karen Black, interview by author.

87: "I was so happy . . ." Karen Black, interview by author.

89: "the most important actor since Brando . . ." Mike Nichols, quoted by Robert Sellers, *Hollywood Hellraisers*.

89: "a cheerleader and a supporter . . ." Peter Guber, interview by author.

91: The casting couch anecdote is from "Happy Jack: Nicholson Is the Easiest Rider of Them All," *Life*, March 1970.

91: "I want to make only . . ." Jack Nicholson, quoted by Ross, *Movie Digest*, January 1972.

91: "If you suck a tit . . ." Jack Nicholson, to David Sheff, *Playboy*, January 2004.

92: "We were enthusiastic . . ." Peter Guber, interview by author.

92: "almost incoherent . . ." Harry Dean Stanton, quoted by Leo Janos, *Cosmopolitan*, December 1976.

92: "The production was disorganized . . ." Karen Black, interview by author.

95: "I personally had . . ." Henry Jaglom, interview by author.

96: "Pick yourself a bedroom . . ." Jack Nicholson, quoted by Jay Cocks, *Time*, August 12, 1974.

97: "you can tell . . ." Harry Gittes, quoted by Leo Janos, *Cosmopolitan*, December 1976.

97: "Chicks dig it sexually . . ." *Playboy*, 1972.

100: "I went to every studio . . ." George Lucas, quoted in George Stevens, *Conversations at the American Film Institute*, p. 302.

101: "He had a lot . . ." Jack Nicholson, to Peter Bogdanovich, *Suddeutsche Zeitung Magazin*, 2006.

104: "The film was written . . ." For obvious reasons, the source of this quote insists on anonymity.

106: "The same year . . ." Jack Nicholson, to Peter Bogdanovich, *Suddeutsche Zeitung Magazin*, 2006.

106: "I liked the project . . ." Jack Nicholson, to Aljean Harmetz, *Los Angeles Times*, March 31, 1974.

106: "I could kill myself . . ." Jack Nicholson, to Rosemary Kent, "Andy Warhol's Interview," *Interview*, April 1974.

CHAPTER 7

109: "I'm a fairly common man . . ." Jack Nicholson, quoted by Tag Gallagher, *Village Voice*, June 7, 1975.

109: "a very big player . . ." Robert Evans, *People*, July 8, 1985.

110: "I've been at parties . . ." Robert Evans, to Paul Attanasio, *Washington Post*, June 14, 1985.

111: Jack's choice of albums for his trip to the East Coast was described in *Playboy*, April 1972.

111: "The character was sort of . . ." Jack Nicholson, to Robert Crane and Christopher Fryer, *Genesis*, February 1975.

112: "stupid Irish Mick . . ." Michelle Phillips, quoted by Dennis McDougal, *Five Easy Decades*, p. 141.

112: "Jack always has the same dynamic . . ." Harry Gittes, quoted by Peter Biskind, *Easy Riders, Raging Bulls*, p. 195.

112: "[Michelle]'s the only one . . ." The unnamed source is quoted by Dennis McDougal, *Five Easy Decades*, p. 150.

114: "I usually don't think critics . . ." Jack Nicholson, quoted by Roger Shales, *Los Angeles Times*, March 1, 1973.

115: "I was totally involved . . ." Peter Guber, interview by author.

115: "The project broke down several times . . ." Ibid.

116: "I had to fly to Canada . . ." Ibid.

117: "Jack was a force of nature . . ." Ibid.

119: "I loved the clothes . . ." Anjelica Huston, quoted in *People*, August 1985.

119: "I was invited . . ." Anjelica Huston, to Bob Flynn, *Mail Online*, April 20, 2012.

120: "When I was working in New York . . ." Anjelica Huston, to Rosemary Kent, "Andy Warhol's Interview," *Interview*, April 1974.

120: "a feeling like when you had a good time with your dad . . ." Anjelica Huston, to Gene Siskel, *Chicago Tribune*, June 16, 1985.

CHAPTER 8

121: "Cocaine is in now . . ." Jack Nicholson, quoted in *Playboy*, April 1972.

122: "Toots . . ." Jack Nicholson told columnist Earl Wilson that his nickname for Anjelica was Toots. He also referred to her as "the Moan" when he thought she complained too much. Earl Wilson, syndicated column, February 7, 1974. Guy Flately, in a profile on Jack for the *New York Times*, quoted the nickname as "Tootie." Guy Flately, *New York Times*, February 10, 1974.

123: "Since we've been together . . ." Jack, to the British press upon his arrival in London.

123: "Can you imagine . . ." *Observer Review* (London), January 19, 2003.

123: "Maria has a fantastic screen personality . . ." Jack Nicholson, quoted in *Elle*, British edition, September 1992.

124: "Maria and I . . ." Jack Nicholson, to Guy Flately, *New York Times*, February 10, 1974.

124: "There are movies that you do . . ." Jack Nicholson, to Peter Bogdanovich, *Suddeutsche Zeitung Magazin*, 2006.

124: "[Antonioni was] like a father . . ." Jack Nicholson, quoted in the movie blog *Dispatches from Zembla*.

125: "Having heard of the upcoming publication . . ." Robert Crane and Christopher Fryer, *Jack Nicholson: The Early Years*, pp. 6–7.

127: "devastated and shocked . . ." Unnamed friends, quoted by Bernard Weinraub, "Who's Afraid of the Big Bad Book Editor," *New York Times*, June 12, 1994.

127: "a deep hurt inside . . ." Peter Fonda, to Robert Sellers, *Hollywood Hellraisers*, p. 15.

127: "The [possible publication of] the news was horrible . . ." Michelle Phillips, to Sheila Weller, *Vanity Fair*, December 2007.

129: "Who wants to sit . . ." Jack Nicholson, to Bill Davidson, "The Conquering Antihero," *New York Times Magazine*, October 12, 1975.

130: "I like the idea of winning at Cannes . . ." Jack Nicholson, quoted by Mason Wiley and Damien Bona, *Inside Oscar*, p. 493.

CHAPTER 9

131: "I don't know why a guy goes to a hooker . . ." Jack Nicholson, to Nancy Collins, *Vanity Fair*, April 1994.

131: "The one place . . ." The dinner conversation took place at Dominick's, a popular L.A. restaurant, and is recounted by Peter Biskind in *Easy Riders, Raging Bulls*, p. 160.

135: "ran into my dressing room . . ." Jack Nicholson, to Deborah Caulfield, *Los Angeles Times*, June 16, 1985.

136: "I have done radio . . ." Jack Nicholson, to Roberr Crane and Christopher Fryer, *Genesis*, February 1975.

136: "I think secrecy . . ." Jack Nicholson, to Michael Ventura, *L.A. Weekly*, July 4, 1985.

138: "I was grateful . . ." Jack Nicholson, to Peter Bogdanovich, *Suddeutsche Zeitung Magazin*, 2006.

CHAPTER 10

142: "To succeed—in order to become a Brando . . ." Jack Nicholson, quoted in *Viva*, September 1975.

144: "Why don't you let me . . ." Michael Douglas, to Tim Cahill, "Knocking Round the Nest," *Rolling Stone*, December 4, 1975.

144: "My saga began . . ." Michael Douglas, ibid.

148: "I don't think Jack . . ." Anjelica Huston, to Bob Flynn, *Mail Online*, April 20, 2012.

148: The anecdote about "What's a five-and-ten-cent store?" is from James Bacon, *Los Angeles Herald-Examiner*, September 4, 1975.

148: "Jack was more than of his time . . ." Henry Jaglom, interview by author.

150: "almost incomprehensible . . ." Kirk Douglas, *The Ragman's Son*, p. 401.

151: "He told me . . ." Jack Nicholson, relating an encounter with one of the patients to Tag Gallagher, *Village Voice*, June 9, 1975.

151: "They tell me . . ." Jack Nicholson, to Bob Lardine, "Close Look: Jack Nicholson's Getting Crazier Every Day," *In the Know*, August 1975.

152: "the classical music of sports . . ." Jack Nicholson, to Martin Torgoff, *Interview*, August 1984.

152: "It is really smashing . . ." Jack Nicholson, quoted in *Los Angeles Herald-Examiner*, February 28, 1975.

152: "for more than four months . . ." Jack Nicholson, in *Newsday*, quoted by Dennis McDougal, *Five Easy Decades*.

153: "a nice place . . ." and "What saved the day . . ." are from *Time*, April 21, 1975.

153: "The secret to *Cuckoo's Nest* . . ." Jack Nicholson, to Ron Rosenbaum, *New York Times Magazine*, July 13, 1986.

154: "Poor Nicholson" and "I was very hurt" are from Leo Janos, *Cosmopolitan*, December 1976.

154: "Marlon's still the greatest . . ." Jack Nicholson, quoted by Bill Davidson, *New York Times Magazine* October 12, 1975.

156: "I'm the first friendly Communist . . ." Jack Nicholson, quoted in *Interview*, December 1976.

158: "The Italian interviews . . ." Jack Nicholson, quoted by Army Archerd, *Variety*, March 9, 1976.

158: "Oh no . . ." *People*, May 22, 1976.

158: "With my sunglasses . . ." Jack Nicholson, quoted in *Hello*, January 22, 2009.

158: "I don't want to be mentioned . . ." Jack Nicholson, quoted in *Women's Wear Daily*, March 24, 1976.

160: "I told you . . ." Jack Nicholson, quoted by Michael Douglas, *Playboy*, February 1984.

160: "The people who vote . . ." Jack Nicholson, quoted in *People*, March 1, 1976.

163: "Oscar night should have been . . ." Ken Kesey, quoted by Mason Wiley and Damien Bona, in *Inside Oscar*, p. 522.

CHAPTER 11

167: "I'm from that late '50s . . ." Jack Nicholson, to Lucy Kaylin, *GQ*, January 1996.

167: "my little red house . . ." Jack Nicholson, to Brad Darrach, *Life*, September 1990.

167: "basically alone . . ." Jack Nicholson, to Chris Chase, *Cosmopolitan*, February 1983.

173: "the feral energy lurking . . ." Alan Warren, *Film Buff*, January 1976.

176: "I didn't have much confidence . . ." Anjelica Huston, to Crystal G. Martin, *Oprah*, March 12, 2012.

177: "Living with Jack . . ." Anjelica Huston, to Bob Flynn, *Mail Online*, April 20, 2012.

178: "quiet, ingenuous aura . . ." This and other details of the casting of Mary Steenburgen are from Fiona Lewis, "Nicholson: Both Sides of the Camera," *Los Angeles Times*, November 6, 1977.

178: "I did a screen test . . ." Mary Steenburgen, to Chris Chase, *Cosmopolitan*, February 1983.

179: "All we can hope for . . ." Harry Gittes, to Fiona Lewis, "Nicholson: Both Sides of the Camera," *Los Angeles Times*, November 6, 1977.

180: "actually, I was trying to do a kind of Clark Gable spin on the character . . ." Jack Nicholson, to Deborah Caulfield, *Los Angeles Times*, June 16, 1985.

181: The report of Kubrick shooting up to one hundred takes is from an article by R. Mann that appeared in the *Los Angeles Times*, on October 3, 1978.

183: "I've got to get . . ." and "Well, you have no choice . . ." Warren Beatty and Jack Nicholson, quoted by Peter Biskind, *Star*, p. 264.

183: "I get such a bang . . ." Jack Nicholson, quoted in "Calendar," *Los Angeles Times*, March 15, 1981.

184: "I'm not a superstar . . ." The anecdote is repeated in several places, including "Sunday Woman," December 2, 1979.

CHAPTER 12

185: "I'm not much for birthdays . . ." Jack Nicholson, quoted in "The Outlook," 1, 39.9B

185: "I hadn't done a lot . . ." Jack Nicholson, quoted by Gregg Kilday, "Jack Nicholson's Face Odysseys," GQ, March 1981.

186: Henry Jaglom's remembering Rafelson's on-set fight . . . Henry Jaglom, interview by author.

187: "the most erotic movie . . ." Bob Rafelson, *Variety*, June 8, 1979.

187: "terrific farm girl . . ." Jack Nicholson, quoted in "Calendar," *Los Angeles Times*, March 15, 1981.

190: "I did *Postman* . . ." Jack Nicholson, to Nancy Collins, *Rolling Stone*, March 29, 1984.

190: "I've always viewed . . ." Ibid.

192: "I certainly would say . . ." Jack Nicholson, quoted in *People*, July 28, 1980.

194: "He can go only so many days without enchiladas . . ." Judy Mazel, quoted in *W*, August 14, 1981.

196: Jack's stock answer to why he wasn't making movies . . . Reported in *Variety*, December 16, 1981.

CHAPTER 13

201: "After *Cuckoo's Nest* . . ." Jack Nicholson, to Martin Torgoff, *Interview*, August 1984.

201: "I can think of only a couple of other pictures . . ." Ibid.

201: "My whole career strategy . . ." Jack Nicholson, to Roger Ebert, "Jack's Back," *Marquee*, February 1984.

203: "You mean, we're in danger . . ." James L. Brooks, quoted by Stephen Farber, "Jack Nicholson Comes to Terms with Middle Age," *Los Angeles Herald-Examiner* (syndicated by the *New York Times*), November 27, 1983.

203: "you needed a male star . . ." James L. Brooks, quoted by Mason Wiley and Damien Bona, *Inside Oscar*, p. 631.

203: "Jack was always too much . . ." James L. Brooks, to Michael Rechtshaffen, *Hollywood Reporter*, January 19, 1999.

204: "He lived in that robe . . ." James L. Brooks, to Bernard Weinraub, *New York Times*, June 12, 1994.

206: "I'm in my forties . . ." Jack Nicholson, quoted by Mason Wiley and Damien Bona, *Inside Oscar*, p. 631..

207: "Look at what he did . . ." Mike Nichols, to Ron Rosenbaum, *New York Times Magazine*, July 13, 1986.

207: "One of the things . . ." Jack Nicholson, ibid.

CHAPTER 14

210: "I've been overweight . . ." Jack Nicholson, to Nancy Collins, *Rolling Stone*, March 29, 1984.

211: "ghoul and an exploiter of emotionally disturbed widows . . ." Jack Nicholson, to Martin Torgoff, *Interview*, August 1984.

213: "In the beginning . . ." Jack Nicholson, to Diana Maychick, *New York Post*, June 13, 1985.

214: "He's been my idol . . ." Jack Nicholson, to Deborah Caulfield, *Los Angeles Times*, June 16, 1985.

214: "Jack's a virtuoso. He can do the acting scales on one hand . . ." John Huston, ibid.

215: "Mainly [Anjelica and I] just ran down . . ." Jack Nicholson, to Richard Stayton, *Los Angeles Herald-Examiner*, June 7, 1985.

217: "Let's face it, certain parts . . . need un–Jack Nicholsoning . . ." Jack Nicholson, to Deborah Caulfield, *Los Angeles Times*, June 16, 1985.

220: "I was specifically . . ." Jack Nicholson, to Fred Schreurs, *Rolling Stone*, August 14, 1986.

220: "It was like meeting . . ." Meryl Streep, to Bernard Weinraub, *New York Times*, June 12, 1994.

220: "Jack is the guy . . ." Mike Nichols, ibid.

CHAPTER 15

223: "I hate being one of the older people in films . . ." Jack Nicholson, to Nancy Collins, *Vanity Fair*, April 1992.

224: "We had bought . . ." Peter Guber, interview by author.

226: "In fact . . ." Ibid.

226: "Early on in our shoot . . ." George Miller, quoted in *Time Out* (London), May 25, 1988.

227: "I would like playing an Irish bum . . ." Jack Nicholson, quoted in *Variety*, December 5, 1985.

228: "I turned around . . ." Bono, quoted in *People*, January 18, 1988.

229: "For a certain period . . ." Jack Nicholson, to Peter Bogdanovich, *Suddeutsche Zeitung Magazin*, 2006.

229: All quotes from Karen Mayo-Chandler are from *Playboy*, December 1989.

230: "She's what I like . . ." Jack Nicholson, to Nancy Collins, *Vanity Fair*, April 1992.

230: "The first time . . ." Rebecca Broussard, ibid.

231: "It was always . . ." Peter Guber, interview by author.

233: "Crazy, nasty . . ." Kim Basinger, to Richard Brooks, *The Observer*, March 1993.

233: "I considered it . . ." Jack Nicholson, to Peter Bogdanovich, *Suddeutsche Zeitung Magazin*, 2006.

CHAPTER 16

237: "The actor is Camus's ideal existential hero . . ." Jack Nicholson, to Ron Rosenbaum, *New York Times Magazine*, July 13, 1986.

240: "We had everybody helping us . . ." and "She's rich, too . . ." Jack Nicholson, to Nancy Collins, *Vanity Fair*, April 1992.

240: "I'm very moody . . ." Jack Nicholson, quoted in *Elle* (British edition), September 1992.

240: "Jack's sex pen . . ." The source of the quote wishes to remain anonymous.

240: "You got any idea . . ." Jack Nicholson, to Brad Darrach, *Life*, September 1990.

241: "Filming Jack wasn't easy . . ." Vilmos Zsigmond, ibid.

242: "It never feels good . . ." Anjelica Huston, *Vanity Fair*, 1990.

242: "Do you know . . ." Jack Nicholson, quoted in *Long Beach Press-Telegram*, August 9, 1990.

242: "[His sexual] relationships . . ." Don Devlin, quoted by Dennis McDougal, *Five Easy Decades*, p. 50.

CHAPTER 17

246: "I've only borrowed money . . ." Jack Nicholson, quoted in "Calendar," *Los Angeles Times*, December 6, 1992.

248: "sky high" and "the baby looks . . ." Jack Nicholson, quoted in *Variety*, February 24, 1992. *Variety* did not publish the phrase "big dick," using two dashes instead. An anonymous source filled in the blanks.

248: "Rebecca's number one . . ." An unnamed source, to Brad Darrach, *Life*, September 1990.

248: "It's an unusual arrangement . . ." Jack Nicholson, to Nancy Collins, *Vanity Fair*, April 1992.

249: "I'd really rather not . . ." Rebecca Broussard, to Brad Darrach, *Life*, September 1990.

251: "I'm still wild at heart . . ." and "I've been in love . . ." Jack Nicholson, to Louise Gannon, *Mail Online*, January 31, 2011.

CHAPTER 18

254: "I'm one of the very few actors . . ." Jack Nicholson, to Hilary de Vries, "Calendar," *Los Angeles Times*, December 6, 1992.

257: [Nichols] took my wolf . . ." Jim Harrison, quoted by Dennis McDougal, *Five Easy Decades*, p. 333.

257: "I wanted to get involved . . ." Jack Nicholson, to Brian Case, *Time Out* (London), August 17, 1994.

CHAPTER 19

265: "I'd like to take . . ." Jack Nicholson, to Hilary de Vries, "Calendar," *Los Angeles Times*, December 6, 1992.

265: "Since the day he arrived . . ." *The Observer* (unsigned column), July 10, 1994.

265: "The thing I like best . . ." Jack Nicholson, quoted in *Hollywood Reporter*, September 6, 1994.

267: "It was kind of like working . . ." Jack Nicholson, to Lucy Kaylin, *GQ*, January 1996.

268: "I told Ms. Anspach . . ." Jack Nicholson, to Bernard Weinraub, *New York Times*, June 1994.

269: "Unfortunately for Anspach . . ." Ibid.

273: "I can't help but notice that women . . ." Jack Nicholson, quoted in *Rolling Stone*, October 5, 2006.

CHAPTER 20

274: "We wanted to create . . ." Jack Nicholson, to Peter Bogdanovich, *Suddeutsche Zeitung Magazin*, 2006.

275: "a range of incensed . . ." Molly Haskell, "Where the Old Boy Always Gets the Girl," *New York Times*, August 8, 1998.

275: "Well, Molly could answer . . ." Jack Nicholson, to Fred Scheurs, *Rolling Stone*, March 19, 1998.

276: "They're the closest . . ." An unnamed source, to *People*, February 23, 1998.

276: "I'm on a constant . . ." Jack Nicholson, quoted in *Us*, May 1998.

277: "I dropped about three quarts . . ." Jack Nicholson, quoted by Gail Kinn and Jim Piazza, *The Academy Awards*, p. 295.

277: "I have a career . . ." Jack Nicholson, quoted in *Variety*, March 24, 1998.

278: "Castro is a genius . . ." Jack Nicholson, quoted by Army Archerd, *Variety*, July 16, 1998.

281: "liked to crack the sexual whip . . ." An unnamed source, Liz Smith's syndicated column, December 12, 1999.

282: "I couldn't look at myself . . ." Jack Nicholson, to Dalya Alberge, *The Times* (London), May 23, 2002.

282: "I looked at him . . ." Jack Nicholson, quoted in *People*, December 16, 2002.

283: "There are a lot . . ." Jack Nicholson, quoted in *Newsweek*, December 9, 2002.

283: "A younger woman . . ." Jack Nicholson, quoted in *People*, December 22, 2003.

285: "Jack's character . . ." Nancy Meyers, quoted in *Variety*, January 7, 2004.

287: "We built this character . . ." Jack Nicholson, to Steven Kotler, *Variety*, December 11, 2006.

287: "The first thing Jack did . . ." Martin Scorsese, quoted in Richard Schickel, *Conversations with Scorsese*.

287: "I was going to set . . ." Jack Nicholson, to Logan Hill, *New York*, October 9, 2006.

290: "One of the toughest parts . . ." Jack Nicholson, to Louise Gannon, *Mail Online*, January 31, 2011.

291: "It was a very singular . . ." Jack Nicholson, quoted in *People*, June 21, 2010.

291: "Keith would stay up . . ." Jack Nicholson, to Peter Biskind, *Vanity Fair*, December 16, 2011.

292: "The reality was . . ." Ibid.

292: "Jack is someone . . ." Anjelica Huston, *Huffington Post*, February 6, 2013.

ACKNOWLEDGMENTS

I FIRST SAW *EASY RIDER* DURING ITS INITIAL RUN AT THE TRANS-LUX East in Manhattan with my then-girlfriend, a transplanted beauty from Ohio hippified via San Francisco. I remember her being upset when we left the theater because of the "injustice," as she put it, of the two senseless murders at the end of the movie. To me, though, the greater injustice was the equally senseless murder of Hanson, a character superbly played by an actor I wasn't as yet aware of, but whose relatively brief appearance moved me far more than the endless paranoid blather that poured out of two-dimensional Captain America and Billy for two hours. Their murder was as convenient as it was cliché. Hanson's midfilm slaying was a genuine shock. It was my first exposure to Jack magic.

I was never a real hippie, I just played one on TV (true story, another time), but I did (and still do) love 1960s longhair rock. The first time I heard the songs from the soundtrack of the movie was on New York's late, lamented WNEW-FM one night, a cream-of-the-crop collection including songs and performances, sometimes both, by Roger McGuinn, Jimi Hendrix, the Byrds, Robbie Robertson, the Electric Prunes (yes), Bob Dylan, and the explosive track that drove the film, Steppenwolf's anthemic "Born to Be Wild." I had no idea as yet what the film was about, who was in it, or anything else. I went to see it because I wanted to hear how the music was used in the movie.

My next cinematic encounter with Jack Nicholson was *Five Easy Pieces*. I saw it by myself in a half-filled theater during the day in the middle of the week, as I had no steady job at the time. Not only did I now know who Jack was, he was the reason I went to see the film. I sat through it three times. I was held in my seat by its emotional power, and I wanted to see it the second and third times to somehow figure out how Jack had transformed himself out of Hanson and into Bobby Dupea, a character as far removed from Hanson as was imaginable. I couldn't do it. Jack's magic was too good.

THIS BOOK IS about the extraordinary power of that magic and the man who made it. Writing it I discovered many fascinating things; the most compelling, I think, was that when Jack was at his best, when the magic fairly shimmered on the silver screen, he was a cinematic spiritualist, able to somehow use the pieces of his difficult, deceptive, angry, at times ruinous life of endless charm, physical excess, emotional emptiness, and familial deception to conjure up characters of cinematic grace and beauty. Writing about him was a pleasure and a privilege and an experience of enlightenment; I think I finally did figure out how at least some of the tricks were done.

That is not to say that everything I found out about him was enjoyable or that I wrote on my knees in hagiographic worship. It just confirmed to me all over again how much I love watching great films and writing about the complex lives of those who help turn them into works of art.

We learn about the power of film through repetition; that doesn't necessarily mean seeing the same film over and over again (although that too can be a surprisingly effective method) but watching a collective, hopefully chronological body of one actor's (or director's, or screenwriter's or in some cases even producer's) work, which for this biography I was fortunately able to do with Jack's movies. I managed to see every Jack Nicholson film in existence in one form or another first to last—I caution you, not an easy task, but an imensely rewarding one. Even those I thought were unwatchable, and there were more than a few, held some value in the context of the body of his work. Today we have advantages that allow us to do what earlier generations could not. Because of it, we can more easily see how movies of a chosen subject are connected, that there are threads that run through them. We don't have to wait years between each release to try to understand what they are and why they are important in the context of an entire career. Viewing films this way, semioticians might suggest, tells us that in terms of a filmmaker's work, a single film is not the whole sentence (*phrase*) but a word in it (*mot*); to understand the language, then, of Jack Nicholson's art requires an immersion into all of it. Seeing one Jack Nicholson film is a pleasure. Seeing fifty Jack Nicholson films is a revelation.

Finally, film has always been mislabeled as a great form of escape. It isn't. Film brings us closer to ourselves. We learn more about who we are, not less, by watching characters up on the screen. In that sense, film is both a window and a mirror. Its emotional power and strength reassures all of us, in the temple of the theater, that we are not alone. The films of Jack Nicholson tell us more about who we are by showing us more about who he is.

Or maybe not. When I asked Henry Jaglom one time who Jack really was, he said, "I'm not sure that anybody knows Jack."

"Not even Jack?" I asked. Henry only smiled.

Many thanks to all those who helped with this book, especially Toni Basil, Peter Biskind, Karen Black, Roger Corman, Peter Davis, Mickey Dolenz, Peter Guber, Monte Hellman, Henry Jaglom, Helena Kallianiotes, Mike Medavoy, and a host of others who in one way or another helped connect me to people and organizations that could help, with interviews and off-the-record information, or made it clear they didn't want to participate on or off the record. There are only a few of them, and they are identified as such. They include Mick Sullivan, Alan Somers, Bryan Lourd, Ashton Fontana, Leslie Dart, Jay Sikura, Jolene Wolff, Alec Cast, Lauren Gibson, Quaid Films, Rand Holston, Jeff Berg, Dennis Aspland, Chris Donnelly, Julie McDonald, Charlie Nadler, Mandalay Entertainment, Julia Buchwald, Ari Emanuel, and David Salidor. And there were several people who, because of their personal proximity or professional positions, did not wish to be named. I am grateful for all of their gracious cooperation in granting original person-to-person interviews for this book. Many have never been interviewed before for any biography of Jack Nicholson.

I wish to thank the Los Angeles Academy of Motion Picture Arts and Sciences Margaret Herrick Library, the London Film Institute, and the Cinémathèque Française in Paris for their help and the availability of their resources.

I wish to thank my dear friend Henry Diltz for his great help. Henry, you are a prince.

I also wish to thank my fact checker and chief researcher, Jesse Herwitz (*Blame him!*); my editor, Suzanne O'Neill, at Crown Archetype; and the rest of the team, including Anna Thompson; and my agent, Alan Nevins of Renaissance Literary and Talent. To my loyal readers. I assure you we will meet again in the not-too-distant future, a little farther up the road.

INDEX

Abbott, Bud, 9

About Schmidt (movie), 281–284

Academy Awards, 78, 80–81, 97–98, 99, 105, 129–130, 138–139, 149, 159–164, 175, 197, 198, 202, 206, 208, 220–221, 252–253, 276–277, 279, 283, 284, 289, 292–293

Adjani, Isabelle, 161, 254

Adler, Lou, 83–84, 94, 113n, 118, 135, 146, 167, 197

Affleck, Ben, 277

African Queen, The (movie), 179

AFTRA (American Federation of Television and Radio Artists), 23

AIDS (acquired immune deficiency syndrome), 211–212

Air National Guard, 30–31

Alda, Alan, 220

Aldrich, Robert, 44

Ali, Muhammad, 128

Altman, Robert, 32, 156n, 161

American Caesar (movie), 280, 281

American Film Institute, 156, 258–259

American International Pictures (AIP), 29, 30, 32, 35, 50, 53, 55, 66, 67, 79

Anderson, Lindsay, 76

Anderson, Roger "Storeroom," 20

Andrews, Dana, 156

Andrews, Julie, 282

Andrews, Luanda, 24

Andrus, Mark, 270

Andy Griffith Show, The (television show), 58

Anger Management (movie), 284

Ann-Margaret, 102, 103, 105, 118, 161

Anne of the Thousand Days (movie), 81n

Ansen, David, 195, 205, 218–219

Anspach, Susan, 87–88, 192, 248, 268–269, 271

Antonioni, Michelangelo, 4, 110, 122–124, 141

Apostle, The (movie), 277

Arkoff, Sam, 29, 50

Arnold, Jack, 174

As Good as It Gets (movie), 270–271, 274–277, 279, 285

Ashby, Hal, 114–118, 121, 128, 145, 146, 147n, 159, 174, 182, 237

Astaire, Fred, 275

Aubrey, Jim, 114

Avco Embassy, 101, 143

Avildsen, John G., 129

Ayres, Gerald, 115, 116, 118

Babenco, Héctor, 227

Bacall, Lauren, 215

Back Door to Hell (movie), 44

Badham, John, 238
BAFTA (British Academy of Film and Television Arts), 128, 139, 152
Ballard, Bruce, 31
Bancroft, Anne, 150, 203
Baratta, Tommy, 217, 256
Barger, Ralph Hubert "Sonny", Jr., 50
Barkin, Ellen, 244
Barry Lyndon (movie), 101, 161, 162, 175
Basil, Toni, 64, 67, 68, 85
Basinger, Kim, 233
Bates, Kathy, 282–284
Batman (movie), 231–233, 243, 275
Batman Returns (movie), 237
BBS, 81–82, 85, 87–89, 98–99, 110, 113–114, 121–122, 130, 179, 186
Bean, Robert, 33
Beatles, the, 60, 64, 65, 73
Beatty, Warren, 82n, 109, 110, 113n, 136, 147, 148, 157, 159, 164, 182–183, 191, 197, 198, 218, 282
Bedknobs and Broomsticks (movie), 105n
Begley, Louis, 281
Bellow, Saul, 212
Belushi, John, 177–180, 210–212
Benedek, László, 14
Bening, Annette, 282
Bergen, Candice, 101, 105, 109, 164, 260
Bergman, Ingmar, 54, 86, 95, 188
Bergman, Ingrid, 277
Berlin Film Festival, 250
Berman, Harvey, 33
Bernstein, Carl, 219–220
Bernstein, Morey, 71
Berry, Halle, 284
Berryman, Michael, 150
Bertolucci, Bernardo, 147n, 255–256
Big Brass Ring, The (movie), 174

Bigstick Productions, 145
Binder, Steve, 162
Biskind, Peter, 27, 46, 76, 99, 291
Black, Karen, 56, 67, 68, 74, 85–87, 90, 92–93, 97
Blake, Robert, 24, 37, 193–194
Blake, William, 43
Blank, Robert Scott, 258, 258n
Blauner, Steve, 60, 62, 67, 81, 89
Blood and Wine (movie), 269–270, 274
Bob and Carol and Ted and Alice (movie), 81n, 93
Bodyguard, The (movie), 147n
Bogart, Humphrey, 20, 173, 178–179, 195, 215, 219
Bogdanovich, Peter, 50, 98–99, 105n, 106, 114, 138, 233
Bonnie and Clyde (movie), 134
Bono, 227, 228
Border, The (movie), 193–194, 195n, 196, 243
Borlaza, Angela, 154
Bound for Glory (movie), 147n
Bourdin, Guy, 119
Bovasso, Julie, 216
Boyce, Tommy, 61
Boyle, Lara Flynn, 279–282
Brando, Marlon, 14–18, 20, 25, 26, 34, 49, 50, 54, 82, 83, 89, 113n, 129, 145, 153–156, 174, 214, 290–291
Braxton, David, 153
Brennan, Walter, 277
Bresler, Sandy, 105, 110, 132, 146, 213, 223, 232n
Brest, Martin, 252
Bridges, James, 202
Bridges, Jeff, 186
Brinkley, Douglas, 86
Britt, Martin, 195
Brody, Adrien, 284
Brooks, Dean R., 150–151

Brooks, James L., 201–204, 206, 227, 270, 273, 276, 277, 289

Brooks, Richard, 195, 223

Brosnan, Pierce, 271

Broussard, Rebecca, 230, 231, 239–240, 244, 248–249, 251–252, 257, 259, 260, 268, 272, 276–279, 292

Brown, David, 246

Brown, Jim, 115

Bucket List, The (movie), 288–289

Buell, Bebe, 191–192

Bulger, James "Whitey," Jr., 287, 288*n*

Burgess, Anthony, 175

Burnett, Carol, 194

Burns, Allan, 202

Burstyn, Ellen, 113, 140, 150

Burton, Tim, 231–232, 271

Butch Cassidy and the Sundance Kid (movie), 80

Byrnes, Edd "Kookie," 23

Caan, James, 146, 214

Cagney, James, 42

Cain, James M., 114, 185, 189, 189*n*

Caine, Michael, 270

Caine Mutiny, The (movie), 247–248

Campbell, W. Stewart, 159

Camus, Albert, 34–35

Canby, Vincent, 128, 155

Cannes Film Festival, 47–48, 76, 93, 118, 184

Capra, Frank, 55

Carnal Knowledge (movie), 89, 101–105, 105*n*, 147, 161, 185

Carney, Art, 139–140, 160*n*, 162

Carradine, David, 147*n*

Carradine, John, 156

Carradine, Keith, 174

Carrière, Claude, 149

Carson, Johnny, 181, 193–194, 198, 208, 237*n*

Carter, Georgianna, 25, 30–34, 37, 41

Cartwright, Veronica, 226, 227, 229, 244

Cassavetes, John, 55

Cassidy, David, 115

Castle Rock Entertainment, 247

Castro, Fidel, 26, 278

Cattaneo, Peter, 277

Cavett, Dick, 191

Chabrol, Claude, 47

Chakiris, George, 50

Chamberlain, Wilt, 84

Champlin, Charles, 137, 160

Chandler, Arthur, 38

Chandler, Raymond, 131

Chaney, Lon, Jr., 255

Channing, Stockard, 147, 148

Chaplin, Charlie, 86, 183

Chatham, Russell, 213

Cher, 225

China Syndrome, The (movie), 175

Chinatown (movie), 4, 5, 5*n*, 124, 127, 131–140, 145, 146, 151, 152, 167*n*, 174, 212–214, 238, 254

Clark, Dick, 57

Clark, Ramsey, 91*n*

Clark, Ron, 174

Clarkson, Patricia, 281

Clayton, Jack, 106

Cliburn, Van, 282

Clockwork Orange, A (movie), 105*n*, 175

Close Encounters of the Third Kind (movie), 174

Cocteau, Jean, 54

Cohn, Harry "King," 59

Colicos, John, 188

Columbia Pictures, 59, 69, 74–76, 89, 91*n*, 115, 116, 118, 121–122, 255–257, 284

Coming Home (movie), 174

Condon, Richard, 213
Conner, Bruce, 68
Coppola, Francis Ford, 35, 39, 139,
    140, 214, 225
Corey, Jeff, 24–25, 29, 36, 45, 156, 233
Corley, Al, 279
Corliss, Richard, 195
Corman, Gene, 32
Corman, Roger, 25–30, 32–33, 35–40,
    45–55, 61, 66, 67, 98, 105, 179
Costa-Gavras, 76
Costello, Elvis, 191
Costello, Lou, 9
Costner, Kevin, 147n, 168, 212
Crane, Robert David, 122, 125, 127,
    137
Cristofer, Michael, 224
Cross, Alison, 269
Crosse, Rupert, 81, 81n, 117n
Crossing Guard, The (movie), 266–
    267, 281
Crothers, Scatman, 150
Crowther, Bosley, 54
Cruise, Tom, 217, 224, 247
Cry Baby Killer, The (movie), 29–30,
    32–33, 44
Crystal, Billy, 252, 276
Cuban Film Festival, 278
Curious Savage, The (Patrick), 13
Curry, Tim, 194
Curtis, Tony, 156

Damon, Matt, 277, 286, 287
Daniels, Jeff, 203
Dargis, Manohla, 141n, 288
Davis, Hope, 282
Davis, Judy, 270
Davis, Sammy, Jr., 139, 140
Day-Lewis, Daniel, 277
Day of the Jackal, The (movie), 106
De Beauvoir, Simone, 190

De Niro, Robert, 12, 139, 212, 214,
    217, 225, 247, 254
De Palma, Brian, 212
Dead, The (movie), 228–229, 239
Dean, James, 23–25, 33–36, 54, 88,
    134, 156
Del Toro, Benicio, 281
Delpy, Julie, 251
Demme, Jonathan, 237, 238
Denby, David, 192
Denver, John, 116n
Departed, The (movie), 286–288
Dern, Bruce, 50, 51, 53, 55, 57, 76, 90,
    96, 110, 111, 113, 148, 174
DeVito, Danny, 9, 150, 151, 179, 203,
    237, 249–250
Devlin, Don, 31, 40, 41, 147, 239, 242
Diamond, Neil, 61
Diamonds Are Forever (movie), 105n
DiCaprio, Leonardo, 286
DiMaggio, Joe, 10, 26
Dirty Harry (movie), 105n
Divorce Court (television show), 23–24
Dmytryk, Edward, 248
Dr. Strangelove, or How I Learned
    to Stop Worrying and Love the
    Bomb (movie), 65, 175, 271
Dog Day Afternoon (movie), 161, 162
Dolenz, Micky, 62–65
Dorff, Stephen, 270
Double Indemnity (movie), 189, 189n
Douglas, Anne, 132
Douglas, Kirk, 132, 142–145, 149–150,
    160, 163, 175
Douglas, Michael, 144–145, 147,
    149–151, 157–158, 160, 162–164,
    167, 175, 278
Dourif, Brad, 150
Dreyfuss, Richard, 174
Drive, He Said (movie), 80, 82, 88–95,
    99, 101, 114, 122, 179, 238

Duell, William, 150
Dunaway, Faye, 134, 135, 140, 150, 239, 243
Duvall, Robert, 214, 277
Dylan, Bob, 12, 26, 75, 90, 96, 128, 147n, 180, 266

East of Eden (movie), 88, 164
Eastman, Carole, 24, 45–48, 84, 85, 88, 98, 111, 147, 244–245, 249, 290
Eastwood, Clint, 110, 182, 252, 260, 280
Easy Rider (movie), 6–7, 58, 59, 70–82, 86, 93, 95, 113, 121, 243, 259
Ebert, Roger, 155, 289
Eckhardt, Aaron, 281
Eckland, Britt, 113n
Ehrenstein, David, 196
EK Corporation, 155n
"Elephant's Child" (Kipling), 227
Ensign Pulver (movie), 42
Entertainer, The (movie), 193
Ephron, Nora, 219, 220
Epitaph (aka To Hold the Mirror) (movie), 43–44
Epstein, Jason, 256
Evans, Bob, 73, 96, 109–110, 131–132, 134, 135, 137, 157, 159, 214, 217–218, 238–241, 243, 254
Evening Star, The (movie), 270, 272
Everly Brothers, 57
Exorcist, The (movie), 106

Fairchild, June, 91
Fantasy Films, 145
Farrell, James T., 36–37
Faulkner, William, 71
Feiffer, Jules, 102
Fellini, Federico, 54, 95, 113, 161
Few Good Men, A (movie), 246–247, 249, 250, 252, 289

Fiddler on the Roof (movie), 105n
Field, Sally, 186
Fiennes, Ralph, 270
Filmgroup, 32
Fink, Mitchell, 227
Finkelstein, Alan, 254
Finney, Albert, 139
Fitzgerald, F. Scott, 156, 157
Five Easy Pieces (movie), 82, 84–88, 92, 97–101, 110, 111, 121, 183, 188, 192
Fleming, Victor, 156n
Fletcher, Louise, 150, 153, 161, 163, 203
Flight to Fury (movie), 44
Flynn, Errol, 121
Flynn, Joe, 22, 24
Fonda, Henry, 42, 50, 80, 174
Fonda, Jane, 43, 76, 101, 134, 146n, 150, 174, 220
Fonda, Peter, 50, 51, 53–54, 58, 59, 65–71, 74–76, 80, 100, 127, 277, 291
Ford, Glenn, 223
Ford, John, 35, 42, 130, 259
Forest, Michael, 32
Forman, Milos, 100, 149, 150, 152, 161–163, 193
Fortune, The (movie), 147–148, 151, 167n, 243, 244
Fosse, Bob, 139, 187
Foster, Jodie, 238, 254
Fox, Michael J., 223
Franciosa, Tony, 106
Frazier, Joe, 128
Freeman, Morgan, 288, 289
French Connection, The (movie), 105, 105n, 253
Frey, Glenn, 57, 167
Friedkin, William, 105, 105n, 106, 253
Fryer, Christopher, 122, 125, 127, 137

Fuller, Robert, 23
Funicello, Annette, 64
Furcillo-Rose, Don, 2, 3, 15, 126, 127,
    137, 169, 260, 274

Gailey, Samantha, 169–171
Gaines, George, 159
Galbraith, John Kenneth, 26
Garfield, John, 114, 185
Garfunkel, Art, 101, 104, 105, 164
Garnett, Ty, 185, 187n, 189
Gazzara, Ben, 106
Geffen, David, 136, 157
George, Nathan, 150
Gere, Richard, 202
Giant (movie), 23, 134
Gibson, Mel, 223, 225, 285
Gielgud, Sir John, 198
Gittes, Harry, 31, 89, 112, 134, 177,
    179, 280, 281
Glory Stompers, The (movie), 53
Godard, Jean-Luc, 47, 61, 95, 118
Goddard, Caleb, 87–88, 248, 268, 271
Godfather, The (movie), 105–106, 129,
    154, 214, 215
Godfather, The: Part II (movie),
    138–140
Goffin, Gerry, 61
Goin' South (movie), 177–182, 187,
    195n, 210, 226, 238, 240, 280
Golden Globe Awards, 128, 139, 149,
    187, 275, 278, 283n
Goldman, Bo, 145, 161
Goldman, William, 80, 247
Goldsmith, Jerry, 135
Gone with the Wind (movie), 156n
Good Will Hunting (movie), 277
Gooding, Cuba, Jr., 270
Gordon, Leo, 39
Gordon, Steve, 198
Gorog, László, 35

Gorshin, Frank, 36
Gould, Elliott, 81, 81n
Graduate, The (movie), 101, 105, 143
Graham, Robert, 242
Grant, Cary, 275
Grant, Lee, 159
Grauman, Sid, 146n
Great Gatsby, The (movie), 106
Greene, Guy, 160
Grey, Brad, 286
Griffith, Charles B., 50
Griffith, Melanie, 180
Grodin, Jim, 171
Guare, John, 149
Guber, Peter, 76, 83, 89, 92, 115–118,
    224–226, 231, 232, 237
Guillerman, John, 187
Guttman, Richard A., 44

Haas, Lukas, 271
Hackett, John, 44
Hackford, Taylor, 202
Hackman, Gene, 146, 252, 253
Hagman, Larry, 43
Hamilton, Guy, 105n
Hanna, Bill, 21, 22
Hanson, Curtis, 277
Hardley, Winny-Lou, 175
Harling, Robert, 270
Harrison, George, 180
Harrison, Jim, 188, 255–257
Harry and Tonto (movie), 139
Hart, Bobby, 61
Hart, Gary, 167
Hartman, Mortimer, 38
Haskell, Molly, 275, 276
Hauben, Laurence, 161
Hawes, Sandra, 13
Hawley, Murray "Bob," 15, 126
Hawn, Goldie, 159
Head (movie), 63–65, 82, 91

Heartburn (movie), 219–220, 226

Hearts and Minds (movie), 122, 130, 140

Hefner, Hugh, 132

Heggen, Thomas, 42

Hellman, Monte, 32, 34, 39, 43–48, 50, 100

Hells Angels on Wheels (movie), 51, 53, 55

Hemingway, Ernest, 212

Henderson the Rain King (Bellow), 212

Henley, Don, 57, 167, 255

Hepburn, Audrey, 162

Hepburn, Katharine, 20, 277

Heston, Charlton, 82*n*

Hickey, William, 215

High Noon (movie), 26

Hill, George Roy, 129

Hill, Gladys, 161

Hill, Jack, 39

Him and Her (movie), 280

Hitchcock, Alfred, 124

Hoffa (movie), 249–251

Hoffman, Dustin, 139, 153, 157, 224, 277

Hogan, Paul, 223

Hollman, Honey, 198*n*, 248

Hollman, Winnie, 198, 198*n*, 248

Hollywood Foreign Press Association, 278–279

Holt, Kathryn, 146

Hope, Bob, 139

Hopkins, Anthony, 238

Hopper, Dennis, 23, 53–54, 58, 59, 64, 65–71, 74–76, 80, 93, 96–97, 99–101, 112*n*, 217, 266, 278, 291

Houston, Whitney, 147*n*

How Do You Know (movie), 289–290

Hudson, Rock, 212

Hunt, Helen, 270, 275, 277, 285

Hunter, Holly, 270

Hurt, William, 221

Hush . . . Hush, Sweet Charlotte (movie), 44

Huston, Anjelica, 5, 118–120, 122– 124, 128–130, 132, 145*n*, 146–148, 151–152, 156–159, 164, 170–172, 174–177, 190, 192, 195, 197, 198, 207, 208, 213, 215–216, 219–222, 225, 226, 229–231, 239, 241–242, 248, 251, 257, 266–267, 268, 292, 293

Huston, Danny, 228

Huston, Jack, 119*n*

Huston, John, 118–120, 129, 132, 133, 157, 161, 176, 194–196, 214–215, 218, 219, 221, 228–229, 237, 239, 243

Huston, Walter, 119, 221*n*

Huston, Walter Anthony "Tony," 119*n*, 229

Hutton, Lauren, 140

Hutton, Timothy, 208

Indian Runner, The (movie), 266, 267

Infernal Affairs (movie), 286, 287

Ireland, John, 28

Ironweed (movie), 224, 227–228

Ivory, James, 256

Jackson, Glenda, 161

Jackspeak, 1, 1*n*, 18, 45, 50, 89, 101, 105, 112, 118, 122, 124, 182, 282

Jagger, Bianca, 181

Jagger, Mick, 96, 176, 180, 191, 255

Jaglom, Henry, 55–56, 67, 74–75, 81, 90, 94, 95, 98, 100, 109, 148, 174, 186

Janiger, "Oz," 38

Jarrott, Charles, 81*n*

Jay, Margaret, 219*n*

Jewison, Norman, 65, 105n
Johnson, Ben, 99
Johnson, Diane, 181
Jones, Davy, 62, 64
Jones, Jennifer, 202
Jones, Quincy, 282

Kael, Pauline, 155–156, 181, 192, 195, 205, 218
Kallianiotes, Helena, 52, 64, 85, 96, 110, 230, 254
Kane, Carol, 161
Karloff, Boris, 39, 98n
Kastner, Peter, 56, 87, 155n
Kauffmann, Stanley, 127–128, 195, 245
Kazan, Elia, 17, 156, 157
Keaton, Diane, 161, 182, 183, 187, 191, 197, 198, 214, 284, 285
Keitel, Harvey, 193, 239
Kellerman, Sally, 24, 32
Kelly, Alex, 279
Kelly, Gene, 159
Kennedy, John F., 41, 143
Kennedy, William, 224, 227
Kerouac, Jack, 18–19, 25, 47, 86
Kesey, Ken, 25, 142–145, 161, 163
Kidman, Nicole, 212
King, Carole, 61
King, Eddie, 125
King, Graham, 286, 288n
King, Stephen, 175
King Kong (1976 remake), 187
King of Marvin Gardens, The (movie), 110–114, 122, 130, 186
Kinnear, Greg, 270, 277
Kirshner, Don, 61, 62
Klein, Dennis, 270n
Klein, John, 149
Kline, Kevin, 270
Klute (movie), 105n

Knight, Christopher, 36
Knight, Sandra, 37–39, 42, 43, 48, 49, 51–53, 64, 72, 74, 153, 160
Kovács, László, 55, 111
Kristofferson, Kris, 100
Kubrick, Stanley, 65, 101, 105n, 142, 161, 175, 177, 180–182, 184, 192, 193, 255, 271

Landau, Martin, 37
Landis, John, 255
Landon, Michael, 23
Lane, Anthony, 265–266
Lang, Stephen, 247
Lange, Jessica, 187–188, 190
Lardner, Ring, Jr., 65
Larner, Jeremy, 89
Lassick, Sydney, 150
Last Detail, The (movie), 4, 115–118, 121, 127–130, 139, 153
Last Movie, The (movie), 99–101
Last Picture Show, The (movie), 98–99, 105n, 114, 121
Last Tango in Paris (movie), 123, 129, 154
Last Tycoon, The (movie), 156–157, 167n, 195n
Lawrence, Jennifer, 292–293
Leachman, Cloris, 99, 105n
Lee, Christopher, 118
Left Handed Gun, The (movie), 153
Légèr, Fernand, 83
Leibovitz, Annie, 248
Lelouch, Claude, 149
Lemmon, Jack, 42, 129–130, 160n, 175
Lennon, John, 96, 180
Lenny (movie), 139
Leone, Sergio, 123
Lerner, Alan J., 72
Lerner, Irving, 36

LeRoy, Mervyn, 42, 130
Levine, Joseph E., 101, 104–105, 143
Levinson, Barry, 224, 277
Lewis, Jerry, 204
Lippert, Robert, 40, 41, 44
Little Big Man (movie), 153
Little Shop of Horrors, The (movie), 35–36
Littlefeather, Sacheen, 129
Lloyd, Christopher, 150, 151, 179
Loewe, Frederick, 72
Logan, Josh, 42, 130
Loners, The (movie), 65–69
Longet, Claudine, 167
Look Back in Anger (movie), 193
Lopez, Jennifer, 269
Lopez, Perry, 217
Los Angeles Lakers, 83–84, 135, 197, 213, 218, 228, 237n, 250, 279, 290
Love Story (movie), 159, 205
Lovin' Spoonful, 61
LSD (lysergic acid diethylamide), 37–38, 63
Lucas, George, 100–101, 206
Lumet, Sidney, 129–130, 139, 161

Maccari, Ruggero, 161
MacGraw, Ali, 134, 205
Machu, Mireille "Mimi," 52, 56, 57, 79–80, 83, 87, 92, 94, 230
MacLaine, Shirley, 139, 140, 202–205, 203n, 208, 270, 276
Madonna, 266, 267
Majestic Films, 269
Malick, Terrence, 89
Malle, Louis, 174
Mamet, David, 188–190, 212, 249–250
Man Trouble (movie), 244–245, 249, 251, 269
Manasquan High School, New Jersey, 11–14

Mandel, Alan, 177
Mann's (Grauman's) Chinese Theater, Hollywood, 146
Manson, Charles, 96, 97
Manson murders, 132, 133, 159
Margotta, Michael, 90, 92, 93
Marquand, Christian, 113n
Marquand, Richard, 206
Mars Attacks! (movie), 271, 272
Martin, Mary, 43
Marvin, Lee, 168
M*A*S*H (movie), 32, 156n
Matinee Theatre (television show), 23
Matthau, Carol, 132
Matthau, Charlie, 132
Matthau, Walter, 132, 159, 162, 174
Mature, Victor, 64
May, Elaine, 257
Mayo-Chandler, Karen, 229–230
Mazel, Judy, 194
Mazursky, Paul, 81n, 139, 223–224, 239
McClure, Michael, 66
McConaughey, Matthew, 254
McDormand, Frances, 277, 285
McDugal, Dennis, 145n
McEnroe, John, 237
McFerrin, Bobby, 227
McGillis, Kelly, 217
McMurtry, Larry, 202, 270
McQueen, Steve, 12, 66, 134, 147n
Medallion Pictures, 44
Medavoy, Michael, 27, 28, 48
Mengers, Sue, 157, 197
Meyers, Nancy, 284–285
MGM, 19–23, 114, 185, 195
Midler, Bette, 148, 223
Mikan, George, 84
Milland, Ray, 156
Miller, George, 225–226
Minnelli, Vincente, 71, 74

Miramax, 267

Mirren, Helen, 281

Missouri Breaks, The (movie), 153, 158, 167*n*, 177, 195*n*

Mister Roberts (movie), 42, 130

Mitchell, Joni, 96, 128

Mitchell, Sean, 274

Mitchum, Robert, 156

Monkees, The (television show), 61–63

Monroe, Marilyn, 20

Montand, Yves, 73

Moontrap (aka *Moon Trap*), 168, 174

Moore, Demi, 247

Moore, Joanna, 158

Moore, Mary Tyler, 202, 208

Moreno, Rita, 102, 104

Moriarty, Cathy, 217

Moritz, Louisa, 150

Morse, David, 267

Mulligan, Robert, 105*n*

Murder on the Orient Express (movie), 139

Murphy, Eddie, 223

Murray, Tony, 241

Myth of Sisyphus, The (Camus), 34

Nashville (movie), 161, 162

National Society of Film Critics, 128, 139

Nelson, Gene, 41

Nesmith, Michael, 62

New Line Cinema, 282

New York Film Critics Circle, 128, 139

New York Film Festival, 113

Newman, Paul, 12, 129–130, 203

Newton, Helmut, 119

Nichols, Mike, 89, 101–105, 105*n*, 132, 136, 143, 147, 148, 164, 207, 219, 220, 256, 259, 265

Nicholson, Ethel May, 1–3, 9–11, 14, 16, 18–20, 30, 31, 33–34, 38, 41, 72, 74, 78, 92, 125–127, 137, 138, 168–169, 260

Nicholson, Jack

acting classes and, 24–25, 29, 36, 37

acting in high school by, 12–13

affairs of, 63, 180–181, 191–192, 198, 198*n*, 226–228, 229–230, 273. *See also* specific relationships

in Air National Guard, 30–31

Anjelica Huston, relationship with, 5, 118, 120, 122–124, 128–130, 151–152, 157–159, 164, 170, 172, 175, 177, 190, 192, 195, 197, 213, 215–216, 220–222, 225, 226, 229–231, 239, 241–242, 248, 251, 292, 293

arrest of, 258

art collection of, 167, 173, 213, 233, 243, 280, 291

awards given to, 128, 139, 152, 258–260, 278–279, 283*n*, 290

birth of, 1, 14, 126

Bob Woodward and, 210–211, 219

at Cannes Film Festival, 47–48, 118

cars of, 14, 20–21, 72, 97

childhood of, 3, 9–11

children of, 43, 87–88, 192, 198, 198*n*, 239–240, 243, 248, 268, 290. *See also* Nicholson, Jennifer

death of mother and, 78

as director, 80, 82, 88–93, 101, 177, 179, 181–182, 238, 240–241, 243, 273

divorce from Sandra Knight, 72

drugs and drinking and, 31, 32, 37–38, 42, 56, 59, 63, 71, 87, 90, 97, 117, 121, 171, 173, 207, 211, 224

early days in L.A., 3, 15–25

early jobs of, 13, 18–23

early movie performances by, 4–5

early television appearances of,
    23–24, 58
"Elephant's Child" recording by,
    227
family of, 1–3
family secret and, 4, 5, 14, 125–127,
    137–138, 168–169
finances of, 14, 18, 20, 30, 33, 47–
    49, 51, 53, 58, 70, 72, 73, 82, 83,
    97, 110, 118, 131–132, 136, 141,
    146, 147n, 155, 186, 187, 194, 201,
    206, 209, 224, 232–233
first screen test of, 21–22
Georgianna Carter, relationship
    with, 25, 30–34, 37, 41
hair loss of, 95, 139, 158, 160, 176,
    191, 195, 254
handprint at Mann's (Grauman's)
    Chinese Theater, 146
at high school, 11–14
houses of, 82–83, 110, 167
injuries and, 180–181, 194, 220, 291
Jackspeak of, 1, 1n, 18, 45, 50, 89,
    101, 105, 112, 118, 122, 124, 182,
    282
Joni Mitchell, relationship with, 96
as Kennedy Center honoree, 282
Lara Flynn Boyle, relationship with,
    279–282
LSD used by, 37–38, 63
at Manson murder trial, 97
as Marlon Brando fan, 15–17, 26,
    82, 154, 290–291
marriage to Sandra Knight, 38
Michelle Phillips, relationship with,
    94, 96–98, 110–112, 114
Mireille "Mimi" Machu,
    relationship with, 52, 56, 57,
    79–80, 87, 92, 94
nicknames given to, 11, 12, 13
nightclub of, 254–255

as office worker at MGM, 19–23
Oscar nominations and awards, 78,
    80–81, 97–98, 129–130, 138–139,
    159–164, 197, 198, 206, 208, 221,
    252–253, 276–277, 283, 284
physical appearance of, 11–12, 21,
    29, 95, 136, 148, 191, 194–195,
    197, 204, 205, 207, 209, 217, 225,
    241, 255
with Players' Ring, 22–23
quoted, 1, 9, 15, 18–20, 26, 29, 33,
    36, 38–39, 40, 47, 52–53, 59, 65,
    70–71, 73–74, 78, 79, 81, 84, 85,
    88, 91, 96, 101, 106, 109, 111,
    112, 114, 121, 123, 124, 130, 131,
    136, 138, 142, 151–154, 158–160,
    167, 180, 183, 185, 190, 192, 201,
    206–207, 210, 215–217, 220, 223,
    237, 240–242, 246, 248–249, 251,
    254, 259–260, 265, 268, 274, 275,
    282, 283, 287, 290–292
Rebecca Broussard, relationship
    with, 230, 231, 239–240, 248–249,
    251–252, 260, 276, 278, 279, 292
reviews and, 37, 79, 88, 113,
    127–128, 137, 148, 181–182, 192,
    193, 195, 196, 205, 218–219, 245,
    265–266, 274–275, 288
Roger Corman and, 26, 29, 33,
    35–36, 38–40, 45–51, 53
Sandra Knight, relationship with,
    37–39, 43, 48, 49, 51–53, 72
as screenwriter, 39–41, 43, 45, 46,
    53–55, 57, 61, 63, 168, 175
sexual problems and, 38, 121
sexuality of, 10, 25, 79
sports and, 11–12, 83–84, 135, 152,
    197, 213
stomach problems of, 32
sunglasses and, 158, 160, 162, 164,
    208, 253

Nicholson, Jack (*cont'd*)
  Susan Anspach, relationship with,
      87–88, 192, 248, 268–269, 271
  tantrums of as child, 10
  television interviews and, 136–137
  in therapy, 48, 52
  Time magazine cover story on,
      137–138
  voice of, 21–22, 24, 30
  Winnie Hollman, relationship with,
      198, 198*n*, 248
Nicholson, Jennifer, 43, 52, 72, 74,
      146, 148, 153–154, 160, 196, 230,
      238, 248, 257, 260, 272–273,
      279–280
Nicholson, Jim, 29, 50
Nicholson, John J., 1, 3, 10, 14, 125–
      127, 137, 138, 184
Nicholson, John Joseph. *See*
      Nicholson, Jack
Nicholson, June, 2–3, 15–18, 31, 34,
      41, 125–127, 138, 168–169, 260
Nicholson, Lorraine, 239–240, 248,
      251, 259
Nicholson, Raymond, 248, 251, 259,
      272
Nicholson, Sean Knight, 272
Niven, David, 129
Nixon, Richard M., 115
Nolte, Nick, 224, 254, 255
Norfleet, Mark, 272
North by Northwest (movie), 124
Nunn, Trevor, 161
Nykvist, Sven, 188

Oates, Warren, 193
Obama, Michelle, 292
Obsessione (movie), 187*n*
Ochs, Phil, 266
Old Friends (movie), 270
Olivier, Laurence, 276

On a Clear Day You Can See Forever
      (movie), 72–74, 78, 88, 118, 131,
      241
On the Waterfront (movie), 17, 18, 26,
      154, 164
Onassis, Christina, 180
One Flew over the Cuckoo's Nest
      (Kesey), 142–145, 163
One Flew over the Cuckoo's Nest
      (movie), 142–147, 149–153, 155–
      164, 167*n*, 195, 238, 252
O'Neal, Cynthia, 103
O'Neal, Ryan, 158–159, 170, 190, 197
O'Neill, Eugene, 182–184, 212
O'Neill, Oona, 183–184
Ordung, Wyatt, 28
Osborne, John, 193
Out of the Frying Pan (Swann), 12–13
Owen, Clive, 212

Pacino, Al, 12, 106, 110, 129–130, 139,
      162, 214, 247, 252
Pakula, Alan J., 105*n*, 202
Palminteri, Chazz, 254
Paltrow, Gwyneth, 279
Paramount, 131, 136, 159, 177–179,
      186, 201–203, 217, 218, 243
Parker, Alan, 225
Parker, Sarah Jessica, 271
Passenger, The (aka *Fatal Exit*)
      (movie), 4–5, 122–124, 141, 167*n*
Pasternak, Joe, 21
Patinkin, Mandy, 219
Patrick, John, 13
Patton (movie), 98
Pavarotti, Luciano, 282
Payne, Alexander, 282
Peet, Amanda, 285
Penn, Arthur, 134, 153, 154
Penn, Sean, 260–261, 266–267, 272,
      280–281

Penta Pictures, 244
Perkins, Millie, 38, 42
Perry, Frank, 100
Persky, Lester, 168
Pesci, Joe, 217
Petroff, Boris, 40
Pfeiffer, Michelle, 225, 238, 257
Phillips, Chynna, 96, 110
Phillips, John, 43, 94, 110, 176
Phillips, Michelle, 43, 80, 93–94,
    96–98, 100, 110–112, 112–113n,
    114, 127, 176, 182, 183
Piaf, Édith, 95
Pickford, Mary, 162
Pinter, Harold, 156, 162
Pirates (movie), 174
Pitt, Brad, 286
Players' Ring, 22–23
Pleasence, Donald, 156
Pledge, The (movie), 280–281
Poe, Edgar Allan, 38, 137
Polanski, Emmanuelle, 250
Polanski, Roman, 55, 96, 97, 124,
    132–137, 140, 169–172, 174, 178,
    184, 212–214, 225, 238, 239, 243,
    250, 256, 284
Pollack, Sydney, 76
Ponicsan, Darryl, 115
Porter, Ann, 33
Postman Always Rings Twice, The
    (1946 movie), 185, 187n, 189
Postman Always Rings Twice, The
    (1981 movie), 185–191, 193, 195,
    196, 244, 249
Postman Always Rings Twice, The
    (Cain), 114, 185, 189
Pretty Baby (movie), 174
Prizzi's Honor (movie), 213–219, 221,
    271
Proteus Films, 45, 155n
Psych-Out (movie), 55, 57, 73

Quaid, Randy, 116, 117, 128, 129, 153
Quayle, Anthony, 81, 81n
Queen, The (McClure), 66, 67

Rafelson, Bob, 59–65, 67, 69, 70, 75,
    78, 82, 84, 85, 87, 88, 89, 97–99,
    110, 113, 114, 130, 167, 185–190,
    197, 244–245, 249, 269–270
Rafelson, Toby, 60, 63, 186
Rains, Claude, 255
Ramrus, Al, 177
Raven, The (movie), 38–39
Raven, The (Poe), 38
Ray, Nicholas, 23
Raybert, 60, 63, 65–69, 74
Rebel Rousers, The (movie), 51
Rebel Without a Cause (movie), 23,
    30, 33, 164
Red Harvest (movie), 147n
Redfield, William, 150
Redford, Robert, 12, 106, 110, 129–
    130, 186
Redgrave, Vanessa, 281
Reds (movie), 182–183, 185, 191, 195n,
    196–197, 198, 201, 212
Reed, Rex, 79–80
Reed, Willis, 84
Reiner, Carl, 247
Reiner, Rob, 247, 288, 289
Reivers, The (movie), 81n
Renoir, Jean, 223
Reynolds, Burt, 115, 129, 146, 203
Richards, Keith, 291
Richardson, Bob, 119, 158
Richardson, Tony, 147n, 193, 194
Ride in the Whirlwind (movie), 45–48
Risi, Dino, 161
Riskind, Robert, 54
Roarke, Adam, 55
Robards, Jason, Jr., 49
Robinson, Julia Anne, 113

Rohmer, Eric, 47
Romero, Cesar, 232n
Ronstadt, Linda, 57
Roos, Fred, 44, 45, 57–58, 89, 280
Rosemary's Baby (movie), 55, 225
Rosenberg, Stuart, 186
Ross, Diana, 129, 147n
Rothman, Marion, 33
Rudd, Paul, 289
Rush, Richard, 35, 50, 55, 143
Russell, Ken, 118
Rydell, Mark, 81n

Sabich, Vladimir "Spider," 167
Safe Place, A (movie), 94–96, 122
Saint, Eva Marie, 18
St. John, Jill, 180
St. Valentine's Day Massacre, The
    (movie), 48–49
Salata, Christine, 273
Sampson, Eduard, 28
Sampson, Will, 152
San Francisco Film Festival, 118
Sandler, Adam, 284
Sarandon, Susan, 225
Sarris, Andrew, 113, 128, 137, 141, 192,
    205–206, 276, 288
Sartre, Jean-Paul, 190
Save the Tiger (movie), 129–130
Schaffner, Franklin J., 98
Scheerer, Robert, 187
Schell, Maximilian, 162
Schiavelli, Vincent, 150
Schickel, Richard, 21, 205
Schneider, Abraham, 59, 61, 76, 82,
    122
Schneider, Berton "Bert," 59–63, 65,
    67, 69–71, 74–76, 79, 81–84, 88,
    89, 93, 95, 98, 99, 109, 110, 114,
    121–122, 130, 140, 183–186, 197,
    291

Schneider, Harold, 89, 177, 238
Schneider, Maria, 123–124
Schruers, Fred, 275
Schwarzenegger, Arnold, 186, 290
Scorsese, Martin, 140, 217, 257,
    286–288
Scott, George C., 98
Scott, Ridley, 180
Scott, Tony, 238
Scott, Walter, 168
Screen Gems, 59–61
Seabra, Nelson, 176
Sebring, Jay, 159
Segal, George, 159
Segal, Peter, 284
Sellers, Peter, 118, 271
Serpico (movie), 129–130
Shampoo (movie), 159
Shane, Celeste "Cici," 119
Shaner, John Herman, 177
Shankar, Ravi, 73
Shaw, Robert, 159
Sheehan, Catherine, 271–272
Sheinberg, Sidney, 99–100
Shepard, Sam, 208, 281
Shields, Brooke, 174
Shining, The (movie), 175, 180–182,
    184, 191–193, 195n, 224, 291
Shooting, The (movie), 45–48
Shootist, The (movie), 45
Shyer, Charles, 177
Siegel, Don, 105n
Silence of the Lambs, The (movie),
    238
Silver, Joan Micklin, 161
Simon, John, 128
Simon, Neil, 161
Simon, Paul, 101
Sinatra, Frank, 50, 139, 140
Sinatra, Nancy, 50
Siskel, Gene, 85

Sloan, Taylor, 33
Small, Mews, 150
Smith, Delos, V., Jr., 150
Smith, George W. "Shorty," 2–3, 31, 111, 260
Smith, Lorraine, 2, 3, 10, 31, 78, 111, 125, 260, 274
Soma, Enrica "Ricki," 118, 119
Something's Gotta Give (movie), 284–285
Sorkin, Aaron, 246, 247
Southern, Terry, 65–67, 69, 70, 70n, 71, 80, 113n
Space Cowboys (movie), 280, 281
Spain, Fay, 41
Spartacus (movie), 142, 143n
Spiegel, Sam, 156, 176, 294
Spielberg, Steven, 174, 175n
Springsteen, Bruce, 9
Stallone, Sylvester, 251
Stanton, Harry Dean, 32, 38, 52, 55, 72, 92, 153, 180, 197, 244
Stapleton, Maureen, 197
Starting Over (movie), 202, 203
Steenburgen, Mary, 178, 180, 182, 195
Stephanopoulos, George, 292, 293
Stevens, Cat, 96
Stevens, George, 23, 38
Stevenson, Robert, 105n
Sting, The (movie), 106, 129
Stone, Oliver, 278
Stone, Sharon, 254
Stranger, The (Camus), 35
Strasberg, Susan, 55, 57
Streep, Meryl, 187, 202, 220, 220n, 227–229, 244, 277
Streisand, Barbra, 73, 88
Strick, Wesley, 257
Studs Lonigan (Farrell), 36–37
Studs Lonigan (movie), 36–37

Sturges, Preston, 255
Sullivan, Ed, 60
Sullivan, Tom, 197
Summer of '42 (movie), 105n
Sunshine Boys, The (movie), 161, 162
Susann, Jacqueline, 160
Susskind, David, 60
Sutherland, Donald, 176
Swann, Francis, 12
Sylbert, Richard, 159

Tally, Ted, 238
Talmadge, Norma, 146n
Tamahori, Lee, 254
Tanen, Ned, 99, 100
Targets (movie), 98n
Taste of Honey, A (movie), 193
Tate, Sharon, 96–97, 132, 159, 169
Taylor, Doug, 203n
Taylor, James, 100
Taylor, Jim, 282
Taylor, Jud, 24
Taylor-Young, Leigh, 158
Tepper, William, 90, 93
Terms of Endearment (McMurtry), 202
Terms of Endearment (movie), 201–207, 212, 213, 252, 270, 276
Terror, The (movie), 39, 40
Thalberg, Irving, 156, 157
Thomas, Marlo, 157
They Shoot Horses, Don't They? (movie), 76, 80
Thomas, Danny, 140
Thomas, Marlo, 157
Thompson, Hunter S., 197
Thomson, David, 27, 172n
Three-Cornered Circle (movie), 114, 115
Thunder Island (movie), 40–41
Tilly, Meg, 239
Time magazine, 137–138
Tinker, Grant, 202, 203n

Titanic (movie), 277–278
Tom, Lauren, 244
Tom Jones (movie), 193
Tommy (movie), 118, 161, 167n
Too Soon to Love (movie), 35
Topper, Burt, 33
Tork, Peter, 62
Torn, Elmore Rual "Rip," 69–70
Towne, Robert, 5n, 24, 89, 90, 98, 115,
    117, 129, 131–134, 140, 146, 159,
    174, 214, 217–218, 238, 241
Tracy, Spencer, 20
Travolta, John, 116n, 202
Trenet, Charles, 95
Trip, The (movie), 53–54, 63, 66
Trudeau, Margaret, 180, 197
Truffaut, François, 47, 61
Turner, Kathleen, 215, 219
Turner, Lana, 20, 21n, 114, 187
Twentieth Century-Fox, 28, 40, 49
Two Jakes, The (movie), 214, 217–218,
    228, 230, 238–241, 243, 250

U2, 227, 228
Ulee's Gold (movie), 277
Ulius, Betty, 55, 57
Unforgiven (movie), 252, 260
United Artists, 157
Universal Pictures, 99, 100, 194, 280
Updike, John, 224, 225

Vaccaro, Brenda, 160, 164
Vadim, Roger, 43
Vaughn, Robert, 23
Venice Film Festival, 51, 265
Veruschka, 207
Vidal, Gore, 161
Villiers, Nick, 269
Viner, Mort, 203n
Visconte, Luchino, 187n
Voight, Jon, 174

Voss, Helmut, 278
Vreeland, Diana, 176

Wag the Dog (movie), 277
Waggner, George, 255
Wahlberg, Mark, 286
Wakefield, Dan, 203
Walk with Love and Death, A (movie),
    119
Walker, Robert, Jr., 42
Wallis, Hal, 143
Walter Reade Organization, 47
Ward, Rachel, 192
Warden, Jack, 159
Warhol, Andy, 156, 174, 176, 197–198,
    207, 237
Warner Bros., 180, 191, 192, 213–214,
    224, 249, 254, 280, 287
Warren, Alan, 160n, 173–174
Wasserman, Dale, 143, 144
Wasserman, Lew, 60
Wayne, John, 140
Wechsler, Richard, 98
Weir, Peter, 255
Welch, Raquel, 187
Weld, Tuesday, 94, 95
Welles, Orson, 49, 94, 174
Wells, David, 171
West, Jerry, 84
WGA (Writers Guild of America), 55,
    57
Whale, James, 255
What Women Want (movie), 284–285
Whitmore, James, 162
Wick, Douglas, 256
Wild Angels, The (movie), 50–51, 53,
    66
Wild One, The (movie), 14, 49, 50,
    154, 164, 290
Wild Ride, The (aka *Velocity*) (movie),
    33–35

Wilder, Billy, 189
Willett, E. Hunter, 55, 57
Williams, Andy, 167
Williams, Robin, 220, 277
Willis, Bruce, 238, 282
Wilson, Dennis, 100
Wilson, Owen, 289
Wilson, Scott, 217
Winger, Debra, 187, 202, 203, 203*n*,
    205, 208, 213
*Wired: The Short Life and Fast Times
    of John Belushi* (Woodward),
    210–212
Witches of Eastwick, The (movie),
    224–226, 228, 238
Witherspoon, Reese, 289
Wolf (movie), 255–257, 265–266

Wolf Man, The (movie), 255
Woods, James, 238, 247
Woodward, Bob, 210–212, 219
Wray, Fay, 187
Wright, Robin, 267, 281
Wyler, William, 161

Young, Gig, 80, 81*n*, 160*n*
Young, Otis, 116, 117

Zaentz, Saul, 144–147, 149, 150, 163
Zappa, Frank, 64
Zemeckis, Robert, 254
Zimmerman, Paul D., 128
Zinneman, Fred, 26, 106
Zsigmond, Vilmos, 241

About the Author

New York Times bestselling author Marc Eliot has had his books translated into more than a dozen languages in countries all over the world. They include biographies of Cary Grant, James Stewart, Clint Eastwood, Phil Ochs, and Steve McQueen.

Born and raised in New York City, he graduated from New York's High School of Performing Arts—the "Fame" School—received his BA from the City University of New York, and his MFA in writing from Columbia University's School of the Arts. He did his postgraduate film work at Columbia, studying under Andrew Sarris. He frequently lectures to classes, at film events, and at conventions, speaking about his writing and his auteurist views of film. His work has appeared in several magazines, both in the United States and abroad. He is a favorite guest on several radio and television shows. He is also a member of the legendary Friars Club.

Nicholson is his twenty-fifth book.